E. S. LAWRENCE

THE ORIGINS AND GROWTH OF MODERN EDUCATION

PENGUIN BOOKS

Penguin Books Ltd, Harmondsworth, Middlesex, England
Penguin Books Inc., 7110 Ambassador Road, Baltimore, Maryland 21207, U.S.A.
Penguin Books Australia Ltd, Ringwood, Victoria, Australia

—

First published 1970

—

Copyright © E. S. Lawrence, 1970

—

Made and printed in Great Britain
by Hazell Watson & Viney Ltd
Aylesbury, Bucks
Set in Linotype Times

To John, who helped so much

CONTENTS

8   CONTENTS

INTRODUCTION

TWICE a day the roads of England, and of much of the world, are alive with children going to school and coming home again. What do they go for?

Ask a dozen people the question and you will probably get a dozen different answers, but the idea that they are going to learn something which will help them to get a job will almost certainly appear, in some form, in most of the answers. Going to school has become accepted as a kind of sentence imposed on all, which must be served before one can be let free into the world, but what its purpose is, beyond this, seems both vague and insignificant to many people.

Living, in today's world, is probably more difficult than at any time in the past. The prosperity of our society has brought little stability or security to the young. They see their world sharply and dangerously divided by hunger, beliefs, and the threat of war. Apparently helpless to influence the course of events, they are, at the same time, deprived of an outlet for their urgent need for adventure, and a satisfying channel for their energies; a difficult world in which to keep one's balance. Viewed in this light, 'going to school' takes on a new significance.

The world presents a crazy picture. Never has man been richer in material wealth and techniques, and potentially more able to cure the world's ills, and at the same time more divided and uncertain about the means of doing so, and poorer in convictions about ultimate ends.

In the flux of changing beliefs and values the old guideposts have largely disappeared. Materialistic creeds threaten annihilation, not only on the material but on the spiritual plane. The complexities of modern civilization create a confusion of thought in which the individual gropes blindly for a satisfying way of life.

What shall we believe, and what shall we teach our children? These questions are close to everyone, even if ignored, and the answers finally given are of the greatest consequence. Education is the concern of everyone; its effects touch our lives at every point. The millions of children at this moment receiving education in school and at home, will, in a few years time, be adult, with all that this implies in responsibility and opportunity. What kind of education are they having, what kind should they have, to prepare them for what is to come?

'What we believe about education,' says M. V. C. Jeffreys, 'implicates our beliefs about everything else. The ends and means of education must be seen in relation to the ultimate problems of life. ... Whereas, from one point of view education is a specialized study, with its own techniques, and is the business of experts, from another point of view education is everyone's business and involves everything that living itself involves.' [1]

What, then, is education? The question is as old as civilization, and in every age there have been those who claimed to know the answer, as well as how to apply it, and others who searched for a truth they dimly perceived.

The twentieth century still asks the question and presents the answers. There are still those to whom it is all quite simple, and those who search. There is the conflict between those who believe in, and practise, what are loosely called modern methods, and those who are outraged by what they understand such methods to be; and there are the many between, who have themselves survived the process known as education, or going to school, most of whom cast off as quickly as possible anything to do with it, and many of whom regard themselves in consequence as qualified to speak, write and theorize about it as experts.

In our own day, and particularly in Britain, we see a wide and varied interpretation of educational theories and practice, from the narrowly traditional and formal, all the way to the experimentation of the schools that believe in and practise freedom; but, broadly speaking, the freer methods and ideas are still looked upon with some suspicion. We hear a great deal of criticism of what are called the 'new' methods, and the

1. JEFFREYS, M. V. C., *Glaucon*, p. 3.

more progressive schools are blamed for the lower standard and lack of discipline which are said to be prevalent.

The dust storm of controversy over educational ideas and practice in recent years has had the effect of obscuring many of the real issues. Many people, both those connected with education and laymen, are still confused about the exact aims and methods of the 'newer' ways. Conclusions have often been drawn from the evidence of certain *outré* experiments, without a too careful investigation of the ideas and philosophy which give rise to them. In the eyes of these observers, modern methods are discredited, and they are often unaware of how far such methods have, in fact, been successfully incorporated into the practice of many schools which would not call themselves progressive, with the result that, in certain branches of education, a silent and unobtrusive revolution has already taken place.

Many of the principles underlying the 'newer' methods are, in fact, far from modern. Much of the philosophy of the educational practice of today has its roots deep in the past, and the purpose of this study is to trace historically the genesis of such ideas.

As at the present time, the gulf, in history, lay broadly between those who believed that education is a matter of training the intellect only, of learning from books, and of discipline imposed from without, and those who believe it to be an inner force, a growth from within; that the germ of development lies in the soul and that, given right conditions, it must develop. Education then becomes a matter of nurturing, and of providing the right environment. It concerns not the intellect alone, but the whole man, his feelings, his creative powers, his imagination and his soul.

Where did the idea originate, that education must be literary and second-hand, that wisdom is contained chiefly in books, and that it has as little as possible to do with living and with the work of one's hands? How did education draw apart from life?

Schools and education are not necessarily the same thing. Education is as old as man, but schools are comparatively new. In the first great Elizabethan Age there were few schools, and most people in England were illiterate; but they were not uneducated.

In primitive societies schools have no part at all. Children learn all they need to know in the life of the tribe, by imitating and taking part in its work and its rituals.

The story of education begins in the mists of unrecorded time. There it had nothing to do with books. It was for living. Children learned by experience, by practice and by imitation of adults, mainly in the home. Young people learned through living.

It was only with the invention of writing that a new kind of education arose, first in Egypt and Babylonia, and later in Greece, which gave rise to schools, since the work of teaching was now too skilled to be carried out at home; so the first step was taken on the road which was to lead education farther and farther away from living, through the sterile marshes of scholasticism, until, after many centuries, it was to begin to circle back to its true purposes.

The story of education is not a simple one. It ebbs and flows. Times of enlightenment, often most remarkably modern in their thought and practice, alternate with long periods of dark conformity and sterility. There is a constant breaking off and starting again. The influence of progressive thinkers was not continuous. Most experiments, successful in themselves, had little influence on other writers and practitioners. But a thread, nevertheless, runs through; a spark grows, glows, and then fades away; the same theme appears, disappears, and reappears in differing forms from age to age, and slowly the light grows steadier.

It is very difficult to estimate the education of the past. What did writers *mean* by what they said and wrote? Did the words mean the same for them as they would for us? It is all too easy to read our own meaning into their writings, and therefore to attribute to the authors depths of understanding that they may never have had.

All should be considered in the setting of their times. Education reflects the current values and beliefs of an era. Broadly speaking, what people believe in becomes crystallized in their system of education.

For instance, the nineteenth century in England saw the beginning of a nation-wide provision for elementary education, to meet the need for a population educated sufficiently to man the new machines, and to cast its vote. This was supported by the zeal of men like Lord Shaftesbury, who brought the children out of mines and mills and into the schools, while the work of the scientists and biologists, notably Charles Darwin, and the writings of men like Dickens, helped to change the climate of thought and set a new value on childhood. Education of the present time reflects the influence of industry and technology in the new emphasis in the schools upon science, mathematics and modern languages, while the provision of secondary education for all, the raising of the school leaving age, and the position of the primary school as virtually a common school, reflect the democratic view of life in our time. Possibly the reason for the demand for more higher education is that it may provide some compensation for the standardization of life and the rapidly vanishing opportunities for individuality in twentieth-century western society.

To understand fully the educational ideas of the past, therefore, it is necessary to study and understand the thought and life of the times in which such ideas were current. The educational theory of Plato, for instance, needs to be studied against the background of his philosophy regarding the nature of man and of the state, and in relation to the contemporary history of his times.

This right method of study would require a library, not a single book. The present study selects certain writers, and from them, certain statements. Others are left. It is not possible to give the background and natural setting against which they ought to be viewed. The web of education is worldwide, enormous. It is impossible to follow every thread. There are many omissions, and perhaps some will question the emphases, but the attempt has been made to show that, in education as in everything else, we are the heirs of the past. There has also been an attempt to show that many of the ideas considered most modern can be traced back, not always to the great names to whom credit has generally been given, but to many less-known men and women, whose thought antedated these figures, often by many years. Rousseau, Pestalozzi and Froebel, for instance, have gathered up the glory of the educational reforms of the eighteenth and nineteenth centuries, but it is not always sufficiently recognized how far their ideas were built on the work of those who went before them.

The first written record on the subject of education comes from the fifth century B.C. In the twenty-five centuries which separate us from the Greeks we have added little to their high conception of the purposes of education, and have hardly begun to translate into practice their great ideals.

In the centuries that followed, the beacon flame was almost extinguished. At times it burned dangerously low, but in every age there appeared certain individuals, of faith and vision, who fanned it back into life. Often it seemed as if the darkness must overwhelm it, but slowly the light grew, as each of the great reformers voiced again the same basic philosophy, adding something of his own thought and experience in the process.

So the ideas were passed on and preserved, often in the face of great opposition. Looking back over the succession of writers on education who have contributed to what are considered modern theory and practice, it is clear that one common theme runs through all their work, a theme from which all else develops; that is, the belief in an inner power of growth, that it is in the nature of man to turn towards the light. Development is the unfolding of the latent powers within man, and the educator can trust this power.

In consequence of this belief – that it is in man's nature to grow and develop – the child must have already within him the power to learn, and, unless he has been seriously mishandled, the desire also. Growth is a natural miracle. The task of the teacher then, is not to teach, in the usual sense, but to create the conditions under which the child can most satisfactorily learn for himself. To use the common simile of the garden, the teacher, like the gardener, believing in the power of the seeds to grow, prepares the soil, and does his best to ensure the right conditions for the growth of his plant; but he does not do the growing for it; it is the plant that grows.

From this fundamental belief in 'the inner light' stems the rest of the theory and practice which we call 'modern': education is a drawing out rather than a putting in; the aim of education is a spiritual one, the development of the whole man; attention must therefore be paid not only to the development of intellect, but to the education of the feelings, the judgement and the creative powers; its purpose is the formation of character, not the development of brain alone; knowledge is not enough; true education must distinguish between knowledge and understanding, wisdom and instruction; children learn through their own experience and discovery and should be given things before books; their needs change, as they grow and develop, and education should be adapted to their changing needs and interests; each child must be educated according to his individual abilities; education must therefore be based on a study of children and their ways of learning; they are not little men, and their education must not be a watered-down adult diet; interest should be used as a lever to learning, and the natural forces at work in children can and must be utilized in their education; education should be a natural growth, without coercion, forcing or punishment; the right relationship between teacher and children is of fundamental importance; children develop in company with one another, by living and working together; discipline is a matter of inner self-control, not of order imposed from without.

In the present century we have added little of significance to these educational ideals, whose origins lie far back in the past, and that they still largely await implementation is clear. The schools seem to be at the mercy of many external pressures, in the demands of society for results that can be measured by examinations, and in the limitations imposed on them through lack of adequate material provision, encouragement and inspiration. Public opinion has yet to be convinced that education is equal in importance to defence, medicine and other national expenses.

One new line of thought which the twentieth century has contributed is connected with what writers like Mannheim and Otto Rank term 'spontaneity'. The belief that the feelings and emotions should receive equal attention with the intellect is not new. Its roots lie in the Christian belief in the spiritual destiny of man, and of the value and significance of the soul. The importance of the creative powers in the child and their significance in education have come, in our time, to be more widely recognized, although we are, as yet, a long way from putting fully into practice this belief, whose influence on education will be far reaching.

What is new in this is the impetus given to the idea from a fresh source – the findings of psychoanalysis. This child of the twentieth century has revealed the very great importance of the unconscious mind and its influence on development, and has shown that education must take into account the inner forces working within the personality of each child. Teaching now becomes much more than imparting knowledge, and assessing intellectual growth, and the teacher must not only know his subject, but have a wide and deep understanding of the children he is teaching.

It is being more and more clearly recognized that resistance to learning at the adolescent stage may almost certainly be traced to some form of failure or maltreatment in infancy, but not enough schools or teachers believe this strongly enough to attempt to bring about an effective cure. Those who have tried it know that the best way to treat the problem of backwardness and unwillingness to learn is not to stumble on along the old lines, in some watered-down version of the curriculum which has already produced only failure, but to strike away into something fresh, such as art, movement, drama or even rabbit-keeping, in which the pupils can find success and re-establish their confidence.

One of those who successfully put this into practice was Professor E. B. Castle. He tells how, in his own school, he found over and over again that the way to academic success was by means of creative work. He writes:

The teacher ... has to touch into life the mechanisms of thought and feeling which are part of the child's natural endowment. He has to recognize first the 'given-ness' of the pupil; only secondly the 'given-ness' of the knowledge he is striving to impart. This knowledge is not an absolute value in itself, it is merely a tool, the spoon, which stirs the child's mind. Hence he will ask, 'Where and how can I touch those depths in the child's nature whence spring the desire to know, the desire to reason?' He will not first ask, 'How much of this knowledge I possess can I push into this empty vessel?' For his first task is to liberate energy and desire.[2]

If the curriculum were thought of not so much as a shopping list of the knowledge that we believe children should possess, but as a way of releasing their energies, of helping them to come alive and to find themselves, there would be fewer problems of backwardness and delinquency, and we might have to reconsider, quite drastically, our views on the apparent limitations of intelligence.

The wheels of education have moved slowly, through the centuries. It is in some ways disheartening to read of the splendid theories put forward in past times which seem to have been so little put into practice, but on the other hand, when we hear of low standards of education in our day, or of resistance to newer methods, we can take heart at reading the opinions of those who lived before us on the state of education and morals of their age; of the little attention paid to education, and of the resistance to its spread among 'the poor' in the nineteenth century. Writers deplored then, as they do today, the low standards achieved in the schools. Some, like the Edgeworths, gave a reason for this, which is applicable to our own times:

A boy of seventeen may know all that the utmost stretch of the abilities of Newton discovered in the course of forty years. This general diffusion of knowledge makes it at once more shameful to be ignorant, and more difficult to excel.... This is the real cause of the complaints we sometimes hear of the mediocrity of modern times, and of the scarcity of men of genius, a scarcity which, instead of being gratefully ascribed to the diffusion of knowledge, is erroneously attributed to the injurious effects of tuition and education.[3]

What will be the pattern of education in the future? In Britain it is likely to be less of a pattern than a tapestry. The

2. CASTLE, E. B., *People in School*, pp. 49–50.
3. EDGEWORTH, R. L., *Essays on Professional Education*, pp. 25–6.

freedom which our schools possess, in striking contrast to those of other countries, will ensure that there shall be no uniformity; aims and achievement vary from school to school, in direct relation to the quality of the men and women who teach in them. Some small effect may be produced by influences outside the school; the effect of a progressive and generous Authority can do much to encourage its teachers; but the final result lies with the staffs of the schools, and their personal influence on the children they teach.

Adams, writing in 1912, said:

Perhaps the most important problem in the educational theory of the future is the place the teacher is to occupy . . . The nation may at last realize the importance of education, and may raise the profession to such dignity and honour as shall draw to it the best abilities in the state. The enthusiastic educator is never able to eradicate entirely from his dreams those philosopher kings of the Republic, those schoolmasters who are made the rulers of men. . . .

Perhaps in the future the old fact may be rediscovered . . . that a genuine educator educates as much by what he is as by what he knows . . . The influence of personality upon personality may be recognized as one of the essentials of real education.[4]

But education is not confined to schools, and schools take their colour from the society in which they exist. They are forced to worship the national gods; and the national god of the twentieth century is intellect. Brains take the glory and the crown, and the whole educational system is organized, like some vast factory, to sift out the brains and pass them along the assembly line, shaking out, in the process, three out of four who fall through the intellectual mesh, taking with them some of the finest qualities of rectitude, integrity and sheer solid goodness, which are not necessarily to be found in the most highly intelligent. The ancient belief in the soul of man has been swept away in the worship of his brain.

'The Greeks,' wrote E. B. Castle, 'believed that the greatest work of art they had to create was a Man . . . Today we tend to ask, not how we shall make a child into a complete man, but what technique we shall teach him so that he will become a neat and uncomplain-

4. ADAMS, J., *The Evolution of Educational Theory*, pp. 379–80.

ing cog in a world whose main concern is to produce material wealth.[5]

As long as our aims are confined to solving immediate practical problems, thus neglecting the message of the Greek philosophers and the Hebrew prophets that education is what makes a man, what brings him into obedience to moral law, what presents him with 'the habitual vision of greatness', we have failed to discover a worthy aim for modern education, relevant to the condition of modern boys and girls.[6]

To discover a worthy aim for education is the urgent task of our time, and this can only spring from the beliefs and values held to be important by society.

'We need to gain a faith by which to live,'[7] says M. V. C. Jeffreys.

'Knowledge is important,' writes Livingstone, 'still more so is the power to use it; but most important of all is what a man believes, what he thinks good and bad, whether he has clear values and standards, and is prepared to live by them.'[8]

Education has a limitless responsibility, extending far beyond the school and the social environment, and affecting the very life and being of the State itself. The future of the State, and indeed its survival, depend on the quality of its education; and this is a matter of spiritual values. Livingstone, writing of a community, says:

The quality of its civilization depends ... on its standards, its sense of values, its idea of what is first-rate and what is not. The vocational and social aspects of education are essential, but the most fatal to omit is the spiritual aspect, fatal because its absence may be long unperceived, and, as with an insidious disease, a State may suffer from it and be unconscious of its condition till the complaint has gone too far to cure.[9]

There is, however, an even more important light in which education must be seen.

5. CASTLE, E. B., *Ancient Education and Today*, pp. 102–3.
6. ibid, p. 205.
7. JEFFREYS, M. V. C., *op. cit.*, p. 56.
8. LIVINGSTONE, R. W., *Education for a World Adrift*, Preface, p. xi.
9. ibid, p. 48.

Tensions between individuals disrupt family, business and industrial life, and, eventually, international relationships. Deep-seated, unconscious insecurity, unresolved personal conflicts and dissatisfactions inevitably affect all social relationships. It is therefore vital, for the peace of communities and of the world, that everything possible should be done to ensure that children are helped to grow up free from fear, and from the backdrag of inner conflicts and emotional insecurity. It is more and more being recognized that the inner life of childhood has a profound effect on personal development, and education which neglects the deep drives of human personality and fails to satisfy the basic emotional needs, particularly, but not only, in early childhood, is failing in its responsibility.

The next chapter in education waits to be written. Its form and content will affect profoundly the world of the future. We have, today, the opportunity to put into effect the great ideals set forward by the educators of the past twenty-five centuries, and to create a new education, which, based on the belief in the natural miracle of growth, the importance of personal relations, and the spiritual ends of education, will be adequate for our time.

I

The Greeks · Socrates · Plato · Aristotle

IN Western Europe and America education has five main springs. Working backwards in time, the first is the new emphasis in our day on child study and the findings of psychology. The second was the nineteenth century, when the coming of industrialism gave rise to the demand for clerks and literate workers, and universal franchise required the education of the masses, when 'We must educate our masters' was the rather cynical cry. From this springs the emphasis in schools on what are called the '3 R's'. The third was the Renaissance, with its discovery of the riches of Greece and Rome. These were only open to those who understood Latin and Greek, so these languages became the heart of the curricula of the schools. A Grammar School was what its name implies – a school which taught classical grammar. The fourth was Christianity, with its respect for the personality of the individual and its emphasis on the importance of the soul as well as the intellect. The most remote in time was the Greeks, with their ideal of the whole man, and of education as concerned not with the intellect only, but with the good life, with wisdom. To the Greek and the Christian, education was a spiritual, not a commercial matter.

Of these, the second and third tend to dominate our system of education at the present time, but gleams of the broader ideals first put forward by Plato and his contemporaries are more and more coming to influence what goes on in our schools.

The Greeks were peculiarly fitted to be, after the Hebrews, the first to understand education as a spiritual affair. Surrounded by natural beauty, made more lovely by the clear light of the Greek skies, they were able to spend much of their life out of doors. One of their chief delights, as it is today, was to gather in the open places of the town and talk. Endless discussion of everything under the sun stirred minds already active, and sharpened thought. Naturally quick and intelligent, and unusually aware of the beauty of line and contour, the Greeks had, as well, some inborn love of perfection which expressed itself in every aspect of their life. Above all, they knew, as no other peoples of their time, the value of moderation. The virtues of self-restraint, self-knowledge and self-reverence, expressed their mottoes, 'Nothing to excess' and 'Know thyself', were the influences which moderated the natural excitability of a warm-blooded Mediterranean race.

Religion played its part. In contrast to other peoples, whose gods were far off and unapproachable, the Greek gods had a great measure of humanity. The Greeks, on the whole, did not fear their gods; they never grovelled to them. It was possible to be on something like equal terms with them, to an extent unknown to other nations. Their gods honoured heroes and received honour rather than obeissance in return. Human life had a value, and human beings a respect for themselves, unequalled by other peoples. The civilization of Greece had a morality and spiritual quality quite absent from the life and religion of her neighbours, with the exception of the Hebrews; a morality which showed itself in practical ways from earliest times. Around the Oracle at Delphi, for instance, grew up the first League of Nations, whose members, twelve near-by tribes, entered into a pact of mutual non-aggression and had powers to impose sanctions, or sterner measures, on any member who broke its laws.

The terrain of the Greek mainland led naturally to the growth of little city-states, where sea and mountain separated tribe from tribe, and each had its steep-sided hill with level top on which to build its stronghold, within which developed a loyalty, not to a nation, but to a small community. Within the safety of their walls grew up a unique civilization, comparatively untouched by the barbarism of the rest of the world.

Here, in these small communities, the citizens developed a close sense of unity and mutual responsibility. All adults took their full share in the defence of their city, and in consequence they expected to have an equal share in its government. So, from this life of the city, grew the form of government which we know as democracy. It reached its fullest stature in Athens. Here, all free citizens might speak in the Assembly, and so take a full part in the government. There was here a freedom and equality unknown anywhere else in the world.

Education for such responsibility was obviously essential. Much of it resulted from the very life of the city itself. It was an education simply to live in Athens, to see the beauties of her temples, to listen to her great men, to visit foreign lands in her ships, to hear news of the world from her merchants and travellers, and to take part in her government. Beyond this there was the educational influence of the drama. Pericles considered this of such importance that he not only made it possible for the poorer citizens to have free seats, but he even saw to it that they were paid the wages they lost by their attendance.

Finally, the great victories of Marathon and Salamis, which brought Athens to the peak of power, freed her at last from the Persian peril, and led to the formation of her Empire and her dreams of wide dominion, and in these days of prosperity and greatness everything favoured the production of thinkers and of artists. The social structure of the city-state, with its slaves to perform the menial tasks, left time for contemplation, discussion and the creation of works of art, and in this climate the birth of educational theory took place.

*

The early Greeks did not believe that education was to be had from books. They learned the poems of Homer, but only in order to live a better life. They honoured the heroes, and set them as models for their children. Honour was of first importance to the Greeks, and a man's honour revealed itself in a life of action.

Education was essentially a practical matter – a training in certain activities as preparation for citizenship. Its motive was moral and social. It was given largely in the home and by imitation. Beyond this it was provided in the community, by the training received in the council, and in war. Literary instruction had no place.

Phoenix reminds his pupil Achilles of the education he gave him to fit him for a life of action.

Peleus, he said, sent me to teach thee ... to be both a speaker of words and a doer of deeds.[1]

In the later days of Greece, when the emphasis had shifted away from deeds, these words were often quoted by the critics of the new education, as they looked regretfully back to the days when Greek education was first of all doing, and only secondly instruction.

By the end of the eighth century B.C. the Greeks had a phonetic alphabet and a national book, the epics of Homer, and the schools, which were in being by the beginning of the seventh century, took over much of the education of children. Now literature began to play a part, but its purpose was still a moral one, and its use was to provide worthy objects for imitation. Music, which included all the arts presided over by the Muses, and physical training, were included, not for themselves, but in order that children might

become more civilized, more balanced, and better adjusted in themselves and so more capable in whatever they say or do, for rhythm and harmonious adjustment are essential to the whole of human life,[2]

and so that

a good mind may have a good body to serve it, and no one be forced by physical weakness to play the coward in war and other ordeals.[3]

Throughout the boy's education his teachers were told

to lay much more emphasis on good behaviour than on letters or music.[4]

Gradually, however, there came a change, consequent upon political and social changes in Athens. With the growth of her power and wealth a demand arose for a new kind of education, that would be adequate as a preparation for the new opportunities that were opening out. Professional soldiers took the place of the citizen hoplites. Trained speakers replaced the

1. *Iliad*, Bk. 9, p. 174.   2. *Protagoras*, 326, B.
3. ibid, 326, C.   4. ibid, 325, E.

statesmen of rank and wealth. Men began to question authority, both in politics and religion, and to claim the right to
decide for themselves on questions of ethics. Moral qualities,
then, became subordinate to success and achievements, and
with this change in values came a change of emphasis. Intellectual qualities became all-important, and the demand for an
education that would ensure a successful career in public life
was met by a new kind of teacher – the sophists. They claimed
to be able to impart the necessary knowledge by theoretical
instruction and discussion. This assumption extended to the
realm of morals. Wisdom, it was held, could be taught through
words. The form and structure of language now became more
important than its content, and education, at least in its higher
forms, became almost entirely literary. Greece changed into
'a nation of talkers instead of a nation of doers'.

Education now became a paid profession, and for the first
time divided society into two classes, the educated and the uneducated. Its purpose was no longer primarily moral, but intellectual and aesthetic. The sophists were the founders of
pedagogy, and their influence is still seen today, wherever
education bows to form rather than content.

Educational theory has always appeared in times of upheaval
and change, when men have been forced by circumstances to
seek out new ways, to search beneath the surface for causes
and cures, and to formulate some kind of panacea in the form
of education. The defeat of Athens by the Spartans in the fifth
century threw into immediate and urgent prominence the question of how man should live, and consequently what kind of
education should be given to children; and from this background emerged Socrates, Plato and Aristotle as the first of the
great educational theorists.

In opposition to the doctrine of the sophists that man is the
measure of all things and can decide for himself in matters of
morality, Socrates believed in the existence of laws and principles that are valid for all, and universal. This philosophy led,
in his view, to the idea that virtue is knowledge, and therefore
virtue can be taught. The good man, then, can only be one who
knows the nature of goodness.

This premise underlay Plato's philosophy in the *Republic*,

where he attempted to show how the perfect State might be brought about. Discussion of the means by which it was to be done comprises the first treatise on education.

For Plato the education of the individual was closely bound up with society. Full development can only come about in and through the life of the city-state, while the character of the State itself is dependent upon the quality of education of its citizens, and education must be adapted to the needs and the potentialities of the different types of people that comprise it.

Plato's contribution to education lay in his belief that the seeds of knowledge exist in every human soul and that the function of the teacher is to help the learner to discover the truth for himself. The teacher's task is to help the soul in its movement towards the light, a movement which is entirely natural.

The soul of every man does possess the power of learning the truth and the organ to see it with; and ... just as one might have to turn the whole body round in order that the eye should see light instead of darkness, so the entire soul must be turned away from this changing world, until its eye can bear to contemplate reality and that supreme splendour which we have called the Good.[5]

Teaching, then, is based on the belief that the power of understanding is already present in the one to be taught, and the task of the educator is to help direct this understanding in the right way. Plato distinguishes between teaching, as giving instruction from without, and true education, which is a process of drawing out what is already latent in the learner, and makes clear that education of this kind is an active search, and only possible when the learner takes it on willingly, for himself.

The soul has learned everything, so that when a man has recalled a single piece of knowledge – learned it, in ordinary language – there is no reason why he should not find out all the rest, if he keeps a stout heart and does not grow weary of the search.[6]

He was aware of the dangers of cleverness for itself, without the balance of wisdom and sensitivity to the needs of the community. To avoid the dangers of an over-developed intel-

5. *Republic*, Bk. 7, 518.   6. *Meno*, 81, D.

lect there must be an education which will develop all sides of man's nature in proportion and harmony, and which will give him qualities of temperance and reverence that he may 'have the power of adapting himself to the most varied forms of action with utmost versatility and grace.' Education is 'that training which is given by suitable habits to the first instincts of virtue in children', and virtue is 'harmony of the soul'.[7]

His philosophy was entirely spiritual. He believed that the world as perceived by the material senses is not the true world but only a shadow of the reality which exists elsewhere, a philosophy developed most fully in the later revelation of Christianity, 'Ye shall know the truth and the truth shall make you free', and echoed by thinkers, poets and mystics of all ages, up to the present day. Wordsworth expressed the same thought in the Ode *Intimations of Immortality from Recollections of Early Childhood*:

> Our birth is but a sleep and a forgetting:
> The Soul that rises with us, our life's Star,
> Hath had elsewhere its setting,
> And cometh from afar:
> Not in entire forgetfulness,
> And not in utter nakedness,
> But trailing clouds of glory do we come
> From God, who is our home.[8]

Plato, then, was responsible for the educational ideal, often attributed to Rousseau, that the nature of the learner, and the process of learning, are of greater importance than the subject matter to be studied. For him the purpose of education was not to develop certain abilities, nor to give specific instruction, but to make men able to achieve their true destiny – to know the good.

In the story of the slave in the *Meno* he showed that, before one can learn anything, it is necessary to know oneself and to realize the extent of one's own ignorance. For Plato the chief purpose of life is to gain such knowledge. He calls it the science of right choice, which makes men able to make right decisions.

7. *Laws*, Bk. 2, 653.
8. *Ode on the Intimations of Immortality*, lines 58–65.

He was very much aware of the educational influence of the environment.

> We would not have our Guardians grow up among representations of moral deformity, as in some foul pasture, where, day after day, feeding on every poisonous weed they would, little by little, gather insensibly a mass of corruption in their very souls. Rather we must seek out those craftsmen whose instinct guides them to whatsoever is lovely and gracious; so that our young men, dwelling in a wholesome climate, may drink in good from every quarter, whence, like a breeze bearing health from happy regions, some influence from noble works constantly falls upon eye and ear from childhood upward, and imperceptibly draws them into sympathy and harmony with the beauty of reason, whose impress they take.[9]

Critics of the 'play-way' of education castigate it as a recent and unfruitful innovation, but in the *Republic* we are told that children should make 'a good beginning in plays'.

> For the free man there should be no element of slavery in learning. Enforced exercise does no harm to the body, but enforced learning will not stay in the mind. So avoid compulsion, and let your children's lessons take the form of play.[10]

And in the *Laws*, play is said to be the best training for the work of later life:

> He who is to be a good builder, should play at building children's houses: he who is to be a good husbandman, at tilling the ground; and those who have the care of their education should provide them when young with mimic tools. ... The future carpenter should learn to measure or apply the line in play; and the future warrior should learn riding, or some other exercise, for amusement, and the teacher should endeavour to direct the children's inclinations and pleasures, by the help of amusements, to their final aim in life.

> The most important part of education is right training in the nursery. The soul of the child in his play should be guided to the love of that sort of excellence in which when he grows up to manhood he will have to be perfected.[11]

Although Plato's conception of play is very different from that of modern educators, he gives what is perhaps the first hint of the value of studying children at play:

9. *Republic*, Bk. 3, 401.   10. ibid, Bk. 7, 536.
11. *Laws*, Bk. 1, 643.

'This will ... help you to see what they are naturally fitted for.'[12]

He understood that it was in the nature of children to be constantly in movement:

'The young of all creatures cannot be quiet in their bodies or in their voices; they are always wanting to move and cry out.'[13]
This movement is the 'origin of rhythm and gymnastic. ...'[14] The whole choral art is ... in our view the whole of education. ...[15] The uneducated is he who has not been trained in the chorus, and the educated is he who has been well trained.'[16]

He was fully aware of the importance of the first beginnings:

The direction in which education starts a man will determine his future life.[17]
'The first shoot of any plant, if it makes a good start, has the greatest effect in helping it to attain its mature natural excellence.[18] The beginning is always the most important part especially when you are dealing with anything young and tender. That is the time when the character is being moulded and easily takes any impress one may wish to stamp on it.'[19]

The office of Minister of Education, in Plato's view, should be the greatest 'of all the great offices of State ... the legislator ought not to allow the education of children to become a secondary or accidental matter'.[20]

In these respects Plato, twenty-five centuries ago, laid out the groundplan of modern educational theory. If much of this philosophy was ignored by later educators, and lay dormant through the centuries that followed, if more notice was taken of his contempt for anything 'real', and his belief that knowledge came, not from observation, but from theory, and if these facets of his teaching then fathered a tradition of reverence for abstract learning and the written word, the fault lies not with Plato but with those who, misunderstanding his spiritual conception of education, twisted his philosophy into lifelessness.

12. *Republic*, Bk. 7, 536.   13. *Laws*, Bk. 2, 653.
14. ibid, Bk. 2, 672.   15. ibid.
16. ibid, Bk. 2, 654.   17. *Republic*, Bk. 4, 424.
18. *Laws*, Bk. 6, 765.   19. *Republic*, Bk. 2, 377.
20. *Laws*, Bk. 6, 765, 766.

For in spite of Plato's contempt for 'reality', he never believed that education was a matter for the intellect only. To him it was always a process of growth, which concerned all sides of man's nature, of which the most important outcome was the formation of character. In this, art and music played an important part.

'Rhythm and harmony sink deep into the recesses of the soul and take the strongest hold there, bringing that grace of body and mind which is only to be found in one who is brought up in the right way.' [21]

Plato's description, in the *Republic*, of the decline of the human soul emphasizes the importance of educating the emotions as well as the intellect. Education must help the soul to know the reality which lies beyond the world as it is perceived by the physical senses, and so to free itself from the limitations which result from ignorance of the truth. This is education of the emotions, of the whole person, not of the intellect alone. It involves attitudes as well as information, morality as well as scholarship, beliefs as well as book learning.

For Plato, instruction from outside was not true education. Socrates in the *Meno* says:

The truth about reality is always in our soul.[22]

The significance of the episode with the slave, described in the *Meno*, lies in the fact that he understood the truth of the mathematical theorem, not from being taught, but because he himself produced the knowledge out of himself.

Of the ideas embodied in the *Republic,* Professor Nettleship says:

In the way of its literal execution we can do hardly anything; but we might do a little towards carrying out some of its spirit. We might introduce more continuity into the curriculum of our schools and universities, trying to give the mind its natural food at the right times, and not letting it be still sprawling on the ground when it ought to be able to walk, nor asking it to climb a mountain before it can find its way about the house.[23]

21. *Republic*, Bk. 3, 401.   22. *Meno*, 86, B.
23. NETTLESHIP, *The Theory of Education in Plato's Republic,* p. 141.

Aristotle also saw education as closely connected with the life of the community. To him it was a part of the art of politics, but he was concerned to a greater degree than Plato with education as an individual matter. He too saw it as a process of development from within, an unfolding and realization of the self, but he also understood that full development cannot be achieved within the narrow limits of the life of the State, but must include all aspects of human life.

He recognized three periods in the development of an individual, in each of which one aspect of growth is most evident: first, the period of physical growth; second, the period when the appetites are predominant; and thrid, the period of the dominance of reason.

To meet the needs of these three periods there must be three stages in education. The education of the body will be followed by the education of the character, and finally will come the education of the intellect.

Aristotle warns against an imbalance in the education of the body which would produce muscle at the expense of mind. The aim of gymnastics should be to give a liberal education, not to produce experts.

It is grace, and not brute strength that should count for most; for it is not the wolf or any of the lower animals that can engage in any fine and dangerous contest, but the good man.[24]

In his understanding of the importance of a balanced education, Aristotle drew attention to a fundamental too frequently ignored by later educators, whose conception of education was often confined to the development of intellect and the neglect of other aspects of growth. He, like Plato, realized the importance of the feelings and the need for their education.

A right disposition of the feelings seems to be the principle that leads to virtue rather than the reason.[25]

He was one of the first to show some understanding of the needs of little children. Up to the age of five they should

24. *Politics*, Bk. V, ch. 4.
25. *Magna Moralia*, 1206 b. trans. ST GEORGE STACK.

learn by means of amusement, and from five to seven there
should be objects for them to look at, and other means of
illustrating oral lessons. They

> should be taught nothing not even necessary labour, lest it
> hinder growth; but should be accustomed to use so much motion as
> to avoid an indolent habit of body; and this can be acquired by
> various means, among others by play.[26]

What, for the Greeks, was the way to this balanced and harmonious development? It came largely from first-hand experience, in the market place, in the Assembly, in the theatre
and in the religious celebrations; through what the Greek
youth saw and heard, not through books. From such experience he learned to think and to make wise decisions.

Professor Boyd describes the first-hand education which the
Greek youth experienced, and which was his preparation for
living:

> As he went along the streets he saw on every side products of
> the noblest art the world has ever known. Day by day he might
> hear the discussions of men of apt speech and wide experience, on
> political questions; and in the springtime he might witness the per-
> formance of the tragedies. Here, if ever, life was the real
> educator.[27]

It was always the whole man which must be developed. It
was the Greeks who first understood and gave expression to
the ideal of perfecting the whole man, of unfolding all his
powers and abilities and developing them to the full. Self-
realization, development from within, was the means and aim
of education. It was a process of evolution of the soul.

'True education, in Plato's view,' says Professor Jaeger, 'means
the awakening of abilities asleep in the soul. It starts the func-
tioning of the organ by which we learn and understand.'[28]

The story of Telemachus, in his transformation from a
weak youth to a hero, shows clearly how the Greeks believed
that education was a release of power, a natural miracle,

26. *Politics*, VII, 17.
27. BOYD, *History of Western Education*, p. 20.
28. JAEGER, *Paideia*, Vol. II, p. 295.

brought about by divine influence, and the part they assigned
to 'music' in education showed how important they considered
the development of creative power as an educative force.

Poetry, music and rhythm were always dominant in Greek
education; even gymnastics was included for its power to
develop, not bodily strength, but courage. All of these were
important for their influence on the whole nature of man.

Intelligence and intellectual qualities were respected and
admired by the Greeks, but unless balanced by other qualities
of character, they believed that they could be dangerous and
undesirable. Chief of these balancing qualities was self-control.
Plato makes Socrates say that the young prince must learn to
overcome his physical needs and to master his appetites.

We allow [children] to go free only when we have established in
each one of them as it were a constitutional ruler, whom we have
trained to take over the guardianship from the same principle in
ourselves.[29]

To the Greeks of the classical period, education was of
great significance. The aim of all their living was the development of a more noble type of man, and they believed that
education, as the means to this end, was of supreme importance.

The ideal of education was the new man, fully developed in
all his powers, able to play his part in society; and this respect
for personality, and provision for its development, is the
great legacy which Greece has given to the western world.

Professor Jaeger describes this achievement: 'Other nations
made gods, kings, spirits; the Greeks alone made men.' [30]

In this they foreshadowed what we still only dimly perceive,
that the making of men is not only a training of the intellect,
but a development of all those qualities which make them able
to know the good.

The culture we call Hellenism [writes Professor Castle] was,
then, an entirely personal thing, no longer rooted in the *polis*, but in
the city which men may find 'in their own hearts'. For Hellenistic
man the aim of life was to make oneself; to produce from the

29. *Republic*, Bk. 9, 590.
30. JAEGER, op. cit., Vol. I, intro. p. xxiii.

original childish material, and from the imperfectly formed creature one may so easily remain, the man who is fully a man, whose ideal proportions one can just perceive. . . . This is *paideia*, the final word of Greece on the meaning of culture.[31]

31. CASTLE, E. B., *Ancient Education and Today*, p. 104.

2

The Romans · Pliny · Quintilian · Seneca · Plutarch

THE Romans derived most of their system of education from Greece, but their more practical outlook – everything must be useful – and their interest in organization and method rejected much of the liberality and breadth of the Greek ideal, and narrowed education to those skills which would produce the good orator and the 'good' citizen. Their methods achieved such perfection in their limited way that they became the accepted methods in use in the schools for centuries afterwards, so that analytical study of language alone formed the main body of the curriculum right into the nineteenth century. The struggle, carried on by small groups and individual educators of vision, to throw off the Roman tradition and to bring back the rich and broad conception of Greek education has been carried on through the centuries, and continues in our own times.

In early times, as with the Greeks, experience of life was the means of education for the Romans. Children and youths learned by watching and imitating, at home, on the farms, in the army and in the forum. Little value was set on knowledge which had no direct bearing on practical life, and books played a negligible part in such training. Scipio says, in the *De Republica*:

Thanks to my father I got a liberal education and from childhood I have sought eagerly to instruct myself. Nevertheless, experience and home education have done more to make me what I am than books.[1]

The younger Pliny wrote:

It was the ancient custom that we should learn from our elders, not only through the ear but also through the eye, those things that

1. CICERO, *De Republica*, 1, 22.

we should soon have to do ... Each one was instructed by his own father.[2]

Cato the Censor taught his son to read and also to fence, to ride, to box, to throw a dart and to swim. To be able to swim was considered as important as to be able to read, and an ill-educated person was described as one who had learned neither to read nor to swim.

Pliny, in a letter of advice to a certain lady on the choice of a tutor for her son, recommended her to find a teacher who will teach him morals first and afterwards eloquence.

Morals were learned in the home, where self-control, modesty and obedience were considered of greater importance than intellectual achievement. All that was considered necessary in the way of a literary education was enough skill in reading to be able to master the Laws of the Twelve Tables, which in time became the chief matter of instruction.

Gradually, however, the simplicity and austerity of Roman life was overlaid, and in time fundamentally altered, by the influence of Greek ideas and culture. Schools took the place of homes as the means of education, schools where the means of instruction were literary and formal, and the material of instruction remote from real life.

The grammar schools which were established, in imitation of those of later Greece, concentrated on the detailed analysis of language, and the functions of words were considered of far greater importance than what they had to say.

The Roman's practical outlook on life was reflected in their system of education. More concerned with the uses of knowledge than with the disinterested pursuit of truth, they showed little understanding of the Greek ideal of the development of the whole man and of education as the means by which he might learn to live the good life.

The aim of education, carried out in the schools of the Rhetors, was the making of orators, but it must be admitted that oratory, to the more thoughtful Romans at least, was something much wider than its literal meaning would imply. Cicero said:

2. PLINY, *Letters*, VIII, 1.

The art of eloquence is something greater, and collected from more sciences and studies, than people imagine... A knowledge of a vast number of things is necessary, without which volubility of words is empty and ridiculous... In my opinion ... no man can be an orator ... unless he has attained the knowledge of everything important and of all liberal arts.[3]

And Quintilian:

It is the perfect orator that we are training and he cannot even exist unless he is a good man. We therefore demand in him not only exceptional powers of eloquence but also every mental excellence.[4]

No one will be an orator unless he is a good man ... Does not he who is called in to plead cases require an integrity which no greed can corrupt, no influence seduce, no fear overawe?[5] Before all else the orator ... must cultivate morality ... no one will be skilled enough even in speaking who has not plumbed the depths of man's nature and formed his own moral character by study and reflection ... fluency in speaking is derived from the deepest springs of wisdom.[6]

Unfortunately for later education it was not this all-embracing ideal which was passed on to succeeding ages, but rather the worship of form, and the mechanical methods of language study which the Romans brought to such perfection. This artificial idea of education gained so strong a hold over the schools of Europe, that even after the Renaissance had restored some of the Greek spirit to the world, it has taken three hundred years to break down the tradition and bring back into education some of the liberal ideas of Greek culture.

There were certain of the Romans, however, who voiced important educational principals which are valued and acted on today. Juvenal said: 'The greatest reverence is due the child,'[7] and Seneca wrote: 'We should learn for life, not for school.' The purpose of learning was to produce virtue and this must

3. CICERO, De Oratore, Monroe, Source Book in the History of Education, Greek and Roman period, pp. 429–30.
4. QUINTILIAN, Education of an Orator, Bk. I, ch. 9, SMAIL, p. 5.
5. ibid, Bk. XII, ch. 1, 3, SMAIL, pp. 108, 113.
6. ibid, Bk. XII, ch. 2, 1.4.6, SMAIL, pp. 120–21.
7. JUVENAL, Satire, XIV.

be found within the soul itself, in which the seeds of wisdom lie. Seneca continued:

Cast about rather for some good which will abide. But there can be no such good except as the soul discovers it for itself within itself.[8]

There is only one really liberal study – that which gives a man his liberty. It is the study of wisdom, and that is lofty, brave and great-souled.[9]

Growth is from within:

Although the body needs many things in order to be strong, yet the mind grows from within, giving to itself nourishment and exercise.[10]

Wisdom and understanding result from the work of the mind on the experiences presented to it.

The food we have eaten, as long as it retains its original quality and floats in our stomachs as an undiluted mass, is a burden; but it passes into tissue and blood only when it has been changed from its original form. So it is with the food which nourishes our higher nature – we should see to it that whatever we have absorbed should not be allowed to remain unchanged, or it will be no part of us. We must digest it; otherwise it will merely enter the memory and not the reasoning power.[11]

Knowledge alone is not enough. Education must go deeper and teach one how to live.

The scholar busies himself with investigations into language, and if it be his desire to go farther afield, he works on history, or, if he would extend his range to the farthest limits, on poetry. But which of these paves the way to virtue? Pronouncing syllables, investigating words, memorizing plays, or making rules for the scansion of poetry – what is there in all this that rids one of fear, roots out desire, or bridles the passions? [12]

Now I will transfer my attention to the musician. You, sir, are teaching me how the treble and the bass are in accord with one another, and how, though the strings produce different notes, the result is a harmony; rather bring my soul into harmony with it-

---

8. SENECA, *Epistulae Morales*, Bk. 1, ed. CAPPS, PAGE, ROUSE, p. 195.
9. ibid, Ep. LXXXVIII.   10. ibid, Ep. LXXX.
11. ibid, Ep. LXXXIV.   12. ibid, Ep. LXXXVIII.

self, and let not my purposes be out of tune. You are showing me what the doleful keys are; show me rather how, in the midst of adversity, I may keep from uttering a doleful note. The mathematician teaches me how to lay out the dimensions of my estates; but I should rather be taught how to lay out what is enough for a man to own ... What good is there for me in knowing how to parcel out a piece of land if I know not how to share it with my brother?

O what marvellous skill! You know how to measure the circle; you find the square of any shape which is set before you; you compute the distances between the stars; there is nothing which does not come within the scope of your calculations. But if you are a real master of your profession, measure me the mind of man! Tell me how great it is, or how puny! You know what a straight line is; but how does it benefit you if you do not know what is straight in this life of ours? [13]

The old form of education was active:

Our ancestors used to teach their children nothing that could be learned while lying down, but neither the new system nor the old teaches virtue,

while the new way actually prevents men from learning what is important.

This desire to know more than is sufficient is a sort of intemperance. Why? Because this unseemly pursuit of the liberal arts makes men troublesome, wordy, tactless, self-satisfied bores, who fail to learn the essentials just because they have learned the non-essentials,

and the philosophers

know more about careful speaking than about careful living. [14]

Plutarch also was aware of the importance of early education.

Childhood is a tender thing and easily wrought into any shape. The very spring and root of honesty lies in the felicity of lighting on good education. [15]

13. ibid.   14. ibid.
15. MONROE, Source Book of the History of Education, Greek and Roman Period, pp. 308, 9.

He quotes Socrates:

What mean you, fellow citizen, that you thus turn every stone to scrape wealth together, and take so little care of your children? [16]

He warns against unwise fathers who

make haste, that their chyldren may the soner excel other, they do put into them infynite labours, whereof bynge werye and oppressed with intollerable paynes, fynallye they fynde lyttell pleasures or swetenes in lernynge. A lyttell water maketh herbes to growe, and with to moche they be soone glutted, wherefore in studyes and labours some recreacion is to be gyven to children. [17]

Education is a process of growth and the educator's work resembles that of the farmer.

For lyke as in tyllage fyrste it behoveth that the moulde ... be good. Secondarily that the husbande or ploughman be experte in sowinge. Thirdely that the sede be clene and withoute faute. So (in bringinge up of youre children) ye shall applie and resemble to the moulde your childrens nature, to the ploughman, their instructour or maister, to the sede, instruction of lernynge and preceptes. ... If a grounde fertile of nature be yll housbandried for lacke of good tillage it appereth foule and yl favored. [18]

He perhaps understood better than we do today the meaning of ability. Unlike many modern educators with their reverence for intelligence tests and selection techniques, Plutarch saw that there is more to the matter than so-called 'inborn ability'. What hope his beliefs in education, in 'labour and industry' hold out for those in whom 'Nature hath not thoroughly done her part'.

And yet if anyone thinks that those in whom Nature hath not thoroughly done her part may not in some measure make up her defects, if they be so happy as to light upon good teaching, and withal apply their own industry towards the attainment of virtue, he is to know that he is very much, nay, altogether, mistaken. For as a good natural capacity may be impaired by slothfulness, so dull and heavy natural parts may be improved by instruction; and whereas negligent students arrive not at the capacity of under-

16. ibid, p. 310.
17. *The Education or Bringinge Up of Children*, no pagination.
18. ibid.

standing the most easy things, those who are industrious conquer the greatest difficulties.[19]

He believed that a child's mind is 'not a vessel to be filled, but a fire to be kindled' and saw that true education could never be forced.

Labour is to be kepte in, as it were in a closet or celle, and so moderately used, that children beynge tendre and flexible, be not in study overmoche fatigated. For as Plate sayth, laboure and slepe be ennemyes to lernynge.[20]

I do affirme surely in myne opinion, chyldren oughte not to be brought up to honest exercise, by beatynge and strokes, but by exhortacion and reasonyng. ... For punishment is meter for villaynes and slaves than for them that be franke or of gentill bloud; whiche with travaile be hardned, and some tyme beinge aferde of the whippe applieth them to labour. ... Children of gentyll nature take more profite by praise or lyghte rebuke, than by stripes.[21]

Plutarch emphasized what was always of such significance to the Greeks, the importance of balance, of the middle way:

The active lyfe, lackynge philosophie, is of littell purpose. ... The contemplative life ... if it be not jointed with the active, it is of none effecte or profite. ... The meane waye to holde in every thynge, it is a high and perfecte craft.[22]

Quintilian was strongly aware of the importance of the early years:

We are by nature most tenacious of what we have imbibed in our infant years.[23]

He believed that children must enjoy learning:

One thing especially must be guarded against, viz. lest one who cannot yet love studies come to hate them and even after the passing of childhood's years shrink from a bitter task once undergone.[24]

19. MONROE, *Source Book of the History of Education, Greek and Roman period*, p. 308.
20. *The Education or Bringinge Up of Children*, no pagination.
21. ibid.   22. ibid.
23. QUINTILIAN, *Education of an Orator*, Bk. I, ch. 1, 5. WATSON, p. 10.
24. ibid, SMAIL, *Quintilian on Education*, Bk. I, ch. 1, 20, p. 16.

He saw the necessity of gaining the co-operation of the child and realized that this could never be done by force:

Zeal for learning depends upon inclination, a thing which cannot be forced ... the mind as a rule refuses tasks imposed by harsh compulsion.[25]

He looked upon play as 'in itself a mark of activity of mind' and regarded it as a sign of a lively disposition. He believed that the boy who lacked the natural impulse of boyhood would be unlikely to show alertness of mind in his work. 'I cannot expect that he who is always dull and spiritless will be of an eager disposition in his studies, when he is indifferent even to that excitement which is natural to his age,'[26] he wrote, and he saw the educative value of play as a means of developing character. 'True character ... reveals itself with less reserve in play,'[27] and in play even very young children may learn the difference between right and wrong.

He made some practical suggestions about how children might be taught by handling things in play:

I approve of a practice devised to stimulate the child to learn, viz. that of giving him ivory letters to play with and anything else that can be proved to add to the child's pleasure, which may be a delight to him to handle, look at, and name.[28]

Corporal punishment is undesirable:

I am altogether opposed to it, first because it is disgusting ... in the next place, because a pupil ... will remain obdurate even in the face of blows ... and finally because such chastisement will be quite unnecessary if there is someone ever present to supervise the boy's studies with diligence. ...

If you coerce the young child by means of blows, how would you deal with the grown youth who cannot thus be driven by fear and has more important things to learn?[29]

Haste can be harmful:

25. ibid, Bk. I, ch. 3, 8.9, p. 31.   26. ibid, WATSON, pp. 26–7.
27. ibid, SMAIL, *Quintilian on Education*, Bk. I, ch. 3, 12, p. 32.
28. ibid, Bk. I, ch. 1, 26, pp. 17–18.
29. ibid, Bk. I, ch. 3, 14.15, pp. 32–3

It is incredible how reading is retarded by undue haste. ... Let reading, then, be first of all, confident.[30]

He realized the need to adapt work to the ability of the learner:

the teacher must be a sensible man with a good knowledge of teaching and must be prepared to stoop to his pupil's level, just as a rapid walker, if walking with a small child, will give him his hand and lessen his own speed and avoid advancing at a pace beyond the powers of his little companion.[31]

The master . . . must make it his business, in dealing with minds still unformed, not to start by overloading the feeble intellects of his pupils, but to control his own powers and come down to the level of their understanding. For just as narrow-necked jars spill a flood of liquid poured over them, whereas they fill up when it flows in gradually or even drop by drop, so we must observe carefully the capacity of youthful minds. For that which is too difficult for their understanding will not find entrance to the boys' minds which, if we may put it so, have too narrow an opening for its reception.[32]

He suggested that a teacher should study the individual differences of his pupils:

The skilled teacher, when a pupil is entrusted to his care, will first of all seek to discover his ability and natural disposition.[33]

When the teacher has noticed the points I have mentioned, let him next observe how the mind of his pupil is to be handled.[34]

Children should be taught according to their abilities:

It is usually and rightly esteemed an excellent thing in a teacher that he should be careful to mark diversity of gifts in those whose education he has undertaken, and to know in what direction nature inclines each one most. For in this respect there is an unbelievable variety, and types of mind are no less numerous than types of body.[35]

He saw the importance of using the child's own impulses in his education:

30. ibid, Bk. I, ch. 1, 32.33, p. 19.
31. ibid, BUTLER, *Quintilian*. Inst. Ora., Bk. II, ch. 3, 7, p. 221.
32. ibid, SMAIL, *Quintilian on Education*, Bk. I, ch. 2, 27.28, pp. 27–8.
33. ibid, Bk. I, ch. 3, 1, p. 30.   34. ibid, Bk. I, ch. 3, 6, p. 31.
35. ibid, Bk. II, ch. 8, 1, p. 101.

Most teachers have thought it expedient to train each pupil in such a way as to foster by sound instruction his peculiar gifts, and so to develop varied endowments most effectively in the direction of their natural bent . . . that each may be brought on in the style in which he excels. Nature . . . gains strength when assisted by careful training, whereas one who is drawn away from his natural bent cannot achieve success in studies for which he is less well fitted, and he also by neglect enfeebles those gifts for the exercise of which he seems to have been born.[36]

The right relationship between teacher and pupil is important:

We must be careful above all things else to secure the intimate friendship of such a master, so that in teaching he may not simply be guided by a sense of duty, but also by affection for his pupil.[37]

Nineteen hundred years ago, Quintilian recognized the problem of backward children and suggested how to deal with it:

We must so far accommodate ourselves . . . to feeble intellects, that they may be trained only to that to which nature invites them; for thus they will do with more success the only thing which they can do.[38]

Quintilian was amongst the first of educators to express a strong belief in the inborn capacity to learn, that reasoning is as natural to man as flying to birds, speed to horses, and ferocity to birds of prey. He understood also something of the problem of resistance to learning, and showed himself aware of the importance of studying the effect of teaching upon children and the need for them to understand what they learn. His influence on later educators and writers was such that Erasmus, writing in 1512, gave his opinion that the subject of methods and aims in teaching had been fully dealt with, 'seeing that Quintilian has said in effect the last word on the matter'.

36. ibid, Bk. II, ch. 8, 3.5, pp. 101, 102.
37. ibid, Bk. I, ch. 2, 15, p. 25.
38. ibid, WATSON, *Quintilian*, Inst. Ora., Bk. II, 8.12, Vol. I, p. 124.

3

The Hebrews

THE feature most characteristic of early Jewish education was that it was basically spiritual. Surrounded by materialistic and barbaric tribes, the little Hebrew people were the first to attempt to base their national life on spiritual values. Far in advance of the rest of the world in their understanding of moral and spiritual principles, they are revealed in their history, as recorded in the Bible, as an intelligent and sensitive people, in the highest sense educated. But education, to them, was not primarily a matter of the intellect, but of the spirit. 'All thy children shall be taught of the Lord' was its theory, and although from the time of Ezra a book was the centre of Jewish religion, learning was never an end in itself. Book learning and intellectual activity were subordinate to a greater purpose. 'The fear of the Lord is the beginning of wisdom' was the keynote of education.

Moral education was not a matter of precepts only, but was learned in living. It was a matter of training, rather than of instruction. Children learned to work hard by taking part in the work of the home, or the fields. They learned courage and loyalty in real situations. From early years they took part in the life of the tribe or community, with its customs and institutions, and by this means their thought was shaped and their character formed.

Much use was made of learning by heart, but this was not entirely divorced from experience, for it must be remembered that much of what children had to learn described what they had themselves seen many times. The situations were not abstract and divorced from experience, but had been vividly witnessed, long before the children were required to learn by heart.

In the earliest times, before the Exile, when there were no schools, education was the concern of the tribe and the family. In the main it was a training in living, and was gained through experience rather than instruction. The means of education were, first, play and, later, active participation in work and in the use of weapons. The boy learned all that was necessary under the guidance of his father and his kinsmen in the tribe. Since the scribes and rabbis themselves frequently carried on a trade, it is likely that arts and crafts and the use of the hands played a part in the education of every child, and that a boy received his training by working alongside his father or older brothers.

Gradually the need for the '3 Rs' developed. The appearance of a written law produced the need for instruction in reading and, with the growth of commerce, came the demand for a knowledge of money and weights and measures. The scribes were the first members of the teaching profession, and after the Exile written literature became increasingly the means of education.

Nevertheless, the scope of the Scriptures shows how broad a field of study was provided by this literature. Law, history, morals, manners and the '3 Rs' were all contained in it, as well as a study of the world of nature, and who shall say that it did not teach the child to observe and to think for himself?

Professor Castle writes:

It is in the Talmud . . . that we meet for the first time 'the effort to understand the child, to awaken his interest, to win his active sympathy' (Nathan Morris).[1] In the first centuries of the Christian era Talmudic literature reveals the same tender attitude towards children that we encounter in the New Testament, when Jesus makes them first citizens of the Kingdom of Heaven. Talmudic writers begin to regard children no longer as possessions but as personalities in their own right. The glimpse Nathan Morris gives us of family life in Talmudic times, of learned scholars on their knees among their children, of that saintly rabbi who bought earthenware dishes for his children to play with, 'in order to satisfy their impulses for breaking things', reveals a picture of almost Froebelian freedom. Further evidence of this change of attitude is revealed in the frequent reference in Talmudic books to children's toys, a matter on which the Bible remains silent.[2]

1. MORRIS, NATHAN, *The Jewish School*, p. 221.
2. CASTLE, E. B., *Ancient Education and Today*, p. 170.

The great movements of thought and culture, however, which stirred the Greek and Roman world, and permeated its ideals of education, in general passed the Hebrews by. They ignored the riches of their pagan neighbours and conquerors, and allowed no part of them to enter their schools. As a result their education may have remained narrow in one sense, but by so doing, they were able to retain their national and spiritual individuality, which in time was to give birth to the new freedom which came with Christianity.

4

The Roman Emperors · Alexandria the Centre of Learning
The Christian Fathers · Clement, Origen, St Jerome, St Augustine
The Dark Ages · The Castle, the Church and the Kings · Alcuin
The Universities · Peter Abelard

WHEREVER the Romans carried their conquests they set up
schools. Grammar and rhetoric were the chief subjects taught,
and the form and method of education remained the same
over many centuries.

During the period of the Roman Empire two important influences were brought to bear on education. The first was the
founding of schools and educational institutions by certain of
the Emperors, which eventually brought education under state
control. The second was the influence of Christianity.

As Rome extended her power the need for, and value of
education became recognized, and successive Emperors began
to be its patrons. Under Augustus and those who followed
him, Alexandria became the great centre of learning. Here the
course of study included not only rhetoric but history, geography, philosophy, philology, politics and religion, natural history, botany and anatomy. Hadrian, an admirer of all things
Greek, followed by Antoninus and Marcus Aurelius, helped
to create a new enthusiasm for learning, but Alexandria never
became a second Athens. Its product was not the true scholar
or the philosopher, but rather the sophist, the rhetorician. Remote from life and concerned almost entirely with language
and verbal ability, its learning carried the seeds of its own
decay, and into this dying culture came the new and living
power of the Christian Church.

The coming of Christianity, that great landmark in the history of man, brought with it a new ideal of human freedom
and restored to education a sense of purpose, which in time
was to have a profound effect on the schools.

In Alexandria, the work of the Christian Fathers, notably

Clement and Origen, lifted Christianity on to a plane where it began to appeal to thinkers and scholars, and where its adherents could challenge the pagan culture of the schools and prove itself superior. Bold in their search for truth, they encouraged all forms of education which helped men to think and to develop their mental powers and judgement, but, in their view, education was a much wider and deeper affair than the training of the intellect.

Clement wrote:

The aim is not to teach, but to improve the soul, to train it to a virtuous, not to an intellectual life. . . . To become as a little child – does not mean that adults should be unlearned or childish, but that, loosed from the world, they should touch the earth on tiptoe. That is the secret of the life-long springtime of youth.[1]

Clement was succeeded by Origen. One of his pupils, Gregory Thaumaturgus, writing of him, proclaims his belief in the seed within, in the natural miracle:

For the soul is free, and cannot be coerced by any means, not even though one should confine it and keep guard over it in some secret prison-house.[2]

In his description of Origen's method he gives a sketch of the ideal relationship between a teacher and his pupils:

In suchwise, then . . . did he receive us at first; and surveying us, as it were, with a husbandman's skill, and gauging us thoroughly and not confining his notice to those things only which are patent to the eye of all . . . but penetrating into us more deeply, and probing what is most inward in us, he put us to the question, and made propositions to us, and listened to our replies; and whenever he thereby detected anything in us not wholly fruitless and profitless and waste, he set about clearing the soil, and turning it up and irrigating it and putting all things in movement, and brought his whole skill and care to bear on us, and wrought upon our mind . . . by teaching us to search into things within us, and to put them all individually to the test, lest any of them should give back a hollow sound.[3]

1. CLEMENT, *The Pedagogue*, trans Ante-Nicene Library, Vol. IV, 5.
2. *Panegyric VI*, Ante-Nicene Library, Vol. XX, p. 54.
3. *Panegyric VII*, Ante-Nicene Library, pp. 56–9.

Gregory tells how Origen's methods encouraged his pupils to think for themselves, without prejudice, always emphasizing the importance of developing moral powers before intellectual.

St Jerome, in a letter on the education of a daughter, forecasts much of what is generally accepted today in the education of young children. McCallister writes,

> Everything that makes learning pleasant and that promotes effort is commended. The teaching of the elements . . . is to be done through play. . . . She is not to be scolded if she is slow to learn; praise must be the main inducement to real effort. . . . Care is to be taken that her lessons are not made distasteful, lest she may conceive a dislike for them in childhood which will continue in maturer years.[4]

St Augustine, one of the greatest of educational thinkers, founded his doctrine on his belief in 'the inner teacher'. He said:

> We consult not the speaker who utters words, but the guardian truth within the mind itself.[5]
> When things are discussed which we perceive through the mind . . . these are said to be things which we see immediately in that interior light of truth by virtue of which he himself who is called the interior man is illumined. . . . He is taught not through my words but by means of the things themselves which God reveals within the soul.[6]

The work of the teacher, then, is not to give information. His task is rather to stimulate his pupils to think for themselves, so that they may be guided by the 'interior light of truth', and to free their minds to receive the flash of insight by which ideas are perceived.

The pupils learn for themselves, the teacher merely reminds them of truth they already inwardly know:

> When the interior truth makes known to them that true things have been said, they applaud, but without knowing that instead of applauding teachers they are applauding learners. . . . And since

4. MCCALLISTER, *Growth of freedom in education*, pp. 91–2.
5. AUGUSTINE, *Concerning the Teacher*, Basic Writings of St Augustine, Vol. I, p. 390.
6. ibid, p. 391.

after the speaker has reminded them, the pupils quickly learn within, they think that they have been taught outwardly by him who prompts them.[7]

Education is not a matter of words, of collecting facts and information, but of growth in understanding, of the endless search for the truth which lies within the soul.

Looking back at his own education, Augustine sees clearly the importance of the delight of children in imaginative experience and the natural curiosity of childhood:

'One and one are two, and two and two are four' ... was a loathsome jingle, while the wooden horse and its crew of soldiers, the burning of Troy and even the ghost of Creusa made a most enchanting dream.[8] I suppose that Greek boys think the same about Virgil when they are forced to study him, as I was forced to study Homer. ... For I understood not a single word and I was constantly subjected to violent threats and cruel punishments to make me learn.[9]

Latin, however, was no hardship to him, for he says:

I learned it without being forced by threats of punishment, because it was my own wish to be able to give expression to my thoughts. ... This clearly shows that we learn better in a free spirit of curiosity than under fear and compulsion.[10]

He puts as clearly as any modern writer on education the value of the direct method of learning by doing rather than listening; that education is an active process:

And, therefore, as infants cannot learn to speak, except by learning words and phrases from those who speak, why should not men become eloquent without being taught any art of speech, simply by reading and learning the speeches of eloquent men, and by imitating them as far as they can? [11] It is just as if a man wishing to give rules for walking should warn you not to lift the hinder foot before you set down the front one, and then should describe minutely the way you ought to move the hinges of the joints and knees. For what he says is true and one cannot walk in any other way:

7. ibid, pp. 394–5.
8. AUGUSTINE, *Confessions*, 1, 13.   9. ibid, 1, 14.   10. ibid
11. AUGUSTINE, *On Christian Doctrine*, 4, 3.5, Fans Dods Works, Vol. IX, p. 12.

but men find it easier to walk by executing these movements than to attend to them while they are going through them.[12]

In his treatise on the Catechism of the Uninstructed St Augustine underlines two of the principles that are basic to all modern education: that teaching should be related to the ability of the pupil, and that help should only be given when needed. To Augustine, teaching was 'a dwelling in each other', a mutual working together, based on a belief in the pupil's capacity for mental growth, a conception which foreshadows the finest thought of the present day concerning the relationship between teacher and taught.

The enlightened thought of the early Christian writers seems to have had little direct influence on the education of the time. The work of the schools, as the Dark Ages approached, appears to have been divorced from real life, consisting mostly of rote learning, with little attempt to encourage the development of thought and search for truth which had been considered of such importance by the Christian Fathers. The ideals put forward with such sincerity by these men, although fated to remain dormant for a period, could not be finally lost, and were in time to reappear, in all their freshness and vigour, in the renaissance of educational thought of a later age.

*

With the end of the Roman Empire in the fifth century, a curtain of darkness descended over Europe. The schools which had flourished for so long disappeared almost entirely, and with them vanished culture and learning. Into this educational void stepped the Castle, the Church and the Kings.

In the Castle, the young knight received his training, which was mainly practical. He learned to ride, swim, box, hawk, shoot with a bow, play chess and compose romantic verses.

The Church was forced to provide the means of learning in order that its clergy should be able to read the sacred writings and to carry on its duties, and by the eleventh century it had established schools over much of Europe.

12. ibid, 2, 37.55, Vol. IX, p. 73.

Authorities differ on the subject of the Church's attitude to education, but it seems likely that the aims of the new schools were very different from those of the Roman Empire. Their purposes were not of this world, and the content of education was in the main limited to what would further the life of faith. It is generally believed that fields of study were confined to those which served the purposes of religion, that intellectual curiosity which might lead beyond such fields was discouraged, and that inquiry was limited to discovering again the learning of classical times and stating it in forms acceptable to the Christian religion.

The usually accepted picture of education at this period is one in which all notions of education as a pleasant affair were discarded, and liberal ideas of earlier, more enlightened thinkers gave place to a régime of harsh discipline, in which learning was considered to be effective only in proportion to the difficulty and unpleasantness of the task. The thoughts and words of other men formed the material of education, and little attempt was made to encourage individual thought or the pursuit of truth. Adams writes:

Scholasticism supplies one of the longest beats in the rhythm of educational theory. The keenest intellects of Europe had been sharpening themselves for something like five centuries on problems of ever increasing abstraction and subtlety.... Under the conditions imposed on scholastic thinking by the Church, a satisfactory solution was out of the question. Observation and thought pointed one way, theology directed in another.[13]

It is possible, however, that this may not have been a true picture of the state of education during these ages. Certain authorities consider that it was by no means as narrow as is generally believed. The influence of certain of the kings, who became the patrons of learning as the Roman Emperors had been, probably did much to keep alive a more liberal view of education. They promoted the establishment of schools and encouraged learning. Greatest of these was Charles the Great, who set about the revival of learning, first among the clergy. In the Palace School, its master, Alcuin, who had a set of puzzles for teaching arithmetical problems, was

13. ADAMS, J., *The Evolution of Educational Theory*, pp. 157-8.

patient, enthusiastic, indefatigable, careful not to load the mind of the learner by giving him too much to learn, striving literally to educate, to call out in each the latent intellectual power; as – to use his own simile – a man strikes out of the flint the fire which has all along only been hidden in it.[14]

McCallister writes:

The early traditions of the monasteries gave abundant evidence of a paternal regard for the children under their care. St Pachomius had a deep affection for childhood; St Basil ... advocated the idea of discipline through consequences closely related to the child's own action; Alcuin observed the natural disposition of his pupils and distributed studies according to their gifts; Ekkehard I, arguing that Nature was an economist in her gifts and that often a slow head was accompanied by skilful fingers, alternated mental and manual activity; St Ethelwold allured his pupils to study by cheerful and encouraging words.[15]

At the Cathedral School at Rheims in the tenth century Gerbert made use of globes and the abacus, and succeeded in making difficult studies pleasant and easy.

Anselm, in a conversation with a neighbouring Abbot who complained how difficult his pupils were, gives a philosophy of education as enlightened as any of our own day: 'We do our best to correct them. We beat them from morning till night, but I own I can see no improvement,' said the Abbot.

'And how do they grow up?' inquired Anselm. 'Just as dull and stupid as so many beasts' was the reply,

'A famous system of education, truly,' replied the Abbot of Bec, which changes men into beasts. Now tell me, what would be the result, if, after having planted a tree in your garden, you were to compress it so tightly that it should have no room to extend its branches? These poor children were given to you that you might help them to grow, and be fruitful in good thoughts; but if you allow them no liberty their minds will grow crooked. Finding no kindness on your part, they will give you no confidence, and never having been brought up to know the meaning of love and charity, they will see everything in a distorted aspect.' [16]

14. GASKOIN, *Alcuin, His Life and Work*, p. 197.
15. MCCALLISTER, *The Growth of Freedom in Education*, p. 111.
16. DRANE, *Christian Schools and Scholars*, Vol. I, p. 419.

The Middle Ages [McCallister observes] were an anticipation on the grand scale of Rousseau's negative education. They aimed at keeping the heart from vice and the mind from error. They were wonderfully efficient within a narrow field, but the lesson they teach us is the impossibility of keeping the mind in leading strings. The soul, as Gregory and Origen taught, cannot be coerced; the body may be shackled but thought must be free or it ceases to be.[17]

The bright light surrounding the School of Charlemagne in the eighth century faded. Charles's Empire dissolved, and Europe was engulfed in strife and in warfare against invaders. In these troubled times most men were too preoccupied to concern themselves with education. Darkness descended once more, but the darkness was not as deep as formerly. Though little was added, in these years, to the sum of knowledge, the old was not entirely lost, so that when, four centuries later, the light began to return, the foundations on which the revival of learning might be built were still there.

The revival came largely through the new centres of education that had come into being, the Universities. Here, scholars like Peter Abelard were stirring men's minds once again. 'Constant questioning,' he said, 'is the first key to wisdom. For through doubt we are led to inquiry, and by inquiry we discern the truth.' [18]

The hold of authority on men's mind was being challenged and the way opened again for honest thought. The Greek ideal of the search for truth was once more to be restored as the end and aim of education.

17. MCCALLISTER, *The Growth of Freedom in Education*, p. 118.
18. ABELARD, *Sic et Non, Prologue*, BOYD, p. 137.

5

The Renaissance · Vergerius · Vittorino da Feltre · D'Arezzo
Sadoleto · Huarte · The Schools of the Jeromites
Rudolph Agricola · Jacob Wimpheline · Luther
Melancthon and Sturm · Jesuits · Erasmus · Rabelais
Ramus · Montaigne

THE great rebirth of the human spirit, known to history as the
Renaissance, was the means by which the mind of man finally
broke out of its narrow medieval servitude. In the desire to
create a larger and fuller life men turned to the past, as they
discovered again the rich world of Greece and Rome. En-
tranced and fascinated by its treasures of beauty, their minds
were broadened as never before by the Greek ideas of individuality and of free intellectual activity.

The key to this new world was the ancient languages, and it
was natural that learning Greek and Latin should be made the
heart of education. It was also inevitable, since there was little
else to take their place, for writing in the vernacular had
scarcely begun, and science was in its infancy.

Had there been an alternative, and had the men of the age
been able to recreate the spirit of the Greeks, the story of education might have been very different. As it was, the life gradually died away, as the letter replaced the spirit in the schools.
Education became a narrow study of the classical languages as
an end in itself. Form became more important than content,
and instead of Greek literature, the schools came to study the
rules of grammar; instead of life, words. As the great dawn
passed into the light of common day the schools settled down
into a dead rigidity, a true rigor mortis.

But before this happened the educational ideals of the true
spirit of the Renaissance were put into writing by Petrus Paulus
Vergerius of Padua. These ideals were carried out in practice in
a school in Mantua by Vittorino da Feltre, 'the first great
school of the Renaissance',[1] where it was said he

1. WOODWARD, *Vittorino da Feltre*, p. 24.

refused, after fair trial made, to force learning upon an unwilling scholar, holding that nature had not endowed all with taste or capacity for study.[2]

Vergerius saw education as the development of gifts that lie in every individual, and his belief that these gifts were good, reflects the emerging faith in man of the humanists. 'Follow the instincts of your best self and you will be found worthy,' [3] he wrote.

He describes a liberal education as one

by which we attain and practise virtue and wisdom; that education which calls forth, trains and develops those highest gifts of body and mind which ennoble men . . . For we allow that soundness of judgment, wisdom of speech, integrity of conduct are the marks of a truly liberal temper.[4]

He anticipated by five and a half centuries much of modern educational theory and practice:

We must remember that mental endowments differ. . . . The choice of studies will depend to some extent upon the character of individual minds. . . . The natural bent should be recognized and followed in education. Let the boy of limited capacity work only at that subject in which he shows he can attain some result.[5]

He gave the study of nature and science a new importance:

The knowledge of Nature . . . the laws and properties of things in heaven and in earth, their causes, mutations and effects . . . this is a most delightful and at the same time most profitable, study for youth,[6]

and he showed clearly that he did not believe that education was to be found exclusively in books:

For it is with character as with instruction: 'the living voice' is of far more avail than the written letter.[6a]

There were others who expressed tht same beliefs: Leonardi Bruni d'Arezzo wrote, probably in 1405:

2. ibid, p. 34.   3. ibid, p. 118.   4. ibid, pp. 102, 107.
5. ibid, pp. 109, 111.   6. ibid, p. 108.   6a. ibid, p. 98.

Proficiency in literary form, not accompanied by broad acquaintance with facts and truths, is a barren attainment.[7]

Jacopo Sadoleto was another who fully understood the meaning of the Renaissance as it applied to learning. He expressed his belief in education as a development of the powers within.

We receive from Nature what is central in ourselves, what indeed makes us truly and individually what we are, but in a rough and unfinished form; it is the function of letters to bring this to its highest perfection and to work out in it a beauty comparable to its divine original.[8]

Education is as much the result of our own mental activity as of the effect of what we are taught.

Character is a composite thing, and cannot be treated upon a uniform plan. One element clearly is that which is impressed upon us by the careful systematic teaching of others: another and a different element is that which we acquire for ourselves by the purposive effort of our own minds.[9]

He makes a clear distinction between discipline imposed from without and that which comes from within, and which is the result of one's own choice, and this he calls virtue. 'The habit that is imposed from without we call 'disciplined training', but that which is our personal choice, virtue. Discipline consists in habituation to the authority of another's virtue: virtue in obedience to its own authority.'[10]

Juan Huarte, the Spanish physician, in the *Examination of Men's Wits*, has much to say on the theme of the individual endowments given to every man by nature, and the importance, as far as education is concerned, of discovering what these are and using them:

If I were a teacher before I received any scholer into my schoole, I would grow to many trials and experiments with him, untill I might discover the qualitie of his wit.[11]

7. ibid, p. 132.
8. SADOLETO, *On Education*, p. 12.
9. ibid, p. 13.   10. ibid, pp. 16–17.
11. HUARTE, J., *Examination of Men's Wits*, p. 4.

It cannot be denied, but that ... there are wits found capable of one science, which are untoward for another: and therefore it behooves, before the child be set to studie, to discover the manner of his wit, and to see what science agreeth with his capacitie, and then to provide that he may applie the same.[12]

He restates the Platonic ideal, that the inner heart of a man knows what is right.

Nature hath so great force, to cause that (of plants, brute beasts, and man) each one set himselfe to performe those workes which are proper to his kind, that they arive to that utmost bound of perfection which may be attained, sodainly and without any others teaching them; the plants know how to forme roots under ground . . . and the brute beasts likewise so soone as they are borne, know that which is agreeable to their nature, and flie the the things which are naughtie and noisome. And that which makes them most to marvell who are seene in naturall Philosophie, is, that a man having his braine well tempered, and of that disposition which is requisit for this or that science, sodainly, and without having ever learned it of any, he speaketh and uttereth such exquisit matters, as could hardly win credit. . . .

Nature . . . is the schoolemaister who teacheth the soules in what sort they are to worke.[13]

The way of following nature is the most effective way of learning:

Verily, there is no Science or Art . . . which if a man wanting capacitie for himselfe to apply, he shall reape anie profit thereof; albeit he toyle all the daies of his life in the precepts and rules of the same. But if he applie himselfe to that which is agreeable with his naturall abilitie, we see that he will learne in two daies.[14]

He recognizes the importance of the first years of childhood: 'His first age . . . is the most pliant of all others to learning,'[15] and suggests the need to wait for the right moment to teach a child. The conception of education as negative, usually attributed to Rousseau and echoing Plato and Augustine, appears in his assertion: 'Hippocrates had great reason to say, that soules were skilfull without the instruction of any teacher.'[16]

12. ibid, p. 6.   13. ibid, ROGERS, p. 33.
14. ibid, p. 102.   15. ibid, p. 6.
16. ibid, p. 36.

The Renaissance appeared later in Northern Europe. In the field of education the ground was already prepared in the schools of the Jeromites, or Brethren of the Common Life, in the Netherlands. When Rudolph Agricola of Friesland came from Italy, bringing with him the new ideas of the Italian Renaissance, these schools readily put them into practice. Agricola wrote:

> If there is anything that has a contradictory name, it is the school. The Greeks called it σχολή which means *leisure, recreation*; and the Latins, *ludus*, that is, *play*. But there is nothing farther removed from recreation and play.[17]

Most men, however, were swept away by their enthusiasm for books, so that by the sixteenth century education had narrowed into a pedantic study of language for its own sake, which left its mark on the schools for nearly three hundred years, and today we still suffer from the idea that education is a matter of form rather than content, and of second-hand ideas to be found from books rather than from life.

In 1497 appeared the first treatise on education by a German, Jacob Wimpheline. He believed that the purpose of education was moral; that humility, nobility of character and the power to think for oneself were of greater importance than book learning:

> Let study be for the quickening of independent thought. What profits all our learning if our characters be not correspondingly noble, all of our industry without piety, all of our knowledge without love of our neighbour, all of our wisdom without humility, all of our studying if we are not kind and charitable? [18]

The Reformation brought into prominence the need for new schools, not only to replace those which had disappeared with the removal of the authority of Rome, but in order that the Bible and the catechism could be read at first hand. Schools for the children of ordinary people, as well as for scholars, were required. Luther's 'Discourse on the Duty of sending Children to School' drew attention to the obligation of the State to pro-

17. COMPAYRÉ, p. 87.
18. MONROE, *History of Education*, p. 378.

vide compulsory education which would be free from the
authority and power of the Church. He would wish education
to free children from restrictions and allow them a wide range
of experience:

The monks have imprisoned the youth whom they have had in
charge, as men put birds in dark cages, so that they could neither
see nor converse with any one. But it is dangerous for youth to be
thus alone. . . . Wherefore, we ought to permit young people to see,
and hear, and know what is taking place around them in the world.[19]
Since the young must leap and jump, or have something to do,
because they have a natural desire for it that should not be restrained . . . why should we not provide such schools, and lay before
them such studies? By the gracious arrangement of God, children
take delight in acquiring knowledge.[20]

He would have a wider curriculum:

If I had children . . . I would have them learn not only the languages and history, but singing, instrumental music, and a full course
of mathematics.[21]

The child's life was not to be wholly made up of work and
drudgery:

Enjoyment and recreation are as necessary for children as food
and drink.[22]

'If we are to teach children, we must become children. Would to
God we had more of this child's play!'[23]

The teacher was to be properly valued:

I tell you, in a word, that a diligent, devoted school teacher
. . . who faithfully trains and teaches boys, can never receive an
adequate reward, and no money is sufficient to pay the debt you owe
him.[24]

Unfortunately for the future of education, others like
Melancthon and Sturm had a most lasting influence on the
schools. 'The teachers,' Melancthon wrote in 1528, 'should see

19. ibid, p. 411.
20. *Letters to the Mayors and Aldermen*, PAINTER, p. 154.
21. WOODWARD, *Education in the Age of the Renaissance*, p. 240.
22. COMPAYRÉ, p. 119.   23. PAINTER, p. 155.
24. MONROE, *History of Education*, p. 414.

to it that the children learn only Latin, not German, or Greek, or Hebrew.' [25] Grammar was the main content of the syllabus. Even those few Latin writers who were read were studied, not as literature, but to provide examples of grammatical rules. In the Strasburg Gymnasium, of which Sturm was Rector for over forty years, the boys spent nine years in learning to speak Latin, followed by five more years in College, doing the same thing. The clouds had indeed gathered across the bright morning sky.

The essence of the religious reformation lay in the principle that spiritual life was to be found in first-hand experience. It would have been natural for education to prepare for this by including some study of the mother tongue and the national literature, and to be more closely related to life than hitherto, but nothing of the kind was even considered, and the influence of Melancthon and those who followed him was to bind the schools for three hundred years to an arid study of the classics, and a lifeless preoccupation with the form and structure of language.

The Catholic Church was not slow to follow the Protestant lead in establishing schools, schools which were highly successful and even rivalled those of the Reformed Church in their own countries. It was a Spaniard, Ignatius Loyola, who was responsible for the movement and who formed, in 1534, the religious order known as the Society of Jesus. Its purpose was to make a stand against the advance of Protestantism and its members quickly realized the value and importance of education in their campaign.

The Schools of the Jesuits spread rapidly, until by the end of the century they had control over much of higher education in the Catholic countries.

These schools exerted a strong influence on education and helped to postpone the dawn of more liberal ideas. They were not interested in the importance of individuality; their concern was for the strength of the Catholic Church. Quick says of the system:

Originality and independence of mind, love of truth for its own

25. ibid, p. 416.

sake, the power of reflecting and forming correct judgements were
not merely neglected – they were suppressed.[26]

Yet they were aware of, and based their teaching on, principles which, had they followed them to their logical conclusion, might have led to as broad a conception of education as
that of any later thinkers.

They understood the importance of gaining the co-operation
of the pupils in learning:

That which enters into willing ears the mind as it were runs to
welcome, seizes with avidity, carefully stows away, and faithfully
preserves,[27]

and they were fully aware that such a response depends largely
on the relationship between the teacher and his pupils:

When pupils love the master they will soon love his teaching. Let
him, therefore, show an interest in everything that concerns them
and not merely in their studies.[28]

They realized the need to study the individual abilities of
the pupils. Each master had to keep a book in which he recorded details of each boy in his class and on this observation
he based his teaching.

They were aware of the fact of maturation, and its importance in education:

His mind expanding and his judgment ripening as he grows
older, the pupil will often see for himself that which he could hardly
be made to see by others.[29]

Their conception of the work of a teacher might be taken
as a model for today. At the heart of his task was a sympathetic
understanding of children, a firm belief in each child's potentialities, and an unending search for the right way to help in
his development:

The true teacher must understand, appreciate and sympathize with
those who are committed to him. He must be daily discovering
what there is (and undoubtedly there is something in each of them)
capable of fruitful development, and contriving how better to get

26. QUICK, *Educational Reformers*, pp. 50–51.
27. ibid, p. 52.   28. ibid, p. 55.   29. ibid, p. 54.

at them and evoke whatever possibilities there are in them for good.[30]

Such principles, applied in a more liberal spirit, could have anticipated by centuries the developments in education of our own time.

But even in the darkness there were gleams of the dawn which would not break for another two centuries. No one, then, considered childhood worthy of study. Children were 'little men', their interests and needs thought to differ from those of adults only in degree; but few doubted the importance of the early stages of life.

Erasmus, the greatest educational thinker of his time, has much to say about making sure that children's first impressions are both good and happy. It is of first importance to gain the affection of the pupil and to bring him to enjoy his work. He suggests that children should be taught in the beginning by play and 'the artifice of an attractive method'. Fear should have no place. Sympathy and gentleness are essential.

The fyrste care is to be belovd, by lytle and lytle followeth after, not feare, but a certen liberall and gentle reverence which is of more value than feare.[31]
A master muste in maner play the childe again, that he may be loved of the chylde.[32]

He stresses the value of interest in learning, although he is far from understanding its full implications, and suggests that teaching should be by means of pictures and objects, rather than words and the learning of rules of grammar.

He had no patience with the methods of teaching of his day and 'the stupidity of the average teacher of grammar who wastes precious years hammering rules into children's heads' and instead, suggests the direct method:

It is not by learning rules that we acquire the power of speaking a language, but by daily intercourse with those accustomed to express themselves with exactness and refinement, and by copious reading of the best authors.[33]

30. ibid, pp. 57–8.   31. SHERRY, p. 173.   32. ibid, p. 199.
33. WOODWARD, *Erasmus Concerning Education*, p. 164.

Content and subject matter of language should come first in importance, before grammar, and therefore, before children are asked to learn rules, they should have opportunities to talk informally, in the language they are learning, about things around them. At a later stage, the study of language should be kept in touch with reality by linking it with the study of agriculture, geography, history, military science, astronomy and other subjects. The study of language should help to develop the pupil's mental powers, and widen his knowledge of life.

Erasmus advises teachers to study the natural capacities and abilities of children, and not to imagine that their interests are the same as those of adults, nor expect them to behave as though they were men in miniature. Teaching should be gradual and adapted to the capacity of children to learn, as their food is adapted to their growing bodies.

Thys man shulde do in fashionyng his wytte, that parentes and nurses be wont to do in formynge the bodye. Howe do they fyrste teache the infante to speake lyke a man? They applye their wordes by lyspyng accordyng to the chyldes tattlynge. Howe do they teache them to eat? They chaw fyrst their milke soppes, and when they have done, by lytle and litle put it in to the chyldes mouthe. ... Neyther do they fede them with everye meate, nor putte more in then they bee able to take; and as they increase in age, they leave them to bigger thinges. First they seeke for noryshemente that is meete for them ... whych yet if it be thrust into the mouthe to muche, either it choketh the chylde, or beynge caste oute defileth hys garmente. When it is softelye and pretelye put in, it doth good. ... So then as by small morsels, and geven now and then, the lytle tender bodies are noryshed: in lyke manner chyldrens wyttes by instrucctions meete for them taught easely, and as it were by playe by lytle and litle accustume theselves to greater thyngs. ... But there be some that looke that chyldren shulde strayghtwaye become olde men, havyng no regarde of their age, but measure the tender wittes, by their owne strengthe.[34]

Erasmus had great faith in the power of education and believed it capable of almost anything. There has been planted in each, he believed, an inner striving for growth, and the right method of education is that which follows the line of the pupil's own nature, which uses his own activity:

34. SHERRY, pp. 200–202.

Nature ... claims the help of the schoolmaster in carrying forward the special gifts with which she has endowed the child. By
following the path which she points out the toil of learning is
reduced.[35]

With extraordinary insight he understood that children were
not 'little men':

Wholly wrong are those masters who expect their little pupils to
act as though they were but diminutive adults.[36]

It was to be four hundred years before this fact was to be
fully realized, and its consequences to affect the education of
young children.

Erasmus is perhaps the first to recognize clearly the value
of natural and spontaneous activity as the foundation and
most effective way of teaching:

Lead the beginner to face his unfamiliar matter with self-confi-
dence, to attack it slowly but with persistence. We must not under-
rate the capacity of youth to respond to suitable demands upon the
intelligence. . . . The child, like every other creature, excels in the
precise activity which belongs to it. . . . Follow Nature, therefore,
in this, and so far as is possible take from the work of the school
all that implies toilsomeness, and strive to give to learning the
quality of freedom and enjoyment.[37]

He works out an elaborate system of teaching aids, which includes alphabets in bone and even biscuit, pictures, maps,
charts and real objects: 'Material for the study of Archaeology
is to be found not only in literary sources, but in ancient coins,
inscriptions and monuments,' [38] he wrote.

In one passage he seems to show an almost Rousseau-like
understanding of the value of nature study:

Let the boy learn to consider the glory of the heavens, the rich
harvest of the earth, the hidden fountains of rivers and their courses,
hurrying to the sea, the illimitable ocean, the countless families of
living creatures, all created expressly to serve the needs of men.[39]

But it is doubtful if he really intended this to be interpreted

35. *De Pueris Instituendis*, WOODWARD, p. 213.
36. ibid, p. 211.   37. ibid, p. 217.
38. ibid, p. 168.   39. ibid, p. 140.

as Rousseau would have done, for, elsewhere, he says: 'What can *men* learn from *trees*?'

He was not concerned with scholarship for its own sake – the chief task of education in his view was to 'give children the seeds of piety' – and he had little time for first-hand experience. Geography and knowledge of Nature were to be learned from the writings of the ancients, and he believed that philosophy taught more in a year than any experience in thirty; but he would have boys 'to learn something of the mechanic arts upon their less undignified side, for example, painting, sculpture, modelling, architecture,'[40] and justifies this, rather apologetically, by saying: 'We cannot forget that our Lord was not only the son of a craftsman, but was one himself.'[41]

These flickers of light, however, had little effect on the prevailing dark, in which the schools sought all wisdom in the literature and language of Greece and Rome, and much history was to pass by before they were at last to illumine education in the eighteenth and nineteenth centuries.

In France, the reaction against scholasticism appeared at first quite independently of the direct stream of education. Rabelais, in *Gargantua and Pantagruel*, tears to pieces the accepted methods of the day. He says, of Gargantua's education, which, after twenty years of book learning, turned him into a 'madcap, a ninny, dreamy and infatuated':

It were better for him to learn nothing at all than to be taught such like books under such schoolmasters.[42]

Under his new tutor, he was to learn from things first, not from books. His days began and ended by observing 'the face of the sky' and at the close of each of his superhuman days he had to 'briefly recapitulate ... that which he had read, seen, learned, done and understood in the whole course of that day'.[43]

40. *Similica*.
41. *Dialog De Pronun*, WOODWARD, *Erasmus concerning education*, p. 98.
42. RABELAIS, *Gargantua and Pantagruel*, Bk. I, Everyman, Vol. I, p. 38.
43. ibid, pp. 54, 58.

He learned from books, but what he learnt he applied to 'practical cases concerning the estate of man'.[44] He was to study while playing, and to learn mathematics 'through recreation and amusement'.[45]

He learned from using his hands. In rainy weather he and his Master

did recreate themselves in botteling up of hay, in cleaving and sawing of wood, and in threshing sheaves of corn at the Barn. Then they studied the Art of painting or carving.[46]

He learned from first-hand observation:

They went likewise to see the drawing of mettals, or the casting of great ordnance: how the Lapidaries did work, as also the Goldsmiths and Cutters of precious stones: nor did they omit to visit the Alchymists, Money-coiners, Upholsterers, Weavers, Velvetworkers, Watchmakers, Looking-glasse-framers, Printers, Organists, and other such kinde of Artificers, and . . . did learne and consider the industry and invention of the trades. . . . And in stead of herborising, they visited the shops of Druggists, Herbalists, and Apothecaries, and diligently considered the fruits, roots, leaves, gums, seeds . . . of some foreign parts.[47]

Gargantua would have his son learn from nature:

As to the knowledge of the works of nature, I would have you to devote yourself to the study of it. Let there be no sea, river or pool of which you do not know the fishes. Learn about all the fowls of the air, all the shrubs and trees in forest and orchard, all the herbs and flowers of the ground, all the metals hid in the bowels of the earth, all the precious stones of the East and the South.[48]

Only then was he to consult books, and that not for themselves, but in order to study man:

Then faile not most carefully to peruse the books of the Greek, Arabian and Latine physicians, . . . and by frequent Anatomies get thee the perfect knowledge of the other world, called the Microcosme, which is man.[49]

44. ibid, p. 54.   45. COMPAYRÉ, p. 98.
46. ibid, Works, Bk. 1, p. 73.   47. ibid, Bk. 1, pp. 73–4.
48. ibid, Urquhart and Molleux, Bk. 2, p. 224.
49. ibid, Bk. 2, pp. 232, 233.

As a result he was able to maintain 'argument against all the Theologians or Divines' at the Sorbonne 'and made it visibly appear to the world, that compared to him, they were but monkies, and a knot of mufled calves', and 'everybody began to say, that Solomon . . . shewed never in his time such a Masterpiece of wisdom, as the good Pantagruel hath done.'[50]

Gargantua's name has passed into common use to describe a more than life-size task, but behind the caricature can be detected the longing for universal knowledge that was deeply felt by Rabelais and many of his contemporaries, and the recognition that the key to this omniscience is experience.

In Gargantua's single rule to the Thelemites – 'Do what thou wilt' – Rabelais shows his belief in the individual worth of each man, and the emerging passion for freedom which was beginning to capture men's minds:

Men that are free, well-borne, well-bred, and conversant in honest companies, have naturally an instinct and spurre that prompteth them unto vertuous actions, and withdraws them from vice, which is called honour. Those same men, when by base subjection and constraint they are brought under and kept down, turn aside from that noble disposition . . . to shake off and break that bond of servitude, wherein they are so tyrannously inslaved: for it is agreeable with the nature of man to long after things forbidden, and to desire what is denied us.[51]

Rousseau was later to echo this in his great principle: 'Everything is good as it comes from the hands of the Creator; everything degenerates in the hands of man,'[52] and to make the educational application: 'The first education . . . should be purely negative. It consists . . . in guarding the heart from vice and the mind from error.'[53]

Peter Ramus, who paid dearly for his attempts to free higher education from the bonds of tradition and to establish the right of men to think for themselves, was a popular and successful teacher whose ideas were to have a strong influence on the course of education. He outlined a scheme for schools

50. ibid, Works, Bk. 2, pp. 212–13, 229.
51. ibid, Bk. 1, p. 163.
52. ROUSSEAU, *On Education*, R. L. ARCHER, p. 55.
53. ibid, p. 99.

much on the lines of the Dalton plan. The major part of the work was to be carried out by the pupils, the proportion being one hour's work by the teacher to five of the student. Private study was to alternate with lectures and discussions.

His efforts helped to free men from bondage to medieval authority and the hold of Aristotle over the human mind, and to encourage the pursuit of truth. In so doing he helped to break the stranglehold of scholasticism and to prepare the way for a new philosophy of education.

The progress of a more liberal idea of education took a remarkable step forward in Montaigne. In his thought and writing is to be found much that today we consider most modern in our conception of education. A rebel against the narrowness of the medieval spirit, he was as critical of the new humanistic learning as of the old. Neither, in his view, was adequate as education. More far-seeing and perceptive than any of his contemporaries, he has much that is fresh to say on the subject .

He took the thought of Rabelais, 'Knowledge without conscience is the ruin of the soul', and developed his great theme – the distinction between knowledge and wisdom, with its echoes of Seneca:

We are constantly asking about a man, 'Does he know Greek or Latin? Can he write in verse or prose?' What is really important is whether he has grown better or wiser; and that is overlooked. We direct all our efforts to the memory and leave the understanding and the conscience empty.[54]

Study should make us wiser. . . .[55]

Of what use is knowledge without understanding? Would to God . . . our Law Societies were as well provided with understanding and conscience as they are with knowledge![56]

All other learning is hurtful to him who has not the knowledge of honesty and goodness.[57]

I again fall to talking of the vanity of our education, the end of which is not to make us good and wise, but learned. Education has not taught us to follow and embrace virtue and prudence, but she

54. *Essay on Pedantry*, BOYD, pp. 222–3.
55. *Education of Children*, RECTOR, p. 32.
56. *Essay on Pedantry*, HODGSON, p. 91.
57. ibid, RECTOR, p. 102.

has imprinted in us their derivation and etymology. We know how to decline the word virtue, even if we know not how to love it.[58]

The cares and expense our parents are at in our education point at nothing but to furnish our heads with knowledge; but not a word of judgment and virtue.[59]

Such men, he says, think to teach wisdom by describing it, not by giving opportunities to the young to practise it:

Glad would I be to find one that would teach us how to manage a horse, to tosse a pike, to shoot-off a peece, to play upon the lute, or to warble with the voice, without any exercise, as these kind of men would teach us to judge . . . without any exercise . . . of judging.[60]

Even if we could become learned with other men's learning . . . wise we cannot be except by our own wisdom.[61]

He put forward the revolutionary idea that 'the greatest clerks are not the greatest sages' and suggested that true learning comes 'not from knowing the past, but the present'.

Books were not the source of wisdom, but life:

I would not have this pupil of ours imprisoned and made a slave to his book . . . Neither should I think it good to encourage an abnormal taste for books, if it be discovered that he is too much addicted to reading. Too much study diverts him from better employment and renders him unfit for the society of men. Many a time have I seen men totally useless on account of an immoderate thirst for knowledge.[62]

I would have the world my scholar's . . . book.[63] Everything that comes to our eyes is book enough.[64]

To know by rote, is no knowledge, and signifies no more but only to retain what one has intrusted to our memory. That which a man rightly knows and understands, he is the free disposer of at his own full liberty, without any regard to the author from whence he had it or fumbling over the leaves of his book. A mere bookish learning is a poor, paltry learning.[65]

58. *Of Presumption*, RECTOR, p. 127.
59. *Essay on Pedantry*, HAZLITT, p. 54.
60. *Education of Children*, Everyman, Vol. 1, p. 158.
61. *Essay on Pedantry*, FRAME, p. 101.
62. *Education of Children*, RECTOR, pp. 58-9.
63. ibid, HODGSON, p. 118.   64. ibid, FRAME, p. 112.
65. ibid, HAZLITT, p. 178.

We can say, 'Cicero speaks thus'; 'These were the ideas of Plato'; 'these are the very words of Aristotle'. A parrot could say as much. But what do we say that is our own? What can we do? How do we judge?·[66]

Things, rather than books, should be the means of education:

Let our pupils be furnished with things – words will come only too fast.[67]

The young scholar is to be taught to think for himself, sometimes to have the way opened for him, and sometimes to open it by himself. He is not to rely on authority:

Let the tutor make his pupil thoroughly sift everything he reads, and lodge nothing in his head upon simple authority and upon trust. ... Who follows another, follows nothing, finds nothing.[68]
We take other men's knowledge and opinions upon trust, but we should make them our own.[69]

Curiosity about his immediate environment was to be one of the foundations of learning:

Let an honest curiosity be awakened in him to search out the nature and design of all things. Let him investigate whatever is singular and rare about him – a fine building, a fountain, an eminent man, the place where a battle was anciently fought.[70]

Self-knowledge was an essential preliminary:

It is very silly to teach our children ... the knowledge of the stars and the movement of the eighth sphere, before we teach them the knowledge of themselves.[71]

The choice of a tutor is of the utmost importance. He should be one 'who has rather a well-balanced head than a well-filled one'. Those who choose him should look more for character

66. *Essay on Pedantry*, RECTOR, p. 94.
67. *Education of Children*, RECTOR, p. 68.
68. ibid, HAZLITT, p. 62.
69. *Essay on Pedantry*, RECTOR, p. 95.
70. *Education of Children*, RECTOR, p. 41.
71. ibid, FRAME, p. 117.

and intelligence than for learning, 'and the tutor must know to the second and how far forth he shall condescend to (the) childish proceedings' of his pupil 'and how to guide them'.[72]

The pupil was to learn to do things for himself:

By depriving a pupil of liberty to do things for himself we make him servile and cowardly.[73]

True education comes from present experience.

In my opinion, we are never wise except by present learning; not by that which is past, and as little by that which is to come.[74]

The pupil was not to be compelled to learn but encouraged through enjoyment and pleasure, a philosophy which even today calls forth the strongest criticism:

This method ought to be carried on with a firm gentleness, quite contrary to the practice of our pedants, who, instead of tempting and alluring children to study, present nothing before them but rods and ferrules, horror and cruelty. Away with this violence! away with this compulsion! nothing, I believe, more dulls and degenerates a well-born nature. ... How much more respectable it would be to see our classrooms strewn with green boughs and flowers than with bloody birch rods. ... Where their profit is there should also be their pleasure. Such viands as are proper and wholesome for children should be seasoned with sugar, and such as are dangerous with gall.[75]

There is nothing like alluring the appetite and affection, otherwise you make nothing but so many asses laden with books.[76]

Montaigne was one of the earliest of educators to suggest that play was to be taken seriously:

It should be noted here that the play of children is not really play, but must be judged as their most serious actions,[77]

and might be made the means of education:

72, ibid, Everyman, p. 155.   73. ibid, RECTOR, p. 33.
74. *Essay on Pedantry*, RECTOR, p. 93.
75. *Education of Children*, RECTOR, pp 61–3.
76. ibid, p. 85.   77. *Of Habit*, RECTOR, pp. 125–6.

As to Greek . . . my father proposed to teach it by a new device, making of it a sort of sport and recreation.[78]

Education was not to be merely negative, as Rousseau was to urge later:

It is not enough that our education does not spoil us, it must change us for the better.[79]

Montaigne's four-hundred-year-old advice about the right method of teaching might well be followed today:

Our tutors never stop bawling into our ears, as though they were pouring water into a funnel; and our task is only to repeat what has been told us. I should like the tutor to correct this practice, and right from the start, according to the capacity of the mind he has in hand, to begin putting it through its paces, making it taste things, choose them, and discern them by itself. ... I don't want him to talk and talk alone, I want him to listen to his pupil speaking in his turn. ... *The authority of those who teach is often an obstacle to those who want to learn.* [Cicero] [80]

He believed in the natural urge in every man to learn: 'We are borne to quest and seeke after truethe' and at last education is to be based on the pupil's own activity; the teacher is to watch him, to respond to him, and use the abilities he shows, but the process of education is one which takes place within the pupil himself, and by means of his own activity, as 'the Bees doe here and there sucke this, and cull that flower, but afterward they produce the hony, which is peculiarly their owne'.[81] For

it is a sign of cruditie and indigestion for a man to yeeld up his meat, even as he swallowed the same: the stomacke hath not wrought his full operation unlesse it have changed forme, and altered fashion of that which was given him to boyle and concoct.[82]

More clearly than anyone since the Greeks, Montaigne states that the purpose of education concerns the whole man.

78. *Education of Children*, RECTOR, p. 79.
79. *Essay on Pedantry*, RECTOR, p. 100.
80. *Education of Children*, FRAME, p. 110.
81. ibid, Everyman, Vol. 1, p. 157.
82. ibid, p. 156.

It is not a mind, it is not a body that we are educating: it is a man,
... and, as Plato says, we must not cultivate one without the other,
we must develop them equally, like a pair of horses harnessed to
the same pole. [83]

83. ibid, HODGSON, p. 130.

6

Vives

IN the year in which Columbus discovered America, there was born a man whose name is far less well-known than Rousseau and Froebel and yet who foreshadowed all the main principles of education which, today, are regarded as progressive. He was Juan Luis Vives, a Spaniard, and one-time student of Erasmus. It is likely that his educational ideas influenced many later writers and thinkers, including Roger Ascham, Mulcaster, Milton, Sir Thomas Elyot and Ignatius Loyola, the founder of the Jesuit schools, among many others.

Many of the ideas for which Mulcaster and later educators have been given credit had been already suggested by Vives: the use of the vernacular; the dangers of forcing children; the importance of the senses, and the suggestion that teachers should confer together at regular intervals in order to find what kind of education was suitable for each child.

Ben Jonson, writing a hundred years after Vives, gives as his own the idea that

wisdom without honesty is mere craft and cozenage. And therefore the reputation of honesty must first be gotten, which cannot be but by living well. A good life is a main argument.[1]

Knowingly or unwittingly he was reaffirming Vives's view of life, of which the ancestry can be clearly traced back to the Greeks. But, as Foster Watson says, 'the fact that such passages have been regarded as highly suggestive and significant for Jonson to have written, shows that the ideas of Vives, written a hundred years before, could be still regarded as original or as representative of the best progressive thought of a full century later'.[2]

1. JONSON, *Timber or Discoveries*, pp. 5, 6.
2. WATSON, *Vives on Education*, pp. xxxiii–xxxiv.

Vives has been called the father of modern psychology.
Watson writes:

> When, nearly three hundred years afterwards, Pestalozzi expressed
> his aim in the memorable words, 'I want to psychologize education',
> his attitude was in continuous development from the starting point
> first established by Vives.[3]

He held the ancient belief that education is a growth from
within:

> There be certain fires or seeds . . . bred by nature in us, of the
> same justice, in the which that first father of mankind was made
> by almighty God: that little fire, if it might increase in us, it would
> bring us up unto perfection of virtue and blessed living.[4]

> As a certain power is given to the earth to produce herbs of every
> kind, so our minds are as it were endued with a certain power of
> seeds over all arts and all learning; and a certain proneness to those
> first and most simple truths, by which tendency the mind is carried
> on; a wish for the aims that are most clearly good; a quickness of
> mind for the most manifest truths . . . That is the reason why the
> boy agrees at once to the most evident truth which he has never
> seen before.[5]

The first essential is self-knowledge and humility –

> The first gryce, that men clymme unto wysedome by, is that that
> so many ancient writers speake of ... Every man to knowe him-
> selfe.[6]

– and to think moderately or humbly of oneself is the foundation of the best education.

Vives's *De Anima et Vita* has been called the first modern
work on psychology, which led ultimately to the idea that
education must be based on an understanding of the mind of
the learner. It is necessary to learn about the mind and its
mental activities so that we can understand ourselves:

> We cannot rightly declare what the soul is in its essence . . . but
> we can set it forth, clothed and as if painted in a picture, in its own

3. WATSON, *Father of Modern Psychology*, p. cxviii.
4. WATSON, *Vives and the Renascence Education of Women*, p. 127.
5. WATSON, *Vives on Education*, p. 21.
6. *An Introduction to Wisedome*, no pagination.

most apt colors, so that it is seen in *its own actions* . . . Nor did he who bid us know ourselves, refer to the essence, but to the actions of our mind, so that they may be ordered for moral life.[7]

Vives gives examples, drawn from his own experience, of the workings of association, and, for the first time since the Renaissance, we have an empirical, introspective approach to workings of the mind, in line with modern psychological method.

Writing in 1872, Sir William Hamilton, 'the most erudite of all British philosophers, in the history of psychology',[8] says of Vives's work on association:

Vives's observations comprise, in brief, nearly all of principal moment that has been said upon this subject *either before or since*.[9]

Vives gives a remarkably astute analysis of the differing abilities of minds:

Natural powers of the mind are: sharpness in observing, capacity for comprehending, power in comparing and judging . . . Some minds are acute and see separate things clearly, but cannot grasp them nor retain them when they are connected; their comprehension is narrow, or their memory short and fleeting. Others grasp, but do not reflect on those things which are intuited, so as to judge and determine their nature and properties . . . There are some minds who look intently and diligently at what they are doing, and who rejoice to get bound up in their work; there are others who look remiss and as if they were doing something else, and who . . . do not wish to exert themselves . . . Some discern dimly, others clearly: the latter look deeply into things and are said to have 'acumen' (or sharpness of mind); the former come to a stop at the most obvious part of things, and are said to be, mentally, dull and blunt.

Some scholars find the first beginnings of things easy but soon are perplexed, over whose mental eye, as it were, a kind of mist spreads while they are working . . . Others, eager and strong, most happily continue steadfastly . . . Some advance tardily and slowly, but at length arrive at their goal, and of these, some with their slow steps

7. WATSON, *Vives, Father of Modern Psychology*, p. 337.
8. ibid, p. 339.
9. Quoted by Foster Watson from *The Works of Thomas Reid* (including Hamilton's 'Dissertations'), 7th ed., Vol. II, p. 896.

advance farther than those who were before them in their course
. . . Variations of mind arise from the different nature of each
person.[10]

He has much to say of memory, with practical suggestions
of how it may best be trained; in particular, the importance of
understanding what is to be learned:

Memory consists of two factors: quick comprehension and faithful retention; we quickly comprehend what we understand, we retain what we have often and carefully confided to our memory.
Both are helped by arrangement of facts, so that we can even recall
what has passed away . . . What we want to remember must be impressed on our memory while others are silent; but we need not be
silent ourselves, for those things which we have read aloud are
often more deeply retained . . . It is a very useful practice to write
down what we want to remember, for it is not less impressed on
the mind than on the paper by the pen, and indeed the attention
is kept fixed longer by the fact that we are writing it down.[11]

The first to write of psychology as an empirical science, he
gives full weight to the importance of experience and of the
senses as the basis of intellectual activity:

The process is to the unknown through the known and *we can
only attain the verdict of the mind's judgment by first employing
the functions of the senses.*[12]

The course of learning is from the senses to the imagination, and
from that to the mind of which it is the life and nature, and so progress is made from individual facts to groups of facts, from individual facts to the universal. . . . And so *the senses are our first
teachers*[13] *for the senses open the way to all knowledge.*[14]

Here is the germ of the inductive method, for the discovery
of which Bacon has been given the credit. Fifty years before
him, Vives was saying:

I only call that knowledge which we receive when the senses are
properly brought to observe things and in a methodical way to
which clear reason leads us on.[15]

10. WATSON, *Vives on Education*, pp. 73–6.
11. ibid, p. 109.
12. ibid, p. lx, *De Causis Corruptarum Artium*.
13. WATSON, *Father of Modern Psychology*, p. 344.
14. WATSON, *Vives on Education*, p. 168.   15. ibid, p. 22.

Investigation, and individual thought and judgement were to take the place of the authority of the old writers, who had held the field for so long:

> It is fare more profitable to learning to form a critical judgment on the writings of the great authors, than to merely acquiesce in their authority and to receive everything on trust from others.[16]

> Man has received from God a great gift, viz. a mind, and the power of inquiring into things: with which power he can behold not only the present, but also cast his gaze over the past and the future. In all this, man considered the chief use of so great an instrument to be to examine all things, to collect, to compare, and to roam through the universe of nature as if it were his own possession.[17]

> The soul is nourished . . . by that which brings light . . . to it, so that it may know how to pursue what should be desired in life, or to escape what ought to be avoided. To this end we must partly learn and accept what has been handed down to us, and partly think it out for ourselves and learn by practising it.[18]

One of the most important aims of education is to develop a true power of judgement:

> True and very wysdome is . . . trewely to judge of thynges, that we esteeme every thynge to be as it is . . .[19]

> Let every man, even from his childhode, use to have ryght opinions of all thynges.[20]

Having cast aside the weight of authority, Vives saw clearly that the alternative was experience:

> Practical wisdom is increased by experience, which is supported by the memory.[21]

This was logical and not surprising. What was surprising, and strikes the modern reader with delight, is Vives's intense interest in nature study. Nearly three hundred years before Pestalozzi and Froebel he wrote:

> Those things which serve for observation and knowledge involve first the exercise of sight on the external face of Nature. . . . Let the

---

16. ibid, p. 8, *De Disciplinis.* Preface.
17. ibid, p. 11.　　　　　　　　18. ibid, p. 36.
19. *An Introduction to Wysedome,* no pagination.
20. ibid.　　　　21. WATSON, *Vives on Education*, p. 38.

keenness of sight of the mind descend from its height to the intimate working of Nature which is concerned with the inner essence
of everything. For in this study an entrance is found to the essential heart of things more readily by the mind than by the eye, although observation begins through the eye.[22]

These might have been the words of Froebel himself, with
their mystical reference to the inner meaning of nature. 'In
these studies,' Vives says, 'there is no disputation necessary;
there is nothing needed but the silent contemplation of Nature.
... It is at once school and schoolmaster.' [23]

It has been suggested that Vives's love of nature came from
his boyhood experiences in Valencia. Certainly the detailed
description, in *Tudor Schoolboy Life*, of the song of a nightin-
gale, and of the countryside in May, sounds like a memory of
a real experience. The student, he says,

will observe the nature of things in the heavens, in cloudy and in
clear weather, in the plains, on the mountains, in the woods. Hence
he will seek out, and get to know, many things from those who
inhabit those spots. Let him have recourse, for instance, to gar-
deners, husbandmen, shepherds and hunters. ... But whether he
observes anything himself, or hears anyone relating his experience,
not only let him keep eyes and ears intent, but his whole mind also,
for great and exact concentration is necessary in observing every
part of nature, in its seasons.[24]

Vives's psychology was to have practical application. The
teacher was to try to assess the differences in abilities between
his pupils, and to adapt his teaching to suit them:

In determining the instruction to be given to each person, the
disposition is to be regarded; the close consideration of this subject belongs to psychological inquiry.[25]

Different subjects of study require, in each case, a distinct type
of natural mental ability for its successful pursuance.[26]

Let the boy remain one or two months in the preparatory school
that his disposition may be investigated. Four times a year let the
masters meet in some place apart where they may discuss together

22. ibid, p. 41.   23. ibid, pp. 169, 171.
24. ibid, pp. 170–71.   25. ibid, p. 73.
26. ibid, p. 33.

the natures of their pupils and consult about them. And let them apply each boy to that study for which he seems most fit.[27]

The disposition of the boy and what he is specially fitted for, can be found out by relatives and friends, and the boy himself will every day give many signs of it. If he is not apt at his letters but trifles with the school tasks, . . . let him be early transferred to that work for which he seems fitted.[28]

Vives understood how children can vary, in their ability to learn, from one period to another in their lives:

Some boys are not fit for study at one time but are at another, and *vice versa*.[29]

He was very aware, too, of the difficulties of the beginners and of the slow learners:

The wise teacher will remember what a difference there is between the beginner, the one who is getting on, and the one who is fully accomplished; that he cannot require from a boy, who is beginning, that which he expects from a youth, who has made progress in self-control and moral character. Nothing is so foolish as to expect ripe fruit when the trees begin to bud in early spring.[30]

Let some extra time be added for those who are somewhat slow, for it is not expedient to have one time for all; nothing would be more unequal than an equality of that kind.[31]

In all forms of teaching, whether intellectual or moral, the subject matter is to be adapted to the ability of the children. It must be within the scope of the children's power to comprehend. Here again is the realization that children are not merely small adults:

The teacher should choose what is suited to the age of his pupils and to the knowledge which he is imparting.[32]

Above all, boys must be accustomed to delight in good things and to love them, and to be grieved at evil things and to detest them; yet their ideas [of good and evil] should be suited to their mental grasp, for they cannot at once apprehend the highest and the absolute.[33]

Vives realized that children must come before subjects:

27. ibid, p. 62.   28. ibid, p. 70.   29. ibid, p. 86.
30. ibid, p. 118.   31. ibid, p. 59.   32. ibid, p. 164.
33. ibid, p. 64.

The teacher in the school ought to look at his audience, . . . that he may teach those topics of the arts most suited to the capacity of his pupils.[34]

The children are to take an active part in the learning process:

Subject matter is to be presented to the boy so that his mind may elevate itself by movement and action. For nothing of this nature can be judged of when it is quiescent.[35]

The pupils are to keep notebooks in which they make their own notes. They are to compare their work, not with one another, but with their own previous efforts. They are to learn from first-hand experience and observation, rather than from books. They

should not be ashamed to enter into shops and factories, and to ask questions from craftsmen, and get to know about the details of their work.[36]

The children are to be encouraged by praise, and in this he echoes the words of Plutarch:

Small rewards and praise should be allowed to those of childish age.[37]

Urge the pupils by praise and approval as though with a pricking spur to a race, that they may not be made ashamed by the constant strange and subtle derision of their teacher and companions, and thus despair before they have tested their powers, for those who are hindered by the possibility of being exposed to ridicule never venture to make any advance.[38]

They are not to be forced into learning nor be over-pressed:

Boys . . . must not be pressed too much or driven to study, but they must be allowed some respite from attention, 'lest they should begin to hate work before they begin to love it'. . . . The human mind is wonderfully inclined to freedom. It allows itself to be set to work, but it will not suffer itself to be compelled. . . .[39] When unwilling minds are driven to uncongenial work, we see that almost all things turn out wrong and distorted.[40]

34. ibid, p. 89.   35. ibid, p. 81.   36. ibid, p. 209.
37. ibid, p. 117.   38. ibid, p. 119.   39. ibid, p. 121.
40. ibid, p. 82.

The relationship between teacher and pupil is to be that of a wise and loving father with his sons:

> The affection of the master for his pupils will be that of a father; he will love him truly and from his heart, as if he were his own offspring. . .
> It is incredible what great influence the affections of the master and the pupil exercise upon both good teaching and good learning.[41]

Pupils are to be taught in groups:

> Let the boy be taught by him, . . . only not alone, for, as Quintilian shows, he will in that case make less progress.[42]

Vives believes in the value of play, both for learning and as a means of assessing children's abilities:

> Children should be exercised in play, for that reveals their sharpness and their characters.[43]
> The boy should be taught, through play, both to rule and to command. The Spaniards rather wisely say in a proverb that 'office and play are the touchstones of minds'.[44]

Vives, the great 'way-breaker', as Lange called him, foreshadowed many of the important principles now generally accepted as essential in education, and for which others, later, were given the credit.

41. ibid, pp. 86–7.   42. ibid, p. 66.
43. ibid, p. 82.   44. ibid.

7

The New Learning in England · Sir Thomas Elyot
Roger Ascham · Mulcaster · Brinsley · Francis Bacon

IN England the new learning was associated at first with a group
of men who were friends of Sir Thomas More: Dean Colet,
the founder of St Paul's, Erasmus, Fisher and Sir Thomas
Linacre; and the first book on education written in English appeared in 1531, *The Boke named the Governour* by Sir Thomas
Elyot, a pupil of More and a friend of Roger Ascham. Elyot
was also a political figure of some stature, a friend of Thomas
Wolsey and Thomas Cromwell, chief clerk to the King's
Council and Henry VIII's ambassador to the Emperor Charles
V at the time of his proposed divorce from Catherine of
Aragon. His book shows the influence of the Italian Renais-
sance, and stresses the importance of the environment, par-
ticularly in the first years:

I will use the policie of a wyse and counnynge gardener: who
purposynge to have in his gardeine a fyne and preciouse herbe,
... he will first serche throughout his gardeyne where he can finde
the most melowe and fertile erth: and therin wil he put the sede of
the herbe to growe and be norisshed; and in most diligent wise
attende that no weede be suffred to growe or approche nyghe unto
it: and to the entent it may thrive the faster, as soone as the fourme
of an herbe ones appereth, he will set a vessell of water by hit, in
such wyse that it may continually distille on the rote swete droppes;
and as it spryngeth in stalke, under sette it with some thyng that
it breake nat, and alway kepe it cleane from weedes. Semblable
ordre will I ensue in the fourmynge the gentill wittes of noble
mennes children.[1]

First in importance was the child, not the subject. He was to
be considered as an individual, and his powers and abilities
understood:

1. ELYOT, SIR THOMAS, *The Boke named the Governour*, Everyman,
pp. 18–19.

The office of a tutor is firste to knowe the nature of his pupil.[2]

Children were to be taught, as Plato and Quintilian had urged, by persuasion and praise, and were to learn by play rather than force:

I wolde nat haue them inforced by violence to lerne but ... to be swetely allured therto with praises and suche praty gyftes as children delite in.[3]

And they were to be encouraged to use their hands, if their interests lay that way:

If a childe be of nature inclined ... to paint with a penne, or to fourme images in stone or tree: he shulde nat be therfrom withdrawen ... but puttyng one to him, whiche is in that crafte, wherein he deliteth, moste excellent ... he shulde be, in the moste pure wise, enstructed in painting or keruinge,[4] and all is to be done by the child's 'owne naturall disposition, and nat by coertion'.

The importance of experience is emphasized:

Experience ... is of no small moment ... in the acquiringe of sapience, in so much that it semeth that no operation or affaire may be perfecte, nor no science or arte may be complete, except experience bee there unto added.[5]

The value of visual aids was recognized:

I dare affirme a man shal more profite, in one wike, by figures and chartis ... than he shall by the only reding or herying the rules of that science by the space of halfe a yere at the lest.[6]

Elyot followed this two years later with *Of the knowledge which maketh a wise man*, in which he, as Vives had done, gives his belief in an education which leads to action. The book consists of a dialogue between Plato and Aristippus. After they have agreed that wisdom means self-knowledge, Aristippus says:

For now me thinketh that none may be called a wise man, excepte unto that knowledge, wherein is wysedome, he joyneth operation.[7]

2. ibid, p. 24.   3. ibid, p. 21.
4. ibid, p. 28.   5. ibid, pp. 284–5.
6. ibid, p. 30.
7. *Of the knowledge which maketh a wise man*, p. 197.

The influence of Elyot's work on educational thought in England was considerable – no doubt his translation of Plutarch's work on the education of children was widely read – and would have been greater but for the interruption of the Reformation and the far-reaching changes which followed it.

Fortunately for England, her Tudor monarchs were zealous for learning, while the prosperity and virility of the nation, particularly under Elizabeth, created a new and widespread interest in education.

Elizabeth's own tutor, Roger Ascham, reflected in his *Scholemaster* much of the thought of Erasmus, Vives and earlier writers. The teacher must study his pupils, he says, and he shares the Jesuits' belief in the possibilities of each. He anticipated the chief problem of our modern methods of selection for secondary education – how to distinguish real ability from frothy brightness – and gives a warning, which is as timely now as in the sixteenth century, against overlooking the children who do not appear to shine as early as others:

Even the wisest of your great beaters, do as oft punishe nature, as they do correcte faultes. Yea, many times the better nature is sorer punished: For, if one, by quicknes of witte, take his lesson readelie, an other, by hardnes of witte, taketh it not so speedelie; the first is alwaies commended, the other is commonlie punished: whan a wise scholemaster should rather discretelie consider the right disposition of both their natures, and not so much wey what either of them is able to do now, as what either of them is likelie to do hereafter. For this I know, not onelie by reading of bookes in my studie, but also by experience of life, abrode in the world, that those which be commonlie the wisest, the best learned, and best men also, when they be olde, were never commonlie the quickest of witte when they were yonge.[8]

Like the Jesuits, Ascham believed that learning goes with love and, with Sir Thomas Elyot and many before him, he stresses the value of praise:

I have now wished twice or thrice this gentle nature to be in a scholemaster. . . . In mine opinion love is fitter than feare, jentlenes better than beating, to bring up a child rightlie in learninge.[9] I

8. ASCHAM, ROGER, *The Scholemaster*, p. 20.
9. ibid, p. 25.

assure you, there is no such whetstone, to sharpen a good witte, and encourage a will to learninge, as is praise.[10]

With Plato, he believed that ignorance was the beginning of wisdom:

In yougthe, . . . som ignorance is as necessarie as moch knowledge.[11]

Many of the educational ideas we think most up to date in the twentieth century were in fact put into practice by a schoolmaster of the sixteenth, Richard Mulcaster, headmaster of the Merchant Taylors' School and highmaster of St Paul's.

He believed that education was not merely a matter of intellectual training, but of all-round development:

Why is it not good to have every parte of the body and every power of the soul to be fined to his best?[12]

Such education must be according to nature:

The end of education . . . is to help natur unto hir perfection.[13]

He stressed the importance of the early stages of education:

The first groundworke would be layd by the best workeman.[14] It is the foundacion well and soundly laid, which makes all the upper building muster, with countenaunce and continuaunce,[15]

and went so far as to say that the teachers of the youngest children should be paid the most, and have the smallest classes, an ideal of common sense in which we are still well behind him:

For that the first grounding would be handled by the best, and his reward would be greatest, bycause both his paines and his judgement should be with the greatest. . . The first maister can deale with but a few, the next with moe, and so still upward as reason groweth on, and receives without forcing. . . If I were to strike the stroke . . . the first paines truely taken should in good truth be most liberally recompensed: and lesse allowed still upward, as the paines diminish and the ease encreaseth.[16]

10. ibid, p. 20.   11. ibid, p. 50.
12. MULCASTER, SIR R., *Positions*, p. 34.
13. MULCASTER, SIR R., *Elementarie*, p. 31.
14. MULCASTER, SIR R., *Positions*, p. 30.
15. ibid, p. 234.   16. ibid, pp. 233–4.

Mulcaster saw clearly the dangers of attempting to force a child to learn before he is ready:

> Bycause of the to timely onset, to litle is done in to long a time, and the schoole is made a torture.[17]

He realized the importance of finding the right time to teach so that children gain confidence:

> Haste is most harmefull, where so ever it setts foote. . . For the poore children when they perceive their own weaknesse, . . . they both faint and feare, and very hardly get forward; and we that teach do meet with to much toile, when poore young babes be committed to our charge, before they be ripe.[18]

Nature is the best guide 'that anie man can follow', and all must 'proceede voluntarily, and not with violence'.

He was well aware of the fact that children mature at different rates. In discussing the question at what age schooling should begin, he says:

> At what yeares I cannot say, bycause ripenes in children is not tyed to one time, no more than all corne is ripe for one reaping.[19]

In this he shows himself more enlightened than we ourselves, who base our educational system on the idea that all five-year-olds are ready for school, and all seven-year-olds are mature enough for formal education.

Mulcaster knew that it was natural for children to be active, and that the educator must realize what he is doing when he asks children to be still for long:

> For if by causing them learne so and sitting still in schooles, we did not force them from their ingenerate heat, and naturall stirring, to an unnaturall stillnesse, then their owne stirring without restraint, might seeme to serve their tourne, without more adoe. But stillnesse more than ordinarie must have stirring more than ordinarie.[20]

Finally, this sixteenth-century schoolmaster helped to lay the foundation of a science of education, as he groped towards an understanding of the process of learning:

17. ibid, p. 33.   18. ibid, pp. 23–4.
19. MULCASTER, SIR R., *Elementarie*, ibid, p. 18.
20. MULCASTER, SIR R., *Positions*, ibid, p. 23.

We haue ... a perceiving by outward senses to fele, to hear, to se, to smell, to tast all sensible things, which qualities of the outward, being receiued in by the *common sense*, and examined by *fantsie*, are deliuered to *remembrance*, and afterwards proue our great and onelie grounds unto further knowledge.[21] The hand, the ear, the eie be the greatest instruments.[22]

Anothery practising schoolmaster, who anticipated in theory at least much of what is now considered modern, was John Brinsley, headmaster of Ashby de la Zouche school. In 1612 he wrote, for those of 'tender yeeres',

Let the schoole be made unto them a place of play.[23] The foundation well layd, the building must needs goe forward much more happily.[24]

Their learning is for the most part as a play to them who are ingenuous.[25]

The masters must not be ashamed, nor weary to doe as the nurse with the child, as it were stammering and playing with them, to seeke by all meanes to breed in the little ones a love of their masters, with delight in their bookes.[26]

Unfortunately, however, much of this was mere lip-service. There is little sign of play in the programme of his school day, which began at six a.m. It seems clear that his idea of play was a very limited one. Play was to be the reward, rather the means of learning, although he says the Schoolhouse should be ... *ludus literarius* indeed a Schoole of play and pleasure ... and not feare and bondage'.[27]

He stressed the value of praise and encouragement, and suggested

that there be most heedfull care, chiefly amongst all the yongest, that not one of them be any way discouraged, either by bitternesse of speech, or by taunting disgrace; or else by severitie of correction, to cause them to hate the Schoole before they know it, or to distast good learning before they have felt the sweetnesse of it: but in stead hereof, that all things in Schooles be done by emula-

21. MULCASTER, SIR R., *Elementarie*, p. 36.
22. ibid, p. 39.
23. BRINSLEY, J., *Ludus literarius*, p. 10.
24. ibid, p. 14.   25. ibid, p. 302.
26. ibid, p. 55.   27. ibid, p. 50.

tion, and honest contention, through a wise commending in them everything, which in any way deserveth praise.[28]

The master

should be of a loving and gentle disposition with gravitie; . . . and to incourage his scholars by due praise, rewards, and an honest emulation.[29]

Let every man's experience teach whether extremitie or excesse of feare . . . doth not deprive and robbe the minde of all the helpes which reason offers. So as that the minde running about that which it feares so much, forgets that which it should wholly intend; whereby in timorous natures, you shall see some to stand as very sotts, and senselesse, through an apprehension of some extreme evill, or by extremity of feare: whereas they are otherwise as wise and learned as the best. Insomuch as all devices are to be used to rid children of that kind of overwhelming feare.[30]

Fear should be replaced by love, a truly educative force:

All things should be done in the Schoole, so as to worke in the children a love of learning; and also of their teachers; for that this love is well knowne to be the most effectual meanes, to increase and nourish learning in them the fastest; and also that government which consists in love, is ever the firmest.[31]

Education must be of practical value, and children should be taught to understand what they learn:
They should

learne onely such bookes and matters, as whereof they have the best use.[32] This is a matter which of all other concerneth the credit of Schooles, and furthereth learning wonderfully; to teach Schollers to understand whatsoever they learne, and to be able to give a reason of everything why it is so.[33]

A brake was put on educational progress during the seventeenth century owing to the exhausting effect of the religious wars in Germany, France and England, and the grammar schools continued to work in much the same limited spirit as

28. ibid, p. 49.
30. ibid, pp. 277–8.
32. ibid, p. 45.

29. ibid, p. 268.
31. ibid, p. 278.
33. ibid, pp. 41–2,

they had always done. They had their critics, and individuals
attempted to show a better way, both in theory and practice.
One whose influence, though indirect, was to prove revolutionary was Francis Bacon, and the application of his methods
by others such as Comenius was fundamentally to alter education.

His challenge was that men should no longer be content to
accept the authority of books but to go themselves to nature
and learn by first-hand observation:

Another error proceeds from too great a reverence ... paid to the
human understanding; whence men have withdrawn themselves
from the contemplation of nature and experience, and sported with
their own reason and the fictions of fancy. These intellectualists
... are censured by Heraclitus, when he says 'Men seek for truth
in their own little worlds, and not in the great world without them:
and as they disdain to spell, they can never come to read in the
volume of God's works.' [34]

Be not wrapt up in the past; there is an actual present lying all
about you, look up, and behold it in its grandeur.[35]

Here, therefore is the first distemper of learning, when men study
words and not matter ... for words are but the images of matter;
and except they have life of reason and invention, to fall in love
with them is all one as to fall in love with a picture.[36]

Men have sought to make a world from their own conceptions
and to draw from their own minds all the materials which they
employed; but if instead of doing so, they had consulted experience
and observation, they would have had facts and not opinions to
reason about.[37]

He urges men

to abjure all traditional and inherited views and notions, and
to come as new-born children, with open and unworn sense, to the
observation of nature. For it is no less true in this human kingdom
of knowledge than in God's kingdom of heaven, that no man shall
enter into it except he become first as a little child.[38]

34. BACON, FRANCIS, *Advancement of Learning*, Bk. 1, p. 33.
35. LAURIE, *John Amos Comenius*, p. 19.
36. ibid, pp. 24–5.
37. *Novum Organum*, LAURIE, *John Amos Comenius*, p. 16.
38. BARNARD, *English Pedagogy*, p. 82.

He shows the same understanding as Plato and Roger
Ascham of the necessity of humility and ignorance as pre-
liminaries to learning. Had he applied the same principle to
the study of children, a science of education might have been
born much earlier than it was, for he was aware of many
principles of education:

– the importance of the first beginnings –

A gardener . . . takes more pains with the young than with the
full-grown plant, and men commonly find it needful in any under-
taking to begin well.[39]

– the need to understand the part played by the feelings, and
their nature –

For as in medicining of the body, it is in order first to know the
divers complexions and constitutions; secondly, the diseases; and
lastly the cures: so in medicining of the mind, after knowledge of
the divers characters of men's natures, it followeth, in order, to
know the diseases and infirmities of the mind, which are no other
than the perturbations and distempers of the affections.[40]

– the need to study individual children and to adapt work to
their abilities, and the importance of following children's
natural interests –

And so to select and assign topics of instruction, as to adapt them
to the individual capabilities of the pupils, – this, too, requires a
special experience and judgment.
A close observation and an accurate knowledge of the different
natures of pupils is due from teachers. . . And note further, that
not only does every one make more rapid progress in those studies
to which his nature inclines him, but again that a natural disinclination . . . may be overcome by the help of special studies.[41]

For the age that followed, Bacon became the great authority
for both learning and teaching. His theories were put into practice by Wolfgang Ratke in Germany, of whom it was said he

39. De Augmentis, LAURIE, John Amos Comenius, p. 19.
40. Advancement of Learning, Bk. 2, p. 171.
41. BARNARD, English Pedagogy, p. 91.

'has discovered the art of teaching according to nature', and formed into a philosophy by Descartes, the heart of which was his belief in reasoning as a natural activity of man, and the necessity to know oneself.

8

Comenius

MUCH of what is thought to be most characteristic of the
great nineteenth-century educators and today regarded as
'modern' is the echo of an earlier and less famous voice, that
of the Moravian John Amos Comenius, the last of the Protestant educators. Hezekiah Woodward called him 'the greatest
light to this kinde of Learning, that ever was set up in the
World'. Practically forgotten for nearly two hundred years, his
writings reappeared in the time of the great upsurge of educational thought of the nineteenth century, and their influence
can be traced in all of the great writers of that time. Froebel's
comparison of children to plants and of the educator to a
gardener, his conception of the 'inner' and 'outer', and that
growth is from within; Rousseau's belief in the importance of
educating according to nature; Pestalozzi's claim that teaching
must be by means of sensible objects; and Herbert Spencer's
emphasis on the importance of sense training were all voiced
in the seventeenth century by the man whom Michelet called
'the first evangelist of modern pedagogy'.

Nicholas Murray Butler said of Comenius that his place in
education is one

of commanding importance. He introduces and dominates the
whole modern movement in the field of elementary and secondary
education. His relation to our present teaching is similar to that
held by Copernicus and Newton toward modern science, and Bacon
and Descartes toward modern philosophy,[1] and Keatinge calls
him 'the prince of schoolmasters'.[2]

The Great Didactic, in which he set out his ideas has been

1. BUTLER, N. M., *The Place of Comenius in the History of Education*,
p. 19.
2. KEATINGE, *The Great Didactic*, p. 98.

called 'one of the greatest treatises on education ever written'.
Its main object, he said was to find a way by which

schools may cease to *persuade* and begin to *demonstrate*; cease
to *dispute* and begin to *look*; cease lastly to *believe* and begin to
know.[3]

In it most of the problems which still face education were
discussed in detail, and many of its suggestions still wait to be
implemented.

Himself a practising teacher, he began, not with subjects, but
with children. He defined a pedagogue as a leader, not a driver,
of children and was convinced that education, if handled
rightly, was both natural and easy:

The action of teaching and learning is in its own nature pleasing
and agreeable.[4]
What is natural takes place without compulsion. Water need not
be forced to run down a mountain-side.[5]
Each individual creature not only suffers itself to be easily led in
the direction which its nature finds congenial, but is actually impelled towards its desired goal, and suffers pain if any obstacle be
interposed.[6]
A bird learns to fly, a fish to swim, and a beast to run without
any compulsion. They do these things of their own accord as soon
as they feel that their limbs are sufficiently strong.[7]

It must follow, then, that

if we learn without very great difficulty to perform the functions of
the body, ... why should we not learn to perform those of the
mind with similar ease, if proper instruction be given?... And
shall not a man be easily taught those things to which nature ...
urges and impels him?[8]

Education, therefore, will be easy, if the course of nature is
followed, that is, if it is suited to the needs of the children at
the different stages of their development:

Nothing should be taught to the young, unless it is not only
permitted but actually demanded by their age and mental strength.[9]

3. QUICK, *Educational Reformers*, p. 152.
4. *The School of Infancy*, ELLER, p. 68.
5. *The Great Didactic*, p. 131.   6. ibid, p. 84.
7. ibid.   8. ibid, p. 85.   9. ibid, p. 138.

The teacher, like the physician, is the servant and not the master of nature and must adapt his teaching to the abilities of his pupils. He uses Quintilian's imagery:

If we take a jar with a narrow mouth (for to this we may compare a boy's intellect) and attempt to pour a quantity of water into it violently, instead of allowing it to trickle in drop by drop, what will be the result? Without doubt the greater part of the liquid will flow over the side, and ultimately the jar will contain less than if the operation had taken place gradually. Quite as foolish is the action of those who try to teach their pupils, not as much as they can assimilate, but as much as they themselves wish.[10]

Comenius recognized that difference in ability was a matter not only of the intellect, but of temperament and character:

There is naturally a difference in intellects.[11] Some men are sharp, others dull; some soft and yielding, others hard and unbending; some eager after knowledge, others more anxious to acquire mechanical skill.[12]

He realized that children develop at different rates.

All children do not develop at the same time, some beginning to speak in the first year, some in the second, and some in the third.[13]

He was aware that it was not always the quick-wit who, in the end, bore the best fruit. Some, he says,

are flexible and anxious to learn, but ... at the same time are slow and heavy... Though such pupils take longer to come to maturity, they will probably last all the better, like fruit that ripens late... At school, therefore, they should be given every opportunity.[14]

All work must be not only suitable to the children but must also please them:

Knowledge is unsuitable when it is uncongenial to the mind of this or that scholar. For there is as great a difference between the minds of men as exists between the various kinds of plants, of trees, or of animals; one must be treated in one way, and another in

10. ibid, pp. 136–7.   11. ibid, p. 86.   12. ibid, p. 88.
13. *The School of Infancy*, ELLER, p. 74.
14. *The Great Didactic*, p. 89.

another, and the same method cannot be applied to all alike. . . If we attempt to counteract a natural disinclination we are fighting against nature and such effort is useless. The teacher should never attempt to force a scholar to study any subject if he sees that it is uncongenial to his natural disposition.[15]

Comenius saw clearly the importance of rousing interest, of creating the desire to learn before attempting to teach:

How many of those who undertake to educate the young appreciate the necessity of first teaching them how to acquire knowledge? . . . Who, I ask, ever thinks it necessary that the teacher . . . should make his pupils anxious for information . . . before he begins to place knowledge before them?[16] A master, if he wish to illumine with knowledge a pupil shrouded in the darkness of ignorance, must first excite his attention, that he may drink in information with a greedy mind.[17] Every study should be commenced in such a manner as to awaken a real liking for it on the part of the scholars.[18]

He saw what is today still hardly recognized, that the surest way to create such appetite for learning is to give children something to do:

If you give the pupil something to do, you will quickly rouse and capture his interest, so that he will throw himself into the work.[19]

Comenius anticipated the best of modern practice in his emphasis on the value of praise, on the need to link different subjects together, and for children to understand fully what they learn:

The scholar should be taught first to understand things, and then to remember them, and no stress should be laid on the use of speech or pen, till after a training on the first two points.[20]

He would be disappointed to find how many schools today reject such advice as too modern, believing that they are fulfilling their function as long as their children can give a right answer on paper or in words.

15. ibid, p. 181.   16. ibid, pp. 87–8.
17. ibid, p. 187.   18. ibid, p. 146.
19. *The Analytical Didactic of Comenius*, p. 108.
20. *The Great Didactic* p. 120.

All learning was to be of definite use and practical value, and he insisted on the use of visual aids, of learning by means of the senses, and of first-hand experience:

The understanding possesses nothing that it has not first derived from the senses. Surely then, the beginning of wisdom should consist, not in the mere learning the names of things, but in the actual perception of the things themselves![21] Man's senses ... must be early brought to bear on the world that surrounds him, since throughout his whole life he has much to learn, to experience and to accomplish.[22]

Pupils should

get to know, first, that which lies nearest to their mental vision, then that which lies moderately near, then that which is more remote, and lastly, that which is farthest off.[23]

Things, therefore, must come before words:

Things are the kernel, words the shells and husks.[24] The proper education of the young does not consist in stuffing their heads with a mass of words, sentences, and ideas dragged together out of various authors, but in opening their understanding to the outer world, so that a living stream may flow from their own minds, just as leaves, flowers and fruit spring from the buds on a tree.[25] Men must as far as is possible be taught to become wise by studying the heavens, the earth, oaks, and beeches, but not by studying books; that is to say, they must learn to know and investigate the things themselves, and not the observations that other people have made about the things.[26] Why ... should we not instead of these dead books, lay open the living book of Nature?[27]

Such first-hand experience should begin long before children come to school. In his description of the Mother School, Comenius laid down the principle of the modern kindergarten and infant school:

In its first six years a child may begin to know *natural things*, the names of fire, air, water and earth; of rain, snow, ice, lead, iron; trees and some of the better known and more common plants; ... likewise the difference between animals; ... finally, the

21. ibid, p. 185.   22. ibid, p. 58.   23. ibid, p. 135.
24. ibid, p. 115.   25. ibid, p. 147.   26. ibid, p. 150.
27. Preface to *Naturall Philosophie Reformed*, LAURIE, p. 69.

outward members of its own body, how they ought to be named, for what use designed.[28]

He will learn the difference between darkness and light and the names of the common colours; he will come to know the sun, moon and stars; the place of his birth, whether he lives in a village, city, town or citadel; what is a field, a fountain, a forest, a meadow, a river.

He will learn to know what is an hour, a day, a week, a month, a year; what is spring, what summer, the meaning of 'yesterday' and 'tomorrow'.

The foundation of arithmetic will be laid when he knows that something is much or little, is able to count to ten and to understand that three are more than two, and that three and one make four.

He will be learning Geometry as he comes to know what is small and large, short or long, narrow or broad, thin or thick; what is meant by a line, a cross or a circle, and how we measure in feet and yards. He will see objects weighed in scales and learn to guess weights by holding objects in his hands.

He will be encouraged to use his hands

to cut, to split, to carve, to strew, to arrange, to tie, to untie, to roll up, and to unroll – such things being familiar to all children.[29] Infants try to imitate what they see others do. Let them therefore have all things except those that might cause injury to themselves or anything. . . When it is not convenient to give them real instruments, let them have toys like leaden knives, wooden swords, ploughs, little carriages, sledges, mills, buildings. . . They love to construct little houses and to erect walls of clay, chips, wood, stone. . . In a word, whatever children delight to play with, provided it be not hurtful, they ought rather to be gratified than restrained from it, for inactivity is more injurious both to mind and body than anything in which they can be occupied.[30]

Even some infant schools have today still to catch up on this three-hundred-year-old vision of the true nature and needs of childhood:

Too much sitting still ... is not a good sign; for the child to be always running or doing something is a sure sign of a sound

28. *The School of Infancy,* ELLER, p. 73.
29. ibid, p. 74.   30. ibid, pp. 91–2.

body and vigorous intellect.[31] Boys ever delight in being employed in something, for their youthful blood does not allow them to be at rest. ... Let them be like ants, continually occupied in doing something, carrying, drawing, constructing and conveying, provided always that whatever they do be done prudently.[32]

Doing is, in fact, the means by which learning takes place, and schools should become workshops:

Artisans do not detain their apprentices with theories, but set them to do practical work at an early stage; thus they learn to forge by forging, to carve by carving, to paint by painting, and to dance by dancing. In schools, therefore, let the students learn to write by writing, to talk by talking, to sing by singing, and to reason by reasoning. In this way schools will become workshops humming with work.[33]

This education through first-hand experience, through the use of the hands, and by play was to continue in the Vernacular School, up to the age of twelve.

Comenius warned against the dangers of beginning formal schooling too soon, and of forcing:

The attempt is generally made to engraft that noblest graft of knowledge, virtue and piety, too early, before the stock itself has taken root; that is to say, before the desire to learn has been excited in those who have no natural bent in that direction.[34] Those who drive boys to their studies do them great harm... If a man has no appetite, but yet takes food when urged to do, the result can only be sickness and vomiting, or at least indigestion and indisposition. On the other hand, if a man be hungry, he is eager to take food, digests it readily and easily converts it into flesh and blood.[35]

Comenius believed that a school should do more than train the intellect; his perfect school would train the heart as well as the head:

I call a school that fulfils its functions perfectly, one which is a true forging place of men; where the minds of those who learn are illuminated by the light of wisdom, ... where the emotions and

31. ibid, p. 92. 32. ibid, p. 91.
33. *The Great Didactic*, p. 195. 34. ibid, p. 117.
35. ibid, pp. 129–30

o.m.e. – 6

the desires are brought into harmony with virtue, and where the heart is filled with . . . divine love.[36]

The most significant contribution that Comenius made to education, and that which is slowly bringing about the greatest change in our schools, lies in his firmly held belief, following Aristotle, Plato, Seneca and Cicero, that all growth, all learning, all development, comes from within, and that the educator's part is to lead and guide, and make that development fruitful:

The seeds of knowledge, of virtue and of piety are . . . naturally implanted in us.[37] Man is not a block of wood from which you carve a statue which is completely subject to your will; he is a living image, shaping, misshaping and reshaping itself.[38]

He speaks of 'the foundation of knowledge that is hidden in the scholars', which the schools have neglected to open and have instead 'watered them with water from other sources'. His true educator, like that of Froebel, is a gardener, who watches and tends his plants, but always respects their own natural growth:

The mind . . . of a man who enters this world is very justly compared to a seed or to a kernel in which the plant or tree really does exist, although its image cannot actually be seen. . . It is not necessary, therefore, that anything be brought to a man from without, but only that which he possesses rolled up within himself be unfolded and disclosed.[39] In very truth, all things exist in man; . . . the lamp, the oil, the tinder and all the appliances are there and if only he be sufficiently skilled to strike sparks, to catch them, and to kindle the lamp, he can forthwith see and can reap the fullest enjoyment of the marvellous treasures of God's wisdom, both in himself and in the larger world.[40] It is God who operates in everything, and nothing remains for man but to receive the seeds of instruction with a devout heart; the processes of growth and of ripening will then continue of themselves, unperceived by him. The duty of the teachers of the young, therefore, is none other than

36. ibid, p. 76.   37. ibid, p. 40.
38. *The Analytical Didactic of Comenius*, p. 108.
39. *The Great Didactic*, p. 42.
40. ibid, pp. 43–4.

to skilfully scatter the seeds of instruction in their minds, and to carefully water God's plants. Increase and growth will come from above.[41]

After three centuries, our schools today still await the implementation of this great belief.

41. ibid, p. 111.

9

Education during the Commonwealth · Hartlib · Petty · Milton
Dury · Charles Hoole · Hezekiah Woodward · Cowley

DURING the Commonwealth, the light of education brightened
once more through a group of English social reformers headed
by Samuel Hartlib, and the cause of education might have
been saved a hundred years of waiting for reform, had it not
been for the Civil War and the reaction of the Restoration.

Hartlib himself urged that schools should be provided where
children, from eight or nine up to thirteen or fourteen, might
'observe all things natural and artificial extant in the world'.

In 1640 the House of Commons was asked to invite to England 'two great public spirits, who have laboured much for
truth and peace' – Comenius and John Dury – with the purpose
of founding a college on the lines of Bacon's 'Solomon's
House', which he had described in the *New Atlantis*. The
meeting took place in 1641–2 and although Comenius' plan for
a pansophic college in London came to nothing because of the
outbreak of war, the work for reform in education was pursued
by Hartlib, under whose influence three educational treatises
were published.

The first appeared in 1647, written by William Petty, a
doctor in Cromwell's Irish Army. It includes one of the earliest
and most delightful pieces of detailed child study:

We see Children do delight in Drums, Pipes, Fiddels, Guns made
of Elder sticks, and bellowes noses, piped Keys, etc., painting Flags
and Ensignes with Elder-berries and Corn poppy, making ships with
Paper, and setting even Nut-shells a swimming, handling the tooles
of workemen as soon as they turne their backs, and trying to worke
themselves; fishing, fowling, hunting, setting sprenges, and traps
for birds and other animals, making pictures in the writing bookes,
making Tops, Gigs, and Whirligigs, guilting balls, practising divers
juggling tricks upon the cards, etc., with a million more besides.[1]

1. PETTY, WILLIAM, *Advice of W.P. to Mr Samuel Hartlib*, p. 24.

Here at last someone has watched real children. Even Froebel never gave such a picture of children's play.

Petty observed the girls too:

And for the Females they will be making Pyes with Clay, making their Babies clothes and dressing them therewith; they will spit leaves on sticks, as if they were roasting meate, they will imitate all the talke and Actions which they observe in their Mother, and her gossips, and punctually act the Comedy or the Tragedy (I know not whether to call it) of a Woman's lying-in.[2]

From this he concludes that children

do most naturally delight in things, and are most capable of learning them, having Quick Sences to receive them and unpre-occupied memories to retaine them.[3]

Therefore

it would be more profitable to boyes, to spend ten or twelve years in the study of Things.[4] Since few children have need of reading before they know, or can be acquainted with the things they read of, or of writing before their thoughts are worth the recording; ... our opinion is, that those things ... be deferred awhile, and others more needful for them, such as in the order of nature before those afore mentioned, be studied before them... We wish therefore that the educands be taught to observe and remember all sensible objects and actions... If a child, before he learned to read and write, were made acquainted with all things and actions, how easily would he understand all good books afterwards and smell out the fopperies of bad ones.[5]

The second treatise was John Milton's *Tractate on Education*. He would not replace books as the source of authority on matters such as farming and medicine – 'Physick' may be 'read to them out of some not tedious writer' – but he would supplement books by observation:

In those vernal seasons of the year, when the air is calm and pleasant, it were an injury and sullenness against nature not to go out, and see her riches, and partake in her rejoycing with Heaven and Earth.[6]

2. ibid.   3. ibid.
4. ibid.   5. ibid, pp. 4, 8.
   6. MILTON, JOHN, *Tractate on Education*, p. 21.

He suggests that pupils should

> ride out in Companies with prudent and staid Guides to all quarters of the Land: learning and observing all places of strength, all commodities of building and of soil for Towns and Tillage, Harbours, and Ports for Trade.[7]

He advocates daily 'conning of sensible things' and suggests that the knowledge of experts should be used as a means of education:

> What hinders, but that they may procure, as oft as shal be needful, the helpful experiences of Hunters, Fowlers, Fishermen, Shepherds, Gardeners, Apothecaries; and in the other sciences, Architects, Engineers, Mariners, Anatomists, ... and this will give them such a real tincture of natural knowledge, as they shall never forget.[8]

Learning was to be by means of the senses, and things were to be understood before languages were learnt:

> Because our understanding cannot in this body found it self but on sensible things, ... the same method is necessarily to be follow'd in all discreet teaching.
> Language is but the Instrument conveying to us things usefull to be known. And though a Linguist should pride himself to have all the Tongues that *Babel* cleft the world into, yet, if he have not studied the solid things in them as well as the Words and Lexicons, he were nothing so much to be esteem'd a learned man, as any Yeoman or Tradesman competently wise in his Mother-Dialect only. Hence appear the many mistakes which have made Learning so unpleasing and so unsucccessful. ... And these are the fruits of misspending our prime youth at the Schools and Universities, as we do, either in learning meer words or such things chiefly, as were better unlearnt.[9]

In the *Areopagitica* he proclaims that freedom is God's gift to man, freedom to choose. Liberty, to him, is the best school of virtue, and education, in his view, must be positive, not negative:

> God sure esteems the growth and completing of one virtuous person more than the restraint of ten vicious.[10]

7. ibid.   8. ibid, p. 13.   9. ibid, pp. 4–7.
10. *Areopagitica*, Prose Works, ii, pp. 74–5, MCCALLISTER, *The Growth of Freedom in Education*, p. 164.

Milton's idea of education, although chiefly concerned with books and information, attacked the formal, linguistic views of his day through the emphasis he put on thought rather than language, on content rather than form, and in his broad view of the practical end to be achieved:

I call therefore a compleat and generous Education that which fits a man to perform, justly, skilfully and magnanimously all the offices both private and publick of Peace and War.[11]

The last of the three treatises, published in 1650, was written by John Dury, tutor to both the Princess Mary and the children of Charles I, and was called *The Reformed School*. Like most other reformers, he puts training of character before intellectual development:

Good manners ... are far to be preferred unto all human learning of what kind soever; because without moral honesty all the perfection of learning is nothing else but an instrument of wickedness to increase and aggravate the miseries of mankind.[12]

Teaching was to be adapted to the children's abilities:

Concerning the children, we must reflect upon their ordinary capacities and distinguish the same into their natural degrees. Concerning the things which are to be taught, we must reflect upon a twofold proportion therein: first, we must find out that which is proportionate to the degree of everyone's capacity; secondly, we must order everything which is suitable to each capacity proportionally to the end for which it is to be taught.[13]

This, then, is the masterpiece of the whole art of education, to watch over the children's behaviour in their actions of all sorts, so as their true inclinations may be discovered.[14]

The child's co-operation was to be sought by making him aware of the reasons for the treatment given to him. The governor and ushers were

to determine the way how to deal with him, that is, not only how to correct his outward visible misbehaviours and to encourage him

11. *Tractate on Education*, p. 8.
12. DURY, JOHN, *The Reformed School*, pp. 32-3.
13. ibid, p. 43.   14. ibid, p. 33.

in what is good and decent, but how to make him sensible and
rationally apprehensive of the true grounds, both of the correction
and encouragement.[15]

Learning was to be pleasant, and to follow the natural order
of development:

The chief rule of the whole work is that nothing may be made
tedious and grievous to the children.[16]
As children faculties break forth in them by degrees to be
vigorous with their years, and the growth of their bodies, so they
are to be filled with objects whereof they are capable.[17]

The first means of learning, following the natural stages of
development, were to be through the senses:

While children are not capable of the acts of reasoning, the
method of filling their senses and imaginations with outward objects should be plied. ... No general rules are to be given unto
any ... till sense, imagination, and memory have received their
impressions concerning that whereunto the rule is to be applied....
The arts or science which flow not immediately from particular
and sensual objects, but tend immediately to direct the universall
acts of reasoning, must be taught after all the rest.[18]

Learning of words without understanding was deplored, as
it had been by Comenius and Milton:

The teaching of words is no further useful than the things signified therby are familiar to the imagination, and ... the teaching
of rules before the material sense of the words is known, ... is
wholly preposterous and unprofitable to the memory.[19]

Up to the age of thirteen or fourteen children were to learn
by 'observing all things natural and artificial extant in the
world'; by using instruments of measuring, by observing husbandry, gardening, fishing and fowling, and by means of
models, pictures, globes and 'plain tables'.

From thirteen or fourteen to nineteen or twenty, their earlier
observations would be supplemented by reading the natural
history of Pliny and others, and medicine and distilling would

15. ibid, p. 34.   16. ibid, p. 28.   17. ibid, p. 40.
18. ibid, pp. 40–41.   19. ibid, p. 42.

be learned partly from books and partly by watching and
carrying out operations themselves.

Dury makes a special point of rousing a desire to learn in
the children before teaching is attempted:

> The governor shall ... give directions unto the ushers how to be-
> have themselves towards the scholars to make them affectionat
> towards the task that is to be offered unto them, that is, attentive and
> greedy to receive it.[20]

One way of doing this was to make clear to the children the
value and purpose of what they were asked to learn: 'The
scholars, before the thing be proposed,' should

> be made sensible of the end, wherefore it is taught them and
> they ought to learn it, viz. what the necessity, use, excellency and
> perfection thereof is in the life of man.[21]

Dury believed that the environment chosen for the school
was of great importance. It should be in the country, but not
too far from the city,

> large and spacious, ... with large gardens and orchards, near the
> places of tillage and of pasturage; that the country may afford unto
> the scholars the aspect and observation of all natural things wherein
> they are to be taught, and the city may afford them the sight of all
> artificial things, of all trades and manufactures wherewith they are
> to be made acquainted,[22]

and the school was to be equipped with a wide variety of visual
aids:

> The large common room ought to be furnished with all manner
> of mathematical, natural, philosophical, historical, medicinal, hiero-
> glyphic and other sort of pictures, maps, globes, instruments,
> models, engines, and whatsoever is an object of sense in reference
> to any art or science.[23]

Some of the educational theories of the treatises and those of
Comenius and Bacon were put into practice at this time by
certain schoolmasters.

One of these was Charles Hoole, who translated the *Orbis*

20. ibid, p. 55.   21. ibid, p. 56.
22. ibid, p. 57.   23. ibid, p. 58.

Pictus and *Janua*, and in his own grammar schools taught by means of object lessons.

He suggests that the first task of teachers is to study the way children learn:

> It being *the very basis of our profession to search into the way of children's taking hold by little and little of what we teach them*, that so we may apply ourselves to their reach.[24]

He has some ingenious suggestions for teaching aids, including 'pictures in a little book or upon a scroll of paper wrapt upon two sticks within a box of iceing glass' and

> a little wheel, with all the Capital Romane letters made upon a paper to wrap round it, and ... fitted to turn in a little round box, which had a hole so made in the side of it, that onely one letter might be seen to peep out at once.[25]

He realized, in theory at least, that children are not the same as adults, and that teaching must proceed from the known to the unknown.

> There is a great difference betwixt a man that teacheth, and a Childe that is to be taught; ... the more condescention is made to a Childes capacity, by proceeding orderly and plainly from what he knoweth already, to what doth naturally and necessarily follow thereupon, the more easily he will learn.[26]

The relationship between teacher and taught should be similar to that between nurse and child or between a gardener and his plants:

> I would advise him that hath to deal with a childe, to imitate the nurse in helping him how to go forward, or the Gardiner in furthering the growth of his young plant.[27]

He believed that

the nature of man is restlessly desirous to know things, and were discouragements taken out of the way, and meet helps afforded young learners, they would doubtless go on with a great deal more

24. *Orbis sensualium pictus*, preface, CHARLES HOOLE, no pagination.
25. HOOLE, CHARLES, *A New Discovery of the Old Art of Teaching Schoole*, The Petty School, p. 8.
26. ibid, The Usher's Duty, pp. 8–9.
27. ibid, p. 10.

cherefulness, and make more proficiency at their books then usually they do.[28]

Childrens wits are weak, active, and lively, whereas Grammar notions are abstractive, dull and livelesse; boyes finde no sap, nor sweetnesse in them, because they know not what they mean. ... *It is very hard to teach a childe in doing of a thing to heed, much lesse to judge what he doth, till he feel some use of reason*, in the mean time, he will profit more by continual practice and being kept still (as he loves to be) doing, then by knowing why, and being called upon to consider the causes wherefore he doth this or that.[29]

Understanding must keep pace with learning by heart:

Till the memory and understanding go hand in hand, a child learns nothing to any purpose.[30]

The teacher must cultivate the innate aptitudes of each of his pupils and help them by giving them some responsibility for their own progress:

I conceive it very necessary for all such as undertake to teach Grammar to little children, to cherish and exercise those endowments which they see do shew themselves most vigorous and prompt in them, be they memorie, phansie, &c. and to proceed orderly and by degrees ... that they may be able to hold pace with their Teachers, and to perceive how themselves mount higher and higher, and at every ascent to know where they are, and how to adventure boldly to go forward of themselves.[31]

As a general rule, children should be told the reasons why things are to be done or not done. When the master

commands, or forbids anything to be done, he should acquaint his Scholars with the end intended, and the benefits or inconveniences which attend such, or such a course.[32]

Children must understand their work:

It is not only possible, but necessary to make children understand their tasks, from their very first entrance into learning,[33]

28. ibid, *The Petty School*, p. 12.
29. ibid, *The Usher's Duty*, p. 11.
30. ibid, p. 12.   31. ibid, p. 13.
32. ibid, *Scholastide Discipline*, p. 235.
33. ibid, p. 306.

and they must be given encouragement and praise:

Nothing works more upon good natured children, then frequent encouragements and commendations for well-doing.[34]

Like Dury, he was aware of the importance of the environment of a school. He recommends that it

should be healthfully and pleasantly seated in a plentifull country, where the wayes on all sides are most commonly faire. ... The Schoolehouse should be a large and stately building. ... It should have a large piece of ground adjoyning to it, which should be divided into a paved Court to go round about the Schoole, a faire Orchard and Garden, with Walks and Arbors, and a spacious green close for Scholars recreations.[35]

Hoole's enlightened philosophy remained largely theoretical. Although he arranged visits for his pupils to Tradescant's museum, in his own school he attempted to teach the same thing to as many as possible at the same time – he considered a hundred to be a reasonable size for a form – seated on benches, their heads in books. His work shows a curious mixture of understanding of principles which he did not put into effect, but it is likely that his views underwent a considerable change in his later years, which may account for some of the apparent contradiction. His educational light seems to have been a flickering one, but at least he helped to mark out boundaries for others to fill in.

Another schoolmaster, and a friend of Samuel Hartlib, whose practice was inspired by the Puritan reformers, was Hezekiah Woodward, who wrote two treatises at the request of Samuel Hartlib. In them he restates much of Comenius's theory, but he makes the unusual statement that many of his ideas were based on his observation of his own children and on memories of his own childhood:

Being a parent myselfe, I obtained of my selfe ... to set downe out of some continued experience and some conversation with Children ... what I thought pertinent.[36]

I spent six yeers and a halfe in the Grammer Schoole, trained

34. ibid, p. 236.   35. ibid, pp. 222–3.
36. WOODWARD (HEZEKIAH), *Of the Child's Portion*, p. 5.

up according to the *bad fashion* … of most Teachers. … In all this time spent in Grammar … I know not which lost me most time, *feare* or *Play*. I know I played away much of the time … but, I know also, feare hindred me most, and cast me farthest back.[37]

There should be no fear in a child's education, he says; he must be led, not driven:

A master must maintaine an *awefulnesse* in the Childe, else little will be done; and he must be as carefull to suppresse *feare*, and the working of it, specially then, when he would give instruction, else no good will be done.[38]

The light you set up in a childs understanding is, at first, as the candle you have newly lighted, and are gone with it by that time you have gone three steps, the candle is out, for you were too hasty, and you did not shelter it well from the winds … 'Our natures, as well as our consciences, are more moved with leading, then dragging, or drawing; and pety errorers will be better reclaimed with gentle meanes, rather than Catechized with hard words, and blowes.'[39]

The child must be brought to love his work if he is to learn:

Our scope is to unfold the understanding, to set up a light there; for the understanding is as the eye to the body, the candle thereof. If you have won your child to the love of his booke, you shall have all at command, hee will use all diligence. But if this love, this delight be not, diligence cannot be.[40]

Both parent and teacher must praise the children and show gentleness and patience, and make the work come alive:

A Parent must look to it that his weake Childe … hath in praise and commendation above his merit and proportion.[41]

We must make things as familiar to children as may be, and we … must draw them on with all pleasingnesse, I mean, in point of instruction. In learning any thing, they seem to pull, as it were, at a dead thing: It is a great point of wisedome, in the Teacher to put some life into it, that the childe may see it stirre, and coming onward, else the work may seem so hard to them, that they can better beare the *smart* of the Rod, then the *labour* of the work; then discouragements follow, such as make them hate the book before they know it. A parent must be very gentle and patient,

37. ibid, pp. 8–9.   38. ibid, pp. 9–10.
39. *A Light to Grammar*.   40. ibid.
41. *Of the Child's Portion*, p. 25.

specially when he is upon the beginnings of things, for they are hardest.[42]

To do this, the teacher must have a sympathetic understanding of children. It will help him if he remembers his own difficulties and puts himself again in the position of a learner:

> If a Teacher would learn something he knows not whilst he is teaching the childe ... he would see his own unaptnesse, and pardon the childes. ... We forget quite what we did, and how unapt we were when we were children, learning something now, would make it fresh again; though the difference is much, betwixt a man and a childe; and it must be considered. What we understand fully, we think a childe might understand more readily, and hence proceeds more hastinesse than is fitting, which shows the Teacher to be the verier child.[43]

Woodward shows here a refreshing insight into children. They are not, as to so many previous educators, men in miniature, but children, who must be understood in their own way, and the teacher has a great responsibility and a great opportunity. He must be one

> who can instruct the *life* of his scholler, as well as his *tongue*; can teach him, as well how to *live,* as how to *speak*.[44] What a faire opportunitie the master hath in his little nurcerie or seminary to prune and manure this little plant.[45]

Education should use what is characteristic of the child at his particular stage of development, and the material for his learning is to be found in the world of nature that lies around him:

> 'Childehood and youth, are ages of fancy. Therefore the Father' – or teacher –

> must make great use of the childes senses, for they have the best agreement with its fancy; hereunto the book of the creatures is very subservient. They speak to the senses, and the senses make report to the minde. So in this way every place will be the childes school, for every where it will meet with its lesson, and no lesson plainer and more legible to a childe, then what he findes in the volume of the Creatures. ...

42. ibid, p. 34.   43. ibid, pp. 34–5.
44. ibid, p. 157.   45. ibid, p. 159.

That parent teacheth best ... who verseth the child most in the open view of the creatures; ... When he cannot carry his childe abroad to view the creatures, he must, what he can, bring the creatures home to the child.[46]

If we walke no further forth then into our *garden*, we see what varietie that yeelds, and the same varietie of instructions. If in our *grove* we may remember what the Father said thereof. '*That he learnt more Divinity* (more of God) in his walk therein, then in his study amongst his paper-books.[47]

The Father was Chrysostom and his words were,

The Booke of the creatures every man may come by; and he that runs may reade it. Their language is easie to be understood; They open, as I may say, the freest schooles and are the fittest to give instruction, of any.[48]

He who fails to understand the lessons in these

freest schooles ... shall never have greater matters committed unto him; and he, who carrieth a negligent eye or eare, towards the works and voice of nature gathering no instruction thence, though the characters are most legible there, and her voice cleare and audible, shall finde no more capacity in himself for higher truths.[49]

Therefore we cannot fit the understanding

with any booke so genuine and naturall as in the booke of Nature, for the worlds are its Book, and every creature there its lesson.[50]

So, for the pupil, 'We must make the world his booke.'

He must learn also from doing, for this is natural to him. Children have an inborn desire to know, and they learn through their own activity. What looks like play is a serious matter to the child, and a means of learning:

Wee will well observe the child first.

Wee shall finde him still in action, here and there and every where, with his sticke, or with his gun, or with his casting stones; perhaps if these be not at hand, he is blowing up a feather: I cannot reckon up his Implements: I beleeve he is as well stored for the driving his pleasant trade, as is the best Merchant in the Towne for his so gainfull: wee suppose him well sorted with com-

46. ibid, p. 98.
47. ibid, p. 90.
48. ibid, pp. 90–91.
49. ibid.
50. *A Light to Grammar*.

modities, he hath his Exchange and Warehouse too, both his boxe and his pocket. And we shall see anon, that by his dealings in the world, he hath learned good part of his Grammar before he came at it. But we observe for present, that the child is all for action, and is very earnest therein, never quiet, except in motion. Wee must observe too that the child is as desirous after knowledge, very curious and enquiring that way. What is this? What is that? All is newes to him ... It is as a little Ape taken up by imitation: what he sees the Governour doe (hee must take heed what hee doth) the childe will make offer to doe the like, nor can you gratifie him better, nor please him more, then to suffer him to try his skill by putting his hand to the work, which you must move altogether, but hee will think he hath done the deed, and by his owne strength: he must enjoy his conceit, and make himselfe merry with it; all such encouragement doth good everywhere: for when the child finds himself a party in the worke, he speaks of it willingly and with delight, remembers it accurately, and much good there is in all that.[51]

In this way the child will learn through his own discovery and active participation, and through play:

Our endeavour shall be to put the Child in a good forwardness, before he knows where he began; he shall be well entred, before he knowes how hee came into the way; hee shall do his worke playing, and play working; hee shall seeme idle and think he is in sport, when he is indeed serious and best imployed. This is done, when the understanding is cleared by its owne light; when the Childs owne door, which he thinks shut, is opened by a natural key, of the childs owne framing, and using. And this is a familiar way of teaching, when the Schoole is indeed a profitable kind of play.[52]

A clearer picture could scarcely have been given of the ideal school which recognizes that, to a child, the adult line of demarcation between work and play has no significance.

He continues, with the same sensitive understanding,

We are fully concluded, That the child must be set straight to his work, and not sit long at it, but while he is sitting there, he must make it his play. Observe him with his little stick puddering in the ashes, drawing lines there, or upon the dirt where he can make an impression; and almost as busie he is, as one was, who would not be driven from it with the sword.[53]

51. ibid.   52. ibid.   53. ibid.

In all this, language must go along with understanding, not ahead of it:

> The childe goes on with ease and delight, when the understanding and the tongue are drawn along like *parallel* lines, not one a jot before another.[54]

It is essential to observe and understand the child's capacity and to adapt teaching thereto:

> We must looke through, and through the childe; we must well understand him, before he can understand us,[55]

and the best teacher will say to himself:

> It is not what I understand, but how I can fit myself to the Child's capacity.
> Hee that goes with a child in his hand, must goe as the child can goe; and he must drop in instruction, as the Nurse fed him, by little spoonefuls, and even that little, by little degrees too. Hee that poures altogether upon a child, or gives it him in a lumpe, loseth all his labour, and choaketh the understanding.[56]

The method of education must be to follow nature and to give instruction by means of the senses first, followed by understanding, with memory taking last place:

> We must follow *nature* as close as we can, and use all the helps this way to make discovery of the childes inclination.[57]
> Nothing comes into the understanding in a naturall way, but through the doore of the senses. If the eye hath no seen that, we are speaking of, it can make no report of it to the minde.[58]

The usual method, however, ignores this:

> Our scope is the Child's good, but we invert the order: ... wee begin with the Child at the wrong end, and we proceed like a Wiardrawer, backward.[59]

This practical and sympathetic schoolmaster shows a remarkable understanding of the slow child, and reveals his belief in the ability of all children to reach fulfilment:

54. *Of the Child's Portion*, p. 98.   55. *A Light to Grammar*.
56. ibid.   57. *Of the Child's Portion*, p. 179.
58. ibid, p. 98.   59. *A Light to Grammar*.

Some have compared children to the Earth, different moulds there: All must be tilled, which we would have fruitfull, but notwithstanding all our tillage, all are not alike fruitfull. Some have compared them to fruits of the earth, some earlyripe, some not yet, some yet later: everything is good in its season. Some children are like Summer fruits, quickly ripe, Commonly as quickly rotten. Other some not so quick for speed, but more sure for use. Some also, whom we miscall, (and misuse too, the more should be the pity) dullards, hard-heads etc. And yet if we could have patience and wait their full time and growth, we may take them good, very good in their season.[60]

The Dull-wit would offer faire, praise must help him; when he hath it, he holds fast, and may prove somebody.

We goe on then, and take the Childe as hee is, and so apply our selves to him as wee can.[61]

The dull Boy, ... may prove a solid and understanding Man,[62]

but sometimes it is the teacher who makes the dullard:

The childe seems the duller because [the Master] leades on the childe in a *dull* way.[63]

There is a place for children of all abilities, and a function for them to perform, but the slow child needs especial encouragement and praise:

We must deale with our Children, as with our fingers [it is Plutarch's comparison] ... at writing and at our musicke ...; so likewise in other employments, we bring all five fingers. All doe help, and the very least finger comes in with its grace, and hath its share, as well as the formost, though it hath not the like strength, nor can it adde much to the furthering the worke: Just so with Children; and then we have the scope of the similitude, which tends but to this; That we use all gentlenesse towards the weake Childe, and that we give it no discouragement, but praise and encouragement rather above its proportion.[64]

The wise teacher will know how to bring the best from all children, because he believes in the power within each of them:

The Master finds that in the childe, which he works upon, he doth not put it there, he findes wit and abilities, and nature forward to

60. ibid.
62. *Of the Child's Portion*, p. 160.
64. ibid, pp. 25–6.

61. ibid.
63. ibid.

put all forth, and now the Master, as the Midwife, promotes exceedingly.[65]

In 1661 the poet Cowley put forward his Plan of a Philosophical College. In many particulars, and in its spirit, it echoes Comenius. He deplored

the loss which Children make of their time at most Schools, employing or rather casting away six or seven years in the learning of words only, and that too very imperfectly.[66]

Ample provision is made, in the universities, he believed, for learning a knowledge of God and for those studies which depend on

Memory and Wit, that is, Reading and Invention. . . . But the other two Parts, the Inquisition into the Nature of Gods Creatures, and the Application of them to Humane Uses ... seem to be very slenderly provided for, or rather almost totally neglected, except onely some small assistances to Physick, and the Mathematicks.[67]

He made the complaint, still often heard today, that insufficient equipment was provided for the study of science:

Partly, because the necessary expence thereof is much greater, then of the other; and partly from that idle and pernicious opinion which had long possest the World, that all things to be searcht in Nature, had been already found and discovered by the Ancients.[68]

To supply this defect in the educational provision Cowley proposed to found a Philosophical College, to which children should go from the age of thirteen. They were to learn the truth about animals and plants, to use and understand globes

and in all this travel be rather led on by familiarity, encouragement, and emulation, then driven by severity, punishment and terrour.[69]

65. *A Light to Grammar.*
66. COWLEY, *A Proposition for the Advancement of Experimental Philosophy,* Essays, p. 39.
67. ibid, p. 25.　　　68. ibid, pp. 25–6.　　　69. ibid, p. 41

10

Locke

WITH the Restoration, the Puritan belief in the importance of education, which might have brought wide reforms, became overshadowed, but much of its philosophy was embodied and preserved in an educational work of great importance, John Locke's *Thoughts Concerning Education*. It is said to be the first book on education that deals primarily with the child. Locke was certainly interested in individuals and considered that children could only be educated as such:

> Let the Master's Industry and Skill be never so great, it is impossible he should have fifty or an hundred Scholars under his Eye any longer than they are in the school together; Nor can it be expected that he should instruct them successfully in any thing but their Books; the forming of their Minds and Manners requiring a constant Attention, and particular Application to every single Boy.[1]

There are marked differences between children, and it is necessary to study the natures and abilities of every one and help each to develop on his own lines. Methods must be as various as individuals:

> Each Man's Mind has some Peculiarity, as well as his Face, that distinguishes him from all others; and there are possibly scarce two Children, who can be conducted by exactly the same Method.[2]

> He therefore that is about Children should well study their Natures and Aptitudes, and see by often Trials what Turn they easily take, and what becomes them; observe what their native Stock is, how it may be improv'd, and what it is fit for.[3]

Education, to Locke, was not primarily a matter of book learning but included character, judgement, a knowledge of men, good manners and responsibility for oneself. Virtue was put ahead of intellectual ability, and common sense before

1. LOCKE, J., *Thoughts Concerning Education*, QUICK, p. 48.
2. ibid, p. 187. 3. ibid, p. 40.

great learning. What he said about learning over three hundred years ago is still pertinent today:

> You will wonder, perhaps, that I put *Learning* last, especially if I tell you I think it the least Part. This may seem strange in the Mouth of a bookish Man. . . .
> Reading and Writing and *Learning* I allow to be necessary, but yet not the chief Business. I imagine you would think him a very foolish Fellow, that should not value a virtuous, or a wise Man infinitely before a great Scholar. . . . *Learning* must be had, but in the second Place, as subservient only to greater Qualities.[4]

> The business of education . . . is not, as I think to make [the young] perfect in any one of the sciences, but so to open and dispose their minds as may best make them capable of any, when they shall apply themselves to it. . . . It is therefore to give them this freedom, that I think they should be made to look into all sorts of knowledge, and exercise their understanding in so wide a variety and stock of knowledge. But I do not propose it as a variety and stock of knowledge, but a variety and freedom of thinking as an increase of the powers and activities of the mind, not as an enlargement of its possessions.[5]

Freedom, this was Locke's theme: freedom for children to be themselves and to learn in their own way. More clearly than anyone before him he saw the importance of liberty. They were to be restrained only from doing wrong:

> [Children] should be allow'd the Liberties and Freedoms suitable to their Ages, and not be held under unnecessary Restraints . . . They must not be hinder'd from being Children, or from playing, or doing as Children, but from doing ill; all other Liberty is to be allow'd them.[6]

> None of the Things they are to learn, should ever be made a Burthen to them, or impos'd on them as a *Task*. Whatever is so propos'd, presently becomes irksome; the Mind takes an Aversion to it, though before it were a Thing of Delight or Indifference.[7]

This had been said many times before, but Locke saw the importance of the liberty of the learner to choose:

4. ibid, p. 128.
5. *Conduct of the Understanding*, p. 19.
6. *Thoughts Concerning Education*, QUICK, p. 45.
7. ibid, p. 52.

Let a Child be but order'd to whip his Top at a certain Time every Day, whether he has or has not a Mind to it; let this be but requir'd of him as a Duty, wherein he must spend so many Hours Morning and Afternoon, and see whether he will not soon be weary of any Play at this Rate. Is it not so with grown Men? What they do chearfully of themselves, do they not presently grow sick of, and can no more endure, as soon as they find it is expected of them as a Duty?[8]

As a consequence of this, children

should seldom be put about doing even those Things you have got an Inclination in them to, but when they have a Mind and *Disposition* to it.[9]

This conception of liberty did not, however, mean that the teacher was to be a merely negative influence. Locke goes on:

If they are not often enough forward of themselves, a good Disposition should be talk'd into them, before they be set upon any thing. ... By this Means a great deal of Time and Tiring would be sav'd: For a Child will learn three times as much when he is *in Tune*, as he will with double the Time and Pains when he goes awkwardly or is dragg'd unwillingly to it. If this were minded as it should, Children might be permitted to weary themselves with Play, and yet have Time enough to learn what is suited to the Capacity of each Age.[10]

What the Mind is intent upon and careful of, that it remembers best.[11]

This theory was not, in Locke's view, to result in softness, in 'doing what you like' and licence. He believed that the mind must be master of itself, and his idea of discipline was far from being soft:

Children should ... be us'd to submit their Desires and go without their Longings, *even from their very Cradles*. The first Thing they should learn to know, should be that they were not to have any Thing because it pleas'd them, but because it was thought fit for them.[12]

Much misunderstanding in regard to modern educational ideas arises on this very point: the meaning of freedom.

8. ibid.   9. ibid, p. 53.   10. ibid.
11. ibid, pp. 154–5.   12. ibid, pp. 25–6.

Locke made quite clear that to him freedom was not the same as licence, and the best of modern educators follow him both in theory and practice.

To ensure successful learning, children should understand the purpose of what they are taught in terms of its value to them, and teaching can only be done in a spirit of love:

The great Skill of a Teacher is to get and keep the Attention of his Scholar; whilst he has that, he is sure to advance as fast as the Learner's Abilities will carry him; and without that, all his Bustle and Pother will be to little or no Purpose. To attain this, he should make the Child comprehend (as much as may be) the Usefulness of what he teaches him, and let him see, by what he has learnt, that he can do something which he could not do before; something, which gives him some Power and real Advantage above others who are ignorant of it. To this he should add Sweetness in all his Instructions, and by a certain Tenderness in his whole Carriage, make the Child sensible that he loves him and designs nothing but his Good; the only way to beget Love in the Child, which will make him hearken to his Lessons, and relish what he teaches him.[13]

Here, for the first time, is the appeal to the senses of achievement and of power as specific motives.

I told you before, that Children love *Liberty*; and therefore they should be brought to do the Things that are fit for them, without feeling any Restraint laid upon them. I now tell you, they love something more; and that is *Dominion*.[14]

Fear was never to be used as a motive. Its effect was wholly bad.

I am very apt to think, that *great Severity* of Punishment does but very little Good, nay, great Harm in Education; and I believe that it will be found that . . . those Children who have been most *chastis'd*, seldom make the best Men.[15]

Corporal punishment he described as a lazy way of disciplining children, and quite ineffective:

The usual lazy and short Way, by Chastisement, and the Rod, which is the only Instrument of Government that Tutors generally

13. ibid, pp. 143-4.   14. ibid, p. 83.   15. ibid, p. 79.

know, or ever think of, is the most unfit of any to be us'd in Education.

This Kind of Punishment contributes not at all to the Mastery of our natural Propensity to indulge corporal and present Pleasure, and to avoid Pain at any rate, but rather encourages it.[16]

Such correction produces an outward change in behaviour but alters nothing within, and in the end, a greater problem has been created:

If *Severity* carry'd to the highest Pitch does prevail, and works a Cure upon the present unruly Distemper, it often brings in the room of it, worse and more dangerous Disease, by breaking the Mind, and then in the Place of a disorderly young Fellow, you have a *low-spirited moaped* Creature, who, however, with his unnatural Sobriety he may please silly People, who commend tame, unactive Children, because they make no Noise, nor give them any Trouble; yet, at last, will probably prove as uncomfortable a Thing to his Friends, as he will be, all his Life, a useless Thing to himself and others.[17]

Incentives, therefore, must be of another kind:

The *Rewards* and *Punishments*, then, whereby we should keep Children in Order, are quite of another Kind ... If you can once get into Children a Love of Credit, and an Apprehension of Shame and Disgrace, you have put into 'em the true Principle, which will constantly work and incline them to the right.[18]

To those who contended that some children would never learn without fear of punishment and the use of force, Locke replied:

This, I fear, is nothing but the Language of ordinary Schools and Fashion, which have never suffer'd the other to be try'd as it should. ... Children learn to dance and Fence without Whipping; nay, Arithmetic, Drawing etc., they apply themselves well enough to without Beating: Which would make one suspect, that there is something strange, unnatural and disagreeable to that Age, in the Things required in Grammar Schools, or in the Methods us'd there, that Children cannot be brought to, without the Severity of the Lash, and hardly with that too.[19]

16. ibid, p. 30.   17. ibid, p. 31.
18. ibid, p. 34.   19. ibid, p. 64.

How the child learns is of more significance than what he learns; and in this the child's natural curiosity is to be employed:

Curiosity should be as carefully *cherish'd* in Children, as other Appetites suppress'd.[20]

With remarkable insight for his time, Locke gives a reason why some children appear lazy and idle, and while away their time in useless occupations:

And I doubt not but one great Reason why many Children abandon themselves wholly to silly Sports, and trifle away all their Time insipidly, is, because they have found their *Curiosity* baulk'd, and their *Enquiries* neglected.[21]

His suggestion for dealing with the child who takes no interest in work might have come from a twentieth-century textbook:

If . . . he be naturally listless and dreaming, this unpromising Disposition is none of the easiest to be dealt with, because . . . it wants the two great Springs of Action, *Foresight* and *Desire*. . . . As soon as you are satisfied that this is the Case, you must carefully enquire whether there be nothing he delights in: Inform your self what it is he is most pleased with; and if you can find any particular Tendency his Mind hath, increase it all you can, and make use of that to set him on Work, and to excite his Industry.[22]

It is natural for children to want to learn. They have no dislike of hard work. The only difference to them between work and play is a matter of compulsion, but they must be active if they are to learn effectively:

This I think is sufficiently evident, that Children generally hate to be idle. All the Care then is, that their busy Humour should be constantly employ'd in something of Use to them.[23]

Were Matters order'd right, learning anything they should be taught might be made as much a Recreation to their Play, as their Play is to their Learning. The Pains are equal on both Sides: Nor is that which troubles them; for they love to be busy. . . . The only Odds is, in that which we call Play they act at Liberty, and employ their Pains (whereof you may observe them never sparing) freely;

20. ibid, p. 87.   21. ibid, p. 104.
22. ibid, p. 109.   23. ibid, pp. 110–11.

but what they are to learn is forc'd upon them, they are call'd, compell'd, and driven to it.[24]

From his own observation he has seen how hard children will work to achieve some skill they have chosen to master, and he draws attention to the age-old problem of how this energy can be canalized and directed for the purposes of education:

Children, if you observe them, take abundance of Pains to learn several Games, which, if they should be enjoined them, they would abhor as a Task and Business.... I have seen little Girls exercise whnle Hours together and take abundance of Pains to be expert at *Dibstones* as they call it. Whilst I have been looking on, I have thought it only wanted some good Contrivance to make them employ all that Industry about something that might be more useful to them.[25]

He puts his finger on the root of the trouble:

Methinks 'tis only the Fault and Negligence of elder People that it is not so. Children are much less apt to be idle than Men.[26]

Play, then, should be used as a means of learning, and although he saw only the fringes of its value and application, the principle was a right one:

I have therefore thought, that if *Play-things* were fitted to this Purpose, ... Contrivances might be made *to teach Children to read*, whilst they thought they were only playing. ... Thus much for *learning to read*, which let him never be driven to, nor chid for; cheat him into it if you can, but make it not a Business for him. 'Tis better it be a Year later *before he can read*, than that he should this Way get an Aversion to Learning.[27]

If learning were to be made 'a Recreation' and not a 'Business':

A set of Children thus ordered ... would all of them, I suppose ... learn to read, write, and what else one would have them, as others do their ordinary Plays.[28]

24. ibid, pp. 53–4.   25. ibid, pp. 131–2.
26. ibid, p. 132.   27. ibid, pp. 131, 132–3.
28. ibid, p. 111.

II

Education in France · Fénelon

THE first classical work on education in France was that of François de Salignac de la Mothe Fénelon, tutor to the grandson of Louis XIV. Though written in 1681, much of *The Education of Daughters* might have come directly out of a modern work on educational method, and Fénelon's warm and human feeling towards children is a refreshing contrast to some of the more pompous and pious utterances of the time.

He would have, first of all, a relationship of complete trust between children and those who have charge of them. To achieve this, adults must be prepared to be quite honest about their own failings, and one is reminded of the kind of friendship which has now become the normal relationship between parents and children in our own day:

> It is most important that you should know your own faults, as well as the children will know them whom you have to bring up ... Generally, those who bring up children pardon nothing in them, though they pardon every thing in themselves ... Fear not to speak of those defects which are visible in yourself....[1]

> Make yourself beloved by them, and they will be open with you; and they will not fear to let you see their faults.[2]

His wise counsel on correction reveals his understanding of the psychology of children: tell your daughter 'of the same errors of which you were guilty at her age',[3] and never find fault with a child 'either in his first emotion, or in yours; if you do it in yours, he will perceive that you are governed by humor and impatience, and not by reason and friendship: you will lose, without resource, your authority'.[4]

Such a relationship of trust and love 'gives you the opportunity of seeing children act in their natural state, and of

1. FÉNELON, *Of the Education of Daughters*, p. 22.
2. ibid, p. 24.   3. ibid, p. 39.   4. ibid, p. 25.

knowing their characters thoroughly', and this study of children is essential:

> We must always know them to the bottom, before we can correct them.[5]

Fénelon goes so far as to suggest, foreshadowing the child guidance clinic, that the difficult children 'upon whose dispositions education can do nothing' should be given 'from their earliest infancy, an entire liberty of displaying their inclinations',[6] in order that they may be helped.

Indeed, Fénelon shows a remarkable insight into the psychology of fear and jealousy, and the importance of praise, encouragement and confidence:

> Joy and confidence must be their general feeling, otherwise we shall damp their spirit and abate their courage. . . . Fear is like those violent remedies which we employ in extreme cases of illness; they purge, but they alter the temperament, and exhaust the organs. The mind led by fear, is always the most weak.[7] We run the risk of discouraging children, if we never praise them when they do well.[8]

> Do not fear to show him, with discretion, of what he is capable; content yourself with little; make him remark his most trifling success; represent to him how mal-à-propos his fears were that he should not succeed in what he had done well. . . .

> Jealousy is more violent in children than we know well how to believe; we see them sometimes from it shutting up their minds, and wasting with a secret languuor, because others are more loved and more caressed than they are.[9]

Learning should be made pleasant, and should follow nature, in contrast to what was usual:

> No liberty, no enjoyment, always lessons, always silence, restrained posture, correction and menace.[10] We often demand from them an exactitude and seriousness of which we should ourselves be incapable. We make even a dangerous impression of ennui and of sadness on their temperament, by speaking to them always of words and of things which they do not understand.[11]

> It is necessary to find out every means of rendering agreeable to the child those things which you exact of him; . . . always show him the utility of what you teach him. . . .[12]

5. ibid, p. 37.   6. ibid.   7. ibid, p. 27.
8. ibid, p. 39.   9. ibid, p. 35.   10. ibid, p. 26.
11. ibid.   12. ibid, p. 23.

The taste of the child must not be forced, we should only offer them openings to exercise it.[13] Let us render study agreeable, let us hide it under the appearance of liberty and pleasure.[14]

This might have been attributed to Froebel, and how well Fénelon lays bare what is sometimes the true motive for using formal methods:

A too great regularity in exacting from them an uninterrupted aplication to study, hurts them much: those who govern often affect this regularity, because it is more convenient to themselves, than subjecting themselves continually to profit by the moments which offer.[15]

His suggestions on how to profit by 'the moments which offer' are entirely up to date and practical:

All that can refresh the mind, all that can offer an agreeable variety to them, that can satisfy their curiosity for useful things, that can exercise their bodies to agreeable arts; all these should be employed in the diversions of children. Those which they like the best, are such as keep the body in motion; they are content provided they often change their place ... it is not necessary to be in trouble for their amusements, they will invent enough for themselves; it is sufficient to suffer them to act, to observe with a gay countenance and to moderate them as soon as they become overheated.[16]

This wise tutor and cleric of three centuries ago fully appreciated the value of curiosity as an aid to learning:

A free curiosity, says St Augustine from his own experience, excites much more the mind of a child, than a rule and a necessity imposed through fear,[17]

and how well he understood the fleeting attention of children and the best way to make use of it:

The brain of a child is like a lit taper exposed to the wind; its light always staggering. The child puts a question to you, and before you have answered it, his eyes are raised towards the ceiling, he has counted all the figures which are painted there, or all the panes of glass in the window: if you would drive him back to his first object, you constrain him as much as if you were to put him in

13. ibid, p. 31. 14. ibid, p. 30. 15. ibid.
16. ibid. 17. ibid, p. 29.

prison ... answer quickly and shortly to their questions, and leave them to make others according to their own inclination. Satisfy simply their curiosity, and let the memory amass for itself a store of good materials. The time will come when they will assemble them; and when the brain, having more consistency, the child will be able to follow a continued reasoning.[18]

By means of their natural curiosity, children will learn more than by direct teaching. The environment provides opportunities for them to learn by observation and by asking questions:

For example, in the country they see a mill, and they wish to know what it is: let them see how the food is prepared with which man is nourished. When they see reapers, explain to them what they are; how the seed is sown and how it multiplies in the earth. In the city they see shops, where many arts are exercised, and where many merchandizes are disposed of ... by this means they will insensibly become acquainted with every thing which serves for the use of man, and on which commerce depends. By degrees, and without particular study, they will know how to make ... all those things which they want for their own use; and the just price of every thing, which is the true foundation of economy.[19]

A hundred years before the birth of Froebel, Fénelon put forward a theory of education by play which might have come from a modern textbook on infant method:

I have known many children who have learned to read whilst they were at play ... We should give them a book well ornamented, even on the outside, with the most beautiful pictures, and characters well formed; every thing which pleases the imagination facilitates study. We should endeavour to choose a book full of short and marvellous histories; this done, be not in trouble about the child's learning to read correctly.[20]

And here is his three-hundred-year-old advice on teaching children to write:

Children of their own accord will apply themselves to make figures on paper; if we assist this inclination a very little, without restraining them too much, they will form them into letters as they play, and accustom themselves by degrees to write. ... Write me a note, you may say to the child; ask something for your brother

18. ibid, p. 21.   19. ibid, p. 15.   20. ibid, p. 29.

or your cousin; all this gives pleasure to children, provided no
dull images or regulated lessons be found in it.[21]

He even suggests acting:

If you have many children, accustom them by degrees to represent
the personages of the histories which they have learned.[22]

Suffer then a child to play, and mix instruction with his play.[23]
The less we give them of set lessons the better. . . . Take great care
not to overcharge his memory, for it is this which stuns and weighs
down the brain.[24]

A century before *Emile*, Fénelon wrote: 'We must content
ourselves with following, and with aiding nature,'[25] and, as
one reads his book, one feels that this was no airy theory but
a belief, founded on close and sympathetic contact with children, one which he had himself put into successful practice.

21. ibid, p. 29.   22. ibid, p. 42.   23. ibid, p. 21.
24. ibid, p. 28.   25. ibid, p. 35.

12

The Little Schools of Port Royal · Charles Rollin

In the great and continuous movement by which education gradually broke away from the supremacy of authority, substituting for it the right of the individual to think for himself, an important part was played by the Little Schools of Port Royal in France. Though they lasted for a very brief period, their influence on French education was considerable. They, too, believed in the inner light of which St Augustine and Comenius wrote. Nicole wrote:

Properly speaking, neither Masters nor outward instructions they give, make Learners comprehend things. These only expose them to the interior light of the mind, by which alone they are comprehended. So that when one does not meet with this light, instructions prove as useless as it would be to expose and shew Pictures in the dark.[1]

Their theories were based on practice, and founded on love and understanding of children. In contrast to the harsh methods generally employed to force children to learn, they advocated methods by which learning might be made pleasant and, most important, based these on the right relationship between teacher and pupils.

Coustel says the master must fill his heart with 'the tenderness and love of a parent'[2] and follow the instructions of St Bernard: ' "Labour rather to make yourselves loved by children than feared".'[3]

'I wish you could read in my heart,' wrote M. de Saint-Cyran, 'the affection that I have for children'[4] and Lancelot says of him that he 'used ... to show towards children a kindness which amounted almost to a sort of respect, in order to express

1. NICOLE, *Education of a Prince*, p. 18.
2. CADET, *Port Royal Education*, p. 204.
3. ibid, p. 207.   4. ibid, p. 69.

his reverence for their innocence and for the Holy Ghost dwelling in them.' [5]

Here was a new attitude to childhood, expressed in the clear recognition of love as the great educative force, the principle towards which the best of the Greeks and Romans had groped, and which was most fully revealed and demonstrated in Christianity.

Pascal wrote:

We must treat them with courtesy and speak to them with deference, and give way to them as far as possible. This wins them over, and it is well to condescend to them sometimes in things which in themselves are indifferent, in order to gain their hearts.[6]

Lancelot tells us M. de Saint-Cyran used to say

that we ought to be, not only the guardian angels but in some sort the providence of children who were committed to our charge, because our chief care should be always to attach them to what is good with gentleness and charity ... He usually reduced what is necessary to do with children to three things: to speak little, bear with much, and pray more.[7] He used to add that we ought to show special love and pity for those who appear most defective and backward.

He often condescended in prison to play at ball on a table with children of seven or eight years old.[8]

Père Louis de la Rivière wrote:

Especially did he seem to be in his element when he was surrounded by little children; they were his daily delight and pleasure.[9]

'Children should see that we can keep a secret,' [10] said Pascal. We should understand that they are different from adults; remembering our own childhood we should treat them with tolerance.

Guyot wrote that Masters

must not imagine that what they find pleasure in knowing children can learn without trouble, but they should rather remember their own childhood, and the difficulties which they themselves had

5. BARNARD, *Port Royalists on Education*, p. 67.
6. CADET, *Port Royal Education*, p. 232.
7. ibid, p. 74.   8. ibid, p. 75.
9. SAINTE BEUVE, vol. i, p. 236, quoted in BEARD, *Port Royal*, p. 83.
10. *Port Royal Education*, p. 229.

in becoming learned. Thus they will adapt themselves to the weakness of their scholars, and not give them more than they can help.[11]

Children ought to be so helped in every possible way, as to make, if it may be, study more pleasant than play and amusement.[12]

M. le Maître de Saci wrote to one of his friends:

We must not be too uneasy about their faults, or too precise in marking them.[13] They are like the young wheat, which often produces more or less than was expected.[14]

It was necessary to have reciprocal love; it was also necessary for the masters to understand their pupils and to study children. Nicole wrote:

The greatest Wits have but limited understandings. In them there are always some cloudy and darksom corners; but the understandings of children are almost totally over-cast, they discover only some little glimpses of light. So that the great work consists in managing these small rays, in increasing them, and placing therein whatsoever one would make them comprehend.

Hence it is that 'tis so difficult to give general Rules for the Instruction of any one, because they ought to be proportion'd to that mixture of light and darkness, which is various according to the difference of Wits, particularly in Children.[15]

'Constant vigilance is necessary in order to form an opinion of them and to discover their tempers and inclinations,' [16] says Pascal.

There is nothing more difficult than to find this proportion to the Understanding of Children; and it is with reason that a Man of the World said, That it *is the part of a strong and elevated Soul, to be able to proportion and frame it self to the ways and humours of Children.* 'Tis an easie matter to make a discourse of Morality for an hour together; but to reduce all things to it, so that the Child neither perceives nor takes distaste thereat, is what requires an admirable address, and such as is to be found in very few.[17]

Coustel said:

If a physician cannot prescribe remedies suitable for the healing

11. ibid, p. 154.
12. BEARD, *Port Royal*, Vol. 2, p. 150.
13. *Port Royal Education*, p. 94.   14. ibid.
15. *Education of a Prince*, p. 18.   16. *Port Royal Education*, p. 238.
17. *Education of a Prince*, p. 16.

of the body, without knowing its varying temperaments, and if a farmer ought not to set about sowing a field without knowing the quality of its soil, then beyond doubt a schoolmaster should also know the different kinds of intellect which he has to educate.[18]

The kind of education provided must then be based on a study of children, and be adapted to individual needs and capacities. Nicole wrote:

Instruction aims at advancing the Mind to the highest point it is capable of.[19]

Its aims were two: first, to develop character; second, to make children think. The order was important. Coustel said that the goal of Christians 'is heaven, for which the sciences are far less necessary than good character'. Indeed, a strong intellect was often regarded as a possible danger, a weak point at which the devil might find entry into the soul.

Lancelot says that Saint-Cyran, the founder of Port Royal, 'remarked that generally speaking knowledge did more harm than good to the young'.[20] He was acutely aware of the danger of knowledge without moral purpose, without wisdom. 'There is nothing I hate more,' he said, 'than those seekers after truth who are not truly devoted to God and who are not led solely by love of Him in their researches.'[21]

Love of God was the basic principle of the education of Port Royal, but, given that, the children were to be encouraged to have a lively spirit of inquiry, and to seek after truth.

Nicole wrote:

To educate is to form the judgment – that is, to give the mind a taste for the good and the power to recognize it; to make the mind keen to recognise false reasoning when it is somewhat obscured; to teach it not to be dazzled by a show of vain talk with no sense in it, or satisfied with mere words or vague principles, and never to be content until one has penetrated to the very bottom of a thing. It is to make the mind quick to see the point at issue in an involved matter and to recognize what is irrelevant. It is to

18. BARNARD, *Lancelot, Memoires de S.C.*, Vol. II, pp. 73–4.
19. *Education of a Prince*, p. 17.
20. BARNARD, *Little Schools of Port Royal*, p. 63.
21. ibid, p. 63.

fill the mind with those principles which help it to find the truth of all matters.[22]

These men valued highly the feeling side of man's nature, giving it even greater importance than the intellect and realized the need for an education of the heart. In their criticism of current methods of education, which trained the intellect but failed to educate the heart, they drew attention to a problem which is still unsolved today. Guyot wrote:

Since then the heart is the most important part of a man, we must pay far more heed to it than to the intellect; and one of the greatest though commonest faults in the education of children is that the intellect is highly trained, but the heart very little.[23]

Arnauld said:

Prizes will be distributed to those who have most distinguished themselves, ... but the first prizes should be given to those who have shown most religion and whose morals are irreproachable. ... The heart should be rewarded before the head.[24]

The way in which children were to be trained and educated was not by force, but by persuasion and enjoyment. In so doing, the teacher was able to use the power of the pupil's will to reinforce his learning.

Coustel would have the teacher

contrive that their studies appear as a kind of pastime or game, rather than as a troublesome and tedious occupation. This is the reason why the school is called ludus literarius and the schoolmaster ludimagister. We must not then exact from children while they are of a tender age an application and devotion to study equal to that which we have a right to demand from fully formed minds. This would mean giving them a dislike for study, which might have undesirable consequences and which also might possibly persist as they grew older.[25]

22. *Education of a Prince*, BARNARD, *Port Royalists on Education*, p. 71.
23. CADET, *Port Royal Education*, p. 124.
24. ibid, p. 124.
25. *Education of a Prince*, p. 6.

'Nothing sinks less into the mind, than what enters there under the unpleasant shape of a Lesson or Instruction,' says Nicole. 'A master shows his skill by setting the pupils under his care to those tasks which are most congenial to them.' [26]

Coustel emphasizes the value of free choice:

What a man does against his will and by a sort of constraint not only is not praiseworthy, but cannot even be lasting; for what is forced soon returns to its previous state, as a tree that has been forcibly bent soon returns to its former direction, whereas what is done from free choice is usually stable and permanent.[27]

It is a general rule that, as far as possible, everything should be made easy for children. We should always proceed from the known to the unknown.

Curiosity, says Nicole, should be encouraged and children should be trained to think for themselves:

One ought to endeavour to incline the minds of Children to a commendable curiosity of seeing things that are strange and curious, and encourage them to be inquisitive of the reasons of whatsoever occurs. This curiosity ... opens and enlarges their minds.[28]

and it was of first importance that children should learn self-knowledge. Pascal wrote:

Children should be strongly exhorted to know themselves.[29]

Then, as now, the temptation for the teacher was to look for results that can be seen and measured and, in order to produce such results, to push children on beyond their understanding. Nicole wrote:

As this method of instruction is not apparent, the benefit resulting therefrom is also in a way not apparent − i.e. it does not manifest itself by obvious and outward signs; and it is this fact which leads unthinking people astray, for they imagine that a child educated in this way has made less progress than another.[30]

26. ibid, Vol. II, pp. 277–8, BARNARD, *Port Royalists on Education*, p. 71.

27. *Port Royal Education*, p. 208.

28. *Education of a Prince*, p. 21.

29. *Port Royal Education*, p. 235.

30. *Education of a Prince*, BARNARD, *Port Royalists on Education*, p. 94.

An earlier translation gives, for 'unthinking people', 'shallow Considerers', a term which might well describe certain present-day critics of modern methods.

Nevertheless, there was to be nothing soft about this. For those who do not respond to this pleasant approach to learning, some other way must be found, and Coustel quotes St Augustine: 'They must be compelled to do it.'

Teaching through the senses, particularly through sight, is recommended, and pictures and maps were to be used as well as objects. Nicole says:

It may nevertheless in general be said, That the light or knowledge of Children depending very much on sense, one ought, as much as possible, fasten to sensible things the Instructions that are given them; and, not onely to make them enter by the ear, but also by the Eye; there being no sense that makes a more lively an impression on the Soul, nor that forms therein Ideas more distinct and clear.[31]

Learning was to begin with the familiar and the concrete. Children were to be asked to write about what they knew. Guyot wrote:

Care must be taken in exercising pupils in speaking or writing that they do it with clearness and precision . . . and with clear and definite knowledge of things. . . . For this reason they should usually be set to write about things of which they know most.[32]

Geography was to be practical, learned from nature and not from a book. Maps were to be used, and pictures of animals, towns, Roman antiquities or historical characters shown to the children.

In their theories the Port Royalists were far in advance of their time, but they were practical schoolmasters, and their doctrines grew out of their experience in the classroom. There is a refreshing sincerity and lack of bombast in their writings, and the influence they had on subsequent French education was profound. It has been said that with their schools, and the view of life for which they stood, a new spirit entered into French education. Professor Barnard, writing in 1913, said

31. *Education of a Prince*, p. 18.
32. BARNARD, *Little Schools of Port Royal*, p. 95.

that their influence 'can be traced in the writings of French educationalists and in the laws and proposals of the French Government during the last two centuries'. Rousseau, although on many points diametrically opposed to them, was one who read their treatises with deep interest. He is said to have 'devoured them'. Locke was another. The *Essai d'Education Nationale*, drawn up by La Chalotais for the Parlement of Paris in 1762, was inspired by their doctrines. Their ideas anticipated both Pestalozzi and Froebel, and much of what they wrote, and carried into effect in the classroom, still waits to be put into practice today.

The Port Royal Schools played a notable part in bringing to an end the scholasticism of the Middle Ages, in which authority was supreme, and in giving birth to the modern era of freedom of thought, and the supremacy of reason and truth.

Charles Rollin, professor of history in the college of France, and three times rector of the university, had a considerable influence on the reform of French education. Writing over three hundred years ago, and influenced himself by Fénelon, he showed a perfect understanding of the truth, still obscure to some today:

Study depends upon the will, which admits of no constraint. ... The will therefore must be gained; and this can only be done by mildness, affectionate behaviour and persuasion, and above all by the allurement of pleasure.[33]

He believed that education, at least as far as girls are concerned, is a matter not only of the intellect, but of the feelings:

Parents and masters should propose a double end in ... education, ... viz. the fashioning of the heart or affections, and the cultivating of the mind.[34]

Play should be used in learning, and children should not be forced:

The skill of the master lies in making study agreeable, and teaching his scholar to find a pleasure in it. To which end play and recreation may very much contribute ... This gives me an oppor-

33. ROLLIN, CHARLES, *The Method of Teaching and Studying the Belles Lettres.*
34. *New Thoughts Concerning Education*, p. 28.

tunity of advising and entreating parents not to push children too much upon study in their early years.[35]

Such untimely efforts

if they are prejudicial to the body, they are no less dangerous to the mind which exhausts itself, and grows dull by a continual application.[36]

He quotes Quintilian's suggestion that children could start learning at three, but he 'would have it a play, not a study, an amusement, not a serious occupation'. He warns against pressing children too early to learn to read. Of the three- to seven-year-olds he says:

It would be of very dangerous consequence, should reading, in the beginning, be made a serious occupation; or children be ever so little chagrin'd, whilst they are learning the elements. Possibly, this may be one cause, of the great disgust which several children entertain, not only in that age, but all their life-time, for everything that bears the name of study and learning. The bare sight of a book fills 'em with melancholy, because it wakes a confus'd remembrance of reproaches and tears, which were inseparable from their infant studies.[37]

He describes a new method of teaching reading, the Typographical Structure or Bureau, invented by a Mr Du Mas. The child picks letter sounds from boxes and sets them out in words, as a printer sets up type, anticipating the principle of modern infant teaching, by which children learn by doing and handling material. Rollin realizes the need for little children to move about and use their limbs in action.

Nothing is more tedious and fatiguing in childhood, than for the mind to be on the stretch, and the body at rest ... At the typographical structure, [the child's] hands, his feet, his whole body is in motion.[38]

The pupil will learn when he has an affection for his teacher.

In order to engage the scholar's affection for learning, the master himself must first win his love.[39]

35. *The Method of Teaching and Studying the Belles Lettres*, Vol. 3, pp. 357–8.   36. ibid, Vol. 3, p. 357.
37. *New Thoughts Concerning Education*, p. 5.
38. ibid, pp. 7–8.   39. ibid, p. 26.

The teacher must know his pupils:

> The master's first care is thoroughly to study and search into the genius and character of the children ... to become acquainted with their humour, their disposition and talents.[40]

This can only be done if the pupils are given freedom:

> The way of growing acquainted in this manner with children, is to give them great liberty to discover their inclinations whilst young, to let them follow their natural bent in order to discern it the better ... to observe them whilst they think least of it, especially at their play.[41]

He recognizes the value of curiosity and suggests that children should be allowed some freedom of choice:

> There is implanted in children, as in all mankind, a natural spirit of curiosity, or desire of knowledge and information, of which a good use may be made towards rendering their study agreeable ... A careful and skilful master ... seems to leave the choice to them.[42]

His ideal lesson, however, reveals the limitation in his understanding: the children are required to read a Latin sentence, syllable by syllable and, when a mistake is made the master strikes the table with his cane, and this method he himself saw practised 'with singular pleasure ... in a most happy manner at Orleans. There was upwards of an hundred boys in the school I visited,' he wrote, 'and a deep silence reigned in every part of it.' [43]

40. *The Method of Teaching and Studying the Belles Lettres,* Vol. 3, pp. 326–7.
41. ibid, p. 328.   42. ibid, pp. 355–6.
43. *New Thoughts Concerning Education,* p. 12.

13

Isaac Watts

THE educational ideas of Issac Watts, the hymn writer, anticipated by some fifty years many of the ideas of Rousseau. He
drew attention, in particular, to the importance of appealing
to the pupil's understanding. In his treatise on the education of
the boy Eugenio, he says:

There was nothing required of his Memory but what was first
(as far as possible) let into his Understanding; and by proper
Images and Representations, suited to his Years, he was taught to
form some Conception of the Things described, before he was bid
to learn the Words by Heart. Thus he was freed from the Danger of
treasuring up the Cant and Jargon of mere Names, instead of the
riches of solid Knowlege.[1]

and elsewhere,

If all your Learning be nothing else but a mere Amassment of
what others have written, without a due Penetration into their
Meaning, ... I do not see what Title your *Head* has to true Learning. . . .[2]

Take heed ... that you do not take up with *Words* instead of
Things, nor mere *Sounds* instead of real *Sentiments* and *Ideas*.
Many a *Lad* forgets what has been taught him, merely because he
never well understood it.[3]

There should be no learning by rote without understanding:

No Word, Phrase, or Sentiment (should) might be admitted
which could not be brought in some measure within the Reach
of a Child's Understanding.[4]

Teaching should be by means of things:

The Business and Duty of the Teacher is not merely to teach
them Words but Things.[5]

1. WATTS, ISAAC, *Improvement of the Mind*, 2nd Part, p. 210.
2. ibid, 1st Part, p. 13.   3. ibid, 1st Part, p. 262.
4. *Discourse on the Way of Instruction by Catechism*, p. ix.
5. ibid, p. 16.

Learning by rote, without understanding, only deadens:

The Sound and Chime of Words that has past over the Ears and the Tongue five hundred Times, without any Signification, will rather go on to pass over still in the same mechanical Manner, and will not seem to want a Signification afterwards . . . If children are trained up to use Words without Meaning, they will get a Habit of dealing in Sounds instead of Ideas and of mistaking Words for Things.[6]

Learning by rote is an ineffective method:

Words which are not understood are much more difficult to be remembered. Words and Things are most easily learnt together. . . .[7]

He answers the question, 'Why should children not learn something they do not understand, for they may come to understand it later?'

Is it the best Method for the feeding and nourishing the Bodies of young Children, to bestow upon them Nuts and Almonds, in hopes that they will taste thee Sweetness of them when their Teeth are strong enough to break the Shell? Will they not be far better nourished by Children's Bread, and by Food which they can immediately taste and relish?[8]

He seems to be on the verge of insight, in this reference to Children's Bread, into an understanding of the needs of little children. Speaking of parents he writes:

If they will put a Man's Coat on a Child, the Child may be cumbered with his long and loose Habiliments, and yet be starved with Cold.[9]

A teacher, he says, should

always accommodate himself to the Genius, Temper, and Capacity of his Disciples, and practise various Methods of Prudence to allure, persuade, and assist, every one of them in their Pursuit of Knowledge.[10]

Love and encouragement are powerful motives in educating the young:

Let not the Teacher demand or expect Things too sublime and difficult from the humble, modest, and fearful Disciple: And where

6. ibid, pp. 29, 34.			7. ibid, p. 28.
8 ibid, pp. 25–6.			9. ibid, p. 35.
10. Improvement of the Mind, 2nd Part, p. 9.

such a one gives a just and happy Answer, even to plain and easy Questions, let him have Words of Commendation and Love ready for him.[11]

He must educate his pupils so that they are able to educate themselves:

Labour as much as possible to make the Person you would teach his own Instructor. Human Nature may be allured, by a secret Pleasure and Pride in its own Reasoning, to seem to find out by itself the very Thing you would teach.[12]

Curiosity is a means to learning and should be encouraged:

Curiosity is a useful spring of Knowledge: It should be encouraged in *Children.*[13]

Their natural powers must be used, and they should follow inclination and learn by play; the path to learning is the road of enjoyment:

Children should be taught the true Use, the Exercise and Improvement, of their natural Powers.[14]

Get a good liking to the Study or Knowledge you would pursue. We may observe that there is not much Difficulty in confining the Mind to contemplate what we have a great Desire to know ... *Pleasure and Delight in the Things we learn* give great Assistance towards the Remembrance of them. ... Children may be taught to remember many Things in a Way or Sport or Play.[15]

Observation, especially of nature, is of the greatest importance, and leads to self-knowledge, as well as to the knowledge of God:

Almost every Thing is new to a child, and Novelty will entice them onward to new Acquisitions. Shew them the Birds, the Beasts, the Fishes and the Insects, Trees, Herbs, Fruits and all the several Parts and Properties of the Vegetable and Animal World: Teach them to observe the various Occurences in Nature and Providence, the Sun, Moon and Stars, the Day and Night, Summer and Winter, the Clouds and the Sky, the Hail, Snow and Ice, Winds, Fire, Water, Earth, Air, Fields, Woods, Mountains, Rivers, etc. Teach them that the great God made all these Things.[16]

11. ibid, 2nd Part, pp. 10–11.   12. ibid, 2nd Part, p. 30.
13. ibid, 2nd Part, p. 10.   14. ibid, 2nd Part, p. 109.
15. ibid, 1st Part, pp. 212, 269, 270.   16. ibid, p. 110.

Observation is the Notice that we take of all Occurrences in human Life....

It is this that furnishes us, even from our Infancy, with a rich variety of Ideas and Propositions, Words and Phrases.[17]

Observation is the path to all knowledge; but it must include not only outward but inward experience:

It is owing to *Obversation* that our Mind is furnished with the first, simple and complex Ideas. It is this lays the Ground-work and Foundation of all Knowledge, and makes us capable of using any of the other Methods for improving the Mind; For if we did not attain a Variety of sensible and intellectual Ideas by the *Sensation* of outward Objects, by the *Consciousness*, of our own Appetites and Passions, Pleasures and Pains, and by inward *Experience* of the Actings of our own Spirits, it would be impossible either for Men or Books to teach us anything.[18]

He stresses the difference between first- and second-hand experience:

All our Knowledge derived from *Observation* ... is *Knowledge gotten at first hand*. Hereby we see and know Things as they are, or as they appear to us; ... from the original Objects themselves, which give a clearer and stronger Conception of Things; ...

What Knowledge we derive from *Lectures, Reading and Conversation*, is but the Copy of other Men's Ideas, that is the picture of a Picture; and it is one Remove further from the Original.[19]

Education therefore, should bring a child into contact with the world around him:

Where time and fortune allows it, young people should be led into company at proper seasons, should be carried abroad to see the fields, and the woods, and the rivers, the buildings, towns and cities distant from their own dwelling.

17. ibid, 1st Part, p. 30.   18. ibid, 1st Part, p. 34.
19. ibid, 1st Part, pp. 34–5.

14

J. P. de Crousaz · David Fordyce · David Manson

EDUCATIONAL ideas that had been lightly sketched in outline through hundreds of years – the place of play in education,
the importance of using children's own abilities and interests,
the necessity for child study and the significance of love as an
educative force – now, with the coming of the eighteenth and
nineteenth centuries, began to be worked out on a wider canvas
by the great educational artists, Rousseau, Pestalozzi and
Froebel. Men like Erasmus, Montaigne, Comenius, the Port
Royalists, Fénelon and many others had given the cartoons,
but it was not until the social and political climate of the
eighteenth century, with its thunderstorms of revolutionary
change, had produced a new idea of man and his place in the
world, that the cartoons could be worked up into the master-
pieces which were to influence profoundly the course not only
of education, but of politics.

More than forty years before the appearance of *Émile* a
Professor of Philosophy and Mathematics at the University of
Lausanne, J. P. de Crousaz, wrote in satirical vein much of
what was later to be read in Rousseau: 'Speak *Latin* readily,
without being acquainted with any Thing else, and you will
be accounted a learned Man'[1] – so he castigated the current
view of education.

If a Tutor endeavours to improve the Understanding of his
Pupil, what does he get by that? Does not the Father know, that
his Son will not fail to be like him, and, consequently, arrive in
Time to Reason, as well as he, without the Tutor's troubling his
head about that.[2]

Teaching of religion must be done with authority, in case
children are tempted to question and discuss the matter:

1. DE CROUSAZ, J. P., *New Maxims Concerning Education*, p. 74.
2. ibid, p. 78.

Therefore every thing that is proposed to them in their younger Years, must be proposed to them with a definite Air and Voice. Not only every Objection, but even every Question, every Desire of Explanation ought to be rejected with extreme Impatience; ... when they take it into their Heads to start Objections or Questions, their Tutors must take them up short, more than for a Lie.[3]

These are young Plants, which the Church may be sure of.[4]

De Crousaz was clearly influenced by Locke but, says Mc-Callister, there is in his philosophy

a keener appreciation of the value of curiosity and of the presentation of ideas within the pupil's mental grasp. The secret of education is to place the pupil in such a position as will enable him to give himself lessons, the opportunities and the materials only being supplied by the teacher. . . .[5]

Even if Rousseau was not influenced by this amusing presentation of common prejudices, it must have prepared the minds of some for the paradoxes of *Émile*.[6]

The little-known writings of David Fordyce, professor of Aberdeen, forecast most of the principal ideas of Rousseau's *Émile* and draw together much of the enlightened thoughts of his predecessors, Erasmus, Vives, Comenius, Locke and others.

In the *Dialogues Concerning Education* he gives a picture of an academy under the guidance of one Euphranor, whom McCallister calls 'this eighteenth-century Socrates'. This wise tutor believed, as did Socrates

that the human Mind was richly impregnated with the Principles of all Knowledge, but that these lay hid like rude Embryo's in the dark Womb of Thought – and that it required an artful Midwife to deliver it of them.[7]

'Yet how few [teachers],' he said,

have the necessary Stock of Patience? and indeed a vast deal is necessary, to help forward the Births, and let the Conceptions of

---

3. ibid, p. 80.   4. ibid, p. 81.
5. MCCALLISTER, *The Growth of Freedom in Education*, p. 212.
6. ibid, p. 218.
7. FORDYCE, DAVID, *Dialogues Concerning Education*, VIII, Vol. I, p. 209.

the Mind go out their time. Without this, it will bring forth nothing but ill shaped and monstrous Productions, crude Ideas and lame, unconnected Reasonings.[8]

He compares the mind to a seed

which contains all the Stamina of the future Plant, and all those Principles of Perfection, to which it aspires in its After-growth, and regularly arrives by gradual Stages, unless it is obstructed in its Progress by external Violence.[9]

The mind has within itself all necessary powers. It is 'completely organized' and wants

no Powers, no Capacities of Perception, no Instincts or Affections that are essential ... but these are, in a manner locked up, and are purposely left rude and unfinished. ... Tis the Business of Education, therefore, like a second Creation, to improve Nature, to give Form, and Proportion, and Comeliness to those unwrought Materials.[10]

There is, within us, a sense which makes us responsive to the idea of moral obligation.

It is interwoven with the very Frame and Constitution of our Nature, and by it We are in the strictest Sense a Law to Ourselves; ... it is *within* us, ever present with us, ever active and incumbent on the Mind, and engraven on the Heart in the fair and large Signatures of Conscience, Natural Affection, Compassion, Gratitude and universal Benevolence.[11]

This basic belief in the innate goodness, or power to good, of every human being, underlies his faith in the method of following nature.

'Gentlemen,' says Eugenio,

what a mighty pother is made by you and a great many others, about the Affair of *Education!* What a Noise about instilling Principles into the Minds of Youth, forming their Tempers by an early Culture, ... crouding their Heads with a number of Names and Notions and dead Languages, and anticipating their Genius and Choice by the Restraints of a severe Discipline! I do not know whether it would not be much better to leave the Mind open and

8. ibid, VIII, Vol. I, p. 210.   9. ibid, VI, Vol. I, pp. 116–17.
10. ibid, VI, Vol. I, p. 117.
11. *Elements of Moral Philosophy,* p. 73.

untinctured with the Prejudices of Education, to trust to the genuine
Dictates of Nature and good Sense, which will teach a truer and
more useful Knowledge than most Masters have themselves. After
the Rudiments of Language are attained, what is learnt in most
Schools and Colleges, but a Set of hard Words, with an insignificant Parade of Knowledge, or a vain Conceit, that we have imbibed the very *Arcana* of Science, joined with a thorough Contempt
of all others whom we fancy less knowing?... Does it not happen
from hence, that one half of our Life is spent in unlearning the
Prejudices and popular Errors we acquired in the other Part of
it?[12]

What then is the method that should be used, asks Constant,
and in Eugenio's reply we see the foreshadowing of Rousseau's negative education:

Why truly, ... my Method is neither nice nor far-fetched; but
quite simple, and such as Nature itself dictates. Instead of putting
the Mind into a Mould, and hampering it with the Trammels of Education, in my Opinion it would be better to give unlimited Scope
to Nature, to lay no Bias on Judgement and Genius, to infuse no
positive Opinions; but to let the young Adventurer, like the industrious Bee, wander about in quest of Intellectual Food, rifle every
precious Flower and Blossom, and, after he has picked up Materials
from every Quarter, range and digest them into a well-compacted
and useful Body.[13]

'The whole ART of Education,' says Philander,

lies within a narrow Compass, and is reduceable to a very Simple
Practice; namely *'to assist us in unfolding and exercising those
NATURAL and MORAL Powers with which Man is endued by
presenting proper Objects and Occasions; to watch their Growth
that they be not diverted from their End, or disturbed in their
Operation by any Foreign Violence; and gently to conduct and
apply them to all the Purposes of PRIVATE and PUBLIC Life.'*
This is but repeating the Maxim of Ancient Wisdom to FOLLOW
NATURE.[14] The great Author of our Nature would never have
made it susceptible of such various Pleasures, unless by those he
had designed to influence our Actions, and mould us for Society.[15]

12. *Dialogues*, VI, Vol. I, pp. 108–9.
13. ibid, VI, Vol. I, pp. 109–10.
14. ibid. XIII, Vol 2, p. 97.   15. ibid, XV, Vol. 2, p. 206.

In his suggestions for the right development of character he anticipates the best of modern psychological thought:

All Unnatural and Fantastic Desires and Passions, are best supplanted and expelled, by giving proper Scope to those which are natural and just.[16]

Education is to be for practical and social life, as Rousseau was to maintain soon after:

A *grand Secret* of teaching ... is to inform [the pupil] fully, why he learns this or the other Piece of Knowledge, what Use or End they answer, and how they will qualify him for social and active life.[17]

The chief aim of education is to form character. Hiero says:

What Pains soever may be taken in furnishing the Infant-Mind with a Stock of Ideas, the principal Care ought to be bestowed in forming the HEART, and planting there, firm Habits of Piety and Virtue.[18]

To this end, the study of nature can be of practical value in the education of children:

If, therefore, before they are hurried into the World, their minds could be seasoned with the Love of Nature, if they could be brought to admire the Charms of Still-Life, and the Delights of rural Innocence and Simplicity, I am apt to believe, it would give their thoughts a sober and sedate Turn, make them better acquainted with themselves and their Connections with the Universe, cherish a Spirit of Devotion, and be a kind of Antidote against the Corruptions of the World.[19]

Give children a good reason for learning, and make it enjoyable, and you will have no difficulty in teaching them, whether in matters of conduct or in learning to read:

Do but once convince a Child fairly, that this Conduct is fit, honourable and advantageous to him, and immediately he is on Wing to pursue it, and will continue to do so while he retains that Opinion. Show him the other to be mean, little, and prejudicial to him, and you excite his Horror and Aversion to that Conduct.[20]

16. ibid, XV, Vol. 2, pp. 206–7.   17. ibid, VIII, Vol. 1, p. 217.
18. ibid, VIII, Vol. 1, p. 218.   19. ibid, IX, Vol. 1, p. 266.
20. ibid, XV, Vol. 2, p. 153.

To make him take Pleasure in learning those, I would inscribe the Letters on their different Play-things, and contrive various Games and Diversions, which shall oblige them to learn and pronounce them distinctly. . . . But whatever Exercises are prescribed to them, or whatever Lessons are taught them, they should not be imposed as Tasks, but recommended to them as Diversions, and chiefly by those Persons who do them good, and whom they love most themselves. . . . The Grand Art is to excite their Curiosity, and keep it continually awake; to lead them forward gently, and convince them how manly and honourable those Exercises are in which they are employed.[21]

Fordyce was by no means the first to see the importance of curiosity, but he was one of the first to state clearly that learning follows appetite, and that the child's innate love of inquiry is his implanted guide, and in this he anticipated the modern method of basing education on the needs and interests of children at their varying stages of development.

In the whole of this Affair therefore, I would not anticipate, but follow Nature. No discreet Nurse would give a Child Nourishment till it craved it; nor continue cramming it, when its Hunger was allayed; but patiently wait the Return of Appetite. The Mind too has its Cravings and Capacities. I would not give it intellectual Food, till it showed Some Desire of it, nor bid it judge, till it discovered a Capacity of judging. We find that the Appetites and Capacities always go together; so that Nature never stings with the former, till it has bestowed the latter. Whenever, therefore, Curiosity and the Love of Enquiry begin to disclose themselves, it is a natural Indication that Reason is now in a Capacity to act and digest such Nourishment as is proper for it.[22]

He suggests practical ways in which curiosity may be used as a lever to learning, in a first-hand study of everyday things:

In order to keep their Curiosity and Attention awake . . . I would let them see the various Changes some Things must undergo, before they are fitted for Use, such as Wool, Flax, Metal, which they should see in their different States, together with the Instruments which work them.[23]

21. ibid, XV, Vol. 2, pp. 191–3.   22. ibid, VI, Vol. 1, pp. 118–19.
23. ibid, VIII, Vol. 1, p 208.

But the curiosity of children is something more. With unusual insight he recognizes in them a spirit of wonder, that intangible response to the beauty and grandeur of their world which is characteristic of them:

They are full of Quesions ... they are still apt to wonder, and are frequently amazed, without knowing why. ... This *Spirit of Wonder*, and *Love of Novelty*, are two admirable Handles, by which to catch hold of such slippery Creatures.[24]

All education must lead the mind to activity; therefore it must not be trained to rely on authority and the judgements of others:

Tis certain, that Opinions which the Mind receives from others, upon their bare Authority, without perceiving their Reasons and Connections, may take fast hold of the Judgement, especially of the young and unexperienced; but all such Opinions fill the Mind without enlightening it, they give no Exercise to the mental Faculties, but rather teach them to rely on the Activity of others, and consequently lull the Mind into a stupid Indolence.[25]

How then is the problem to be solved? If the child is to be made something more than a parrot he must be taught to teach himself:

How is it possible to communicate Truth to the open and credulous Mind, without secretly and insensibly influencing its Judgement, by the Authority of the Teacher? Nothing more practicable or easy, if you will let it teach itself.[26]

Nature will do more than half the work since there are, within, natural faculties and capacities which function of themselves:

By these simple but powerful springs ... the life of man ... is preserved and secured, and the creature is prompted to a constant round of action.[27]

Nature is ever teaching the tender Infant, even while we think him a Subject incapable of Instruction.[28]

24. ibid, VIII, Vol. 1, p. 207.   25. ibid, VI, Vol. 1, pp. 117–18.
26. ibid, VI, Vol. 1, p. 119.
27. *Elements of Moral Philosophy*, pp. 15–20, MCCALLISTER, *The Growth of Freedom in Education*, p. 22.
28. *Dialogues, VIII*, Vol. 1, p. 199.

It seems clear that Fordyce was here anticipating the modern theory of instincts, with the important difference that he believed these faculties or instincts to be good, and to work always towards truth and understanding:

All therefore we have to do . . . is to furnish Materials, and store the Mind with plenty of Ideas; it will range and combine them itself, and by a natural kind of Instinct, cleave to Truth while it rejects Error.[29]

Few writers of the present time can have put more clearly the basic principles of the modern approach to teaching. Education must be a journey of discovery and experience for every individual. It can never be got at second hand:

The principal Advantage of this kind of Instruction . . . is this, that here they instruct themselves, plod to find out a Meaning, and are charmed with every Discovery, as *their own*.[30] For . . . the human Mind opens its Powers spontaneously, the Buds of Knowledge unfold themselves by insensible Degrees, and one Branch of Truth makes way for another, if we remove all Obstructions and give Nature full scope.[31]

Fordyce understood as clearly as any twentieth-century educator that education must be a matter of activity. Even, or perhaps, primarily, is this true in the field of morals:

The Science of *Good* may be taught Children much sooner than we imagine; but it must be in the *Experimental*, rather than the *Speculative or Literary* Way.[32]
There is a wonderful Activity or Propensity to Action in human Creatures, but especially in Children: They love to be always playing, leaping, prattling or doing something; and cannot enjoy themselves, when they have nothing to do. . . . It is therefore a great Secret in *Moral* Culture, 'to find proper Work and Employment for them, such as is at once most suited to their Capacities, in the different stages of their Growth'.[33]

He must, then, be given freedom to develop through a wide

---

29. ibid, VI, Vol. 1, p. 120.
31. ibid, VIII, Vol. 1, p. 206.
33. ibid, XV, Vol. 2, p. 212.

30. ibid, VIII, Vol. 1, pp. 204–5.
32. ibid, XV, Vol. 2, p. 200.

variety of experiences, reminiscent of the best primary schools of today:

> Let him mark out his own Sphere of Action, and chuse his own Amusements, to exercise his Invention, and explore his Genius. Many innocent Employments, besides Reading and Study, may be proposed to him; such as gathering, sometimes buying his Food, ordering Breakfasts or Suppers, chusing or disposing the Furniture of his own Apartments, laying out little Gardens, and furnishing them with proper Kitchen Fruits. . . . Let him have proper Materials and Instruments for Building little Houses, Wind and Water-Mills, making Castles, Fortifications, Models, Machines, whether for Play or Use, Turning, Graving, Designing and other Works of Ingenuity or Labour.[34]

In his understanding that a moral sense is only developed through practice and experience he was well ahead of his time:

> But it is chiefly *Moral* Improvements which I have in my Eye. How then are these to be attained? Not, I conceive, by fatiguing their Memories with rigid Rules, or disgusting them with dry Discourses concerning *Abstinence, Austerity* and *Self-denial*; nor so much by setting before them the Example of those who have excelled in the Practice of such Virtues, in which possibly they may think themselves but little interested; the true Way, as I take it, is by engaging them in *Moral Exercises*.[35]

This practice alone will touch the heart and so influence conduct, and here perhaps is the core of Fordyce's philosophy, in his recognition that true education can never be a matter of the intellect alone, but must include the feelings, the imagination, the heart. Children 'must be led by Feeling, rather than Reasoning,' says Philander, echoing Aristotle.

> Unless the Mind sees the Reasons of its Actions, and be accustomed to observe the Nature and Tendency of the Course to which it is habituated, and unless that Course be agreeable to its Original Feelings and Affections, it will never act with Vigour and Complacence, and though it may contract a strong Propensity to a certain Object, or Scheme of Action, yet the Habit, wanting its main

34. ibid, XV, Vol. 2, p. 214.   35. ibid, XV, Vol. 2, p. 215.

Basis and Support, will be easily displaced, when the particular
Influence ... ceases to act; or when a better Scheme of Conduct,
which approves itself to its genuine and uncorrupted Feelings, is
proposed.[36]

Philander foreshadows the theory of the growth and influence of sentiments upon human conduct, and the importance
of educating the imagination.

It is in the *Imagination* . . . that those *Images of Beauty and
Good* are formed, which sway our Resolution and guide our Passions. Truth, unsupported by these, or separate from them, makes
but a faint impression on our Minds.[37]

Euphranor says:

I take it to be no small Error in the Affair of Education, to
regard it as a Matter of meer SCIENCE or SPECULATION, rather
than of PRACTICE; an *Art or Method of furnishing* the HEAD,
rather than a *Discipline of the* HEART *and* LIFE.[38]

Hiero continues:

I had got a Notion in my Head, that a *benevolent* Heart gives
a Man more Pleasure than a *learned* Head, and a rich stock of
Goodness a better Treasure than a great Estate.[39]

The practical problem of educating children produced many
experiments, notably that of the Play School of David Man-
son. Ten years before the appearance of *Émile*, his school was
founded in the North of Ireland,

whose regulations were so perfect that every scholar must have
been made insensibly to teach himself while he all the time considered himself as assisting the master in teaching others. All were
actively engaged but so regulated as to produce not the least confusion and disturbance.[40]

'No one who preceded him,' said the *Belfast News Letter*,

36. ibid, VI, Vol. 1, p. 121.   37. ibid, X, Vol. 1, p. 270.
38. ibid, XVII, Vol. 2, pp. 294–5.   39. ibid, XVIII, Vol. 2, p. 338.
40. MCCALLISTER, *The Growth of Freedom in Education*, p. 333.

studied more to blend pleasure with instruction and to incite scholars to diligence by kindness and rewards. For this purpose he contrived amusements of different sorts, suited to the several ages of those under his care, some of them on a very extensive scale and attended with much expense.[41]

41. ibid.

15

Rousseau · La Chalotais

THE revolt against the social and political régime began in France, under Voltaire. In his rebellion against authority he was the heir of men like Peter Ramus, as well as of Newton, Locke and Pope. In place of authority, reason was to be enthroned, and nothing was to be accepted which could not satisfy human reason. The logical sequence of such a creed was a new belief in man and a new estimate of his worth.

In the field of education it was Rousseau who stated the new belief in the worth of man, as Luther had stated it in the field of religion, and this philosophy had an immediate political implication.

Man is too noble a being to be obliged to ... serve simply as an instrument for others, and should not be employed at what he is fit for, without also taking into account what is fit for him; for men are not made for their stations, but their stations for men.[1]

Here was the beginning of a new era in social history, and consequently in education, for, if this were true, then every man had the right to receive the kind of education which would develop in him those powers which were his by natural endowment; consequently no education could be adequate which was not based on the nature of children, and educationalists must therefore begin by studying them, and their attitude must be one of reverence:

'Hold childhood in reverence ... Give nature time to work before you take over her business.'[2]

Before developing character, we must study it.[3]

A prudent tutor will observe his pupil well before he speaks the first word.[4]

1. ROUSSEAU, J. J., *New Héloise*, Vol. 2, MCCALLISTER, *The Growth of Freedom in Education*, pp. 286-7.   2. *Émile*, Bk. 2, p. 71.

3. *Julie*, ARCHER, *Rousseau on Education*, p. 33.

4. *Émile*, ibid, p. 99.

'I wish some trustworthy person would give us a treatise on the art of child-study. This art is well worth studying, but neither parents nor teachers have mastered its elements.'[5]

A child should choose his own occupation; but you should always be at his side, to observe him continually and to watch his movements without his knowing it.[6]

Rousseau emphasizes, as many before him, the need for a sympathetic understanding of the fact that children are different from grown men.

We are unable to put ourselves in the child's place, we fail to enter into his thoughts, we invest him with our own ideas, and while we are following our own chain of reasoning, we merely fill his head with errors and absurdities.[7]

Children are all different, and education must take account of this fact:

Each individual is born with a distinctive temperament which determines his genius and character. . . .[8]

Each mind has a form of its own in accordance with which it must be directed; and for the success of the teacher's efforts it is important that it should be directed in accordance with this form and no other.[9] I cannot too strongly urge the tutor to adapt his instances to the capacity of his scholar.[10] One nature needs wings, another shackles. One has to be flattered, another repressed. One man is made to carry human knowledge to its furthest point, another may find the ability to read a dangerous power.[11]

We must learn to draw out of men all that nature has implanted in them.[12]

Rousseau, more clearly than any of his predecessors, saw that not only are children intrinsically different from adults, but that

'Every age, every station in life, has a perfection, a ripeness, of its

5. ibid, Bk. 3, p. 162.
6. ibid, ARCHER, *Rousseau on Education*, p. 166.
7. ibid, Bk. 3, p. 133.
8. *Julie*, ARCHER, *Rousseau on Education*, p. 29.
9. *Émile*, Bk. 2, BOYD, p. 297.   10. *Émile*, Bk. 3, p. 144.
11. *New Héloise*, BOYD, p. 297.
12. *Julie*, ARCHER, *Rousseau on Éducation*, p. 34.

own. We have often heard the phrase "a grown man"; but we will consider "a grown child".' [13]

What is to be thought therefore, of that cruel education which sacrifices the present to an uncertain future, that burdens a child with all sorts of restrictions and begins by making him miserable, in order to prepare him for some far-off happiness which he may never enjoy? [14]

Nature would have them children before they are men. If we try to invert this order we shall produce a forced fruit immature and flavourless, fruit which will be rotten before it is ripe . . . Childhood has its own ways of seeing, thinking and feeling; nothing is more foolish than to try and substitute our ways. [15]

Why urge him [the child] to the studies of an age he may never reach to the neglect of those studies which meet his present needs? 'But,' you ask, 'will it not be too late to learn what he ought to know when the time comes to use it?' I cannot tell; but this I do know, it is impossible to teach it sooner, for our real teachers are experience and emotion, and man will never learn what befits a man except under its own conditions. A child . . . should remain in complete ignorance of those ideas which are beyond his grasp. My whole book is one continued argument in support of this fundamental principle of education. [16]

Leave childhood to ripen in your children. [17]

We must therefore teach children only what they are ready to learn at the particular stage of development they have reached: We know nothing of childhood; and with our mistaken notions the further we advance the further we go astray. The wisest writers devote themselves to what a man ought to know, without asking what a child is capable of learning. They are always looking for the man in the child, without considering what he is before he becomes a man. [18]

The whole of *Émile* is an attempt to carry out this principle.

The aim of the education given to him – not to make him a scholar and give him knowledge, but to make him wise and good and a lover of truth – echoes the thought of many of Rousseau's wise predecessors:

There will always be time to learn; but there is not a moment to be lost in forming the disposition. . . . There is not the least need

13. *Émile*, Bk. 2, p. 122.   14. ibid, Bk. 2, pp. 42–3.
15. ibid, Bk. 2, p. 54.   16. ibid, Bk. 3, p. 141.
17. ibid, Bk. 2, p. 58.   18. ibid, Preface, p. 1.

for a man to be a scholar, but nothing is more needful for him than to be wise and good.[19]

To live is the profession I would teach him. ... To live is not merely to breathe. ... He has not had most life who has lived most years, but he who has felt life the most.[20]

As a result,

Émile knows little, but what he knows is really his own. ... Among the few things he knows and knows thoroughly this is the most valuable, that there are many things he does not know now but may know some day, many more that other men know but he will never know, and an infinite number which nobody will ever know. He is large-minded, not through knowledge, but through the power of acquiring it; he is open-minded, intelligent, ready for anything, and, as Montaigne says, capable of learning if not learned. I am content if he knows the 'Wherefore' of his actions and the 'Why' of his beliefs. For once more my object is not to supply him with exact knowledge, but the means of getting it when required, to teach him to value it at its true worth, and to love truth above all things.[21]

Émile is industrious, temperate, patient, stedfast, and full of courage ... he is all that a boy can be at his age. He has no errors, or at least only such as are inevitable; he has no vices, or only those from which no man can escape. His body is healthy, his limbs are supple, his mind is accurate and unprejudiced, his heart is free and untroubled by passion. ... Without disturbing the peace of others, he has passed his life contented, happy and free, so far as nature allows. Do you think that the earlier years of a child, who has reached his fifteenth year in this condition, have been wasted? [22]

His ideas are few but precise, he knows nothing by rote but much by experience. If he reads our books worse than other children, he reads far better in the book of nature: his thoughts are not in his tongue, but in his brain.[23]

The book of Nature, first-hand experience, personal discovery – these were to be the means of his education, rather than books and words:

Give your scholar no verbal lesson, he should be taught by experience alone.[24]

19. *Julie*, ARCHER, *Rousseau on Education*, pp. 49–50.
20. *Émile*, Bk. 1, ARCHER, *Rousseau on Education*, pp. 62, 63, 64.
21. *Émile*, Bk. 3, pp. 169–70.   22. ibid, Bk. 3, pp. 170–1.
23. ibid, Bk. 2, p. 124.   24. ibid, Bk. 2, p. 56.

ROUSSEAU 161

Things! Things! I cannot repeat it too often. We lay too much stress upon words; we teachers babble, and our scholars follow our example.[25]

His whole environment is the book from which he unconsciously enriches his memory till his judgment is able to profit by it.[26]

I am never weary of repeating: let all the lessons of young people take the form of doing rather than talking; let them learn nothing from books which they can learn from experience.[27]

Never expect a child to learn anything which he cannot understand. In doing so, we do more serious harm than we know:

Is it a small thing to teach a child to be content with words, to believe that he knows what he cannot even understand? [28]

Let us transform our sensations into ideas, but let us not jump all at once from the objects of sense to objects of thought. The latter are attained by means of the former. Let the senses be the only guide for the first workings of reason. No book but the world, no teaching but that of fact. The child who reads ceases to think, he only reads. He is acquiring words not knowledge.[29]

Rousseau gives a powerful argument in favour of reality and first-hand experience in education:

As a general rule – never substitute the symbol for the thing signified, unless it is impossible to show the thing itself; for the child's attention is so taken up with the symbol that he will forget what it signifies.[30]

What is the use of inscribing on their brains a list of symbols which mean nothing to them? They will learn the symbols when they learn the things signified ... what dangerous prejudices are you implanting when you teach them to accept as knowledge words which have no meaning for them.[31]

What a wealth of interesting objects, towards which the curiosity of our pupil may be directed without ever quitting the real and material relations he can understand, and without permitting the formation of a single idea beyond his grasp! [32]

25. ibid, Bk. 3, p. 143.　26. ibid, Bk. 2, p. 76.　27. ibid, Bk. 4, p. 214.
28. *Julie*, ARCHER, *Rousseau on Education*, p. 49.
29. *Émile*, Bk. 3, p. 131.　　　　30. ibid, Bk. 3, p. 133.
31. ibid, Bk. 2, p. 76.　　　　　32. ibid, Bk. 3, p. 153.

The apparent ease with which children learn is their ruin. You fail to see that this very facility proves that they are not learning. Their shining, polished brain reflects as in a mirror the things you show them, but nothing sinks in. The child remembers the words and the ideas are reflected back.[33] It is a great disadvantage for him to have more words than ideas, and to know how to say more things than he can think.[34]

We are in danger of never finding anything of our own in a memory over-burdened with indigested knowledge.[35]

This method will reveal that children are surprisingly capable of perception and of reasoning when they are asked to exercise these faculties on themselves and their environment:

If you proceed on the plan which I have begun to sketch; . . . if you no longer carry your pupil's thoughts to a distance and make him ceaselessly wander in strange countries, climates, and ages; if, instead of transferring him to the extremities of the earth and even to the skies, you keep his attention fixed on himself and his immediate surroundings; you will then find him capable of perception, of memory, and even of reason.[36]

The child 'judges, forsees, reasons on everything which is directly related to him'.

Education must be based on the experience of the senses, as Vives had pointed out two hundred years before:

Since everything that comes into the human mind enters through the gates of sense, man's first reason is a reason of sense experience. It is this that serves as a foundation for the reason of the intelligence; our first teachers in natural philosophy are our feet, hands, and eyes. To substitute books for them does not teach us to reason, it teaches us to use the reason of others rather than our own; it teaches us to believe much and know little.[37]

The child must learn, therefore, by his own discovery if he is to know for himself:

Put the problems before him and let him solve them himself. Let him know nothing because you have told him, but because he has

33. ibid, Bk. 2, p. 71.
34. ibid, MONROE, *Text Book in the History of Education,* p. 561.
35. ibid, Bk. 3, p. 169.
36. ibid, Bk. 2, ARCHER, *Rousseau on Education,* p. 121.
37. ibid, Bk. 2, p. 90.

learnt it for himself. Let him not be taught science, let him discover it ... why not begin by showing him the real thing, that he may at least know what you are talking about? [38]

During infancy ... a child attends only to those sensations which actually affect his senses with pain or pleasure. His sensations are the raw materials of his ideas. ... He wants to touch and handle everything which he sees: do not check this restlessness; it is a necessary apprenticeship to learning. [39]

The child's natural curiosity will lead him to discover for himself. He has an inborn desire to learn.

The bodily activity, which seeks an outlet for its energies, is succeeded by the mental activity which seeks for knowledge. Children are first restless, then curious; and this curiosity, rightly directed, is the means of development for the age with which we are dealing. [40]

Undoubtedly the notions of things ... acquired for oneself are clearer and much more convincing than those acquired from the teaching of others. [41]

With our foolish and pedantic methods we are always preventing children from learning what they could learn much better by themselves. [42]

Rousseau indicated the importance of motivation:

Do not forget that it is rarely your business to suggest what he [a child] ought to learn; it is for him to want to learn, to seek and to find it. [43]

People make a great fuss about discovering the best way to teach children to read. They invent bureaux and cards, they turn the nursery into a printer's shop. Locke would have them taught to read by means of dice ... There is a better way than any of those, and one which is generally overlooked – it consists in the desire to learn. Arouse this desire in your scholar and have done with your bureaux and your dice – any method will serve.

Present interest, that is the motive power, the only motive power that takes us far and safely ... I will just add a few words which contain a principle of great importance. It is this – What we are in no hurry to get is usually obtained with speed and certainty. I

38. ibid, Bk. 3, p. 131.
39. ibid, Bk. 1, ARCHER, *Rousseau on Education*, pp. 81–2.
40. ibid, Bk. 3, p. 130.   41. ibid, Bk. 3, p. 139.
42. ibid, Bk. 2, p. 42.   43. ibid, Bk. 3, p. 142.

am pretty sure Émile will learn to read and write before he is ten, just because I care very little whether he can do so before he is fifteen.[44]

Let us then reject from our primary studies those branches of knowledge for which man has not a natural taste, and let us limit ourselves to those which instinct leads us to pursue.[45]

No one, however, has yet made sufficiently clear what these instinctive interests are and how they can be harnessed in the service of education. It is one of the tasks of the future to bring this theory fully into practice and clarify its meaning in terms of effort and discipline.

Rousseau understood that learning comes through play. He pointed out again, as others, particularly Locke, had said before him, the effort which children will put into a self-chosen task:

Children generally acquire speedily and certainly whatever they are not pressed to learn.[46]

In all their games, as long as they are quite sure it is only play, they will suffer, without complaint and even with laughter, pains which would not otherwise have been borne without floods of tears.[47]

Nothing, then, must be done by compulsion:

Attention should never be the result of constraint, but of interest or desire . . . whatever happens stop before he is tired, for it matters little what he learns; it does matter that he should do nothing against his will.[48]

It is of his nature to be on the move:

Children are always in motion; quiet and meditation are their aversion; . . . neither their minds nor their bodies can bear constraint.[49]

All restrictions then must be removed. This is the task of the ideal, the negative, education:

44. ibid, Bk. 2, p. 81.
45. ibid, MONROE, *Textbook in the History of Education*, p. 562.
46. *Émile*, Bk. 2, ARCHER, *Rousseau on education*, p. 121.
47. ibid, p. 126.   48. *Émile*, Bk. 3, p. 135.
49. *Julie*, ARCHER, *Rousseau on Education*, p. 28.

The education of the earliest years should be merely negative. It consists, not in teaching virtue or truth, but in preserving the heart from vice and from the spirit of error.[50]

Later educators seem largely to have misunderstood Rousseau's doctrine of a negative education. They did not fully realize how far his philosophy was a reaction against contemporary methods. What he was trying to do was to educate according to the needs and abilities that were characteristic of the child at each stage of his development, rather than to impose upon him some form of training for which his own inner being was not ready; and his 'negative education' was in fact wholly positive.

I call a positive education one that tends to form the mind prematurely, and to instruct the child in the duties that belong to a man. I call a negative education one that tends to perfect the organs that are the instruments of knowledge before giving this knowledge directly; and that endeavours to prepare the way for reason by the proper exercise of the senses. A negative education does not mean a time of idleness, far from it. . . . It disposes the child to take the path that will lead him to truth, when he has reached the age to understand it; and to goodness, when he has acquired the faculty of recognizing and loving it.[51]

It was particularly important to Rousseau that no attempt 'to form the mind prematurely' should be made in the moral and spiritual field. This would be to give children the form without the reality and to postpone, perhaps for ever, their chances of true spiritual growth and understanding:

Exercise the body, the organs, the senses and powers, but keep the soul lying fallow as long as you can.[52] If he learns about it too soon, there is a risk of his never really knowing anything about it.[53]

Moral training in childhood was to be by means of natural consequences, and perhaps one of Rousseau's most original contributions to education which has had far-reaching results consisted in his 'psychology of badness'. Starting from the

50. *Émile*, Bk. 2, p. 57.
51. MONROE, *Textbook in the History of Education*, p. 558.
52. *Émile*, MONROE, *Textbook in the History of Education*, p. 561.
53. ibid, p. 220.

belief that all children are by nature good he maintained that wrong behaviour is the result of wrong training and, even more particularly, of frustration and inferiority. All characters, according to Julie's husband,

are good and healthy in themselves. There are no mistakes ... in nature; all the faults which we impute to innate disposition are the effect of the bad training which it has received. There is no criminal whose tendencies, had they been better directed, would not have produced great virtues.[54]

A child is only naughty because he is weak; make him strong and he will be good; if we could do everything we should never do wrong.[55]

Rousseau is frequently given credit for being the source and fountain head of most of the principles of modern education, whereas, in fact, he was deeply in debt to the past, and the heir of many, whose educational ideals he made his own. Nevertheless his writings gathered together into a significant whole the best thought of past ages, and the appearance of *Émile* made an impact on educational thought and practice of very great moment.

The immediate effect, McCallister says, 'was to stimulate an interest in the *possibility* of freedom'.

Briefly, the contribution of Rousseau to educational thought lay in the following principles:

Education is a process of natural development from within the child, which works by means of the inborn interests and instincts and must be related to needs and characteristics of children at each successive stage of their development. It should be a matter for the present, for life itself, not a preparation for the future, and the material of education should be drawn from the immediate environment, from things rather than books, and in particular, from a study of nature on which the child should work actively himself. Education has a social rather than an intellectual purpose and should enable the child to live in and make his own contribution to society. It is concerned with feeling as well as with intellect.

54. *Julie*, ARCHER, *Rousseau on Education*, p. 29.
55. *Émile*, Bk. 1, p. 33.

Whereas Rousseau's predecessors had concerned themselves with what they believed a child ought to know, he set out to inquire what a child is capable of learning. He was perhaps the first and greatest exponent of a truly child-centred education, based on a belief in the innate goodness of children; and all later efforts to formulate an education related to the psychology of childhood owe him a debt.

*

In the year following the publication of *Émile* appeared La Chalotais's *Essay on National Education*, putting forward a case for the provision of state education. Much of it echoed Rousseau and his predecessors, particularly the Port Royalists:

The principles for instructing children should be those by which nature herself instructs them. Nature is the best of teachers.[56]

Every good method should be based upon the nature of the human mind.

All that should be known is not contained in books ... Man is made for action ... Almost the whole of our philosophy and our education is concerned merely with words; yet it is things themselves that it is important to know. We must return to the material and the actual ... The successful method is to arouse [young people's] curiosity ... to kindle in them a desire for knowledge, and this will never be done by means of abstract studies. ... Choose for them that knowledge ... which is most closely in touch with the normal course of daily life.[57]

Children should know about the world in which they live:

Most young men know neither the world which they inhabit, the earth which nourishes them, the men who supply their needs, the animals which serve them, nor the workmen and citizens whom they employ. They have not even any desire for this kind of knowledge. No advantage is taken of their natural curiosity for the purpose of increasing it.[58]

56. *Essay on National Education*, COMPAYRÉ, p. 347.
57. ibid, CLARK, LA CHALOTAIS, *Essay on National Education*, pp. 69, 70–7.
58. ibid, COMPAYRÉ, p. 347.

Children should be asked to write, not on abstract subjects, but about their own experiences, 'their occupations, their amusements or their troubles'.

The method of education he suggested was, however, a middle way. He mistrusted Rousseau's negative education, where all is left to nature:

If good is not taught him he will of necessity become preoccupied with evil. The mind and heart cannot remain empty.[59]

La Chalotais's practical and less revolutionary suggestions made an appeal to many who were unable to accept Rousseau's extreme views, and they were directly responsible for ensuing reforms.

59. ibid, CLARK, LA CHALOTAIS, *Essay on National Education*, p. 35.

16

William Godwin

A STRONG sympathizer with the French Revolution, William Godwin – the father-in-law of Shelley – whose book, *Political Justice*, earned him the title of philosophical representative of English radicalism, wrote:

> The true object of education . . . is the generation of happiness. . . . Man is a social being. . . . Men should be taught to assist each other. The first object should be to train a man to be happy; the second to train him to be useful, that is to be virtuous. . . .
>
> To make a man virtuous, we must make him wise. . . . The man of genuine virtue, is a man of vigorous comprehension and long views.[1]

One of the first purposes of the educator of young children must be to awaken the mind. The true object of education is

> to teach no one thing in particular, but to provide against the age of five and twenty a mind well regulated, active, and prepared to learn. . . . It is of less importance, generally speaking, that a child should acquire this or that species of knowledge, than that he should acquire habits of intellectual activity. . . . The first lesson of a judicious education is, Learn to think, to discriminate, to remember and to enquire.[2] Whatever will inspire habits of industry and observation, will sufficiently answer this purpose. . . . Study with desire is real activity: without desire it is but the semblance and mockery of activity.[3]

Here he discusses the crucial question of motivation:

> To the attainment of any accomplishment what is principally necessary, is that the accomplishment should be ardently desired. . . . Give but sufficient motive, and you have given every thing.[4]
>
> The only possible method in which I can excite a sensitive being

1. GODWIN, W., *The Enquirer*, Essay 1, Pt. 1, pp. 1–2.
2. ibid, Pt. 1, pp. 5, 6.   3. ibid, Essay IX, Pt. 1, p. 78.
4. ibid Essay I, Pt. 1, p. 3.

to the performance of a voluntary action, is by the exhibition of motive.[5] The first object of a system of instruction, is to give to the pupil a motive to learn. . . .

This plan is calculated entirely to change the face of education.[6]

The pupil would then learn for himself:

Strictly speaking, no such characters are left upon the scene as either preceptor or pupil. The boy, like the man, studies, because he desires it. He proceeds upon a plan of his own invention, or which, by adopting, he has made his own. . . .[7]

There are three considerable advantages which would attend upon this species of education:

First, liberty. Three fourths of the slavery and restraint that are now imposed upon young persons would be annihilated at a stroke.

Secondly, the judgement would be strengthened by continual exercise. Boys would no longer learn their lessons after the manner of parrots. No one would learn without a reason, satisfactory to himself, why he learned. . . .

Thirdly, to study for ourselves is the true method of acquiring habits of activity. The horse that goes round in a mill, and the boy that is anticipated and led by the hand in all his acquirements, are not active.[8]

He gives here the true definition of activity: 'Activity is a mental quality',[9] and shows that, to be active, a child must learn for himself:

'Turn the boy loose in the fields of science,' he advises.

Let him explore the path for himself. Without increasing his difficulties, you may venture to leave him for a moment, and suffer him to ask himself the question before he asks you, or, in other words to ask the question before he receives the information.[10]

The pupil, not the teacher, then must be the leader in education:

According to the received modes of education, the master goes first, and the pupil follows. According to the method here recommended, it is probable that the pupil should go first, and the master

5. ibid, Essay IX, Pt. 1, p. 76.   6. ibid, Pt. 1, pp. 79, 80.
7. ibid, Pt. 1, p. 80.   8. ibid, Pt. 1, pp. 81, 82.
9. ibid, Pt. 1, p. 82.   10. ibid, Pt. 1, p. 82.

follow. If I learn nothing but what I desire to learn, what should hinder me from being my own preceptor? [11]

The pupil should be allowed in some instances to select his own course of reading, for he may know best himself the right time for learning:

There is a principle in the human mind by which a man seems to know his own time, and it will sometimes be much better that he should engage in the perusal of books at the period of his own choice, than at the time that you may recollect to put them in his hands. Man is a creature that loves to act from himself; and actions performed in this way, have infinitely more of sound health and vigour in them, than the actions to which he is prompted by a will foreign to his own.[12]

Whatever each man does for himself, is done well.... He that learns because he desires to learn, will listen to the instructions he receives, and apprehend their meaning.[13]

He must learn through experience. This applies not only to wisdom and knowledge, but, most especially, to morals:

If we would acquire knowledge, we must open our eyes, and contemplate the universe.... There are other ways of attaining wisdom and ability beside the school of adversity, but there is no way of attaining them but through the medium of experience.... We cannot understand books, till we have seen the subjects of which they treat.[14] Morals cannot be effectually taught, but where the topics and occasions of moral conduct afford themselves.[15] The social affections are the chief awakeners of man.[16]

Godwin, like many of his predecessors, understood the importance of early years and the effect of maturity on the ability to learn:

The more inexperienced and immature is the mind of the infant, the greater is its pliability.... Many things that, in the dark and unapprehensive period of youth, are attained with infinite labour, may, by a ripe and judicious understanding, be acquired with an effort inexpressibly inferior.[17]

11. ibid, Pt. 1, p. 79.   12. ibid, Essay XV, Pt. 1, p. 144.
13. *Enquiry Concerning Political Justice*, Bk. VI, ch. 8, p. 669.
14. ibid, Bk. V, ch. 2, pp. 388–9.
15. *The Enquirer*, Essay VII, Pt. 1, p. 63.
16. ibid, Essay VII, Pt. 1, pp. 56–7.   17. ibid, Essay I, Pt. 1, pp. 4, 5.

He was well aware of the differences of ability between children –

What may be the precise degree of difference with respect to capacity that children generally bring into the world with them, is a problem that it is perhaps impossible completely to solve.[18]

– and the consequent need to study children:

How shall I form the mind of a young person unless I am acquainted with it? How shall I superintend his ideas and mould his very soul, if there be a thousand things continually passing there, of which I am ignorant? The first point that a skilful artificer would study, is the power of his tools, and the nature of his materials.[19]

There was nothing in these ideas that was new, but what was novel was the depth of his understanding of the mind and personality of a child, and the relevance of this understanding to education:

The thoughts which a young person specially regards as his personal property, are commonly the very thoughts that he cherishes with the greatest affection. The formal lessons of education pass over without ruffling a fibre of his heart; but his private contemplations cause his heart to leap, and his blood to boil. When he returns to them, he becomes a new creature.[20]

Amongst few educators of his time he realized the essential value of sympathy:

If any man desire to possess himself of the most powerful engine that can be applied to the purposes of education, if he would find the ground upon which he must stand to enable himself to move the whole substance of the mind, he will probably find it in sympathy.[21]

One of the greatest errors of education, is that children are not treated enough like men ... that they are not made to feel their importance and to venerate themselves.[22]

He understood, more clearly perhaps than anyone before him, a child's feeling of inadequacy. He realized that the educator must give him a belief in himself, first of all by praise:

18. ibid, Pt. 1, p. 3.   19. ibid, Essay XIV, Pt. 1, p. 120.
20. ibid, Pt. 1, p. 121.   21. ibid, Pt. 1, p. 124.
22. ibid, Pt. 1, p. 127.

The first thing that gives spring and expansion to the infant learner, is praise. . . . If . . . you would have him eagerly desirous of any attainment, you must thoroughly convince him that it is regarded by you with delight.[23]

There is no more certain source of exultation, than the consciousness that I am of some importance in the world. A child usually feels that he is nobody.

He must be given trust and freedom:

How suddenly does a child rise to an enviable degree of happiness, who feels that he has the honour to be trusted and consulted by his superiors?

But of all the sources of unhappiness to a young person the greatest is a sense of slavery. How grievous the insult, or how contemptible the ignorance, that tells a child that youth is the true season of felicity, when he feels himself checked, controled, and tyrannised over in a thousand ways? [24]

He would therefore take care never to impose knowledge on a pupil, but try to communicate it

without infringing, or with as little as possible violence to, the volition and individual judgment of the person to be instructed.[25]

He is exceedingly critical of what he believes to be Rousseau's hypocritical presentation of liberty. He calls his whole system of education

a series of tricks, a puppet-show exhibition, of which the master holds the wires, and the scholar is never to suspect in what manner they are moved.[26]

Godwin's idea of the relationship between teacher and pupil, in contrast, was to be one of true equality and it is here, perhaps, that he makes his most original and valuable contribution to education. For him, the relationship must be one of respect, even of reverence; an echo of the belief and practice of the Port Royalists:

We should always treat our children with some deference and make them in some degree the confidants of our affairs and our

23. ibid, Essay VII, Pt. 1, pp. 57, 58.
24. ibid, Essay VIII, Pt. 1, pp. 66–7.
25. ibid, Essay IX, Pt. 1, p. 76.
26. ibid, Essay XII, Pt. 1, p. 106.

purposes. We should extract from them some of the benefits of friendship, that they may one day be capable of becoming friends in the utmost extent of the term. We should respect them, that they may respect themselves. We should behold their proceedings with the eyes of men towards men, that they may learn to feel their portion of importance, and regard their actions as the actions of moral and intelligent beings.[27]

There is a reverence that we owe to everything in human shape. . . .

The most fundamental of all the principles of morality is the consideration and deference that man owes to man; nor is the helplessness of childhood by any means unentitled to the benefit of this principle. The neglect of it among mankind at large, is the principal source of all the injustice, the revenge, the bloodshed and the wars, that have so long stained the face of nature.[28]

Here, for the first time, is enunciated that great principle of respect for the child, which was to be developed, with incalculable benefit to children, by Pestalozzi, Froebel, Madame Montessori and the great educators of our own day.

27. ibid, Essay XIII, Pt. 1, p. 118.
28. ibid, Essay X, Pt. 1, pp. 88, 89.

17

David Williams

DAVID WILLIAMS was a practising teacher who had much
to say on the subject of education.

Unlike many of his predecessors he made no claim to having discovered the perfect method, and had no illusions about
the difficulties: 'One of the last and most perfect productions
of the human mind will be a compleat system of education',[1]
he wrote.

'Education is the art of forming children into happy and
useful men', and the way thereto,

if there were but one uniform state of mankind, ... would be to
follow Nature – Nature produces the child; provides for its nourishment; improves its strength, furnishes it with ideas; and forms its
mind, by certain and effectual laws; and these laws are the fundamental principles of education.[2] She wants not our assistance, but
our service.[3]

Education must be active experience:

The body acquires the use of its parts, not by maxims and doctrines, but by trial or experiment; and the mind must obtain the
use of its faculties; the right direction and employment of its passions ... – by repeated trials and experiments, not by doctrines
and commands.... Instructions to the mind should be of the
same kind with those given to the body; and consist of actual
exercises.[4]

True knowledge and judgement can never be obtained from
books. Observation is essential, particularly of nature.

What we learn from reading and commit to memory is very
seldom real knowledge.... Nay, seeing an action performed, though
a nearer step to knowledge than reading of it, yet is not knowledge. A meer student, or a fine gentleman, who has never held a

1. WILLIAMS, DAVID, *A Treatise on Education*, pp. 99–100.
2. ibid, pp. 1–2.   3. ibid, p. 9.
4. *Lectures on Education*, V, pp. 64–5.

plough, or put a spade into the earth, have very imperfect ideas of those actions, though they see them every day.[5]

The memory

should be the repository of things.... A fluctuating credulity is the constant effect of mere reading. A firm and clear knowledge is to be obtained only by observing and copying nature.[6]

Experience is the basis of education.

We have clear and indisputable proofs that our reason and imagination are produced by experience.[7] The business of Education should be, not merely to furnish our memories with arbitrary maxims, but to qualify us for them, by occurrences and incidents.[8]

The only instruction required is that which was understood by the ancients, which we value enough to give to those qualifying for

any inferior occupation or employment.

In that case, we do not furnish maxims, to be committed to memory; – for we see, a good mason or carpenter cannot be formed by rules, on the uses of stone and timber: – we exercise persons, designed for such employments, in their practical branches; and hardly ever fail of accomplishing our purposes.[9]

The primary task of education 'is to stimulate and direct the desire of knowledge', which is a natural instinct in the young.

The general occupation of infancy is to *enquire*; the business of instructors to direct curiosity to proper objects; and to provide for its full and varied gratification. This is the apprenticeship of wisdom.[10]

The usual method of education does not render men

intelligent and virtuous; because children are commanded, not instructed; and obliged to learn maxims, not to acquire information, or practise duties.[11]

His theories are based on his own experience:

I have had occasions to compare the different effects of leading children immediately to books; and of educating them by circum-

5. *A Treatise on Education*, pp. 116–17.
6. ibid, pp. 118–19.
7. *Lectures on Education*, III, p. 44.
8. ibid, IV, pp. 52–3.   9. ibid, IV, p. 53.
10. ibid, IV, p. 55.   11. ibid, V, p. 64.

stances, observation, and facts.[12] I have experienced the effects of the established method. I was educated, according to its severest maxims. I have assisted in the education of youth on the same plan: and its obvious, and invariable error, is to force out purposes prematurely. It is the spring, at its opening; exhibiting the treasures of autumn. Hence the general disappointment in modern education.[13]

'Are we to wait the acquisition of knowledge and virtue', he asks, 'by the experience of young people?'

His reply is: 'There is no other method of producing them.'[14]

There is no need to try any other method, nor to use rewards and punishments:

Fear ... is not an effectual principle of Education.[15]

Bodily punishment is never necessary with children unless they have been injudiciously managed; and then, it would not be used by a wise man, who had time to recourse to inducements.... Wisdom never punishes, because it can adjust; and it corrects errors by removing their causes.[16]

Learning is natural to the child:

If the subject of education was thoroughly understood, and proper people could always be employed in it, punishments and even rewards would be as unnecessary to lead a child to his business as to his food. The disposition to knowledge is as natural to the mind, as the desire of food is to the body.[17]

Attention is natural, and it is the business of education to rouse interest and direct attention:

All the exercises and amusements which a boy could want, might be rendered beneficial to his mind. ... A boy at play is much more intent on his game than he has ever been on his book. We are never inattentive but when we are asleep.[18] There is hardly anything in nature but may be rendered an object of desire to a child by some little management; and when the desire is excited and the instructor humane, the child will exert all its abilities and make every improvement it is capable of.[19]

12. ibid, VI, p. 92.   13. ibid, VII, p. 95.
14. ibid, VII, p. 99.   15. ibid, VII, p. 99.
16. ibid, I, p. 13.
17. *A Treatise on Education,* p. 101.
18. ibid, p. 175.   19. ibid, pp. 230–1.

Here again, is the search after the 'springs of action', innate in every human being.

The art of producing inclinations, and that of directing the attention, are founded on real knowledge of actuating principles in human nature.[20]

If, instead of being forced, children were led into employments and pursuits adapted to their capacities; the various interests engaging them would fill up their time, and divide it into portions, having no intervals of that weary and mischievous idleness to be observed in pupils of common schools. It is probable the name of the person may be lost, who invented the mode of driving hoops in the streets. ... Let it be assigned as a task; and the amusement will disappear, ... and the boy who now overcomes the difficulties of crouds, will be obstructed by the first passenger, and wearied with the slightest exertion. Every pursuit in which we would interest young people, is susceptible of an impulse similar to that which engages the boy to drive his hoop.[21]

He gives an interesting account of his own experiments in teaching a boy through an active education, related to his needs and interests, reminiscent of some of the best work of a modern primary school. A skilled teacher, he was still a learner himself.

My first attempts to lead a child in the path of knowledge, which suited his years ... were made, on a visit to a family. ...

To give the plan its full operation, I resolved to set out with my pupil, in a science, of which I was nearly ignorant. ... I was nearly ignorant of natural history. ...

In the intervals of botanical pursuits, or when confined by the weather, we minutely examined the furniture of the house. ...

It was not difficult to direct his curiosity to the means, by which natural productions were converted into artificial conveniences. He had seen smiths and carpenters; but without ideas of their occupation, or any curiosity respecting them. They became important in his estimation; and he had a solicitude to learn, how they effected the purposes of their arts. ...

The attractions of the blacksmith, made me hasten to stones, earths, and ores, with as little method or knowledge, as I had of botany.[22]

20. *Lectures*, XII, pp. 187–8.   21. ibid, VII, pp. 101–2.
22. ibid, IX, pp. 133, 136–7, 138.

Together they collected iron ore and smelted sufficient to give a clear idea of the production of iron.

This afforded the first ground of an opinion, that chemistry is a science peculiarly suited to children.[23]

He showed he had the teacher's skill of making use of every opportunity, and of using his pupil's own interest and activity rather than imposing on him ideas of his own:

The necessity of marking or distinguishing objects, induced attempts to design and draw. . . . Being a greater proficient in numbers, I availed myself of his desire to class the collections; to compare them with mine; or to barter with me, according to the suggestions of his fancy.[24]

Since the work arose from the child's own interest, he learned rapidly and with ease the basic rules of arithmetic:

The business, arising out of his immediate convenience, the rapidity with which he actually comprehended or converted to his purposes, the four general rules of arithmetic, was beyond any example I have seen in the progress of learning.[25]

The experience was also a lesson to the teacher:

I could not avoid . . . reflecting with wonder on that undefinable faculty, by which I had obeyed the hand of authority; and waded in wretchedness through volumes of arithmetic calculations, without comprehending or annexing an idea of utility, to any of its operations.[26]

As a result of his experience he therefore proposed a school which should be based on active methods of learning

which might unite the general objects of ancient and modern methods. It was my intention, the children should be made acquainted with natural objects, their common relations, and general uses, by actual observation or experiment.[27]

His ideal school was to have the qualities of a family, and the tutor should take the place of a father:

23. ibid, IX, p. 138.   24. ibid, IX, p. 139.
25. ibid, IX, pp. 139–40.   26. ibid, IX, p. 140.
27. ibid, XI, pp. 163–4.

A tutor who cannot raise this affection, whatever his talents or his learning may be, is unfit for education.[28]

The best education would be that of a competent father; and a school is defective and injurious as it departs in its regulations from those of an intelligent and happy family.[29]

Ideally, every man should educate his own children, but few parents are fit for the task, therefore children must be sent to school. In time, however, if these schools are properly run, 'as much like well regulated families ... as it is possible to make them'[30] they may have the eventual effect of making men 'capable of presiding in their families and educating their children; and render schools themselves unnecessary'.[31]

This will never happen in the usual kind of public school, which is an unnatural institution,

where the children are not of the family; but form an unnatural community of themselves: where they are never trained up in those little domestic duties and endearments which are to afford their future happiness, where all the first and most delicate impressions of a social and moral character are never made on them; and they are sent into the world with abundant pedantry about books; but with hearts as unimproved, and manners as offensive, as if they had been brought up in the wilds of America.[32]

The education provided in public schools is entirely wrong and undesirable. 'The finest feelings of our nature have been blunted and checked in childhood.' We are torn from our families,

lodged in those prisons which are called schools, herded together in great numbers, where there can be no idea of relation and friendship, where no family virtues can be exhibited, where everything is sacrificed to silence, order and affectation, where the most amiable parts of God's works are often spoilt and ruined by a cruel pedagogue, or an unfeeling governess.

At best our knowledge consists mostly of prepossessions, instead of being early taught to examine, and led gradually to judge and to discern, we are wholly employed in committing things to memory, and obliged to take every thing on trust. ... We are

28. *A Treatise on Education*, p. 104.
29. ibid, p. 46.   30. ibid, p. 26.
31. ibid, pp. 26–7.   32. ibid, p. 27.

strangely ignorant of that common art of living which might be useful to us every day. We know not the properties of those things which are continually affecting us. We are often unacquainted with the qualities of our common food, and the general means of preserving our health.[33]

In his description of the education of Philo's son, David Williams shows how the desire to read may be roused in a child without any difficulty:

When experience had formed in him ideas of utility; his father would send him home with some fruits of their expedition, and with written messages of kindness to his Amelia. These she read before her boy with proper marks of delight; dropping hints of the advantages of writing; and sending him back with written answers. This was sufficient to raise desire; and this desire was heightened to a degree bordering on impatience, on a little absence of his father.... But what was his delight, when a servant brought a letter similar to that he had been used to convey. ... He was impatient to have it deciphered. Amelia bid him do it himself. He desired to know how; and his first lesson for reading, was from his mother, in his father's letter.[34]

He goes on, in this account, to show the importance of teaching 'at the proper season'.

Philo's son was not taught to read his bible, to learn hymns, or to repeat prayers. He was very sure, that this was the most effectual way to make him disregard, if not dislike them for his whole life. ...[35]
Men begun where they should have ended; and taught their children doctrines of religion, and notions of God. This is the very reason, that religion has had in general so little influence on the morals of the world. It was made a duty and a task when it could not be understood. ... Almost every species of learning has had the same fate with religion, and on the same account; because they have not been taught at the proper season, and have been imposed by mere authority.[36]

Philo's education of his pupil began by first-hand observation of the world around him, and this education led him naturally to an effective use of books:

33. ibid, pp. 187–8.   34. ibid, pp. 228–9.
35. ibid, p. 243.   36. ibid, pp. 242–3.

Philo gradually extended the views of his pupil on the natural surface of the world, and the productions and animals about him, till he thought his understanding might comprehend some very familiar illustrations of the first truths of geography. He gave some reasons for the general opinions which are held of the shape of the world; and its relation to other bodies in the solar system.... He wanted only to make his child avoid the general idea of children that the world is flat and terminated by their horizon. He took pains therefore, to change that horizon, by taking even long journies to prove what he had said.... He taught him the use of the globes and maps; and made him conceive a general idea of the world as divided into continents, seas, kingdoms, and provinces; all furnished with materials of knowledge, in the same manner as the spot they inhabited. ... It was easy therefore, to excite his most ardent curiosity to know everything they contained. Philo told him this was impossible in the way they had begun, as he might easily see by the time they had already spent in their own neighbourhood; and he was capable of forming some judgment of the small proportion of a province or a parish to the surface of the whole globe. Philo, however, encouraged him by letting him know, that some people had always been employed in the same manner with themselves, and committed all their observations to writing. Nothing more was necessary to induce his pupil to go through every book that Philo set before him on natural history.[37]

In his description of the heart of Rousseau's doctrine, which was also his own, he sums up much of the best in modern educational theory:

that in domestic, as in political life, order, harmony, and obedience, ever accompany freedom; that children may be induced to the utmost exertions of body or mind, without tyranny, punishment, or reward; that the great instruments furnished by nature, activity and curiosity, may be directed in extensive and rapid pursuits of natural history, natural philosophy, chemistry, mechanics, arithmetic, or geometry: without obliging the pupils to sit down or commit books to memory.[38]

37. ibid, pp. 247–9.   38. *Lectures*, XII, p. 186.

18

Kant

THE ideal of an education based on the nature of children grew steadily from the time of Rousseau and achieved a new clarity and development in the writings of Immanuel Kant. Davidson called him

the presiding genius of the spiritual life of the nineteenth century, ... the modern Socrates.... He gathered up in himself, and did his best to harmonize, all the forward movements of the three preceding centuries.[1]

His own philosophy took the movements into a fresh field. Davidson continues:

It was no longer [the question of old]. How does the world get into the mind? but, How does it get out of the mind? – no longer, How does the mind appropriate a world already existing? but, How does it build up any world of which it can predicate existence? ... Each man, by his own mental processes, builds up his own world.[2]

Kant was deeply influenced by *Émile*; he is said to have given up his daily afternoon walks in order to read it, but although much of his philosophy reflects the thought of Rousseau, he was far from agreement with him on all points. With Rousseau, he believed in the goodness of man:

The rudiments of evil are not be found in the natural disposition of man. Evil is only the result of nature not being brought under control. In man there are only germs of good.[3]

It is necessary, therefore,

'to ... see to it that men become not only clever, but good'.[4]

1. DAVIDSON, *History of Education*, p. 29.
2. ibid, pp. 29–30.
3. CHURTON, *Kant on Education*, p. 15.
4. ibid, p. 18.

'Early education', in consequence, should be 'only negative'.[5] But it is clear Kant believed that education was to be far from passive:

> There are many germs lying undeveloped in man. It is for us to make these germs grow, by *developing his natural gifts* in their due proportion, and to see that he fulfils his destiny,[6]

and in his development of this theme, Kant took a road which separated him quite fundamentally from the thought of Rousseau. Buchner writes of this development:

> Human actions . . . are the absolute requirements of the supreme law of duty, or conscience. Indeed, it is a 'categorical imperative' which presides over the inner self and its relations of will to other selves. . . . Duty and the moral law are more truly representative of man's nature and the destiny of his earthly career than the intellect and the acquisition of knowledge.[7]

The child must therefore experience restraint, until he is able for himself to guide his own conduct, and the educator is faced with the conflicting claims of freedom and control.

> One of the great problems of education is how to unite submission to the necessary *restraint* with the child's capability of exercising his *freewill* – for restraint is necessary. How am I to develop the sense of freedom in spite of the restraint? I am to accustom my pupil to endure a restraint of his freedom, and at the same time I am to guide him to use his freedom aright. Without this all education is merely mechanical, and the child, when his education is over, will never be able to make a proper use of his freedom.[8] Children are badly educated if their wills are gratified, and quite *falsely* educated if one acts directly contrary to their wills and desires.[9]

'But,' says McCallister,

> even in the restraint and discipline which Kant repeatedly emphasizes there is a clear appreciation of the value of self-activity, a clear enunciation of 'doing' as the best means to 'understanding'. . . . It is not necessary that [children] should know the principles

5. ibid, p. 39.   6. ibid, p. 9.
7. *The Educational Theory of Immanuel Kant*, BUCHNER, pp. 31–2.
8. *Kant on Education*, p. 27.   9. BUCHNER, p. 54.

underlying every part of their education, but 'on the whole we
should try to draw out their own ideas, founded on reason, rather
than introduce ideas into their minds'. ... Although Kant ultimately finds freedom in obedience to law, ... he very definitely
urges ... that children should learn to act according to 'maxims',
the reasonableness of which a child is able to see for himself. ... He
recognizes the problem of the 'fickle' will and wishes to set it free
through a training which reinforces and strengthens its deepest
aspirations.[10]

Education, far from being passive, must teach children to
think, and the aim was to be the development of character
and morality. Buchner writes:

It is morality alone which gives *meaning* to man, and at the same
time puts an *end* into educational thought and effort,[11] and Kant
says: Parents are in the habit of looking out for the inclinations,
for the talents and dexterity, perhaps for the disposition of their
children, and not at all for their heart or character.[12]

and the use of rewards and punishments should be considered
carefully in regard to their effect upon character:

If you punish a child for being naughty, and reward him for
being good, he will do right merely for the sake of the reward.[13]

Kant emphasizes repeatedly the distinction between memory
and understanding. True understanding must be based on experience:

The understanding is first developed by arriving, through experience, at intuitive judgments, and, through these, at concepts. ...
A teacher is expected to make of his hearer first an *intelligent*, then
a *reasonable,* and finally a *learned* man. ... If this method is re-
versed, the pupil snaps up a kind of reason before his understanding
is developed, and he wears borrowed science, which is only, as it
were, stuck on to him, and not grown on, whereby his mental
ability remains as unfruitful as ever, and at the same time has become much more corrupt by the illusion of wisdom. ... In short,

10. MCCALLISTER, *The Growth of Freedom in Education,* pp. 273–4.
11. BUCHNER, p. 69.   12. ibid, p. 228.
13. *Kant on Education,* p. 84.

he is to learn, not *thoughts*, but thinking; he is to be *guided*, not *carried*, if he is to be able to *walk* alone in the future.[14]

'Self-activity,' says Buchner, 'has never received a greater vindication' than in the *Critique of Pure Reason*. 'Instruction,' he writes, 'is seen to be more and more an affair of inner experience and less and less an affair of objects and so-called "content".' [15]

Kant believes firmly in the ability of children to teach themselves:

It would be better ... if children were allowed to learn more things by themselves. They would then learn them more thoroughly.[16]

The best way of cultivating the mental faculties is to *do ourselves* all that we wish to accomplish. ... The best way to understand is to do. That which we learn most thoroughly, and remember the best, is what we have in a way taught ourselves.[17]

Teaching should be adapted to the stage of development the child has reached:

Children should only be taught those things which are suited to their age.[18]

He suggested that learning should come through play,

His interest being absorbed in these plays, the boy denies himself other needs, and thus learns gradually to impose other and greater privations upon himself. At the same time he becomes accustomed to continuous occupation.[19]

but he had little understanding of play as a means of education as it is today understood. His ideas of children's first experience of school was 'that they may become used to sitting doing exactly as they are told'.[20] It is only later, after the child has learned 'positive obedience' that he is 'permitted to make use of his powers of reflection and of his freedom, but under laws'.[21]

14. *Announcement of the Arrangement of his Lectures for the Winter Semester*, 1765–6, Hartenstein, ii, pp. 313–16, BUCHNER, pp. 263–4.

15. BUCHNER, pp. 38, 39.   16. *Kant on Education*, p. 42.

17. ibid, p. 80.   18. ibid, p. 93.

19. BUCHNER, p. 162.   20. *Kant on Education*, p. 3.

21. BUCHNER, p. 130.

Education, in order to be effective, must become a science, based, like other sciences, on experiment and hence, on principles:

Experimental schools must first be established before we can establish *normal schools*. Education and instruction must not be merely mechanical; they must be founded upon fixed principles.[22]

22. *Kant on Education*, pp. 21-2.

19

Pestalozzi

WITH Pestalozzi the educational picture is projected on to a wider screen than ever before, with a depth of colour and reality previously unknown.

There is no doubt that he was deeply influenced by Rousseau. He writes:

My own visionary tendencies were stimulated to a pitch of extraordinary enthusiasm when I read that dream book of his. I compared the education which I had received at home and at school with that which Rousseau demanded for Émile, and I felt how wretchedly inadequate it all had been.[1]

More than any educator before him, Pestalozzi had observed children, and what he believed was the result of what he had tried out in practice. He had a remarkable understanding of the reasons for children's behaviour, particularly when that behaviour was unsatisfactory:

Man of himself is good, and desires to be good; ... if he happens to be evil, surely it is because the road by which he sought to do good was blocked. . . . Many who rave and rant do so only because their love has been scorned and their faith mocked.[2]

This faith in the innate goodness of man, and in love as the vital force in education, underlay and permeated his entire theory and practice:

Whatever is good, whatever is holy and ennobling, whatever tends to promote harmonious perfection in man, springs from a central force which regulates, guides, inspires, and sets limits to, these things in accordance with a lofty ideal of man's inner sanctity.[3]

1. PESTALOZZI, *Swan Song*, Werke (Seyffarth), XIV, 200, BOYD, p. 319.

2. *Aphorisms*, p. 7.   3. 4th Letter, GREEN, p. 160.

Teaching, by itself and in itself, does not make for love, any more than it makes for hatred. That is why teaching is by no means the essence of education. It is love that is its essence. . . .[4]

Without love, neither the physical nor the intellectual powers of the child will develop naturally.[5]

Education must always be a matter of the heart, not of the head:

The first instruction of the child should never be the business of the *head* or of the *reason*; it should always be the business of the senses, of the *heart*, of the *mother*.[6]

Learning is not worth a penny when courage and joy are lost along the way.[7]

Feelings are of fundamental importance:

All that men have done, all progress in civilization, is an outcome of feeling, of action, and of the stimuli to both.[8]

The ideal setting for education is the home:

Home is the great school of character and of citizenship,[9]

but

if the child does not enjoy parental care, the conception of parenthood must still find a place in his education.[10]

Where love, and the capacity for love are present in the domestic circle, one might say beforehand that no form of education can fail to succeed. The child must become good.[11]

The lack of such love is the basic cause of backwardness, delinquency and maladjustment, a truth well confirmed by modern psychology.

One might well-nigh affirm that, whenever a child does not seem to be kind, vigorous and active, it is because his capacity for love has not found that succour and guidance at home which it should.[12]

The only motives to be used are those which will touch the heart:

4. *Aphorisms*, p. 33. 5. ibid, p. 33.
6. *How Gertrude Teaches Her Children*, p. 189.
7. *Aphorisms*, p. 33. 8. 4th Letter, GREEN, p. 160.
9. *Ephemerides*, GREEN, p. 23. 10. 5th Letter, GREEN, p. 162.
11 ibid, p. 163. 12. ibid, p. 163.

Motives like fear or inordinate ambition may stimulate to exertion, . . . but they cannot warm the heart. . . . Such motives are inadequate in their source and inefficient in their application, for they are nothing to the heart and 'out of the heart are the issues of life'.[13]

In his own school Pestalozzi carried this principle into practice, so that a visitor remarked, 'It is not a school that you have here, but a family.'

He had the highest possible estimate of those who were to carry out the business of educating children:

No profession on earth calls for a deeper understanding of human nature, nor for greater skill in guiding it properly.[14]

If the schoolmaster is a man with the spirit of love, of wisdom, of purity; a man who is fitted for his calling, and who enjoys the confidence of young and old; a man who esteems love, order and self-control as higher and more desirable than actual knowledge and learning; a man who, with penetrating foresight, perceives what sort of man or woman the child is likely to develop into, and guides his school-days with that end in view, he will become in the true sense of the word a father to the village.[15]

The aim of education, for Pestalozzi, was the development of the whole person, not in isolation, but in its place in the 'great chain that binds humanity together':

Education is nothing more than the polishing of each single link in the great chain that binds humanity together and gives it unity. The failings of education and human conduct spring as a rule from our disengaging a single link and giving it special treatment as though it were a unit in itself, rather than a part of the chain.[16]

The development of the whole person requires an education which is concerned with all sides of man's nature, the creative powers, the feelings and manual abilities, as well as intellect and morality:

Only that which affects man as an indissoluble unit is educative. . . . It must reach his hand and his heart as well as his head. . . .

13. *Letters to Greaves*, XXXIII, GREEN, p. 264.
14. *Aphorisms*, p. 33.
15. Appendix III, GREEN, pp. 181–2.
16. *Aphorisms*, p. 32.

It is as wrong to think only of morality and religion as it is to have the intellect solely in mind.[17] Specialized development of one side of human nature is unnatural and false. . . . Education worth the name necessarily strives after the perfection of man's powers in their completeness.[18]

Here again is the specific demand for an education which will be balanced and complete, neglecting no part of man's nature, nor ignoring any of his capacities.

The equilibrium of the capacities, which is the key-note of our idea of an Elementary Method, demands the full development of all man's fundamental powers.[19]

The result is to be a harmony of the whole personality, and to this end, knowledge and the development of learning must be kept in proper proportion to the other capacities:

The instruction of the young must in every aspect be directed more toward developing their abilities than toward the enrichment of their knowledge.[20]

This complete education can only be achieved by a gradual process which works in step with a child's unfolding capacities and abilities, and this ideal he put into practice at the Institute at Burgdorf by means of the method, psychologically correct, which makes a child proceed from his own intuition, and leads him by degrees, and through his own efforts, to abstract ideas.

Nature has enclosed man's higher aptitudes as in a shell; if you break the shell before it opens on its own, you will find only a budding pearl. You will have destroyed the treasure you should have preserved for your child.[21]

We cannot put powers to practical use until they are developed:

Parents should not hurry their children into working at things remote from their immediate interests. Let them first attain the strength that comes from dealing efficiently with matters near at hand. . . . By anticipating the ordinary course, they diminish the

17. *Swan Song*, GREEN, pp. 268–9.
18. ibid, p. 269.   19. ibid.
20. *Aphorisms*, p. 35.   21. ibid, p. 34.

powers of their children, and disturb profoundly the equilibrium of their nature. This is what happens when teachers hurry children into lessons that are concerned chiefly with words, before they have passed through the discipline of actual encounter with real things. ...[22]

To arrive at knowledge slowly, by one's own experience, is better than to learn by rote, in a hurry, facts that other people know; and then, glutted with words, to lose one's own free, observant and inquisitive ability to study.[23]

Interest, then, is to be the starting-point of all learning, and it is the teacher's responsibility to see that it is roused:

This *interest* in study is the first thing which a teacher ... should endeavour to excite and keep alive. There are scarcely any circumstances in which a want of application in children does not proceed from a want of interest; and there are, perhaps, none under which a want of interest does not originate in the mode of treating adopted by the teacher. I would go so far as to lay it down for a rule, that whenever children are inattentive, and apparently take no interest in a lesson, the teacher should always first look to himself for the reason.[24]

This generalization, although sweeping, nevertheless drew attention for the first time to an important principle:

As long as teachers will not ... inspire their pupils with a living interest in their studies they must not complain of the want of attention.[25]

Pestalozzi suggests that the best means to prevent idleness

is to adopt a better mode of instruction, by which the children are less left to themselves, less thrown upon the unwelcome employment of passive listening, less harshly treated for little and excusable failings – but more roused by questions, animated by illustrations, interested and won by kindness.[26]

Once roused, interest must lead, as it naturally does, to observation. Life, not books, was to be the great teacher:

22. *Ephemerides,* GREEN, p. 19.   23. *Aphorisms*, p. 35.
24. *Letters to Greaves,* XXX, GREEN, p. 253.
25. ibid, p. 254.   26. ibid, p. 254.

The infant mind should be acted upon by illustrations taken from reality ... we ought to teach by *things* more than by *words*.[27]

Not art, not books, but life itself is the true basis of teaching and education.

Life shapes us and the life that shapes us is not a matter of words but action.... A man learns by action ... have done with words![28]

It is an old saying, and a very true one, that our attention is much more forcibly attracted, and more permanently fixed, by objects which have been brought before our eyes, than by others of which we have merely gathered some notion from hearsay and description.[29]

Whenever we put empty words into a child's mind; and impress them upon his memory, as if they were real knowledge, ... we are ... deviating from the principle, 'Life teaches'.... We are sowing the seeds of callous insincerity and shallowness.[30]

Pestalozzi makes repeated pleas for an education concerned with things and not merely words:

A man who has only word wisdom is less susceptible to truth than a savage. This use of mere words produces men who believe they have reached the goal, because their whole life has been spent in talking about it, but who never ran toward it, because no motive impelled them to make the effort; hence I come to the conviction that the fundamental error – the blind use of words in matters of instruction – must be extirpated before it is possible to resuscitate life with truth.[31]

It is not what children learn, but what they become, that is of prime importance. Pestalozzi makes Gertrude, his ideal peasant mother, say to a schoolmaster:

You should do for the children what their parents fail to do for them. The reading, writing and arithmetic are not after all, what they most need. It is all well and good for them to learn something, but the really important thing for them is to *be* something.[32]

27. ibid, XXXI, GREEN, p. 258.
28. *Aphorisms*, pp. 36, 37.
29. *Letters to Greaves*, XXVIII, GREEN, p. 248.
30. *Swan Song*, GREEN, p. 293.
31. *How Gertrude Teaches Her Children*, MONROE, *Textbook in the History of Education*, p. 616.
32. *How Gertrude Teaches Her Children*, QUICK, p. 307.

Again and again Pestalozzi warns of the dangers of what
he calls 'the artificial methods of the school which prefers the
order of words to the free though slow sequence of Nature.'
These 'may make men superficially brilliant, hiding in this
way their want of native powers,' a process reminiscent of what
A. S. Neill called 'Macdonaldization', and one which has not yet
passed out of our schools.

Pestalozzi says that it was the children who taught him this
great principle of the value of observation of real things:

> I learned from them ... to know the natural relation in which real
> knowledge stands to book knowledge. I learnt from them what
> a disadvantage this one-sided letter-knowledge and entire reliance
> on words ... must be. I saw what a hindrance this may be to the
> real power of observation ... and the firm conception of the
> objects that surround us.[33]

Observation of nature is especially important:

> Any child who has learned to look carefully at water at rest
> and in motion, or in its various forms – dew, rain, mist, steam,
> hail, snow, etc. – and then again has learned to observe its various
> effects on other bodies, and can express himself with clearness con-
> cerning them, has already got the foundations of the physicist's way
> of looking at things. Similarly, the boy who is familiar with such
> phenomena as the solution of salt and sugar, and its recovery by
> evaporation and crystallization, fermentation, the conversion of
> marble into chalk, and of flint into glass, is as well prepared for
> the scientific investigation of these things as the country lad who
> knows thoroughly a few cottages, and can describe them in detail.[34]

Pestalozzi, in his uncompromising statement of what he
believed, sketched with firmer hand than any before him the
chief outlines of the great fresco of education, traced and re-
traced, by all later artists, and still awaiting completion:

> The child learns – that is, develops mentally, through his own
> activities, and only through impressions, experiences, not through
> words.[35]

33. ibid, pp. 18–19.
34. *Swan Song*, GREEN, pp. 316–17.
35. MONROE, *Textbook in the History of Education*, p. 618.

Education is to begin with the concrete, with a child's immediate surroundings:

> The range of knowledge through which man is blessed in his station is narrow, and it is in the beginning narrower still, centred entirely about himself and his immediate neighbourhood.[36]

In the school at Yverdun the first elements of geography were taught on the spot and the children made models of their own valley. Gertrude taught her children arithmetic by helping them to know the difference between 'long' and 'short', 'narrow' and 'wide', 'round' and 'angular', and by making them count the steps across the room and the number of panes in the window.

> How would you make the child understand that two and two make four unless you show it to him first in reality? To begin by abstract notions is absurd and detrimental.[37]

This method, put into practice, had excellent results. It is amusing to see how little the policy of the opposition has changed in a hundred and fifty years:

> It has been objected that children who had been used to a constant and palpable exemplification of the units, by which they were enabled to execute the solution of arithmetical questions, would never be able afterwards to follow the problems of calculations in the abstract, their balls, or other representatives, being taken from them.
>
> Now, experience has shown that those very children, who had acquired the first elements in the concrete and familiar method described, had two great advantages over others. First, they were perfectly aware, not only what they were doing, but also of the reason why. They were acquainted with the principle on which the solution depended; they were not merely following a formula by rote; the state of the question changed, they were not puzzled, as those are who only see as far as their mechanical rule goes, and not farther.[38]

These children

> displayed great skill in *head calculation*. . . . Without repairing to their slate or paper, . . . they not only performed operations with

36. *Ephemerides*, GREEN, p. 20.
37. *Letters to Greaves*, GREEN, p. 256.   38. ibid, p. 257.

large numbers, but they arranged and solved questions which at first might have appeared involved, even had the assistance of memoranda or working on paper been allowed.

Of the numerous travellers . . . who did me the honour to visit my establishment, there was none . . . who did not express his astonishment at the perfect ease, and the quickness, with which arithmetical problems . . . were solved.[39]

Pestalozzi was clearly concerned, not merely with producing the ability to calculate, but with developing an understanding of the true meaning of mathematics, an inner truth of understanding, the importance of which is only beginning in our own day to be fully appreciated.

When . . . we just learn by heart 'three and four make seven', and then build upon this seven, as if we really knew that three and four make seven, we deceive ourselves, for the inner truth of seven is not in us, for we are not conscious of the meaning behind it, which alone can make an empty word a truth for us.[40]

The same approach is as true of reading as of arithmetic:

The child must learn to *talk* before he can be reasonably taught to read

and he

must be brought to a high degree of knowledge, both of things seen and words, before it is reasonable to teach him to spell or read.[41]

How wrong is the usual way of beginning:

We leave children up to their fifth year in the full enjoyment of nature; we let every impression of nature work upon them; . . . they already know full well the joy of unrestrained liberty and all its charms. . . . And after they have enjoyed this happiness of sensuous life for five whole years, we make all nature round them vanish before their eyes; tyrannically stop the delightful course of their unrestrained freedom, pen them up like sheep, whole flocks huddled together, in stinking rooms; pitilessly chain them for hours, days, weeks, months, years, to the contemplation of unattractive and

39. ibid, p. 257.
40. *How Gertrude Teaches Her Children*, pp. 133–4.
41. ibid, pp. 26, 36.

monotonous letters (and, contrasted with their former condition) to
a maddening course of life.[42]

Right beginnings are of the utmost importance. Pestalozzi says
that the ignorance of the children

made me stay long over the beginnings; and this led me to
realize the high degree of inner power to be obtained by perfecting
the first beginnings.[43]

By investigating the early history of the child, he

was soon convinced that the first hour of its teaching is the hour
of its birth. From the moment in which his mind can receive impressions from Nature, Nature teaches him.[44]

All later instruction, then, must be on the same lines, a
following of nature:

All instruction of man is then only the Art of helping Nature to
develop in her own way.[45]

This is the way of wisdom, for nature can be trusted to lead
us aright:

Nature only does us good; she alone leads us uncorrupted and
unshaken to truth and wisdom.[46]

It is not the educator who puts new powers and faculties into man
and imparts to him breath and life. He only takes care that no
untoward influence shall disturb nature's march of development.[47]

This faith is well placed, for it is founded on the ancient
belief that growth is from within, that the soul contains within
itself all that is needed for its full and perfect development, as
the seed contains in itself the future tree:

Sound education stands before me symbolized by a tree planted
near fertilizing waters. A little seed, which contains the design of
the tree, its form and its properties, is placed in the soil. The whole
tree is an uninterrupted chain of organic parts, the plan of which
existed in its seed and its root. Man is similar to the tree. In the

42. ibid, p. 28.   43. ibid, p. 17.   44. ibid, p. 25.
45. ibid, p. 26.   46. ibid, p. 31.
47. MONROE, *Textbook in the History of Education*, p. 612.

new-born child are hidden those faculties which are to unfold during life.[48]

The teacher therefore must make a two-fold study: of the child and of his environment:

The man ... who looks upon conduct as the fruit ripening upon the tree, whose aim it is to bring the inner life of his child to perfection; the man who desires to make of his child that which ... it can and ought to become, must first of all ask himself: 'What is there firstly in the child himself, and secondly in the environment and conditions which are forced upon him, which Nature herself employs in the education of mankind, from which we may learn the principles of education?' [49]

Everything which tends to make the body and the soul of the child thrive has its source in the care of the parents. Its inner sources is in the child himself.[50]

The educator, then, is like a gardener, whose task it is to tend his plants. The plants grow of themselves:

But what is the true type of education? It is like the art of the gardener under whose care a thousand trees blossom and grow. He contributes nothing to their actual growth; the principle of growth lies in the trees themselves. He plants and waters, but God gives the increase; It is not the gardener who opens the roots of the trees ... who divides the pith from the wood and the wood from the bark, and thus helps forward the development of the separate parts.... Of all this he does nothing; he only waters the dry earth that the roots may not strike it as a stone. He only drains away the standing water that the tree may not suffer. He only watches that no external force should injure the roots, the trunk, or the branches, of the tree.... So with the educator: he imparts no single power to men. He gives neither life nor breath. He only watches lest any external force should injure or disturb. He takes care that development runs its course in accordance with its own laws.[51]

Whatever man therefore may attempt to do by his tuition, he

48. Birthday Address, 1818, MONROE, *Textbook in the History of Education*, pp. 611–12.
49. 4th Letter, GREEN, p. 160.
50. 5th Letter, GREEN, p. 162.
51. *Address to my House*, 1818, GREEN, p. 195.

can do no more than assist in the effort which the child makes for his own development.[52]

The care of the gardener is far from being passive however:

It is good to make a child read, and write, and learn, and repeat – but it is still better to make a child think. . . . The mode of doing this is not by any means to talk much *to* a child, but to enter into conversation *with* a child; not to address to him many words, . . . but to bring him to express himself on the subject; not to exhaust the subject, but to question the child about it, and to let him find out, and correct the answers.[53]

Pestalozzi expresses clearly what is now accepted, if not acted upon, as an educational truth: that education can force nothing into children, but only draw out what is already there.

I tried to drive where no driving was possible; where it was only possible to invite into a vehicle, which had its own power of going in itself; (or rather, I tried to force in, where it is only possible to bring out from within the child, that which lies in him, and is only to be stimulated within him, and cannot be put in him).[54]

This was not theory. It was put into practice and it succeeded, as anyone who has tried knows that it does succeed.

At Stanz, Pestalozzi's school for orphans on the shores of Lake Lucerne, it

quickly developed in the children a consciousness of hitherto unknown power. They felt their own power, and the tediousness of the ordinary school tone vanished like a ghost. They wished, – tried, – persevered, – succeeded, and they laughed. Their tone was not that of learners, it was the tone of unknown powers roused from sleep.[55]

Pestalozzi was no mere idealist, but a practical schoolmaster, with no illusions about children. He was well aware of the weakness of human nature and consequently of the need to train the will. Freedom for him was never to become licence. A man is truly free only when he is not the slave of his own passions:

52. MONROE, *Textbook in the History of Education*, p. 611.
53. *Letters to Greaves*, XXIX, GREEN, pp. 249, 252.
54. *How Gertrude Teaches Her Children*, p. 31.
55. ibid, p. 17.

The tree is subject to the influences of inanimate Nature, against which its vital powers can offer no resistance, whereas the higher spirit which dwells in man is free to allow his sensory nature and sensory environment to bring about his ruin, or to work against and overcome them. . . . Through the voice of conscience all men hear God's message concerning what is good and what is evil. . . . They can hear this voice of God within them and continue to be free. They can also shut out that voice. . . . They can deny freedom to their own will, and become the slave of sensuous and worldly pleasures.[56]

He speaks of

the duty of educating the will through faith and love to self-sacrificing devotion to the cause of truth and right.[57]

A child must very early in life be taught a lesson which frequently comes too late, and is then a most painful one – that exertion is indispensable for the attainment of knowledge.[58]

Morality, like everything else, is to be learned not by theory but through practice; and the right moral attitudes have their root in the relationships of earliest childhood:

Take care to teach children to think, feel, and act rightly, . . . before we drill the subjects of . . . theology . . . into their memories. . . .[59]

The most sensible parents, and the ones who do best in bringing up their children, are those who make the least use of those well-worn pedagogical phrases, 'Be good, be obedient, be industrious!' They stimulate the child's obedience without talking much about it; they touch his heart without telling him 'be merciful'; they get him to work without saying 'work brings bread'; they make him love his parents without having to say 'you should' or 'you must'.[60]

The children's moral sense must first be aroused by their feelings being made active and pure; then they must be exercised in self-control . . . finally they must be brought to form for themselves . . . a just notion of the moral rights and duties which are theirs by reason of their position and surroundings.[61]

56. *Address to my House*, 1818, GREEN, p. 191.
57. ibid, p. 198.
58. *Letters to Greaves*, XXX, GREEN, p. 253.
59. *How Gertrude Teaches Her Children*, pp. 50–1.
60. *Aphorisms*, p. 27.
61. QUICK, *Educational Reformers*, p. 329.

Pestalozzi's influence is clearly to be seen in all that is best in modern education: his attitude to children, his plea for a balanced development of all sides of the child, his belief that education of the right kind is attainable by everyone, all these have become part of accepted educational thought. From his time, educators began to think seriously of the child as the centre of education, and the process of education as inextricably interwoven with his natural development.

His demand that 'education must be raised to the level of a science which must spring from, and be based upon, the deepest possible knowledge of human nature'[62] is gradually being fulfilled in our day, while the twentieth-century attitude towards children undoubtedly owes much to Pestalozzi's reverence for personality and to his deep humanity.

Through this great practical teacher, education shook itself free from tradition and the hold of the theorists, and stepped out into the realm of experiment and practice. Most of the best of educational theory was being put into practice in his schools over a hundred and fifty years ago, and it is possibly true that few major or fundamental advances have been made since his time. From then on, however, the way was open as never before for educators to find a way for the schools, more nearly related to the needs and spontaneous development of children, a way which in the latter half of the twentieth century still waits to be thoroughly explored.

62. *Address to my House*, 1818, GREEN, p. 198.

20

The Eighteenth Century · R. L. and Maria Edgeworth

THE eighteenth century saw the beginning of a new era. The discovery of the power of steam altered the economic and social life of nations. New ideas of the rights of man sowed the seeds of the ideal of democratic government, while the enthronement of reason led to the temporary overthrow of authority in the form of traditional religion, and a new belief in the right of the individual to think for himself.

As the bright hopes of the dawn of a new social order faded, after the French Revolution and its aftermath had shown human reason to be insufficient, reaction set in in all fields of human activity, including education. But the reaction was not complete. The ideal of freedom could not be forgotten, and the century which followed was a time of conflict between opposing beliefs and antagonistic claims. Out of the struggle emerged the great educational thinkers of the nineteenth century, notably Herbart and Froebel, whose influence was to turn the tide decisively in the direction of freedom.

Before their time, however, there were others whose names are less famous, whose vision was as clear, and who not only expressed their philosophy in simpler terms, but achieved remarkable success in putting it into practice.

In the first days of the nineteenth century there appeared a book, curiously neglected by historians of education, which in clarity and simplicity sets forth the main principles of modern educational thought and practice. Written by a practising schoolmaster, R. L. Edgeworth, and his daughter, Maria, it has much to offer to the schools of today.

In schools for young children

the first object should not be to teach them reading, or grammar, or Latin, or arithmetic, ... but gradually to give them the desire to learn, and the power to attend.... Most of what they learn should be first taught by conversation; and even their walks and hours of amusement may be usefully employed. Their masters should take them out into the fields; should let them run, and leap, and exercise their limbs, and make observations on the various objects they meet ... they must be taught to think.... Instead of pressing forward the pupils to astonish parents by the rapidity of their progress, masters should patiently and courageously conquer by delay. They should make the children understand, as much as possible, the reason of all they do.[1]

The theories of the Edgeworths were founded on first-hand observation of children. Records of children's conversation were kept by the second Mrs Edgeworth, and continued by Maria and her father, providing for the first time a basis for understanding children's ways of thinking.

Many of the principles in *Practical Education* anticipate Froebel, notably in the presentation of the value of play and of discovery as the means of education. Young people

require to have things which continually exercise their senses or their imagination, their imitative and inventive powers.... A boy, who has the use of his limbs, and whose mind is untainted with prejudice, would in all probability prefer a substantial cart, in which he would carry weeds, earth, and stones, up and down hill, to the finest frail coach and six that ever came out of a toy-shop: for what could he do with a coach, after having admired, and sucked the paint, but drag it cautiously along the carpet of a drawing-room, watching the wheels, which will not turn, and seeming to sympathise with the just terrors of the lady and gentleman within, who appear certain of being overturned every five minutes. When he is tired of this, perhaps, he may set about to unharness horses which were never meant to be unharnessed; or to comb their woollen manes and tails, which usually come off during the operation.

That such toys are frail and useless, may, however, be considered as evils comparatively small: as long as the child has sense and courage to destroy his toys, there is no great harm done; but, in general, he is taught to set a value upon them totally independent of all ideas of utility, or of any regard to his own real feelings. Either he is conjured to take particular care of them, because they cost a great deal of money; or else he is taught to admire them as miniatures of some of the fine things on which fine people pride themselves. Instead of attending to his own sensations, and learning from his own experience, he acquires the habit of estimating his

1. EDGEWORTH, R. L., *Essays on Professional Education*, pp. 40–41.

pleasures by the taste and judgement of those who happen to be near him.

'I liked the cart the best,' says the boy, 'but mamma and every body said that the coach was the prettiest; so I chose the coach.' — Shall we wonder if the same principle afterwards governs him in the choice of 'the toys of age'.[2]

The right kind of toys can lead children to thought and reflection:

It is surprising how much children may learn from playthings when they are judiciously chosen, and when the habit of reflection and observation is associated with the ideas of amusement and happiness. A little boy of nine years old, who had had a hoop to play with, asked,

'why a hoop, or a plate, if rolled upon its edge, keeps up as long as it rolls, but falls as soon as it stops, and will not stand if you try to make it stand still upon its edge.' Was not the boy's understanding as well employed whilst he was thinking of this phenomenon, which he observed while he was beating his hoop, as it could possibly have been by the most learned preceptor?[3]

Another boy, also of nine years old,

was standing without any book in his hand, and seemingly idle; he was amusing himself with looking at what he called a rainbow on the floor: he begged his sister M-- to look at it; then he said he wondered what could make it; how it came there. The sun shone bright through the window; the boy moved several things in the room, so as to place them sometimes between the light and the colours which he saw up on the floor, and sometimes in a corner of the room where the sun did not shine. As he moved the things he said, 'This is not it;' 'Nor this;' 'This hasn't anything to do with it.' At last he found, that when he moved a tumbler of water out of the place where it stood, his rainbow vanished.[4]

There were violets in the tumbler, which he thought might be the cause of the colours which he saw on the floor.

He took the violets out of the water; the colours remained upon the floor. He then thought that 'it might be the water'. He emptied the glass; the colours remained, but they were fainter.[5]

2. *Practical Education*, Vol. 1, pp. 2–3.
3. ibid, Vol. 1, pp. 23–4.   4. ibid, Vol. 1, p. 70.
5. ibid, Vol. 1, pp. 70–71.

The boy then saw that it was the water and the glass together that made the rainbow.

'But,' said he, 'there is no glass in the sky, yet there is a rainbow, so that I think the water alone would do, if we could but hold it together without the glass. Oh, I know how I can manage!' He poured the water slowly out of the glass into a bason, which he placed where the sun shone, and he saw the colours on the floor twinkling behind the water as it fell; this delighted him much; but he asked why it would not do when the sun did not shine. The sun went behind a cloud whilst he was trying his experiments: 'There was light,' said he, 'though there was no sunshine.' He then said that he thought the different thickness of the glass was the cause of the variety of colours: afterwards he said he thought that the clearness or muddiness of the different drops of water was the cause of the different colours.[6]

When a pedantic schoolmaster sees a boy eagerly watching a paper kite, he observes, 'What a pity it is that children cannot be made to mind their grammar as well as their kites!' and he adds perhaps some peevish ejaculation on the natural idleness of boys, and that pernicious love of play against which he is doomed to wage perpetual war. A man of sense will see the same sight with a different eye; in this *pernicious* love of play he will discern the symptoms of a love of science, and, instead of deploring the natural idleness of children, he will admire the activity they display in the pursuit of knowledge. He will feel that it is his business to direct this activity, to furnish his pupil with material for fresh combinations, to put him, or to let him put himself, in situations where he can make useful observations, and acquire that experience which cannot be bought, and which no masters can communicate.[7]

The distinction between play and work is unreal, and it is necessary to define clearly what is meant by play:

Children, it is said, work hard at play, therefore we should let them play at work. Would not this produce effects the very reverse of what we desire? The whole question must at last depend upon the meaning of the word play: if by play he meant every thing that is not usually called a task, then undoubtedly much may be learned at play; if, on the contrary, we mean by the expression to describe that state of fidgeting idleness, or of boisterous activity, in which the intellectual powers are torpid, or stunned with unmeaning noise,

6. Ibid, Vol. 1, p. 71.   7. ibid, Vol. 1, p. 24.

the assertion contradicts itself. At play so defined, children can learn nothing but bodily activity; it is certainly true, that when children are interested about any thing ... they will exert themselves in order to succeed; but from the moment the attention is fixed, no matter on what, children are no longer at idle play, they are at active work.[8]

This philosophy of education must be understood. Teaching by means of play does not mean humouring children, allowing them to do as they like:

The truth is, that useful knowledge cannot be obtained without labour ... There is a material difference between teaching children in play, and making learning a task.[9]

The Edgeworths were the first to draw attention to the serious nature of children's activities and the need to follow the child's own way to learning:

An infant should never be interrupted in its operations; whilst it wishes to use its hands, we should not be impatient to make it walk, nor when it is pacing with all the attention to its centre of gravity that is exerted by a rope-dancer, suddenly arrest its progress, and insist upon its pronouncing the scanty vocabulary which we have compelled it to learn. When children are busily trying experiments upon objects within their reach, we should not ... break the course of their ideas, and totally prevent them from acquiring knowledge by their own experience.[10]

We should never do for children what they are able to do for themselves:

When a foolish nurse sees a child attempting to reach or lift any thing, she runs immediately, 'Oh, dear love, it can't do it, it can't – I'll do it for it, so I will!' – If the child be trying the difference between pushing and pulling, rolling or sliding, the powers of the wedge or the lever, the officious nurse hastens instantly to display her own knowledge of the mechanic powers; 'Stay, love, stay; that is not the way to do it – I'll show it the right way – See here – look at me, love.'[11]

The danger of doing too much in education is greater even than the danger of doing too little. As the merchants in France answered

8. ibid, Vol. 1, pp. 69–70.   9. ibid, Vol. 1, pp. 68, 69.
10. ibid, Vol. 1, pp. 11–12.   11. ibid, Vol. 1, p. 12.

to Colbert, when he desired to know 'how he could best assist them', children might perhaps reply to those who are most officious to amuse them, 'Leave us to ourselves.'[12]

Instead of showing young people the steps of a discovery, we should frequently pause to try if they can invent. In this our pupils will succeed often beyond our expectations.[13]

The ambitions of parents, then as now, could be the cause of irreparable damage:

We see but few examples of children so extremely stupid as not to have been able to learn to read and write between the years of three and thirteen; but we see many whose temper and whose understanding have been materially injured by premature, or injudicious instruction; we see many who are disgusted perhaps irrecoverably with literature, whilst they are fluently reading books which they cannot comprehend, or learning words by rote, to which they affix no ideas. It is scarcely worth while to speak of the vain ambition of those, who long only to have it said that their children read sooner than those of their neighbours; for supposing their utmost wish to be gratified, that their son could read before the age when children commonly articulate, still the triumph must be of short duration, the fame confined to a small circle of 'foes and friends', and probably in a few years the memory of the phenomenon would remain only with his doting grandmother. Surely it is the use which children make of their acquirements which is of consequence, not the possessing them a few years sooner or later.[14]

If a child is to write he must have something to write about:

There is no danger, that those who acquire a variety of knowledge and numerous ideas should not be able to find words to express them; but those who are compelled to find words before they have ideas are in a melancholy situation.[15]

Interest is of paramount importance:

To fix the attention of children, or, in other words, to interest them about those subjects to which we wish them to apply, must be our first object in the early cultivation of the understanding.[16]

12. ibid, Vol. 1, p. 46.   13. ibid, Vol. 1, p. 42.
14. ibid, Vol. 1, pp. 50–51.   15. ibid, Vol. 1, p. 487.
16. ibid, Vol. 1, p. 73.

208   GROWTH OF MODERN EDUCATION

As long as a child is interested in something, there is a starting-point for his learning. The teacher must discover where his interest lies and use this as a beginning:

If by some unlucky mismanagement a lively child acquires a dislike to literary application, he may appear at his books with all the stupid apathy of a dunce. In this state of literary dereliction, we should not force books or tasks of any sort upon him; we should rather watch him when he is eager at amusements of his own selection, observe to what his attention turns, and cultivate it upon that subject, whatever it may be. He may be led to think and to acquire knowledge upon a variety of subjects, without sitting down to read; and thus he may form habits of attention and of application, which will be associated with pleasure. When he returns to books he will find that he understands a variety of things in them which before appeared incomprehensible. . . . As long as a child shows energy upon any occasion, there is hope: if he 'lend his little soul' to whipping a top, there is no danger of being a dunce.[17]

Children learn naturally, through their own experience, when not confronted too early with abstractions. Here we have the first advocates of the 'direct method':

If any person unused to mechanics were to read Dr Desagulier's description of the manner in which a man walks, the number of a-b-cs, and the travels of the centre of gravity, would so amaze and confound him, that he would scarcely believe he could ever again perform such a tremendous operation as that of walking. Children, if they were early to hear grammarians talk of the parts of speech, and of syntax, would conclude that to speak must be one of the most difficult arts in the world; but children, who are not usually so unfortunate as to have grammarians for their preceptors when they first begin to speak, acquire language without being aware of the difficulties which would appear so formidable in theory. . . .

General . . . terms should . . . be as much as possible avoided in early education. . . . General terms are, as it were, but the endorsements upon the bundles of our ideas; they are useful to those who have collected a number of ideas, but utterly useless to those who have no collections ready for classification.[18]

17. ibid, Vol. 1, pp. 118–9.   18. ibid, Vol. 1, pp. 85, 90–91.

The first learning, then, must come through concrete means. The suggestions for the use of mathematical aids might have come from a present-day publication:

In the chapter 'On Toys' we have recommended the use of plain regular solids, cubes, globes, etc., made of wood, as playthings for children. ... For teaching arithmetick, half-inch cubes, which can be easily grasped by infant fingers, may be employed with great advantage; they can be readily arranged in various combinations; the eye can easily take in a sufficient number of them at once, and the mind is insensibly led to consider the assemblages in which they may be grouped, not only as they relate to number, but as they relate to quantity or shape; besides, the terms which are borrowed from some of these shapes, as squares, cubes, etc. will become familiar. As the children advance in arithmetick, to square or cube a number will be more intelligible to them than to a person who has been taught these words merely as the formula of certain rules.[19]

For the first time it is made clear how the natural interests of children in making, finding out and collecting, can be used as levers to learning:

We can connect any species of knowledge with those occupations which are immediately agreeable to young people; for instance, if a child is building a house, we may take that opportunity to teach him how bricks are made, how the arches over doors and windows are made, the nature of the keystone and butments of an arch, the manner in which all the different parts of a house are put together, etc.[20]

It would be highly useful to children to be taken to manufactories, under the care of a person properly qualified to explain them.[21]

To those who acquire habits of observation, every thing that is to be seen or heard becomes a source of amusement. Natural history interests children at an early age; but their curiosity and activity is too often repressed and restrained by the ignorance or indolence of their tutors. ... 'It will dirty the house', puts a stop to many of the operations of the young philosopher.[22]

Opportunities for handwork and physical activity should be provided:

19. ibid, Vol. 2, pp. 57–8.　　20. ibid, Vol. 1, p. 73.
21. ibid, Vol. 1, p. 32.　　22. ibid, Vol 1, p. 38.

Whilst our pupils occupy and amuse themselves with observation, experiment, and invention we must take care that they have a sufficient variety of manual and bodily exercises. ... A turning-lathe, and a workbench, will afford them constant active employment, and when young people can invent, they feel great pleasure in the execution of their own plans.[23]

Teaching should not be a piecemeal affair of separate subjects. We must provide the seamless garment of education:

The persisting to teach things separately, which ought to be taught as a whole, must prevent the progress of mental cultivation. The division and subdivision of different parts of education ... must tend to increase and perpetuate error.[24]

In spite of this hundred-and-fifty-year-old advice it is still possible to find on the timetable of a Junior School the subjects Composition, Comprehension, Literature and Poetry, while it is the general practice to treat History, Geography, Art and Craft and English as totally unrelated 'subjects'.

The aim of education is to encourage thought and judgement:

It is not from want of capacity that so many children are deficient in arithmetical skill, and it is absurd to say, 'such a child has no genius for arithmetick: such a child cannot be made to comprehend any thing about numbers.' These assertions prove nothing, but that the persons who make them are ignorant of the art of teaching. A child's seeming stupidity in learning arithmetick may, perhaps, be a proof of intelligence and good sense. It is easy to make a boy, who does not reason, repeat by rote any technical rules which a common writing master may lay down for him; but a child who reasons will not be thus easily managed; he stops, frowns, hesitates, questions his master, is wretched and refractory, until he can discover why he is to proceed in such and such a manner; he is not content with seeing his preceptor make figures and lines upon a slate, and perform wondrous operations with the self-complacent dexterity of a conjurer. A sensible boy is not satisfied with merely seeing the total of a given sum, or the answer to a given question, *come out right*, he insists upon knowing why it is right. ...

In arithmetick, as in every other branch of education, the prin-

23. ibid, Vol. 1, pp. 42-3.   24. ibid, Vol 2, p. 203.

cipal object should be to preserve the understanding from implicit belief.[25]

Education must provide for the development of the creative and reasoning powers, as well as exercising the memory:

It is not sufficient in education to store up knowledge; it is essential to arrange facts so that they shall be ready for use, as materials for the imagination, or the judgment, to select and combine. The power of retentive memory is exercised too much, the faculty of recollective memory is exercised too little, by the common modes of education. Whilst children are reading the history of kings, and battles, and victories, whilst they are learning tables of chronology and lessons of geography by rote, their inventive and their reasoning faculties are absolutely passive; nor are any of the facts which they learn in this manner associated with circumstances in real life. These trains of ideas may with much pains and labour be fixed in the memory, but they must be recalled precisely in the order in which they were learnt by rote, and this is not the order in which they may be wanted. . . . Many people are obliged to repeat the alphabet before they can recollect the relative place of any given letter; others repeat a column of the multiplication-table before they can recollect the sum of the numbers which they want. . . . The great difference which appears in men of the same profession, and in the same circumstances, depends upon the application of their knowledge more than upon the quantity of their learning.[26]

25. ibid, Vol 2, pp. 53–4, 55.   26. ibid, Vol 1, pp. 444–5, 446.

21

Elizabeth Hamilton and the Cottagers of Glenburnie
Dean Dawes' School
M. de Fellenberg's School of Industry
Arthur Hill and Hazlewood School

IN her account of the imaginary Scottish village of Glenburnie, Elizabeth Hamilton, writing in 1808, gives a conversation between the pastor and William, the new schoolmaster, in which the pastor gives his views of what the aims of education should be:

'Let me ask you,' the pastor said, 'what is the end you aim at, in sending your children to school?'

'I send them,' returned William, 'in order that they may learn to read and write and cast accounts. . . .'

'That is one reason, to be sure,' said Mr Gourlay, 'and a good one; but why do you wish them to be instructed in the branches you have mentioned?'

'I wish them to learn to read,' returned William, 'that their minds may be enlarged by knowledge, and that they may be able to study the word of God; and I have them taught to write and cast accounts, that they may have it in their power to carry on business, if it should be their lot to engage in any.'

'That is to say,' replied Mr Gourlay, 'that you are anxious to give your children such instruction as may enable them faithfully to discharge their religious and social duties; your object is laudable: but it is not merely by teaching them to read and write that it is to be accomplished. If their minds are not in some degree opened, they will never use the means thus put into their hands; and if their hearts are not in some degree cultivated, the means of knowledge will lead them rather to evil than to good.'[1]

The suggestions for the teaching of reading are remarkably modern. Reading must not be taught mechanically. Children must learn to read with understanding and with natural expression, not to 'roar, and sing out what they read'. The schoolmaster should

1. HAMILTON, ELIZABETH, *Cottagers of Glenburnie*, pp. 368–9.

consider it his duty to teach his pupils to read with understanding, and carefully to observe whether they know the meaning and import of the words they utter. This they can never do, if they are not taught to read distinctly, and as nearly as possible in the tone of conversation.[2]

What they read must not be divorced from their own natural speech; a principle still only partially applied even today.

Acquiring the art of reading

will be useless, if the teacher has confined his instruction to the mere sounds of words, especially where these sounds are very different from those which we are accustomed to use in conversing with each other.[3]

No fear must be used. It should be the schoolmaster's first object

to train his pupils to habits of order and subordination, not by means of terror, but by a firmness which is not incompatible with kindness and affection.[4]

Children should never be punished for behaviour which results from having insufficient to do. A master would be wrong

who punished a boy at school, for playing, or making noise, if it appeared that he had provided him with no better employment. This is the great fault in all our country schools. The children spend three fourths of their time in downright idleness, and when fatigued with the listlessness of inaction, have no other resource, but in making noise, or doing mischief.[5]

Morality is learned not by precept but by practice:

The school in which the greatest number of moral habits were acquired, would certainly be the best school of moral instruction.[6]

Intelligence grows by being used in observing and through activity, particularly activity of the hands, which encourages thought. Handwork which becomes merely mechanical is worse than useless. The village benefactress, Mrs Mason, found

2. ibid, p. 372.   3. ibid, p. 369.   4. ibid, p. 373.
5. ibid, p. 374.   6. ibid, p. 376.

that the girls were less intelligent than the boys and she put this
down to the fact that

while the boys, by being constantly engaged in observing the
operations that were going on without doors, or in assisting in
them, had their attention exercised, and their observation called
forth, the girls, till able to spin, were without object or occupation.
After the first week, the labour of the wheel became mechanical,
and required no exertion of the mental faculties. The mind, therefore, remained inert, and the power of perception, from being so
long dormant, became at length extinct.

She therefore

not only contrived varieties of occupation, but made all the girls
sit in judgment on the work that was done.[7]

This seems a pale shadow of the Edgeworths' dynamic and
liberal conception of a school; but the very fact that it was
written at all gives an indication of the darkness that surrounded the education of the ordinary child of the early nineteenth century, a darkness which it was to take another
hundred years to dispel.

*

The darkness was not entirely unrelieved. A small number of
individual schools attempted, in differing ways, to put into
practice more liberal ideas of education: the Quaker school at
Bootham, which was the first school in England to have a
natural history society, and in which the development of the
soul was considered more important than the development of
the mind; the Manchester Grammar School, which had done
away with corporal punishment by 1800, and where, according
to De Quincey, the 'self-discipline of the older boys and the
efficacy of their examples' was enough to keep order; Wordsworth's village school at Hawkshead, with its delightful freedom from formality; and probably others of which no record
remains.

A report made in 1847 by the Inspector on Dean Dawes'
school at Kings Somborne in Hampshire reads:

7. ibid, pp. 390, 391.

On entering the school a stranger ... would ... be struck by
the absence of those things intended to catch the eye, which
have sometimes awakened his suspicions in other schools of local
celebrity. There is a reality in the scene which will impress him
favourably in respect of it. . . .

Here ... where so many other things are taught besides reading,
the children are found in advance, in reading, of others, in the
majority of which scarcely anything else is taught.

And this is always the case, and a fact which seems to point
to the expediency, if not the necessity, of teaching children something else besides reading, that we may be able to teach them to
read ... it is impossible that the instruction they receive in other
things, awakening the intelligence and strengthening the memory,
should not aid them in learning to read. ... I certainly never heard
little children in an elementary school read so well.[8]

One can imagine his delight at discovering this unusual
school, with its evidence of the practical value of a wider
approach to education. Here the children were asked to write
about familiar things,

all the things in the house where it lives ... all it knows ...
about sheep, or cows, or horses ... of the village of Kings Somborne, or the neighbouring downs and hills, of the farms and hold-
ings in the parish ... of the river Teste which runs through it ...
'I certainly never have examined little children', continues the Inspector 'who could spell so well; and that good spelling and good
reading, and skill in the expression of written thoughts, go together,
may be taken as an illustration of the fact that to achieve excellence
in any one subject of instruction in an elementary school ... it is
necessary to unite it with others; and that the singular slowness
with which the children of our National schools learn to read ...
is, in some degree, to be attributed to the unwise concentration of
the labours of the school on that single object. ...'[9]

Mathematics was equally well taught. The Report continues:

'I can bear testimony to the fact that they are "not taught these
things in a parrot-like way, but led to understand them as a matter
of reasoning".'[10]

8. Minutes of the Committee of Council on Education, HMSO, 1848,
Appendix, pp. 9, 12–13.
9. ibid, pp. 13 14.   10. ibid, p. 16.

The system used in the school

'deals ... with things rather than words ... thinking and doing are associated in a pleasureable relation. ... "the science of common things" [has] an important place.' [11]

The Inspector goes on to outline a suitable curriculum for country schools, a kind of early nineteenth-century Handbook of Suggestions in miniature. Geography should 'make the child acquainted with things in other parts of the world', but only in comparison with his own. It is 'a gradual process, beginning at the objects which immediately surround the child, and widening continually its circle'.[12]

History ought to be

'a knowledge in respect to the people who formerly lived here, of things similar in their kind to those which a child knows about the people who now live here. ... What is at present taught under the name of history is a record of events placed by their very magnitude beyond the sphere of a child's sympathies. ...' [13]

'If ever we are to educate the labouring classes it must, in my opinion, be by teaching them to reason and to understand about things which are connected with their ordinary pursuits.' [14]

*

M. de Fellenberg's School of Industry at Hofwyl in Switzerland was a unique experiment, of great interest, for which His Imperial Majesty, the Emperor Alexander, created him Knight of the Order of St Vladimir.

'By the plan adopted ... children have been rescued from the lowest depths of wretchedness and depravity, and rendered useful members of society'.[15]

According to Count Louis de Villevieille its success

'has convinced the most incredulous: it has given to those who would be too unhappy, if they were compelled to despair of the

11. ibid, p. 26.   12. ibid, p. 32.
13. ibid, pp. 32–3.   14. ibid, p. 27.
15. Preface to *Reports of M. le Comte de Capo d'Istria*, p. ix.

human race, another reason for believing that it is not difficult to lead them to good'.[16]

In a letter to one of his friends M. de Fellenberg condemns the usual methods of schools, not all of which have wholly passed away today:

'The only object in view, for the most part, in schools, is the acquisition of imperfect and desultory knowledge: little attention being paid to the general result, essential as yet it is to the education of the higher classes, to the forming their character and their judgment. . . .[17]

By forcing the attention of children, to objects that do not interest them; by compelling their application for so long a continuance as to be painful; by crowding them together in schoolrooms, ill-adapted for the purpose; by employing, in their instruction, methods clashing with one another, and suffering them to be surrounded by ill examples, it is impossible that we should not render them idle, and corrupted from their earliest infancy.[18]

Experience has taught me that *indolence* in young persons is so directly opposite to their natural disposition to activity, that unless it is the consequence of bad education, it is almost invariably connected with some constitutional defect.[19] The individual, independent activity of the pupil is of much greater importance than the ordinary busy officiousness of many who assume the office of educators.'

The school he founded drew its children 'from the most abject and degrading situations'. Some were vagrants and beggars. It was not intended as a school for instruction, but for labour. A Report on the School presented to His Majesty, the Emperor Alexander, in 1814, said:

Instruction is here only an accessory, and scarcely occupies more than two hours in each day. Being a relaxation from bodily labour, it is never carried so far as to produce weariness in the children,

16. COUNT LOUIS DE VILLEVIEILLE, *The Establishments of M. de Fellenberg*, p. 18.

17. *Letter to a friend, Report by M. le Comte de Capo d'Istria*, 1814, p. 42.

18. ibid, p. 38.

19. SPENCER, *Education*, p. 73.

and there is none of that distraction, inattention, and fatigue, which is so commonly seen in other schools.[20]

It goes on to describe the success of the method:

The eager pleasure with which they learn, keeps their attention fixed. . . . In observing, at the evening reading, their countenances, expressive of the steadiest attention, and of the liveliest interest, it is difficult to conceive that these very children have laboured during ten hours in the fields. So strong is the desire of instruction among the elder ones, that they frequently beg to be allowed to go on with their reading and writing, after the others are gone to bed.[21]

The course of instruction given to the children covered the following subjects

which are here mentioned in an order nearly agreeing with the importance which they are taught to attach to them: religion; practical agriculture; reading, writing and arithmetic; elementary geometry, with reference to land surveying; natural history, with reference to husbandry; the history and geography of Switzerland, in a compendious manner, and the rudiments of music.[22]

and the method used was to be such as would

directly tend to cultivate the heart and unfold the reasoning faculties. The great object of education, agreeable to M. de Fellenberg's idea, is to direct the activity of all the faculties of man, towards his internal powers, and their extension.[23]

The spring of true education is interest, and the source of such interest lies both in the world that surrounds the child and in his own inner powers:

It is only by a persevering, and concentrated attention to all that interests man, whether arising from objects around him, or from his own powers, that he can succeed in regulating his thoughts, his feelings, and his actions, by the standard of true wisdom.[24]

Vehrli, the boys' tutor, wrote:

20. *Report of M. Rengger*, p. 14.
21. ibid, pp. 14–15.
22. COUNT LOUIS DE VILLEVIEILLE, *The Establishments of M. de Fellenberg*, p. 16.
23. *Report of M. Rengger*, pp. 13, 78.
24. *Letter to a friend, Report by M. le Comte de Capo d'Istria*, p. 38.

I have now tried, and am perfectly sensible of the difference . . . between a school conducted like ours, and ordinary village schools. . . . A thousand objects, connected with their principal occupations, furnish opportunities for acquiring knowledge, which they could never have enjoyed while seated on the forms of a school, nor would they seek for information and explanation, with that eagerness which, with us, leads to the most gratifying results. Here the children question me repeatedly on every object that strikes them, and never surely can instruction be so effectually given, as when it is previously solicited. . . . If they perceive an insect, bird, or other animal, I am sure to have a hundred questions on the subject: if their curiosity is excited by a plant, a stone, or any sort of earth, they are not satisfied without a full explanation and are never tired of asking questions. Can any thing similar be found in the generality of schools where the children are crowded together not allowed to stir from their seats; for ever occupied on one subject and seeing nothing but the same dead walls? . . . The capacity of investigating, discovering, judging, and observing, is awakened and cultivated in the best possible manner.[25]

A story he tells in his journal illustrates how the method and spirit of the school succeeded in developing, even in the younger children, a sense of responsibility for their own work and an absorption in the tasks which they set themselves to do. An eight-year-old planned a surprise for M. de Fellenberg on his return from a visit to Berne,

by presenting him with four small baskets filled with ears of corn, as the produce of his day's gleaning. Night, however, advanced; Vehrli had already returned home with the rest of the children, and the fourth basket was not yet full: the little fellow remained alone in the field, to complete the task which he had imposed on himself,[26]

and even when M. de Fellenberg went to the field to find him, he was so absorbed in his work that he did not perceive M. de Fellenberg until he was quite close to him.

The Reporters speak of the good results obtained in the school, in mathematics and other work:

We could not but admire the exactness with which pupils of the upper class could estimate the length of lines, the degrees of an

25. *Report of M. Rengger*, pp. 18–19.   26. ibid, p. 24.

angle, and the area of a triangle or of a trapezium; the readiness with which the dimensions being given, they calculated the cube of a stack of hay, and determined the proportion of the sine to the tangent, or the secant in right angle triangles with given angles. . . .

The information which they receive, on natural history, is chiefly intended to make them understand the nature of those objects which they have constantly before their eyes. They not only know what plants are cultivated for agricultural purposes, but those also which are considered to be weeds. Some of the elder ones have made herbals. They can distinguish different stones, which they find in the fields, by their proper appellations, and according to their nature and useful properties. While we were present, one of the children began making a catalogue of all the natural bodies with which he was acquainted, ranged under their proper heads. Not long ago this child was a common beggar.[27]

The greater number [of the children] . . . read with that ease, accuracy and well-placed emphasis which is so seldom met with in schools.[28]

The journal, which is kept by all the elder pupils, is also an excellent exercise of the understanding. On Sunday morning each of them writes on his slate whatever has happened, during the preceding week, which he thinks worthy of remark; this, after being corrected by Vehrli, is copied into a book . . . sometimes a sketch or song supplies the place of such observations. The commissioners could not but admire the good sense predominant throughout the greater part of these journals; and in all of them a freedom from blots and blurs, not commonly found in the copy-book of a schoolboy.[29]

The picture emerges of an unusually happy community of normal boys, full of feeling. The story is told of how the children wanted to give money to a beggar who was watching them; of a child falling asleep during the lesson after supper; of the children going to the room of a sick companion, anxious to know if he were better and wanting to do something for him, and of the boy who said that he might have caught a hare one day, but did not, because 'I thought it was as happy to be alive as we are, and therefore I let it go.' 'But,' says one of the boys, 'hares eat the turnips.' 'Well, even if they do eat a few turnips; what would you say if you were never permitted

27. ibid, pp. 11–13.   28. ibid, p. 5.   29. ibid, p. 14.

to eat anything', and we are told that 'when amidst the noisiest game, or the most lively diversion, the voice of Vehrli is heard, "come, my children, you have had enough", the uproar instantly ceases, and they all follow him without a word'.[30]

Vehrli related how he inquired one day who was responsible for some wrongdoing:

One of them accused his companion, but had no sooner uttered the words, than he began crying and ran to Vehrli, entreating him not to punish the accused.[31]

The account written by the boy who had been a beggar before coming to the school, expresses the effect of the spirit of this remarkable school:

'One evening last week, I was sent on a message to Buchsée. On my road, I noticed a fine apple which I longed for very much, and could easily reach, but I did not touch it. As I came back I remarked the apples again, and wished for it still more; but on looking about me, I beheld the starry heavens, and the moon just rising, and I then no longer wished to take the apple.' [32]

*

A hundred and fifty years ago a school was in existence, near Birmingham, which put into practice original and effective methods of self-government, reminiscent of the ideals of Helvetius, and a theory of education which owed much to the Edgeworths and which would be considered progressive today. At a time when the national urge for education was at its height, when Bell and Lancaster were attempting to provide it on a large scale, and Owen was experimenting with schools for Infants, Arthur Hill, at Hazlewood School, was working out a satisfactory method of educating large numbers of boys, using practical means of teaching and discipline.

The aim of the school was an all-round development.

'Let it never be forgotten,' Hill wrote,

that the first object of education is not so much to impart knowledge as to inculcate sound principles, form good habits, and to develop all human faculties, physical, moral, and intellectual.[33]

30. ibid, p. 37.   31. ibid, p. 38.   32. ibid, p. 40.
33. HILL, ARTHUR, *Hints on the Discipline Appropriate to Schools*, p. 15.

It is our object to produce voluntary mental exertion.... We wish to teach them [the pupils] to educate themselves while we direct their operations. We must teach them to *think*, as well as act.[34]

He quoted Gibbon:

"Every person has two educations, one which he receives from others, and one, more important, which he gives to himself." [35] The latter of these is seldom begun till the former is ended; an earlier commencement of it would perhaps ensure greater success to both.[36]

It is more important to instil the love of knowledge than to impart information:

If it were possible for the pupil to acquire a love of knowledge, and that alone, during the whole time he remained at school, he would have done more towards ensuring a stock of knowledge in maturer age, than if he had been the recipient of as much learning as ever was infused into the passive schoolboy by flogging or coaxing.[37]

The imagination and judgement need education as much as the memory:

A very common error is to overwork the memory; leaving the perception, the judgment, and the imagination but little to do.[38]

The attitude of the teacher was of vital importance:

The master should keep a watchful guard over his own temper; should earnestly endeavour to look upon his pupils as his moral patients; their offences towards himself as disorders to be cured, not wrongs to be avenged.[39]

To gain the respect of his pupils, he must be rigidly careful to respect them; to maintain a strict regard for their rights; to remember that their feelings are easily excited; to abstain, therefore, at all times, from the language of contempt, sarcasm and invective; to remember that dulness and ignorance are objects of pity, not of ridicule.[40]

34. HILL, ARTHUR, *Public Education*, p. 218.
35. GIBBON, *Life and Letters*, HILL, *Public Education*, p. 199.
36. *Public Education*, p. 199.
37. ibid, pp. 192–3.   38. ibid.
39. *Hints on the Discipline Appropriate to Schools*, p. 15.
40. ibid, p. 16.

Hill had the highest respect for teachers and the teaching profession:

everyone considers himself, as a matter of course, a complete adept in the science of education; and it has been for some time held as an axiom, that the only good reason for sending children to school, is want of time on the part of the parent for their instruction at home. We doubt if a man could be found in the three kingdoms, sufficiently vain to make a similar avowal with respect to the repair of his old shoes.[41]

We have never succeeded in ridding ourselves of the prejudice, that it is one thing to have learnt, and another to be able to teach.[42]

The teacher must understand the stages of development of his pupils and know when the right time comes to teach them:

In our eagerness to secure what we deem most important, do we not too often call upon the mind for the exercise of powers as yet but imperfectly developed, if developed at all, or imply the possession of a taste which has not yet been formed? . . .

It is a very common mistake to suppose, that, because a study is important it should therefore be entered upon very early. It would be about as reasonable for an impatient traveller to call on the shoeing-smith to ply the hammer before the fire is kindled, forgetting that his blows will be unavailing unless he strike when the iron is hot.[43]

The educator must therefore study the boy's tastes, 'which are often a true index of his powers',[44] and the course of instruction which ensues is likely to be 'the one best calculated to excite his interest, to awaken his attention, enlarge his capacity, and increase his mental strength'.[45]

An appeal to the natural motives of children is the best means of rousing them to learn:

See how strong the desire of knowledge is in a child, – how prone he is to enquire, how importunate in his questions, how inquisitive and meddlesome in his investigations, – volatile, indeed, and apparently capricious, yet always bent on enlarging his sphere of knowledge, . . . always, that is, until his natural curiosity, that strong

41. *Public Education*, p. 172.   42. ibid.
43. *Hints on the Discipline Appropriate to Schools*, p. 8.
44. ibid, p. 8.   45. ibid, p. 8.

desire – it might almost be called a passion – is either enfeebled by inanition or choked by repletion.[46]

Again, how strong is the natural love of employment! With what eagerness does the child demand it, – how painful does he find inaction, and with what contempt does he often reject mere aimless occupation! It is true, that, as boyhood advances, this desire too often fails, or ... becomes perverted; but are not the causes of this defect often similar to those just referred to? Either suitable employment has not been found, ... or his attention has been overtaxed.[47]

Education must be practical, not only in the sciences but in the learning of morality, for:

it is an acknowledged truth among teachers, that no man can do them [the pupils] a greater service than by reducing every art and science ... to be made a part of juvenile education, under the dominion of 'Practical Instruction'.[48]

Children should be allowed some freedom to move about and to change their occupations:

We look upon all restraint as evil.[49]

In early youth the power of applying to one task for any great length of time, or of remaining with comfort in one position, is very limited; we therefore change the place and occupation of our pupils much more frequently than is generally done.[50]

Children should learn to teach themselves:

We are careful to lose no opportunity of providing motives and means for self-instruction; thoroughly convinced that the great maxim of education ought to be – 'It is better to learn than to be taught.' [51]

Children should see some purpose in what they are learning; they must be aware of a need in themselves:

No man would undergo the trouble of investigating the nature of plants, unless he, or his friends, stood in need of their medicinal virtues. The motions of the heavenly bodies were first observed by sailors and husbandmen.[52]

46. ibid, p. 7.
47. ibid, p. 7.
48. Public Education, p. 176.
49. ibid, p. 5.
50. ibid.
51. ibid, p. 6.
52. ibid, p. 193.

They should be encouraged to learn through interest, and by making sure that everything is thoroughly understood:

Great care is taken to fix the attention of the boys by making the business as interesting as possible; by seeing that every thing is fully comprehended; and by frequently changing the pupil's occupations. We endeavour to lead the pupils to reason upon the different steps as they proceed, and invite them to put questions to the teacher, when any thing transpires which they do not fully comprehend.[53]

The object of the education at Hazlewood was that

as little coercion as possible shall be used in any stage of the pupil's education; and ... that even this little shall be from time to time withdrawn, as he becomes able to direct himself; so that when he leaves the school he may have matured the habit of self-government.[54]

Education must be gained at first hand, not through books and the thoughts of others:

Many a fine mind has been lost by an exclusive attention to books. Reading may degenerate into a very idle method of spending time; the more dangerous, as it has the appearance of something better. ... The inferiority of the *second-hand* ideas acquired by reading, to those gained practically, will readily be seen by comparing the different processes which the mind of the author and his reader undergo.... Numberless associations ... will be suggested to the author by a perusal of his own work, to which the reader must be an utter stranger.... As all the ideas enter the reader's mind by the same process, and with equal ease, he is in danger of not distinguishing accurately between them. . . . Ideas thus received are, so to speak, dead;

– one is reminded of the 'inert ideas' of the Hadow Report on the Primary School of 1931 –

they have lost the generative power, and when, by process of decay, they themselves are gone, they leave no trace behind.[55]

Such inert ideas must be avoided and

The only means of supplying the great defect resulting from receiving the unmodified thoughts of others is for the pupil to observe, reflect, and at a proper age, compose originally.[56]

53. ibid, p. 96.   54. ibid, p. 282.   55. ibid, pp. 320–21.
56. ibid, p. 321.

On the matter of writing, Hill quotes Miss Edgeworth:

'No person should be expected to write, unless he has something to say;' indeed, the utter uselessness of any other composition than that which is employed as a vehicle for the communication of ideas, must excite, even in the mind of a child, a contempt even to loathing.[57]

Those who have endured the infliction of such composition in childhood may wonder why she wrote *even in the mind of a child*, since children are generally more aware of such stupidity and its consequent insincerity than are adults. He goes on:

We dare not calculate the mental injury which must necessarily ensue 'from the Egyptian compulsion, under which some young people are placed, of thus making bricks without straw'. [58] (Locke)

It always appeared to us to be a great advantage to employ the student in composition on subjects with the facts of which he must be practically acquainted, and where his own interests are involved.[59]

Hill has some pungent criticisms to make of current methods of teaching reading:

The business of teaching to read ... is even yet in a state of barbarism. There is not enough for the child to do – not a sufficient number of the faculties employed.[60]

He understands the importance, in relation to learning to read, of a wide speaking vocabulary. He describes a child of three and a half who is playing by his side and who uses the words 'biped' and 'quadruped' with complete understanding. It is clear that such a child will have little difficulty in learning to read.

His recommendations for the teaching of mathematics could still be followed with profit today:

All technical forms and expressions should be avoided, until the detailed plans for which they are substituted are thoroughly understood; ... the pupil should not employ even ideal signs in his calculations, until he has applied his arithmetic to the objects which these signs are intended to represent.[61]

57. ibid, p. 200.   58. ibid, p. 200.   59. ibid, p. 136.
60. ibid, p. 336.   61. ibid, p. 116.

Adding together long rows of meaningless figures is not only useless but injurious:

What master but must have observed that his younger pupils, after working a problem, are sometimes perfectly ignorant of the effect which has been produced, and are unable to write an answer to the question proposed? ... Is not the pupil's mind suffering injury by thus blindly applying means without knowing what end is to be effected, and sometimes without being conscious that any object is intended to be attained beyond that of exercising his patience? [62]

Concrete materials should be used, including marbles and ounce and pound weights. The boys at Hazlewood made surveys out of doors and they were encouraged to make estimates of their answers before working out problems. In geometry they began with guessing lengths of lines and recognizing geometrical figures in walls, floors and ceilings of rooms, and Hill, well ahead of his time, suggests that algebra 'may be studied at a much earlier age than is usually imagined'.

Hill is equally progressive in his suggestions for the teaching of geography. In his school this began with making maps of the school and its neighbourhood, chalked on a horizontal blackboard. This was followed by a map of the country twenty-five miles round Birmingham. The boys were taken on expeditions to Warwick and Stratford, whose history they studied, and to see a Roman road. From first-hand experience they learned the meanings of geographical terms such as land, water, hill, mountain, valley, common, pool, spring, brook, river, ford, cataract. Later they were introduced to a map of the British Isles and discovered the meaning of words such as island, peninsula, strait, coast and cape. Maps were made of the journeys of boys coming to the school, and of visitors. This was followed by a study of Europe, and finally by the use of the globe.

The school was run as a self-governing community with an elaborate system of rewards and punishment which was administered by the staff and boys working together.

The principle on which we have acted has been to leave as much as possible all power in the hands of the boys themselves.[63]

62. ibid, p. 195.   63. ibid, pp. 1–2.

The boys elected a committee which proposed, discussed and enacted the laws of the school, and order was kept by a Jury Court and 'a small but vigorous police'.

To illustrate the serious way in which the boys regarded their duties, Hill tells that, on one occasion, the jury deliberated over a case for eleven and three quarter hours, without food.

A conference of staff 'directs the amount and species of labour to be performed by the different classes, and the time of study' and

usually regulates the amount and species of rewards given for superiority in the classes and for voluntary labour. All regulations which regard either punishment or privilege belong to the Committee [of boys], which must therefore be applied to for the enforcement of the ordinances made by the Conference; this latter body having no power to enforce its decrees by any penal sanction.[64]

There was no corporal punishment and no impositions:

Every measure is avoided which would destroy self-respect.[65]

Artificial rewards and punishments, however necessary, are always evils, and ... should always be rendered as light and infrequent as is compatible with the end in view.... Punishment ... can never be applied without weakening ... the motives (which we should encourage) nor, indeed, without a danger of raising up an antagonistic feeling, strong enough to counteract them all.[66]

The true end of punishment

must be a permanent rather than an immediate effect ... to produce, not show boys, but well-principled, right-minded, able, energetic men: and this result can only be secured by creating durable motives.[67]

In spite of this ideal, the complicated system of privileges and ranks, based on the boys' past records, does seem to have been rather artificial, but Hill claimed that, as a result, 'the great mass of our pupils are secure from all punishment, except the loss of their marks'.[68]

64. ibid, p. 11.   65. ibid, p. 181.
66. *Hints on the Discipline Appropriate to Schools*, pp. 5, 14–15.
67. ibid, p. 6.   68. *Public Education*.

Hill has a timely word to say on the question of parental anxiety:

> One of the most common errors into which he [the parent] falls, is that of too great an anxiety about specific acquirements; forgetting that when the powers of body and mind are thoroughly developed, and the art of their general application is learnt, the pupil will be able to turn them into any particular direction, with comparative ease. Let the first stage of education, therefore, be, to call out the powers both mental and physical: and here we may remark, that the absence of coercion very much promotes this end. ... Variety of pursuit is necessary to a development of all the powers.[69]

Results cannot always be measured:

> It sometimes happens that parents do serious injury by the impatience of which we have spoken. They ought to be satisfied at first with the conviction that a child, whose habits and feelings are well directed, must acquire a great deal of knowledge which cannot be reduced to language, or which does not come under the parents' regard, because it has no conventional rank in education. A boy of inquiring mind, and vigorous bodily powers, even in roving about the fields must of necessity acquire a great deal of information, which, though telling for little in the 'measure and value' of a schoolmaster's 'estimate', is of much, or more practical utility, than many of the subjects which he is called upon to learn. It may be as useful to a boy in after-life to know the difference between parsley and hemlock, at sight, as to recollect the distinction between a rhombus and a rhomboid. Perhaps, if he were to forget both, no great practical evil might follow; but looking to the exercise of the powers of observation and comparison, who will say, that the boy was not as usefully employed when sitting on a bank with a stalk of each plant in his hand, as while poring over the wood-cuts of his Euclid.[70]

The results of the methods used at Hazlewood were such that a large proportion of the school could be relied upon

> to abstain from breaches of the law, and other improprieties, with almost as much care in the master's absence as in his presence ... to draw upon their leisure hours for the completion of their lessons, ... and even spontaneously to apply for an increase in their task when they [found] it insufficient.

69. ibid, p. 348.   70. ibid, p. 349.

It had its great testing time

on the eve of the holidays. At that critical time, when artificial
motives have lost all or nearly all their power, when the master
who has relied upon them feels like the witch in Thalaba who
cries 'Ye rebel spells, obey!', he who has successfully cultivated
this higher sentiment is rewarded by such a manifestation of its
efficacy as yields security for the present, and gives high promise
for the future.[71]

71. *Hints on the Discipline Appropriate to Schools*, p. 12.

22

Robert Owen

M. COLE wrote that Robert Owen's ideas 'were astonishingly modern; so much so, in fact, that New Lanark between 1816 and 1826 might almost be regarded as an epitome of the progress made in English education during the following hundred years'.[1]

His practical and successful methods of education were put into practice amongst the degraded workers in his cotton mills in New Lanark, and the five hundred children who formed about a quarter of the community. He called his work

the most important experiment for the happiness of the human race that had yet been instituted in any part of the world. This was, to ascertain whether the character of man could be better formed, and society better constructed and governed, by falsehood, fraud, force and fear . . . – or by truth, charity and love . . . whether by replacing evil conditions by good, man might not be relieved from evil, and transformed into an intelligent, rational, and good being.[2]

His method, which entirely transformed the workers, was founded on what he called

This great and self-evident truth – 'that the Creating Power gives all the qualities to the forms created'.[3] 'That the made receives all its qualities from its maker, and that, the created receives all its qualities and powers from its Creator.' [4] 'The character of man is formed *for* and not *by* him.' [5]

This knowledge, he believed, is all that is required to change society and bring about the millennium. For,

by withdrawing all responsibility from the created, . . . and by acquiring a knowledge of the science of the influence of surround-

1. COLE, M., *Robert Owen of New Lanark*, p. 79.
2. *Life of Robert Owen by Himself*, p. 82.
3. ibid, Preface, p. xii.   4. ibid, Preface, p. ix.
5. ibid, p. 105.

ings upon humanity, and how to combine them in order and with wisdom, man may now be made a terrestrial angel of goodness and wisdom, and to inhabit a terrestrial paradise.[6]

He was quite certain of the basic goodness of man and the practical possibility of achieving heaven on earth:

By my own experience and reflection I had ascertained that human nature is radically good, and is capable of being trained, educated, and placed from birth in such manner, that all ultimately ... must become united, good, wise, wealthy and happy.[7]

This belief was combined with an unusual understanding of children and their feelings. Writing of his own experience as a child, he describes the feelings of the girls in the dancing class, when they were unable to obtain the partners they liked:

The feelings of some of them ... were so overpowering, that it was afflicting to see how much they suffered. I have long thought that the mind and feelings of young children are seldom duly considered or attended to, and that if adults would patiently encourage them to express candidly what they thought and felt, much suffering would be saved to the children, and much useful knowledge of human nature would be gained by the adults.[8]

With such an attitude of mind it is not surprising that he should be strongly aware of the importance of early childhood, and that he should see the need among the work people of his mills at New Lanark for special schools for little children;

To a great extent the character is made or marred before children enter the usual schoolroom.[9] Much of good or evil is taught to or acquired by a child at a very early period of its life; much of temper or disposition is correctly or incorrectly formed before he attains his second year; and many durable impressions are made at the termination of the first twelve or even six months of his existence. The children, therefore, of the uninstructed and ill-instructed, suffer material injury in the formation of their character during these and the subsequent years of childhood and youth.[10]

6. ibid, Preface, pp. xii–xiii.   7. ibid, p. 181.
8. ibid, p. 13.   9. ibid, p. 242.
10. COLE, M., *Robert Owen of New Lanark*, p. 80.

In searching out the evil conditions in which the workpeople were involved, their domestic arrangements for rearing their children from infancy appeared to me especially to be injurious to parents and children, and my thoughts were now directed to measures which should . . . relieve both from the worst of the evils which they were suffering. . . . These considerations created in me the first thoughts respecting the necessity of an infant school, to be based on the true principle of forming character from the earliest period at which the infants could leave their parents.[11]

In the Infant School which he set up, therefore, the children, from the age of one

were trained and educated without punishment or any fear of it, and were while in school by far the happiest human beings I have ever seen.[12] . . . Punishment . . . will never be required, and should be avoided as much as giving poison in their food.[13]

The children were taught, in every subject, only what they could understand. Robert Owen's son wrote:

We must not expect, that children should like a study, which does not interest them, or should feel interested in a study, which they do not understand,[14]

and Owen himself said,

The infants and young children, besides being instructed by sensible signs, – the things themselves, or models or paintings, – and by familiar conversation, were from two years and upwards daily taught dancing and singing.[15]

The basic principle of the school was happiness. The teachers were instructed

that they were on no account ever to beat any one of the children, or to threaten them in any manner in word or action, or to use abusive terms; but were always to speak to them with a pleasant countenance, and in a kind manner and tone of voice. That they should tell the infants and children . . . that they must on all occasions do all they could to make their playfellows happy, – and that the older ones . . . should take especial care of younger ones, and

11. *Life of Robert Owen by Himself*, p. 115.
12. ibid, p. 186.   13. ibid, pp. 241–2.
14. *Outline of the System of Education at New Lanark*, p. 58.
15. *Life of Robert Owen by Himself*, p. 186.

should assist to teach them to make each other happy.[16] Being always treated with kindness and confidence and altogether without fear, even of a harsh word, ... they exhibited an unaffected grace and natural politeness.[17]

The children were not to be annoyed with books; but were to be taught the uses and nature or qualities of the common things around them, by familiar conversation when the children's curiosity was excited so as to induce them to ask questions respecting them.[18]

Reading and writing are merely instruments by which knowledge ... may be imparted; and, when given to children, are of little comparative value, unless they are also taught to make a proper use of them.[19]

They should be out of doors in good air at play, as much as the weather and their strength will admit. When beginning to be tired of play in their playground, they should be taken within the school-room, and amused by the teacher, by showing and explaining to them some useful object within their capacity to comprehend.[20] ... The schoolroom for infant instruction was ... furnished with paintings, ... with maps, and often supplied with natural objects from the gardens, fields, and woods ... – with these infants everything was made to be amusement.[21]

The results appear to have been remarkably successful. Robert Owen himself wrote:

It was most encouraging and delightful to see the progress which these infants and children made in real knowledge, without the use of books. And when the best means of instruction or forming character shall be known, I doubt whether books will ever be used before children attain their tenth year. And yet without books they will have a superior character formed for them at ten.[22]

The Report of the Leeds Poor Law Guardians of 1819 stated:

In the education of the children the thing that is most remarkable is the general spirit of kindness and affection which is shown towards them, and the entire absence of everything that is likely to give them bad habits, with the presence of whatever is calculated to inspire them with good ones; the consequence is, that

16. ibid, pp. 192–3.   17. ibid, p. 198.   18. ibid, p. 193.
19. ROBERT, OWEN, *A New View of Society*, 4th Essay, Everyman, p. 74.
20. *Life of Robert Owen by Himself*, p. 241.
21. ibid, p. 193.   22. ibid, pp. 193–4.

they appear like one well-regulated family, united together by the ties of the closest affection. We heard no quarrels from the youngest to the eldest; and so strongly impressed are they with the conviction that their interest and duty are the same, and that to be happy themselves it is necessary to make those happy by whom they are surrounded, that they had no strife but in offices of kindness.[23]

23. *Report of Poor Law Guardians*, 1819, PODMORE, Autobiography, p. 147.

23

Herbart

THE claim made for Herbart by Oscar Browning was that he was 'a psychologist of the first rank'. H. and E. Felkin, his translators, believed that he had 'created a natural history of the human mind', while Browning considered that he might be regarded by some as 'the founder of modern psychology'.

It is certainly true that he had a deeper insight into the working of the human mind than anyone before him, and that as a result of his work a great advance was made in psychology, and a new dimension introduced into educational thought. For the first time, the new education was given a scientific basis.

Many of his ideas had their roots deep in the past: the aim of education is to be the production of good men, consequently the education of the will is more important than the education of the intellect.

'The worth of a man consists not in what he knows, but in how he wills'.[1] This had been said by many of his predecessors, but it was Herbart who showed how the good will depends on the enlightenment of the whole man and in what this enlightenment consists:

a large circle of thought closely connected in all its parts, possessing the power of overcoming what is unfavourable in the environment, and of dissolving and absorbing into itself all that is favourable.[2]

The pupil was to achieve this enlightenment and to form his own character by active participation in his own education, by

'a making' which [he] himself discovers when choosing the good and rejecting the bad – this or nothing is formation of character! This rise to self-conscious personality ought without doubt to take place

1. HERBART, *Letters and Lectures*, p. 127.
2. HERBART, *Science of Education*, p. 92.

in the mind of the pupil himself, and be completed through his own activity; it would be nonsense if the teacher desired to create the real essence of the power to do it, and to pour it into the soul of his pupil.[3]

Although he speaks of the soul as a *tabula rasa* and of all ideas as 'a product of time and experience', he yet seems to hold the ancient belief of the power of growth in the soul and its essential goodness. He goes on:

But to place the power already existent and *in its nature trust-worthy* under such conditions that it must infallibly and surely accomplish this rise – this it is which the teacher must look upon as possible, which to attain, to affect, to investigate, to forward, and to guide, he must regard as the great object of all his efforts.[4]

Freedom is essential to the making of a stable character.

Character is inner stability, but how can a human being take root in himself, when he is not allowed to depend on anything, when you do not permit him to trust a single decision to his own will? [5]

He understands, as did Pestalozzi, that a child is not free when left to the tyranny of his own 'wild impetuosity, impelling him hither and thither'. To be truly free he must learn to subordinate his desires to 'a true will, which renders him capable of determination'.

This will can never be achieved by means of 'supervision, prohibition, restraint, checking by threats', for these 'are only negative measures of education. Hindrance of offences is only good when a new activity continually takes the place of that which is restrained.'

Discipline is to be felt as a *forming* principle ... the pupil must on no account be in inward opposition to it ... Discipline finds room only so far as an inward experience persuades its subjects to submit to it willingly.[6]

Children must be free to make mistakes:

The individual ought not to be too simple, too incapable, too indolent to commit faults, otherwise virtue would be at an end also.[7]

3. ibid, p. 61.   4. ibid, p. 61.
5. ibid, p. 85.   6. ibid, p. 234.
7. *Aphor. zur Pädagogik*, MCCALLISTER, *The Growth of Freedom in Education*, p. 325.

Authority and love must be brought to bear if children are to benefit from education. 'To wound the desire to do evil ... is the business of education',[8] and this can only be achieved where the child and the teacher work fully together in a spirit of sympathy:

Only when it is possible for the pupil to unite his activity in some way or other with the teacher's can he contribute force of his own to the relationship between them.[9]

The teacher must be of the highest possible calibre:

It is a matter of course, that teachers, to perceive what is moving in the children's minds, must, themselves possess that same culture, the most subtle traces of which they have to observe in them. This is just the misfortune of education that so many feeble lights which glimmer in tender youth, are long since completely extinguished in adults, who are therefore unfitted to kindle those feeble lights into flame.[10]

The spirit in which education is given must be that of the home, nothing else can be a substitute, and the essence of this spirit is respect for the individuality of the child:

The teacher ought to make it a point of honour to leave the individuality as untouched as possible.[11]

The teacher is, however, to be more than a human gardener, surrounding his plants with the right conditions, in which they will grow of themselves. His part is to have an active influence on the inmost life of his pupils by presenting them with experiences, with thoughts and ideas. Instruction is an essential part of teaching:

Not all kinds of self-activity are desirable, but only the right kind and in the right degree. Otherwise lively children might be left to themselves, and there would be no need either to educate or even to govern them. It is the work of instruction to direct their thoughts and efforts in the right path.[12]

8. *Science of Education*, p. 99.   9. ibid, p. 100.
10. ibid, pp. 143–4.   11. ibid, p. 35.
12. *Letters and Lectures*, pp. 134–5.

The circle of thought begins with interest and ends with action. The appeal to interest is of primary importance:

The supreme final aim of instruction is . . . contained in the concept, – virtue. But the nearer aim which instruction in particular must set before itself in order to reach the final one, may be expressed as – *many-sidedness of interest*. The word *Interest* characterises in general the kind of mental activity which education ought to arouse, since it cannot be satisfied with mere knowledge.[13]

Instruction means much more than the imparting of information. What Herbart considers important is the mental process by which the mind takes hold of the material presented to it. What is needed is a laying hold on information, an active process by which the learner makes the information part of himself. The aim should always be 'the genuine development of mental power'.[14]

Mere information does not suffice,

for we conceive of mere knowledge as a store, which a man may be entirely without, and yet be no other than he is with it.[15]

The means by which this is accomplished is through interest:

Interest means self-activity.[16]

Voluntary attention depends on the pupil's determination; the teacher must often compel it by threats and admonitions. Involuntary attention, on the other hand, is much more desirable and productive. The art of instruction consists in developing it, and in it is contained the interest which we have in view.[17]

Where interest does not awake and cannot be kindled, all compulsory attainment is not only worthless, because it leads to mindless activity, but it is even injurious, for it ruins the tone of the mind.[18] If interest itself were not already the aim of instruction, we should certainly have to consider it here as the only means by which permanence to its results could be given.[19]

Work which comes from the pupil himself is of far greater value than what is imposed:

13. ibid, p. 130.   14. ibid, p. 179.
15. ibid, p. 130.   16. ibid, p. 134.
17. ibid, pp. 136–7.   18. ibid, p. 262.
19. ibid, p. 174.

Three lines of original work are worth more than three pages due to cut and dried direction.[20]

The true way of education is that in which the pupil becomes deeply involved because he himself has chosen something which is meaningful for him:

One hears much of the value of a *hardening* mode of life for the young. I leave the question of physical hardening to stand upon its merits. I am, however, convinced that the proper *hardening* principle for man . . . will not be found until we learn how to arrange a mode of life for the young, whereby they can pursue . . . what in their own eyes is a *serious* activity.

Such activity must 'proceed from the youth's own mind' and consist of '*acts through which the inward desire determines itself as will*'. Without such experience the so-called educated man 'will perhaps one day search in himself painfully, as vainly, for that power of self-manifestation and self-control on which character is based'.[21]

Herbart drew attention to the importance of the correlation of studies, and pointed out in particular that geography can be made the integrating subject of the curriculum.

The teaching must not be divided according to the names of its subjects . . . [22] That which stands isolated is of little importance.[23]

Subject matter is important and must be carefully chosen, since mental activity is not all of the same kind, therefore '*what* is to be taught and learned must not be left to fancy or convenience'.[24]

Of greater importance, however, is the mental activity which results:

In educative instruction all depends on the mental activity which it excites. It must increase, not diminish, ennoble, not deteriorate this mental activity.[25]

This mental activity may be adversely affected if enough opportunity is not given for physical activity:

Mental activity is diminished when much learning, sitting . . .

20. ibid, p. 172.
21. *Science of Education*, p. 219.
22. *Letters and Lectures*, p. 180.
23. ibid, p. 128.
24. ibid, p. 129.
25. ibid, p. 128.

affects the bodily development to such an extent, that sooner or later health suffers.[26] Due satisfaction

must be given to

the craving for bodily activity according to the child's age, in order that the natural restlessness arising from that craving, may be diverted.[27]

Experience is fundamental to education:

Indeed, who can dispense with experience and intercourse in education? To do so would be to dispense with daylight and content ourselves with candlelight! ... [28]

The teacher's address should have the effect of making the pupil hear and see what is told and described, as if it were in the immediate present. The pupils must therefore have actually seen and heard much; and this reminds us of the necessity of expanding the circle of experience, by taking them about, and by demonstrations.[29]

Herbart, in his practical suggestions on how very young children might be given first-hand experiences, gives a picture of many modern infant schools:

I have suggested marking out with bright nails on a board the typical triangles, and placing them continually within sight of the child in its cradle. . . . I, in thought, place near this board, sticks and balls painted with various colours; I constantly change, combine, and vary these sticks, and later on plants and the child's playthings of every kind. I take a little organ into the nursery and sound simple tones and intervals on it for a minute at a time. I add a pendulum to it for the child's eye and for the unpractised player's hand, that its rhythmic proportions may be observed. I would further exercise the child's sense to distinguish cold and heat by the thermometer, and to estimate the degrees of heaviness by weights. Finally, I would send him to school with the cloth manufacturer to learn as correctly as he, to distinguish finer and coarser wool by touch. Yes, who knows whether I would not adorn the walls of the nursery with very large gaily painted letters. At the foundation of all this lies the simple thought that the abrupt and troublesome process of stamping things on the mind, called learn-

26. ibid, p. 128.   27. ibid, p. 120.
28. *Science of Education*, p. 137.   29. *Letters and Lectures*, p. 163.

ing by heart, will either not be necessary, or very easy, if only the elements of synthesis are early made constituent parts of the child's daily experience. They will then, so far as possible, steal imperceptibly in among the incomparably greater accumulation of things with their names which, at the time of learning to speak, can be comprehended with such wonderful facility.[30]

Many of his excellent suggestions for the teaching of mathematics still await implementation:

Mathematics

has too much degenerated into a game assisted by lines and formulae. Let it be led back, as far as possible, to the thinking out of the *concepts* themselves.[31]

The study of mathematics . . . must be connected with knowledge of nature, and at the same time with experience, that it may enter the pupil's circle of thought.[32]

The idea that aptitude is rarer for mathematics than for other subjects is a mere illusion, due to postponing and neglecting the elementary work. . . . In the teaching of arithmetic the combinatory and geometrical elements have been neglected, and proofs are attempted before any power of mathematical abstraction has been developed.

The first step is the observation of magnitudes and their changes as they are met with, by actual counting, weighing and measuring where possible, or failing that, forming estimates . . . by observing the greater or less, the larger or smaller, the nearer or more distant objects.[33]

As in all instruction, 'the most obvious deduction is that the pupil's own activity must be fostered' in the learning of mathematics, 'that mere lecturing is insufficient. Mathematical occupations are what are required.'[34]

In like manner, modern educators have been slow to put into practice Herbart's ideas for the teaching of geography; many syllabuses still begin with 'Children of Other Lands':

In teaching geography there are at least two distinct courses; one starts analytically from the immediate neighbourhood, . . . the other, the reverse of this, begins from the globe. . . .

The usual starting point from the globe would be less open to

30. *Science of Education*, pp. 158–9.
31. ibid, p. 161.   32. *Letters and Lectures*, p. 117.
33. ibid, p. 240.   34. ibid, p. 245.

objections if we, to make the presentation of the earth as a ball clearer, pointed out the moon, and showed it to the child through a telescope. But, granted this is done, it is still wrong to substitute the weak and uncertain presentation of an immense ball for direct observation. Just as unsuitable would be to begin with Spain or Portugal. *The place* where teacher and pupil are sitting at the time, is the point from which the latter should start on his search for knowledge and extend his horizon in thought.[35]

Experience by itself, however, is not enough. Some direction is needed, and this is the function of teaching:

The kernel of our mental being, then, cannot be cultivated with certain results by means of experience and intercourse. Instruction must certainly penetrate deeper into the laboratory of the mind.[36]

Experience, left to itself, is not the kind of teacher that gives methodic instruction. Experience does not follow the law of proceeding from the simple to the compound, but amasses objects and occurrences, mixing them up together, and producing thereby confusion in the pupil's understanding.[37] We must subject the store of experience which the children bring, to a process of reconstruction.[38]

Herbart's theory of education was based firmly on his belief in the pupil's capacity for cultivation:

Growth in every sense is the child's natural destiny.[39] Humanity educates itself continuously by the circle of thought which it begets.[40]

His view that the teacher's task is to cultivate not merely the intellect, but the character, through the development of the aesthetic judgement, helped to strenghen the growing movement towards an education from within, rather than one imposed from without, and his belief that education should be concerned with human relationships prepared the way for the greater developments in educational thought of the century that followed.

35. ibid, p. 249.   36. *Science of Education*, p. 140.
37. *Letters and Lectures*, p. 164.   38. ibid, p. 165.
39. *Letters and Lectures*, p. 108.
40. *Science of Education*, Intro., p. 93.

24

Froebel

WITH the advent of Froebel the educational fresco sprang to life. Its hidden figures, created by the great educators through the centuries, began to glow with colour and the great masterpiece of educational thought emerged in a fresh and vivid form.

Froebel, like every other link in the long chain of educational thinkers, owed much to his predecessors. Even some of the phrases most closely associated with him – 'Live for our children', 'Making the inner outer and the outer inner' – were taken directly from Pestalozzi; but his own contribution was momentous, and brought about a change in education, particularly of young children, the extent of which it is difficult to estimate in these days, when so much of his thought is inextricably woven into the practice of our schools. Professor W. H. Kilpatrick of the Teachers' College, University of Columbia, said, 'with Froebel education took a rightabout face', and Evelyn Lawrence called him 'the prophet of the active nature of the learning process'.

To Froebel is due directly the great advance in the psychology of childhood, with its consequent effect on the work of our infant schools today.

Underlying all his theory was his deeply spiritual philosophy, his belief in the divine within, and the unity of all things:

> It is the destiny and lifework of all things to unfold their essence, hence their divine being, and, therefore, the Divine Unity itself – to reveal God in their external and transient being.[1]

All else follows from this belief in a power within, which strives after perfection and completeness. Man must obey this law of his own being, a law as inevitable as those which govern plants, animals and inanimate nature. Education, therefore, is

1. FROEBEL, F., *The Education of Man*, HAILMANN, p. 2.

a process of development from within, a process in which man, as a conscious being, must take a full and active part:

> *Education consists in leading man, as a thinking, intelligent being, growing into self-consciousness, to a pure and unsullied, conscious and free representation of the inner law of Divine Unity.*[2]

What is to have true, abiding and blessing, instructive and formative effect on the child ... must ... have an arousing and wakening effect on the inner life of the child and must thus spontaneously germinate from that life.[3]

The first task of the teacher, then, is to arouse 'an inner want for the instruction'. In teaching children to write:

> It is imperative that parents and teachers should be careful to render the inner life of their children as rich as possible, not so much in diversity as in inner significance and activity . . . We teach our children without having aroused an inner want for the instruction and after repressing everything that was previously in the child.[4]

This spring of life lies in the inner, instinctive life of man, which must be guided and purified. Froebel fully believed this to be possible. Deeply religious, his vision of education was a vision of greatness:

> The purpose of teaching and instruction is to bring ever more *out* of man rather than to put more and more *into* him; for that which can get *into* man we already know and possess as the property of mankind, and every one, simply because he is a human being, will unfold and develop it out of himself in accordance with the laws of mankind. On the other hand, what is yet to come *out* of mankind, what human nature is yet to develop, that we do not yet know, that is not yet the property of mankind; and, still, human nature, like the spirit of God, is ever unfolding its inner essence.[5]

Education, therefore, must cease to attempt to mould children and to stamp them like coins, and allow this inner growth to take place:

2. ibid, p. 2.
3. *Education as Development*, p. 18.
4. *Education of Man*, HAILMANN, pp. 222–3.
5. ibid, p. 279.

Shall we never cease to stamp human nature, even in childhood, like coins, to overlay it with foreign images and foreign superscriptions instead of letting it develop itself and grow into form according to the life planted in it by God? [6]

From this belief in the divine nature of the child sprang Froebel's characteristic reverence for childhood as something of infinite value in itself, an attitude which gave rise directly to a change in outlook towards childhood, to the great surge of interest in, and study of children of our own time, and to the concept of the child-centred school:

My teachers are the children themselves with their purity and innocence, their unconsciousness, and their inestimable claims, and I follow them like a faithful, trustful scholar.[7]

Education then, must be essentially passive.

Education ... should necessarily be *passive, following* (only guarding and protecting), not *prescriptive, categorical, interfering.*[8]

The child is a plant and the teacher a gardener:

We grant space and time to young plants and animals because we know, that in accordance with the laws that live in them, they will develop properly and grow well; young animals and plants are given rest, and arbitrary interference with their growth is avoided, because it is known that the opposite practice would disturb their pure unfolding and sound development; but the young human being is looked upon as a piece of wax, a lump of clay, which man can mould into what he pleases. ...

The grape-vine must, indeed, be trimmed; but this trimming as such, does not insure wine. ... The trimming, although done with the best intention, may wholly destroy the vine, ... if the gardener fail in his work passively and attentively to follow the nature of the plant. In the treatment of the things of nature we very often take the right road, whereas in the treatment of man we go astray; and yet the forces that act in both proceed from the same source and obey the same law.[9]

6. PAINTER, *History of Education*, p. 312.

7. LAWRENCE, *Letters on the Kindergarten, Friedrich Froebel and English Education*, p. 23.

8. *Education of Man*, HAILMANN, p. 7.

9. ibid, pp. 8–9.

The urge in the child to realize his destiny is a power that can be trusted and must be used:

We now trust too little to the energetic and uniting power in the child and boy — we respect it too little as a spiritually quickening power.[10]

This power he describes as self-activity, and it must be the means of education:

The eternal divine principle . . . demands and requires free self-activity and self-determination on the part of man, the being created for freedom in the image of God.[11]

In the words of an inspector:

Self-activity of the mind is the first law of this instruction; therefore the kind of instruction given here does not make the young mind a strong box, into which, as early as possible, all kinds of coins of the most different values and coinages . . . are stuffed; but slowly, continuously, gradually, and always inwardly, that is, according to a connection found in the nature of the human mind, the instruction steadily goes on, without any tricks, from the simple to the complex, from the concrete to the abstract, so well adapted to the child and his needs that he goes as readily to his learning as to his play.[12]

'Continuously, gradually, . . . adapted to the child and his needs': here for the first time we have the important principle that the child and his own needs are the starting-point for education, that each stage of development has its own requirements, which must be met as they appear:

Powers and tendencies, the activities of the senses and limbs, should be developed in the order in which they appear in the child.[13]

The child should, from the very time of his birth, be viewed in accordance with his nature, treated correctly, and given the free, all-sided use of his powers. By no means should the use of certain powers and members be enhanced at the expense of others, and these hindered in their development; the child should neither be partly chained, fettered, nor swathed; nor, later on, spoiled by too

10. ibid, p. 133.   11. ibid, p. 11.
12. MONROE, *Textbook in the History of Education*, p. 644.
13. *Education of Man*, HAILMANN, p. 36.

much assistance. The child should learn early how to find in himself the center and fulcrum of all his powers and members, to seek his support in this, and, resting therein, to move freely and be active, to grasp and hold with his own hands, to stand and walk on his own feet, to find and observe with his own eyes, to use his members symmetrically and equally.[14]

There are no sudden breaks between stages of development. It is rather a continuous process, in which the needs of one stage change slowly and imperceptibly into those of the next:

In his entire cultivation, it is highly important that his development should proceed continuously from *one* point, and that this *continuous* progress be seen and ever guarded. Sharp limits and definite subdivisions within the continuous series of the years of development, . . . are therefore highly pernicious, and even destructive in their influence.

Thus, it is highly pernicious to consider the stages of human development – infant, child, boy or girl, youth or maiden, man or woman, old man or matron – as really distinct, and not, as life shows them, as continuous in themselves, in unbroken transitions; highly pernicious to consider the child or boy as something wholly different from the youth or man.[15]

Above all, it is essential to understand that full development of each stage depends on the satisfactory development of the stages which precede it; that the needs of each stage must be fully met at the right time if complete development is to take place. Froebel was the first to recognize this important psychological principle:

How different could this be in every respect, if parents were to view and treat the child with reference to all stages of development and age, without breaks and omissions; if, particularly, they were to consider the fact that the vigorous and complete development and cultivation of each successive stage depends on the vigorous, complete and characteristic development of each and all preceding stages of life! . . .

The boy has not become a boy, nor has the youth become a youth, by reaching a certain age, but only by having lived through childhood, and, further on, through boyhood, true to the requirements of his mind, his feelings, and his body; similarly, adult man

14. ibid, p. 21.   15. ibid, p. 27.

has not become an adult man by reaching a certain age, but only
by faithfully satisfying the requirements of his childhood, boyhood
and youth.[16]

Man should live fully through every stage of his life, and
the aim of education should not be to prepare for future life
but to meet the needs of the child at the particular stage he has
reached:

> The child, the boy, man, indeed, should know no other endeavour
> but to be at every stage of development wholly what that stage
> calls for.[17]

Education must be, first of all, development and only later,
instruction. Before a child can learn he must have reached a
certain stage of maturity, of self-development.

A school is a place and a method in and by which a man obtains
knowledge of something outside himself. . . . But the child must first
himself be something, before he can turn to the contemplation of
strange things foreign to his nature. One ought already to have some
firm standpoint of his own, before one begins to acquire things
altogether novel. . . . We must admit that no man can acquire fresh
knowledge . . . beyond the measure which his own mental strength
and stage of development fits him to receive. But little children have
no development at all. . . . Little children . . . ought not to be
schooled and taught, they need merely to be *developed*. It is the
pressing need of our age, and only the idea of a garden can serve to
show us symbolically . . . the proper treatment of children.[17a]

To know what the needs of childhood are, we must study
children:

What, now, shall the school teach? In what shall the human
being, the boy as scholar, be instructed?
Only the consideration of the nature and requirements of human
development at the stage of boyhood will enable us to answer this
question. But the knowledge of this nature and these requirements
can be derived only from the observation of the character of man
in his boyhood.[18]

16. ibid, pp. 28–9.   17. ibid, p. 30.
17a. *Letters on the Kindergarten*, p. 291.
18. *Education of Man*, HAILMANN, p. 137.

The characteristic form of activity, natural and proper to earliest childhood, is play. Froebel was by no means the first to realize this, but he was the first to penetrate below the surface and to find the deeper significance of play, and by so doing to elevate it from being something which must be tolerated, or at best, a pleasant path to learning, to being something worthy of the most serious consideration.

The plays of childhood are the germinal leaves of all later life.[19]

Play is the highest phase of child development – of human development at this period, for *it is self-active representation of the inner – representation of the inner from inner necessity and impulse.*

Play is the purest, most spiritual activity of man at this stage. . . . It holds the sources of all that is good. A child that plays thoroughly, with self-active determination, perseveringly until physical fatigue forbids, will surely be a thorough, determined man, capable of self-sacrifice for the promotion of the welfare of himself and others.[20]

Froebel has his heirs in the best of modern infant and nursery schools, in those who are working to convince the nation of the need to provide suitable and adequate places for the children of the flats and cities to play. To him is due the enrichment of childhood of our own time. Where his ideas have been most fully understood the schools provide an environment to meet the needs of little children, where, through play, they are led gradually and naturally into work, which for them has the same quality of spontaneity and joy which is characteristic of their play.

All work should have this characteristic of play, which may be called free activity. The term has become overlaid in our time and many critics regard it with suspicion. It is valuable to remember that Froebel defined it as 'intelligent action'. For him only action or activity which gave rise to mental activity deserved his name. As Froebel uses the term it has the meaning of all that is the opposite of mechanical, the opposite of all that can be done without thinking. Work

can only become intellectual action . . . when the occupation of the hand is at the same time the occupation of the mind.

19. ibid, p. 55.   20. ibid, pp. 54–5.

To lead children early to think, this I consider the first and fore-most object of child-training.[21]

This can be done in many ways, primarily by encouraging children to find out for themselves, to discover:

Do not . . . tell him in words much more than he could find himself without your words. For it is, of course, easier to hear the answer from another, perhaps to only half hear and understand it, than it is to seek and discover it himself. To have found one fourth of the answer by his own effort is of more value and importance to the child than it is to half hear and half understand it in the words of another; for this causes mental indolence. Do not, there-fore, always answer your children's questions at once and directly; but, *as soon as they have gathered sufficient strength and experience,* furnish them with the means to find the answers.[22]

They should learn to observe. He describes the teacher's task:

Not the communication of knowledge already in their posses-sion is the task, but the calling forth of new knowledge. Let them observe, lead their pupils to observe, and render themselves and their pupils conscious of their observations.[23]

The child must also touch and handle and construct:

It is not enough that we show him objects; it is necessary that he touch them, that he handle them, that he appropriate them to him-self. . . . He takes delight in constructing; he is naturally geo-metrician and artist.[24]

Action and experience are the best means of learning:

'Man understands just as far as he tries to do.'[25]
'Knowledge acquired in our own active experience is more living and fruitful than that conveyed only by words.'[26]

Froebel suggests many ways in which children can learn by doing: making things for the home, including kitchen utensils and mats for the table and floor; chopping wood for the

21 ibid, p. 87.   22. ibid, pp. 86–7.   23. ibid, p. 200.
24. COMPAYRÉ *History of Pedagogy,* p. 449.
25. *Education of Man,* FLETCHER and WELTON, p. 56.
26. ibid, pp. 154–5.

furnace; binding books; making nature and art collections and boxes for storing them; looking after the garden and orchard; working in the fields; tending ducks, chickens and pigeons; drawing, painting and modelling in clay.

The study of nature is given first place, for nature is a revelation of God. 'From every object of nature and life there is a way to God.' The care of plants and animals will help a child to foster his own life:

Teachers should scarcely let a week pass without taking to the country a part of their pupils, . . . making them observe and admire the varied richness which nature displays to their eyes at each season of the year.[27]

Understanding and love of nature is the prelude to religion. Baroness von Marenhaltz-Bülow, one of Froebel's greatest admirers, wrote:

All work, all exercises, which awaken the active powers which form the capacity for rendering loving service to fellow creatures, will help to lay the groundwork of religion in the child.[28]

Education is not wholly from within and as the child grows into boyhood he requires more and more of the outer to be made inner, as well as the inner outer:

As the preceding period of human development, *the period of childhood*, was predominantly that of *life* for the sake merely of living, for making the internal external, so the *period of boyhood* is predominantly the period for *learning*, for making the external internal.[29]

In his remarkable insight into the inner workings of the mind of a child, Froebel was far ahead of his time. He is the first psychologist of early childhood:

Play and speech constitute the element in which the child lives. Therefore, the child at this stage imparts to each thing the faculties of life, feeling, and speech. Of everything he imagines that it can

27. *History of Pedagogy*, p. 456.
28. LAWRENCE, *Friedrich Froebel and English Education*, p. 164.
29. *Education of Man*, HAILMANN, p. 94.

hear. Because the child himself begins to represent his inner being outwardly, he imputes the same activity to all about him, to the pebble and chip of wood, to the plant, the flower, and the animal.[30]

His sympathy with children reveals a rare understanding of their motives and of the damage that can be done by adults who do not have such insight. He tells of a boy shooting at a neighbour's pigeons and speaks of his intense desire to hit his mark:

He did not consider that, if the bullet should hit the mark, the pigeon would be killed.... It is certainly a very great truth ... that it generally is some other human being, not unfrequently the educator himself, that first makes the child or the boy bad. This is accomplished by attributing evil – or at least, wrong – motives to all that the child or the boy does from ignorance, precipitation, or even from a keen and praiseworthy sense of right or wrong. ... Such birds of ill omen ... are the first to bring guilt upon such a child, who, though not wholly innocent, is yet without *guilt*; for they give him motives and incentives which were as yet unknown to him.[31]

Froebel had no doubt about what was of most importance in a school:

Airy, bright school-rooms are a great, precious boon, worthy the daily gratitude of teacher and pupil; but alone they are not sufficient.[32] It is by no means the acquisition of a certain number of miscellaneous external facts that constitutes the essential characteristic of the school, but only the living spirit that animates all things and in which all things move.[33]

So his kindergarten, in the words of Hughes, 'was a little world where responsibility was shared by all, individual rights respected by all, brotherly sympathy developed by all, and voluntary co-operation practised by all'.

Froebel's view of childhood may have been too idealized, taking too little account of the forces which work, both within and without, to frustrate the natural and harmonious development which he believed, given the right education, was inevitable, but his deeply held beliefs in the sacredness of childhood

30. ibid, p. 54.   31. ibid, pp. 124–5.
32. ibid, p. 131.   33. ibid, p. 129.

and his respect for personality, gave to the study of childhood a new dignity and importance. The great advances in the present century in the psychological study of children, which give a fuller and clearer picture of their needs and nature, is a direct outcome.

25

Sir Thomas Wyse

'EDUCATION must be studied as a science,' declared Sir Thomas Wyse, Member of Parliament for Tipperary, whose work for education produced, in Cobden's words, a sort of 'moral intoxication'. Believing in the need of education for all children he put forward a scheme to provide a universal system. Teachers must be trained, he urged, and largely as a result of his work the first training college for teachers was established at Battersea.

It is, unquestionably, a singular circumstance, that, of all problems, the problem of Education is that, to which by far the smallest share of persevering and rigorous analysis has yet been applied. The same empiricism, which once reigned supreme in the domains of chemistry, astronomy, and medicine, still retains possession, in many instances, of those of education.... No journal is kept of the phenomena of infancy or childhood – no parent has yet registered, day after day, ... the marvellous developements of his child. [He adds in a footnote: Perhaps we ought to except the Journal given by Madame Guizot ... and the specimen which forms the *Appendix to Miss Edgeworth's Practical Education*.] Until this is done, there can be no solid base for reasoning.[1]

Education has lost its high purpose:

We make bankers, or attorneys, and not heroes – machines for business or intrigue, *ad nauseam*, but few great men.[2]

True education should be a living thing, dealing in realities, whose aim is

to give the individual entire possession of himself. . . .
Instead of building up a dead mind and a dead heart, it draws forth life to the mind and life to the heart, from the fountain of life within. It teaches numbers, instead of ciphers – living sounds,

1. WYSE, SIR THOMAS, *Education Reform*, pp. 25–6.
2. ibid, p. 94.

instead of dead characters – deeds of faith and love, instead of abstruse creeds – substances, instead of shadows – realities, instead of signs.[3]

Sir Thomas's rather cynical comment on the national attitude towards education is not entirely inappropriate today. Speaking of the evils of large classes, as prevalent in his day as in ours, he writes:

But why not, then, have small ones? We are too economical a generation for that. If we could educate by steam, and by millions, no matter how badly, provided it were also cheaply, I have little doubt we should risk the experiment. . . . Who is there that does not feel that Education is but a section of Finance? 'Virtus *post* nummos.' Our purses first, and our minds afterwards. If both objects can be accomplished, so much the better; but at all events, and under all circumstances, our purses.[4]

For Wyse, education is basically religious:

The best means we can devise for preparing the future man for the ends destined by the Creator.[5]

Even mathematics should contribute to spiritual development:

Geometry is no longer a chaos of conundrums, but a beautiful interweaving of order within order, truth growing upwards out of truth, full of holy influences on the heart, as well as on the head.[6]

The purpose of human life 'is the full perfection of our being in another world through the faithful discharge of duty here', and it is to be achieved through 'the full development of our double nature'.

Thus, education must be of the whole man:

Good Education . . . necessarily embraces the whole man, – body, head and heart.[7] No single chord of our complicated being should be left untouched or unstrung. . . . This feeling of *unity of keeping* in the intellectual and moral man, as well as in the physical, was the *beau ideal* of ancient education.[8]

3. ibid, p. 94.   4. ibid, p. 203.
5. ibid, p. 36.   6. ibid, p. 94.
7. ibid, p. 56.   8. ibid, p. 74.

Those who would separate moral and intellectual education judge erroneously, and thank God, attempt impossibilities. Half of our being cannot thus be torn from the other. They are intertwisted: it is difficult to say, where one begins, and the other ends.[9]

A man *all reason*, as well as a man *all imagination*, like a man wholly physical or wholly intellectual, is only half a man.... Proportion — symmetry — are the first great rules of all education.[10]

The feelings and the imagination, therefore, must receive education along with the reason.

The Imagination should be diligently and lovingly conducted, not for its own sake only, but for the sake of all the other powers which walk with it.[11]

Education of the feelings neglected,

the cold skeleton of knowledge is given; but it wants the muscle, and the flesh, and the 'purple light' of youth — the breathing spirit of life within, by which the man is distingushed from the machine, and wisdom from barren information.[12]

Education is a gradual process and there should be no attempt at forcing:

The senses being educated, next follows the education of the young intellect. It is just in its bud, and is not to be forced open, but allowed to blow.[13]

The method of education should be such as will lead to mental effort and must therefore be the way of discovering, first-hand observation and self-activity:

When we say *taught*, it is meant not only that the teacher should teach, but, what is far more difficult, should enable the pupil to *teach himself*.[14]

The pupil must examine, observe, develop, combine, appropriate, and apply the ideas he acquires; he must do this in a great measure by *himself*. This cannot be effected by heaping on him in a crude form the ideas of *others*.[15]

9. ibid, p. 59.   10. ibid, pp. 73, 74.
11. ibid, p. 91.   12. ibid, p. 194.
13. ibid, pp. 81 2.   14. ibid, p. 109.
15. ibid, p. 213.

The child may be allowed to make his observations without any direct assistance. The teacher is scarcely required to intervene: all he has to do, amounts to little more than to see that nothing thwarts the wise education of nature. . . . The teacher should rather stimulate than satisfy; he should see that his pupil observes, examines, judges; but, so far from forcing on him his own explanations, he should be very cautious how he even answers all the questions which are proposed. . . . A child who desires an answer . . . will think some time, and search himself, before he goes to another. It ought to be the object of the instruction to increase this feeling, to throw the child in upon his own resources, and make it work out its own mind.[16]

The sense of power which comes from learning for oneself should be utilized:

Children delight in thus discovering and using the powers of their own mind – . . . they like the sense of power. . . . This principle may be seized. . . . The child should be allowed and induced to walk, but not forced to grope his way.[17]

Children in their learning should follow the road taken by men in the past.

'No science yet came fully-armed, Minerva-like, from the human intellect',[18] but grew from observation of facts,

then by a collection of observation of deductions from these observations; finally, by the arrangement of these deductions into rules and principles. . . . Precisely in this manner should the child proceed; he should set out by observation of *facts* – by discovering. It will be time later to come to their *arrangement* – to reasoning.[19]

The world around can provide plenty of material for such first-hand observation:

Country walks with their teacher . . . may . . . be applied to the most beneficial purposes. The teacher . . . should extract Education from every thing. To the young, especially, every thing around is a book.[20]

The rudiments of geography can be learned in the daily walk:

16. ibid, pp. 215–16.
17. ibid, pp. 83–4.
18. ibid, p. 129.
19. ibid, p. 129.
20. ibid, p. 69.

A child sees all the definitions which load our geographical catechisms and grammars, far better in the open page of nature, than in books. Here, again, I would pursue the same process ... – the road of invention. I would begin, as men began; – I would lead the child by the same steps by which they were led, to the discovery and arrangement – from observation to rule, and from one rule to the other – until they had embodied the science at last. Man did not set out with a definition of our universe, and a description of the imaginary divisions of our globe: he began with his valley; ... he was, what the child now is, – and the child should be taught, by the same succession, not of theories, but of facts.[21]

In the same way, zoology should as far as possible be a first-hand study

from nature itself, and not from copies.... The child should begin, too, with the animals within his actual observation, instead of at once setting out, as is usually the case, with lions, elephants, etc. A dog, a sheep, an ass, seen and compared every day, will be a better lesson for his faculties, and a better preparation for future enquiries and discoveries, than all the monsters of the African deserts.... The examination of the object being diligently gone through, the classification should follow; but this classification should be the pupil's own.[22]

The teaching of mathematics, in particular, should follow the method of first-hand discovery preceding rules; it can begin as soon as the child can speak: 'The moment it can say "another and another" it has begun.'[23]

Geometry can be taught alongside arithmetic, and solids should be used before plane figures. Apples, balls, squares, cubes may be used,

always something visible and tangible. Additions and subtractions ... should be performed always in reference to real objects.[24]

It is better for children to discover rules for themselves than to be given short methods:

For a considerable period ... the pupil will continue to perform all his multiplications by repeated additions, and his divisions by repeated subtractions ... he will gradually, of himself, abridge

21. ibid, p. 140. 22. ibid, p 138.
23. ibid, p. 120. 24. ibid, p. 121.

these methods, and fall at last into the invention of a multiplication table. . . .

The multifarious names, and formulae put forward with such pretension in [School Arithmetics] are only another of the numerous mystifications of our school learning. The habit of attending more to these formulae, than to principles, has produced precisely the same results, as in the study of language. Taken out of the particular rule, the pupil is at sea. . . . The method now insisted on, is precisely the reverse. It begins at the very beginning; advances gradually; never adopts a rule which is not deduced from practice, or a term before its adoption is felt to be requisite.[25]

The surroundings of the school are important:

Whenever they can be placed in suburbs or open spaces, – wherever most air, most sky, most of the bright and green of nature, can be had – there . . . ought such institutions . . . to be planted. Where this is not possible, compensation should be made for the want, by larger playrooms, and more airy workshops attached to the building. . . . Where so much of our spiritual nature depends upon mere material circumstances, as much life and joyousness should be thrown into them, as is possible.[26]

Wyse realized the importance of early childhood and was one of the first educators to appreciate the rights of young children:

The very youngest child has his rights, as sacred, and as much to be respected, as our own.[27]

If it be true that the man is educated in the child; the man and child are educated in the infant. . . . Yet, of all periods of education, this is the least considered as a period fitted *for* education, – as if the child could . . . be kept in a sort of suspended existence – between knowledge, and no knowledge, all this time. The child is educating, or miseducating; it is moving, thinking, living. We can choose, indeed, whether it shall be educated well, or educated ill; but we can no more put knowledge, or education of some kind or other, in abeyance, than we can life. But these truths are not believed, or not known.[28]

Much of the educational philosophy of Sir Thomas Wyse, written well over a century ago, still waits to be put into

25. ibid, pp. 124, 126.   26. ibid, p. 71.
27. ibid, p. 230.   28. ibid, p. 80.

general practice, along with the theories of so many of his predecessors and contemporaries, and, according to McCallister, his main ideas 'still remain standards of enlightened educational practice. He may be rightly regarded as the first exponent of methods designed to appeal to the pupil's *whole* life, and practical enough to be living forces in the education of the masses.'[29]

29. *The Growth of Freedom in Education*, p. 354.

26

Madame Necker de Saussure · J. P. F. Richter · Karl Rosenkranz

ONE of the effects of State control of education in France was to produce a new interest in home education for those who were not prepared to accept the influence of the Church in the public schools, and a number of French women now began to write on the subject.

It is difficult to understand why the name of Madame Necker de Saussure is not more well known. Her book *Progressive Education* shows a remarkable insight into the importance and needs of early childhood, and states clearly and convincingly most of the basic principles held by modern educationalists, and practised in the best twentieth-century infant schools. This book – probably the first on the subject – deals extensively with the first two years of life. She calls it 'a most important period',[1] and says: 'We do not in general sufficiently appreciate the great importance of the first year of infancy.'[2] This statement, probably made for the first time, has become one of the foundation-stones of modern child psychology.

> Because the infant cannot understand our fine discourses, and is not capable of being regularly instructed, we conclude that it is a mere insignificant little being, requiring only to have its physical wants attended to. Because its life is passed in playfulness we treat it as a plaything.[3]

Her conclusions were based on a careful study of children.

> I had studied my own children, without imagining that I was studying children in general. . . .[4]

It seemed to me that, in the constancy of the phenomena presented to our view by infancy, the effect of general laws was perceptible.[5]

1. DE SAUSSURE, MME N., *Progressive Education*, Vol. 1, Preface, p. xiii.

2. ibid, Vol. 1, Bk. 1, ch. 5, p. 98.   3. ibid, p. 98.
4. ibid, Vol. 1, Preface, pp. x–xi.   5. ibid, p. xi.

It is astonishing, that while in every other science requiring observation, such admirable perseverance has been displayed, no regular and methodical attention has ever been paid to the observation of infancy. . . . Yet what an inexhaustible fund of knowledge would be obtained by an attentive and judicious study of young children; and how much light might be thrown on many most important questions by a series of careful observations! What curious discoveries would these little creatures afford, on the existence of instinct in man; on the formation of language; in short, on the whole history of the human mind![6]

Only when such study of children is carried out thoroughly and systematically will answers be found to the fundamental questions of education:

What can escape the investigating spirit of this age?. . . May we not hope that some association will be formed for solving, by a series of facts, the great problems relating to education?. . .

In the present state of our knowledge on this subject, perhaps the most useful work on education would be a series of explanatory questions, to which answers might be furnished, within the next fifty years, by those enlightened minds who devote their attention to this most important subject.[7]

When institutions founded on entirely new principles, such as those of Pestalozzi, Fellenberg, and Père Girard, in Switzerland, and Hazlewood school, in England, become more common, some progress will be made towards solving the more important questions in education. We shall then learn, for example, whether the use of emulation . . . is absolutely necessary for the complete development of the powers of the mind. . . . And we may, perhaps, also learn to pay more attention to the culture of the feelings and the understanding. . . . Much light has been thrown on a more important branch of education – the formation of the character – by the infant schools which have been recently established. When we see in one of these schools above a hundred children, from two to six years old, acquiring habits of order and regularity, receiving the first elements of instruction, and pursuing their lessons, or their amusements, without a tear, an angry tone, or a quarrel, constantly happy and cheerful, we cannot but feel astonished at the extraordinary effect produced by such simple means; and wonder how it has happened that ages should have elapsed before recourse was had to such methods.[8]

6. ibid, Vol. 1, Bk. 1, ch. 1, pp. 40, 41.
7. ibid, pp. 49–51.   8. ibid, pp. 47–9.

This study is not easy, the reason being the important one that young children differ fundamentally from adults:

Before children can speak, their whole life appears a scene of confusion: their manner of feeling, of connecting ideas, and comparing them together, differs so entirely from ours, that we can neither understand nor explain it. ... At a more advanced period, when our means of communicating with them are increased, and they might themselves be able to throw some light on the subject, the difference between them and us is no longer so decidedly marked, and the child, in appearance at least, already too much resembles the man.[9]

She gives us the results of her own delightful observations, in which is noted, for the first time, the differences in stages of growth and development among young children:

Observe a group of children of different ages. He who can just walk proudly drags along an empty little cart; the noise of the wheels behind him is enough to make him happy. Another, a little older, must have a doll to ride in it: a third, still older, will give the doll a character, and make it act a part: while a child of five or six years old will fill the cart with sand, grass, or straw, thus trying to imitate, with some appearance of reality, any rural occupation. First arises the wish for simple activity – then that for the pleasures of imagination – and lastly that for supposed, or real, utility.[10]

Her careful observation of little children gave her an insight unequalled by any previous writer on education.

Give a child a box containing a sugar-plum, and he will be continually opening it, to see whether the treasure is still there; hide yourself behind a curtain, and his joy at seeing you again will prove, not that he would have been surprised at your non-appearance, but that it would have grieved him. The pleasure felt by children often arises from their being unexpectedly delivered from fears, of whose existence we had no previous suspicion. A sort of obscure personification of inanimate objects will frequently strengthen their impressions. They extend this personification, not only to their dolls, ... but to all their other playthings. Even the furniture, or articles of any kind, of which they are accustomed to make use, seem to them endowed with a kind of animated existence.[11]

9. ibid, Vol. 1, Bk. 2, ch. 1, p. 119.
10. ibid, ch. 3, p. 144.   11. ibid, ch. 5, pp. 166–7.

The part played by imagination is fully realized, and the consequent importance of children being given the right kind of playthings is stressed:

Playthings of their own invention amuse them far more than ready-made toys: imitations of real things, if too exact, soon meet with the fate of any other wearying pleasure. They are admired and valued at first; but their form, too nearly resembling reality, affords no scope to the imagination. . . . A figure of a soldier in full uniform can be nothing but a soldier; it cannot represent by turns the child's father, or brother, or any one else whom he may call upon. How much more originality does his young mind display, when, inspired by the imagination of the moment, he puts every thing within his reach in requisition in order to accomplish his wishes, and sees in all around him only the instruments of his pleasure! A stool turned wrong side up is a boat or a gig; placed on its legs again, it becomes a horse or a table. A pasteboard box may be a house, a cupboard, a coach – any thing in the world. We should be careful to cultivate and assist this talent for inventing playthings, by giving to our children, even before they are old enough for rational toys, the means of making things, rather than the things themselves. Some thick pieces of wood in the shape of books, which may be placed one upon another in different directions, are excellent materials for building. . . . Children, while very young, are also made perfectly happy, by having a quantity of sand or bran to play with; they will have dinners with it, fancy it land and water, or a variety of other things. With such simple materials, capable of becoming any thing suggested by the fancy of the moment, they will procure for themselves a constant variety of pleasures.[12]

This principle is illustrated by the story of a small boy of about two and a half who pretended to be a coachman, using two chairs for his horses: 'Should any one . . . place himself before the chairs, . . . he . . . becomes angry, and cries out, that "they prevent his horses going on". '[13] The same child fed imaginary poultry every day and begged that the door be left open so that the ducks and hens could get out.

'A real and deep feeling is often found to be associated with such illusions in the minds of children,' Madame de Saussure wrote,

12. ibid, pp. 171–2.   13. ibid, p. 173.

and there is something quite touching in the affection which a little girl sometimes shows towards her doll. Even at four years old, if she let her favourite fall, and unhappily its nose be broken, her despair, her tears, are really distressing; and they are re-doubled if a thoughtless father, not imagining the affair to be so very serious, laughs at her, and trying to mend the poor face, buries the rest of the maimed nose in an enormous hole. The child's grief is then mixed with anger, and becomes so violent as to be alarming. They contrive, however, to calm her; they take away the doll, promising to cure it; and at length the poor little creature, overcome by fatigue, falls asleep. Advantage is taken of this time to send the doll to be mended; a beautiful new face is substituted for the old one, and it is fully expected that the child, on awaking, will be satisfied and even delighted. But this is far from being the case; her grief, as lively as ever, has only assumed a more tender and distressing character. It is no longer passion; it is the sorrow of a true mother, to whom they have dared to offer another child instead of her own. Sobs impede her utterance as she exclaims, 'Oh, it is not my own doll! I knew it before, and now I do not know it at all: I shall never like it – take it away, – I won't look at it.' [14]

The imagination, the feelings, these are of paramount importance and in them lies the mainspring of education:

No effort can be obtained from the pupil without the excitement of some moving force in his mind.[15] Instead of cultivating feelings, we inculcate precepts; and thus our dry system of education is reduced to the art of prevention.... Our aim ... must be to influence the motives of children. At every age it is on the heart alone that any salutary effect can be produced; and at this early period it is only by sympathy that we can influence the heart.[16]

The educator must discover and

bring into action some of these moving forces which act most powerfully on the soul. The secret of all success lies in being able either to profit by the natural inclinations, or to create others in their place.... From these natural sources a taste for study may be imbibed; and by them, motives to be employed in education are furnished.[17]

14. ibid, pp. 174–5.
15. ibid, Vol. 2, Preliminary Chapter, p. 18.
16. ibid, Vol. 1, Bk. 1, ch. 3, pp. 78–9.
17. ibid, Vol. 2, Preliminary Chapter, p. 51.

Of these motives, one of the strongest is for the child to have an interest in his own education.

If we frequently consult him on the best means of increasing his application, his industry, his goodness – if we judiciously examine with him the various obstacles which prevent the accomplishment of his good intentions – he will soon begin to have pleasure in pointing out what he thinks would be the best plan to be pursued; he will be interested in the success of what he has suggested, and will at last regard the performance of his duty as the most important object of his life. . . .

By thus teaching a child . . . to find a teacher within his own breast, we are enabled to give him a much clearer idea of duty.[18]

For education is not something put on from without, it is an inner growth. 'The changes which take place in the "inward man" are the real events of life.' [19]

The teacher must take care that he allows this inward growth to take place and for this the child must have some measure of freedom.

Whenever it has been attempted to subject him to perpetual superintendence, the effect has been injurious; his will has been enervated from want of exercise: continually obliged to submit to the control of others, all internal energy has been destroyed; having always been directed, he has never learnt to act for himself; and his morality is of a completely passive character.[20]

Let us . . . be very careful not to throw any restraint over the enjoyments of children, but allow them freely to abandon themselves to the simple impressions natural to their age; and above all let us never endeavour to shackle them by the imposition of our own ideas. If we oblige them to find beauty, where for them it has no existence, we produce only an affectation.[21]

In his unsupervised play the child may show himself to be 'acting like a man':

And why is this? Because what we mean by the expression *acting like a man*, is that he should propose to himself some definite object, and choose certain means in order to attain it.[22]

18. ibid, pp. 60–61. 19. ibid, Vol. 1, Introduction, p. a.2.
20. ibid, Vol. 2, Bk. 4, ch. 5, p. 203.
21. ibid, Vol. 2, Bk. 2, ch. 3, pp. 97–8.
22. Ibid, Vol. 2, Bk. 4, ch. 5, p. 203.

A forerunner of modern nursery and infant educators, Madame de Saussure emphasizes the importance of free choice, and of self-discipline.

If the free choice of children could ever be brought to agree exactly with what we should have chosen for them, this would be the perfection of education. . . . The most praiseworthy obedience is not altogether satisfactory: *not*; it is always accompanied by a degree of restraint. . . . But as he [the child] must at some future time trace out for himself his own line of duty, it would be very desirable that . . . we should endeavour to make him feel the necessity of imposing certain duties on himself.[23]

Educators frequently fail in their object by teaching more than children are ready to learn:

We often fatigue children by our continual instruction.[24]

It is all too easy to do too much:

Sometimes our over anxiety to afford children the means of indulging their tastes, only produces satiety. If they show an interest in natural history, we immediately overwhelm them with books and engravings; or we present them with ready-made little collections, and in so doing are almost sure to disgust them.[25]

The secret of success lies in encouraging children to find out for themselves:

If we really desire to encourage, or to create a taste of this kind, our first endeavour should be to awaken a spirit of research, and to reward its efforts by the pleasure of obtaining the object in question. . . .
You may create a taste for science by means of the pebbles in your garden walk, and destroy it by the possession of a museum.[26]

Discovery and activity are then to be the chief means of education.

For the purpose of keeping the mind really active, we must admit the superiority of the method of teaching by investigation.[27]
We must never forget that the desire of activity, so natural to

23. ibid, pp. 204, 210.
24. ibid, Vol. 2, Bk. 2, ch. 1, p. 74.
25. ibid, p. 72.   26. ibid, pp. 72–3.
27. ibid, Vol. 2, Preliminary Chapter, p. 48.

children, forms the source of all their most lively pleasures. . . . They imagine that their enjoyment is derived from some particular object or amusement; while, in reality, it arises from the activity which is thus excited. . . . They have obtained what they desired, and in seeking for it the powers of their mind are developed.[28]

As clearly as any modern educationalist, Madame de Saussure shows how children's own activity and interest must be the starting-point for all development.

When your children have once learned to receive pleasure from their own activity, this activity may easily be directed towards such objects as will be favourable to the end you have in view.

One mistake into which we are very apt to fall, is that of requiring the first efforts of a child's attention, even before it has been exercised in any other way, to be directed to objects totally uninteresting to him. . . . Let us, in the first place, lead children to observe and examine such things as are likely to interest them.[29]

It is through such interest that intellectual development takes place, and it is of the greatest importance that the children should be allowed to become absorbed in whatever it is that has aroused their interest.

As soon . . . as we perceive their attention fixed on any object, we should carefully avoid disturbing them; every thing which excites their interest, or becomes the subject of their observation, assists in the developement of their intellect.[30]

Learning by doing is recognized as a good means of education.

Children delight so much in manual occupations, that it is always a fortunate circumstance when we are able, at the commencement of our instruction, to connect these with their other employments.[31]

Understanding must precede rote learning, if the children are not to form misconceptions.

Nothing . . . which is not thoroughly understood should be committed to memory. . . . Self-love or indolence often leads children to conceal their ignorance as much as possible; and hence they acquire, without our being aware of it, the most erroneous ideas as to the meaning of words.[32]

28. ibid, Vol. 2, Bk. 3, ch. 2, p. 89.   29. ibid, ch. 1, pp. 68-9.
30. ibid, Vol. 1, Bk. 1, ch. 2, p. 64.
31. ibid, Vol. 2, Bk. 3, ch. 5, p. 128.   32. ibid, p. 133.

Madame de Saussure rightly prophesied that the best education of the future would be based on children's need for activity arising from real experiences.

The idea of making use of the pleasure which children take in active employment, by bringing real life, with all its various interests, sooner within their reach, seems likely to become, at some future time, the *primum mobile* of education.[33]

The fault then, as now, lies in the narrow view as to what are the true values in education:

As long as instructors attach a higher value to temporary success, than to the motives which prompted the efforts by which that success was obtained, – as long as they attend more to external acquisitions than to internal feelings, they will never succeed in bringing the faculties of the mind to their greatest perfection.[34]

This perfection can never be attained by a concentration on the intellect alone. The direct road is not the shortest. Intellect cannot be developed in isolation, but is dependent upon the full development of the whole personality.

No combination of studies can ever entirely develope the full powers of the intellect. Every study requires application and attention; but there are other faculties which will expand only when the mind is free and unoccupied, and whose powers are checked by any effort being demanded from them. These, not being under the control of instruction, require some other exciting cause to bring them into action. Once awakened, they easily obtain materials on which to exercise themselves, in the accumulated stock of ideas which the mind has received through the medium of instruction; but we shall seldom find that the faculties relating to the feelings or the imagination, can be excited in the first instance by mere study.[35]

All worldly success depends so much on the intellectual powers that it is but too common for an instructor to consider the cultivation of these as the only object of his labours. Yet in so doing, he not only endangers the true interests of an immortal soul, but is unable even to form a well-arranged plan of education.[36]

But the intellect must not only be supplied with truths; the focus

33. ibid, Vol. 1, Bk. 2, ch. 3, p. 151.   34. ibid, p. 151.
35. ibid, Vol. 2, Preliminary Chapter, p. 24.   36. ibid, p. 2.

in which these all unite must also be made the center of the affections.[37]

If the moral qualities do not attain their full growth, the intellectual powers will be dwarfed with them.[38]

Intellectual and moral education are closely connected, and correspond in all their parts; it is in vain for the teacher to endeavour to separate them. . . .[39]

It is true enough that every fresh acquirement of knowledge must add to the cultivation of the faculties; but it is equally true, that our being more occupied in merely storing the mind with information, than in the full development of all its powers, is the cause of the greater part of the defects of instruction.[40]

The most common fault of all instruction, and of intellectual education in general, is that it tends too much to the exclusive developement of the reasoning powers.[41]

Instruction, the imparting of knowledge, is not enough. It can, in fact, be a danger. The teacher is tempted to use a method which he knows will bring a quick result, without seeking to know the quality of that result:

The exclusive importance attached to the mere acquisition of knowledge forms one of the dangerous snares of education. We are enticed by it to choose expeditious methods, and to avoid difficulties. The child appears to make a certain progress; he knows the things which you have taught him; he performs what you have showed him how to perform; but try him in a different direction, require of him some new exercise of his faculties, and he is quite at a loss. And even when arrived at manhood, this may continue to be the case, almost without our being aware of it. By the help of memory and imitation, we often see people make their way tolerably well. The degree of civilization at which we are arrived has created a form for almost every thing; a mechanical education extends its influence over the whole course of life; and hence it is that the number of insignificant beings is so great.[42]

The wise educator, however, will

oblige his pupil to reason for himself in applying the knowledge which he has acquired; will lead him to understand the principles

37. ibid, p. 4.
38. ibid, Vol. 1, Bk. 2, ch. 3, p. 151.
39. ibid, Vol. 2, Preliminary Chapter, pp. 18–19.
40. ibid, p. 12.   41. ibid, p. 21.   42. ibid, pp. 12–13.

of every thing, and even to discover, or, if possible, form for himself, practical rules.[43]

There will be no success until the teacher is more concerned with the child than with the subject he is teaching.

It has almost always happened that instructors have been too much influenced by partial and confined views. . . .
And so it will be, as long as the attention of the instructor is bestowed more upon the science he wishes to teach than on the pupil who is to be taught; as long as he is more desirous to form a living encyclopaedia, than an intellectual and moral being.[44]

Education, directed exclusively to the intellect, starves the feelings, and fails to develop the social instincts.

One of the disadvantages attending a studious life for children is, that the motives generally employed are merely personal ones; such as direct the views of the pupil to the future, as connected with himself alone; and do not call into exercise that noble disposition to devote himself to others, which may sometimes be observed even at a very early age, when children are engaged in active life. And when to this defect is added that of cultivating only the argumentative powers, can we wonder that our pupils are deficient in feeling? We instruct, but do not inspire; we scatter seeds in profusion, but have not previously fertilized the soil.[45]
We must never forget . . . that it is by the feelings alone that the soul is affected.[46]

The formation of character is the chief end of education.

To cultivate good dispositions, to give them that stability and permanence which may entitle them to the name of qualities, and to raise these qualities to the rank of virtues by stamping them with the sacred seal of religion, – such is the gradual progress of a good education, as it respects the formation of character.[47]

The method must be to 'overcome evil with good'.

Our best method of stifling or weakening evil inclinations is, to encourage the continual exercise of those that are good.[48]

The foundations are laid in early childhood. Opportunities

43. ibid, p. 13.   44. ibid, pp. 17, 18.
45. ibid, p. 23.   46. ibid, p. 37.
47. ibid, Vol. 1, Bk. 1, ch. 3, p. 66.   48. ibid, p. 66.

must be taken when the time is right. Morality is a matter of the heart, not the head.

If the favourable season of sympathy has been allowed to pass away, without our having gathered the fruits which it ought to have produced; such as a desire to please and oblige, a wish to relieve the afflicted, the power of giving up a pleasure in order to bestow it on another; – we shall soon arrive at a troublesome period, when our children will, to a certain degree, understand our exhortations, but will receive no moral impressions from them. Our reasonings may be listened to, understood, perhaps approved; but they will produce little effect, because we refer to motives which have not acquired any influence over their minds. . . . If the heart be not already well disposed, such an exercise of the understanding will have little influence on the conduct.[49]

Although an admirer of Rousseau, Madame de Saussure was critical of many of his theories; in particular she had no belief in a negative education. She suggests

that education must be positive from the earliest infancy; – not only keeping children from the example of evil, but gently impressing on them a tendency to good.

She recognizes the existence of

that instinct of sympathy in young children, which mothers know so well how to foster and encourage, and of which they make always so gentle, and sometimes so judicious, a use! The greatest service we could render to education would be, to improve and regulate what good sense and tenderness have often dictated to mothers; they understand thoroughly how to influence these little creatures: . . . for, at first, it consists almost entirely in loving them.[50]

More clearly perhaps than anyone before her, she realizes the need of young children for security and love, and draws attention to the importance of sympathy, and to the question of children's fears.

She suggests that the study of the natural sciences is of great value, both intellectually and morally:

The study of nature . . . possesses . . . inestimable advantages as regards his intellectual development. Every things here speaks to

49. ibid, ch. 3, pp. 98–9, 100.   50. ibid, p. 101.

his mind, and, by opening his eyes to what is passing around him, gives rise to an innumerable variety of reflections.[51]

One great advantage which children derive from the study of the natural sciences is, that it teaches them to arrive with certainty at the truth. . . . As every thing in them depends on facts – on real and sensible objects – children perceive at once the connection of cause and effect: they gain a habit of searching thoroughly into a subject; and are not contented, as is too frequently the case in the study of abstract ideas, with mere words.[52] Depending entirely on an attentive and accurate examination of sensible objects and phenomena, they may easily have a desirable tendency given to them, by making them the means of inspiring the pupil with a love of truth. All the facts and secondary causes which he is called upon to observe are referrible to the most sublime of all truths – the existence of one great Primary Cause.[53]

In this understanding of God, children are much closer to the truth than adults.

The chain by which every thing is connected with God is shorter to children than it is to us. . . . Children . . . may be said . . . to approach nearer than we do to eternal truth.[54] Not bound down, as we are, by fixed habits, their connection with earth is not so intimate. They can believe in what is unseen. . . . Religion already slumbers in their breast; requiring, not to be brought into existence, but only to be awakened.[55]

Slow children need especial care.

Though our pupil may be sluggish, heavy, insensible, he is as much entrusted to our care as if he were quick and intelligent. . . . And though the effect of our care may not be so apparent, it will really be much greater. We shall have contributed still more to the developement of his faculties, from their having required artificial heat to make them expand.[56]

In order to afford an exercise to the minds of children of a slow and confused understanding, material objects are far more useful than purely intellectual ideas. In fact, such is the case with almost all children at this age (5–7). . . . A volatile attention will be much sooner fixed by any information . . . which is illustrated by visible

51. ibid, Vol. 2, Bk. 3, ch. 2, p. 83.
52. ibid, Vol. 2, Preliminary Chapter, p. 35.
53. ibid, p. 33.   54. ibid, p. 33.
55. ibid, Vol. 1, Bk. 2, ch. 7, p. 195.
56. ibid, Vol. 2, Bk. 2, ch. 1, p. 70.

and tangible objects. The child is no longer a mere passive agent, but takes an active part in what is going on.[57]

Children who are taught by means of material objects may, perhaps, appear less intellectual, but every thing they possess is really their own.[58]

'What then must we do to ensure our success?' asks Madame de Saussure.

We must in the first place give our attention to the child, as such, and in the next prepare him for his future state of manhood. ... It was formerly too much the custom ... to consider only the future man; and the consequence was that the child was nothing but a pupil, overwhelmed with studies.[59] What then does a child, in his natural state, without any reference to the future, require? Activity, enjoyment, liberty.[60]

In case, however, the criticism should be made, as it is still made today by those who do not fully understand modern education, that this way of education is soft and enervating, and does not require enough of children, Madame de Saussure states the principle which underlies all that is best in the approach to teaching of our own day.

As it is our wish to accustom children to fix their attention even on objects not likely at first to interest them, and to give them a habit of rational and serious application, we should, instead of sparing them every difficulty, require from them a degree of effort proportionate to their strength.[61]

*

'All teaching is warming into life rather than sowing.'[62] In his conception of the child as a plant, and in his understanding of the meaning of play Richter echoes Froebel. In *Levana* he writes:

The plays and actions of children are as serious and full of meaning in themselves and in reference to their future, as ours are to ours.[63]

In beasts the body alone plays, in children the mind.[64]

57. ibid, pp. 70–71.   58. ibid, p. 71.
59. ibid, Vol. 2, Bk. 3, ch. 5, pp. 118, 119–20.
60. ibid, p. 118.   61. ibid, pp. 122–3.
62. RICHTER, J. P. F., *Levana*, p. 103.
63. ibid, p. 158.   64. ibid, p. 134.

If one were to make propositions, ... one might express this: That for every child a circle of games and real actions should be provided, composed of as many different individualities, conditions and years, as can possibly be found, in order to prepare him, in the *orbis pictus* of a diminished play-world, for the larger real one.[65]

Every plaything and playworld is only a distaff of flax from which the soul spins a many coloured coat.[66] Give no plaything whose end is only to be looked at; but let every one be such as to lead to work.[67]

A box of building materials ... will make [a child] as rich and happy as an heir to the throne.... I know no cheaper and more lasting plaything ... than ... – sand.[68]

The second kind of play is the playing of children with children. ... Teach children by children! The entrance into their play-room is for them an entrance into the great world; and their mental school of industry is in the child's play-room and nursery.[69]

The great fault of education is

that filling and cramming of the day with mere lessons; ... and what else ... is this but unceasingly to sow one field full of seed upon seed? A dead corn granary may possibly come out of it, but no living harvest field.... Your watch stops while you wind it up, and you everlastingly wind up children and never let them go.[70]

*

The German philosopher Karl Rosenkranz based his philosophy of education largely on Hegel's belief:

Pedagogy is the art of making man moral. It regards man as one with nature, and points out the way in which he may be born again, and have his first nature changed into a second spiritual nature, in such fashion that the spiritual nature may become habitual to him.[71]

'The nature of education,' Rosenkranz wrote, 'is determined by the nature of mind ... it can develop what is in itself only by its own activity.'[72]

Consequently education cannot impose itself, but can only work through the nature of the pupil himself:

65. ibid, p. 159.   66. ibid, p. 154.   67. ibid, p. 156.
68. ibid, p. 156.   69. ibid, p. 157.   70. ibid, p. 170.
71. MACKENZIE, *Hegel's Educational Theory and Practice*, p. 63.
72. ROSENKRANZ, KARL, *The Philosophy of Education*, p. 19.

It is the nature of education only to assist in the producing of that which the subject would strive most earnestly to develop for himself if he had a clear idea of himself.[73] Education can only lead and assist it; it cannot create.[74] Mind is essentially self-activity. ... Mind lets nothing act upon it unless it has rendered itself receptive to it.[75]

One of the natural desires in children is

to collect things, and this may be so guided that they shall collect and arrange plants, butterflies, beetles, shells, skeletons, etc., and thus gain exactness and reality in their perception.[76]

Ahead of his time, though echoing earlier writers, Rosenkranz expressed the view that full development required the education of all sides of human nature, not the intellect alone, and put forward the idea, only partly accepted in theory even now, and even less in practice, that 'feeling and imagination are not less necessary to a truly complete human being'.

73. ibid, p. 20.
75. ibid, p. 70.

74. ibid, p. 47.
76. ibid, p. 79.

27

Spencer

'How to live? – that is the essential question for us. . . . To prepare us for complete living is the function which education has to discharge.'[1] Such was the basis of Spencer's wide-flung philosophy of education.

It should therefore include education for self-preservation, for parenthood and for citizenship, as well as for the miscellaneous refinements of life; but the education of his time, according to Spencer, failed in all these respects.

In his shop, or his office, in managing his estate or his family, in playing his part as director of a bank or a railway, [a man] is very little aided by this knowledge he took so many years to acquire. . . .[2]

How widely, then, must teaching as it is, differ from teaching as it should be. . . . Under that common limited idea of education which confines it to knowledge gained from books, parents thrust primers into the hands of their little ones years too soon, to their great injury. Not recognizing the truth that the function of books is supplementary – that they form an indirect means to knowledge when direct means fail; . . . teachers are eager to give second-hand facts in place of first-hand facts. Not perceiving the enormous value of that spontaneous education which goes on in early years – not perceiving that a child's restless observation . . . should be diligently ministered to; . . . they insist upon occupying its eyes and thoughts with things that are, for the time being, incomprehensible and repugnant. Possessed of a superstition which worships the symbols of knowledge instead of knowledge itself, they do not see that only when his acquaintance with the objects and processes of the household, the streets, and the fields, is becoming tolerably exhaustive – only then should a child be introduced to the new sources of information which books supply. . . . Observe next, that this formal instruction, far too soon commenced, is carried on with but little reference to the laws of mental development. Intellectual progress is of necessity from the concrete to the abstract. But regardless of

1. SPENCER, HERBERT, *Education*, p. 7.   2. ibid, p. 2.

this, highly abstract studies ... are begun quite early ... See the results. What with perceptions unnaturally dulled by early thwarting, and a coerced attention to books – what with the mental confusion produced by teaching subjects before they can be understood, and in each of them giving generalizations before the facts of which they are the generalizations – what with making the pupil a mere passive recipient of others' ideas, and not in the least leading him to be an active inquirer or self-instructor; ... there are very few minds that become as efficient as they might be. Examinations being once passed, books are laid aside; the greater part of what has been acquired ... soon drops out of recollection; what remains is mostly inert; ... and there is but little power either of accurate observation or independent thinking.[3]

Knowledge can only be possessed satisfactorily through the self-activity of the pupil, through his first-hand experience and discovery, through a process of self-development, which should be encouraged to the uttermost.

Children should be led to make their own investigations, and to draw their own inferences. They should be *told* as little as possible and induced to *discover* as much as possible. ... Those who have been brought up under the ordinary school-drill ... will think it hopeless to make children their own teachers. If, however, they will consider that the all-important knowledge of surrounding objects which a child gets in its early years, is got without help – if they will remember that the child is self-taught in the use of its mother tongue – if they will estimate the amount of that experience of life, that out-of-school wisdom, which every boy gathers for himself, ... they will find it a not unreasonable conclusion, that if the subjects be put before him in right order and right form, any pupil of ordinary capacity will surmount his successive difficulties with but little assistance. ... This need for perpetual telling results from our stupidity, not the child's. We drag it away from the facts in which it is interested, and which it is actively assimilating of itself. We put before it facts far too complex for it to understand, and therefore distasteful to it. ... By thus denying the knowledge it craves, and cramming it with knowledge it cannot digest, we produce a morbid state of its faculties, and a consequent disgust for knowledge in general.[4]

Learning for oneself is the most effective and efficient form of acquiring knowledge.

3. ibid, pp. 27–9.   4. ibid, pp. 71–3.

Any piece of knowledge which the pupil has himself acquired – any problem which he has himself solved, becomes, by virtue of the conquest, much more thoroughly his than it could else be. The preliminary activity of mind which his success implies, the concentration of thought necessary to it, and the excitement consequent on his triumph, conspire to register the facts in his memory in a way that no mere information heard from a teacher, or read in a schoolbook, can be registered.[5]

To *tell* a child this and to *show* it the other, is not to teach it how to observe, but to make it a mere recipient of another's observations: a proceeding which weakens rather than strengthens its powers of self-instruction.[6]

After long years of blindness, men are at last seeing that the spontaneous activity of the observing faculties in children has a meaning and a use. What was once thought mere purposeless action, or play, or mischief ... is now recognized as the process of acquiring a knowledge on which all after-knowledge is based. ... Without an accurate acquaintance with the visible and tangible properties of things, our conceptions must be erroneous, our inferences fallacious, and our operations unsuccessful. ... 'The education of the senses neglected, all after education partakes of a drowsiness, a haziness, an insufficiency which it is impossible to cure.'[7]

Spencer sees clearly the influence of success upon achievement, and suggests that the cure for school failures lies in an active approach by which they learn for themselves. The confidence thus produced releases the power to attack difficulties in a new spirit, a spirit which ensures victory, since it stems from a new belief in their own powers.

It has repeatedly occurred that those who have been stupefied by the ordinary school-drill – by its abstract formulas, its wearisome tasks, its cramming – have suddenly had their intellects roused by thus ceasing to make them passive recipients, and inducing them to become active discoverers. ...

They no longer find themselves incompetent; they, too, can do something. And gradually as success follows success, the incubus of despair disappears, and they attack the difficulties of their other studies with a courage ensuring conquest.[8]

5. ibid, p. 93.　　　　　6. ibid, p. 79.
7. ibid, p. 58.　　　　　8. ibid, pp. 89–90.

Spencer bases his educational ideas on Plato's belief in the innate power within every man which is always working towards perfection and fulfilment. In this development there is a natural order of growth which needs to be followed in education.

Alike in its order and its methods, education must conform to the natural process of mental evolution — ... there is a certain sequence in which the faculties spontaneously develop, and a certain kind of knowledge which each requires during its development; and ... it is for us to ascertain this sequence and supply this knowledge.[9]

The right method of learning is to present the concrete before the abstract. This was the way of learning for the human race, and is the correct way for children:

While the old method of presenting truths in the abstract has been falling out of use, there has been a corresponding adoption of the new method of presenting them in the concrete.... Manifestly, a common trait of these methods is, that they carry each child's mind through a process like that which the mind of humanity at large has gone through. The truths of number, of form, of relationship in position, were all originally drawn from objects; and to present these truths to the child in the concrete is to let him learn them as the race learnt them.[10]

This idea that the child should in learning repeat the experience of the race, generally attributed to Spencer, was in fact put forward almost a hundred years earlier, by Condillac, the founder of Sensationalism, friend of Rousseau and Diderot and tutor to a grandson of Louis XIV. He wrote:

The method which I have followed does not resemble the usual manner of teaching; but is the very way in which men were led to create the arts and the sciences.

Spencer stresses the vital part played by interest in the process of education:

Experience is daily showing with greater clearness, that there is always a method to be found productive of interest — even of delight; and it ever turns out that this is the method proved by all other tests to be the right one.[11]

9. ibid, p. 61.   10. ibid, p. 59.   11. ibid, p. 74.

282 GROWTH OF MODERN EDUCATION

Every one knows that things read, heard or seen with interest, are better remembered than things read, heard, or seen with apathy. In the one case the faculties appealed to are actively occupied with the subject presented; in the other they are inactively occupied with it; and the attention is continually drawn away by more attractive thoughts. Hence the impressions are respectively strong and weak[12]

If education does not conform to the natural order of development –

if the higher faculties are taxed by presenting ... knowledge more complex and abstract than can be readily assimilated ... the ... abnormal advantage gained will inevitably be accompanied by some equivalent, or more than equivalent, evil.[13]

Spencer's conception of discipline is a natural outgrowth of his philosophical beliefs. It is not a separate part of education, but woven into its very fabric. It can never be imposed from without, but must come from within.

What now is the most important attribute of man as a moral being? May we not answer – the faculty of self-control? ...

But the power of self-government ... can be developed only by exercise. Whoso is to rule over his passions in maturity, must be practised in ruling over his passions during youth. Observe, then, the absurdity of the coercive system. Instead of habituating a boy to be a law to himself, as he is required in after-life to be, it administers the law for him. ... No wonder that those who have been brought up under the severest discipline should so frequently turn out the wildest of the wild.[14]

12. ibid, p. 95.   13. ibid, p. 168.   14. *Social Statics*, pp. 84–5.

28

David Stow

DAVID STOW, who began his work in education in his Sunday school in Glasgow in 1816, had much to say in criticism of the education of his time.

Till within the last few years, the term used to define Education was INSTRUCTION. Give elementary and religious *instruction*, it was and is still said, and this will be sufficient. Teach the poor to read the Bible, and forthwith you will make them good, holy, and happy citizens, – kind parents, – obedient children, – compassionate and honourable in their dealings; and crime will diminish. Hundreds of thousands of our population have received such an education. Are such the results?[1]

To be effective, education must be much more than instruction. It must be concerned with the whole man:

Man is not all head, all feeling, or all animal energy. He is a compound being, and must be trained as such.... The most influential and successful mode of cultivating the child is, therefore, the daily and *simultaneous* exercise of his intellectual, physical, and moral powers.[2]

Education, therefore, must be concerned with all sides of man's nature:

The cultivation of mind and body in school has been too much disjoined; and whilst the physical powers have not had their due share of attention, the intellect and verbal memory have been almost exclusively, though but partially, cultivated. The moral affections and habits have not been properly exercised and directed. ... The child has been held to be under cultivation when his intellect or verbal memory was being exercised, as if he were neither a physical nor a moral being; forgetting, or not attending to the fact, that the *simultaneous* cultivation or exercise of all the powers of our compound nature alone trains 'the child', and secures the

1. STOW, DAVID, *The Training System*, p. 5.   2. ibid, pp. 6–7.

highest attainment of each faculty; and that the sympathy of our nature is such, that the non-exercise or overstretching of one power or faculty to a certain extent weakens the others.[3]

He made a clear distinction between knowledge, in the form of telling or teaching, and training, which consists in doing and practice, and the training of the feelings:

'Knowledge indeed is power', but it is a power for evil as well as for good.[4]

Education consists not in the mere amount of knowledge communicated, but in the due exercise of all the faculties whereby the pupil acquires the power of educating himself. It is a mould for the formation of character.[5]

What the education is that will best enable a man to educate himself, ought surely to be the paramount inquiry.... Is it the amount of elementary knowledge communicated, or is it that exercise of mind by which the pupil acquires the power of educating himself? ... Can all the *telling*, or teaching, or instruction in the world enable a man to make a shoe, construct a machine, ride, write, or paint, without *training* – that is, without *doing*? Can the mere *head-knowledge* of religious truth make a good man without the practice of it – without the training of the affections and moral habits? Will teaching to read, write, and cast accounts cultivate the child – the whole man?[6]

Too many school books are put into the hands of children of all ages, and too many tasks are required to be committed to memory. *Knowing* is not equivalent to *doing*.... Morally and intellectually, as well as physically, *we only know a thing when we do it.*[7] Training may be doing not merely with the *hand* or the *tongue*, but the *understanding* and *affections.*[8]

The schoolmaster ... must ... cultivate by exercise *the whole man*, in his thoughts, affections and outward conduct.[9]

The environment, in which such education can take place, has never yet been seriously considered:

What suitable school premises for popular education ought to be, remains, therefore, quite as undefined as the term Education itself. ... School accommodation, to teach or instruct the head, may be

3. ibid, p. 3.
4. ibid, p. 12.
5. ibid, p. 14.
6. ibid, pp. 5–6.
7. ibid, pp. 81, 137, 285.
8. ibid, p. 326.
9. ibid, p. 7.

just what it has hitherto been, viz., the one school-room, not un-frequently *dingy, dirty, and airless.* What a school for 'training' the child ... *must be,* is quite another thing. The physical, intellectual and moral propensities and habits, must have *free* exercise under a proper superintendence, and the opportunity of development in *real* life, which, to a child, is freely at play.[10]

Schools are not so constructed as to enable the child to be super-intended in real life, which is at play; the master has not the opportunity of training, except under the *unnatural* restraint of a covered school-room; and it is imagined, or at least stated, that children are morally trained, without their being placed in circum-stances where their moral dispositions and habits may be developed and cultivated; as if it were possible to train a bird to fly in a cage, or a race-horse to run in a stable.[11]

Real knowledge, understanding, is obtained through self-education, and through the education gained from living in society:

Education ... comprehends that of the family, and the educa-tion ... which we all more or less experience in the intercourse of society.... Above all, it embraces self-education, to which every man is most of all indebted for his *real* knowledge and attain-ments.[12]

Education is '*that system which cultivates the whole nature of the child, instead of the mere head – the affections and habits, as well as the intellect*'.[13]

Stow stresses the importance of the early years of child-hood:

We ought to place the young under the most accomplished masters.... 'Learn early, learn well'.... [14]

It ... is a very generally received opinion that education cannot be properly commenced with children under five or six years of age. This is perfectly true, when the process is confined to books and mere teaching or instruction – stuffing instead of *feeding*, forcing instead of leading or *training.*[15]

Childhood is

one of the most important stages of the life of man ... – a period *by far the most impressible*, when habits are only beginning

10. ibid, pp. 7–8.   11. ibid, p. 6.   12. ibid, p. 2.
13. ibid, p. 32.   14. ibid, p. 277.   15. ibid, p. 11.

to be formed, ideas expanded, and propensities requiring to be regulated.... At a later period, even at six years of age, improper habits, bodily and mental, ... must be undone before correct ones can be established.[16]

He draws attention to what is a fundamental problem in the training of young children, that education, in the true sense of the word, cannot be assessed, and therefore there is always the temptation to look for results that can be seen and measured:

The process of moral training in the school or in the family cannot be rendered so visible to a visitor or inspector, as can the intellectual process and its results.[17]

The great and general mistake appears to arise from the fatal idea and practical error of substituting mere intellectual *instruction* for intellectual and *moral training*, and imagining that the 'child' is under cultivation when the *head* alone is being exercised.[18]

Stow, unfortunately, did not know how to put into practice his splendid theories. A school, for him, was a series of galleries of sixty or seventy children, all answering at once and reading in unison, and it was left to a later generation to develop schools which should really begin to achieve the high and excellent aims of which he wrote.

16. ibid, p. 11.   17. ibid, p. 43.   18. ibid, p. 2.

29

Arnold of Rugby

DR ARNOLD was concerned with wider issues than the life and work within the walls of a school. He was deeply disturbed by the trends in the social and religious life of his time and always saw the problems of education, both in his own school and elsewhere, in the broadest setting. The purpose of his work at Rugby was to a large extent to prevent the spread of moral anarchy which he saw as both the cause and effect of the French Revolution, and his educational theory and practice were a reaction against the theories of Rousseau as its educational mouthpiece.

The aim of education, for him, was not to develop the intellect, nor to impart knowledge, but to bring about the change from childhood to manhood. This, he said, is 'altogether distinct from a premature advance in book-knowledge'. It is rather 'a change from ignorance to wisdom'.[1]

Wisdom is not the same as knowledge. 'Knowledge, unhappily, can exist without wisdom, as wisdom can exist with a very inferior degree of knowledge',[2] and knowledge of the usual school subjects does not bring us 'of necessity any nearer to real thoughtfulness, such as alone gives wisdom, than the knowledge of a well-contrived game', since it may have nothing whatever to do 'with our being better men, or ... with our pleasing God.[3] The great work of education is to make us love what is good, and therefore not only know it, but do it.' [4] Arnold Whitridge writes:

Arnold's conception of the schoolmaster's rôle rested on a hypothesis that was widely challenged in his own lifetime and is not entirely accepted even today. He believed that a boy was a moral being and that a school was a human society.[5]

1. ARNOLD, THOMAS, *Sermon F*, Vol. 4, No. 3, FINDLAY, p. 151.
2. ibid, p. 151.   3. ibid, pp. 151–2.
4. *Sermon L*, Vol. 5, No. 8, FINDLAY, p. 190.
5. WHITRIDGE, ARNOLD, *Arnold of Rugby*, p. 133.

Education should lead the child's natural instincts towards the truth:

We should desire so to raise the understanding as that it may fasten itself, by its own native tendrils, round the pillar of truth,

and the means should be by avoiding

all unnecessary harshness; we should speak and act with all possible kindness; because love, rather than fear, ... is the motive which we particularly wish to awaken. Thus, keeping punishment in the background ... and putting forward encouragement and kindness, we should attract ... the good and noble feelings of those with whom we are dealing.[6]

One of Arnold's chief objects was that his pupils should learn to think for themselves. Writing to a parent, he said:

The difference between a useful education, and one which does not affect the future life, rests mainly on the greater or less activity which it has communicated to the pupil's mind, whether he has learned to think, or to act, and to gain knowledge by himself, or whether he has merely followed passively as long as there was some one to draw him,[7]

and in a letter to Mr Sergeant Coleridge he wrote:

You will be amused when I tell you that I am becoming ... more suspicious of the mere *fact* system, that would cram with knowledge of particular things, and call it information,

and writing to Rev. F. C. Blackstone he says:

I seem to find it more and more hopeless to get men to think and inquire freely and fairly, after they have once taken their side in life. The only hope is with the young, if by any means they can be led to think for themselves without following a party, and to love what is good and true, let them find it where they will.[8]

To Mr Justice Coleridge he wrote:

I am sure that the more active my own mind is, ... the better for the school, ... because education is a dynamical, not a mechanical process, and the more powerful and vigorous the mind of the teacher, ... the better fitted he is to cultivate the mind of another. And to this I find myself coming more and more: I care

6. ARNOLD, *Sermon H*, Vol. 4, FINDLAY, p. 165.
7. STANLEY, *Life and Correspondence of Thomas Arnold*, p. 36.
8. ibid, p. 348.

ARNOLD OF RUGBY

less and less for information, more and more for the pure exercise of the mind.[9]

'His whole method,' wrote Stanley,

was founded on the principle of awakening the intellect of every individual boy. Hence it was his practice to teach by questioning. As a general rule, he never gave information, except as a kind of reward for an answer. ... His explanations were as short as possible. ... 'You come here', he said, 'not to read, but to learn how to read'; and thus the greater part of his instructions were interwoven with the process of their own minds; there was a continual reference to their thoughts, an acknowledgement that, so far as their information and power of reasoning could take them, they ought to have an opinion of their own.[10]

He was always restrained from speaking much or often, both from the extreme difficulty which he felt in saying anything without a real occasion for it, and also from his principle of leaving as much as possible to be filled up by the judgment of the boys themselves, and from his deep conviction that, in the most important matters of all, the movement must come, not from without, but from within.[11]

His wish was that as much as possible should be done *by* the boys, and nothing *for* them; hence arose his practice ... of treating the boys as gentlemen and reasonable beings, of making them respect themselves by the mere respect he showed to them; of showing that he appealed and trusted to their own common sense and conscience.[12]

'I cannot remain here,' he once addressed the school, 'if all is to be carried out by constraint and force; if I am to be here as gaoler, I will resign my office at once.'[13]

He at once made a great alteration in the whole system of punishments in the higher part of the school; 'keeping it as much as possible in the background, and by kindness and encouragement attracting the good and noble feelings of those with whom he had to deal.'[14]

He determined to use, and to improve to the utmost, the existing machinery of the Sixth Form, and of fagging. ... Whilst he made the Praeposters rely upon his support in all just use of their authority, as well as on his severe judgment of all abuse of it, he endeavoured also to make them feel that they were actually fellow-workers with him for the highest good of the school, upon the highest principles and motives – that they had, with him, a moral

9. ibid, p. 396.　　10. ibid, pp. 122–3.　　11. ibid, pp. 152–3.
12. ibid, pp. 99–100.　　13. ibid, p. 101.　　14. ibid, p. 101.

responsibility and a deep interest in the real welfare of the place.[15]
'When I have confidence in the Sixth,' was the end of one of his
farewell addresses, 'there is no post in England which I would
exchange for this; but if they do not support me, I must go.'[16]

Arnold was more concerned with developing character than
with intellect. 'For mere cleverness . . . he had no regard,' wrote
Stanley. 'Mere intellectual acuteness, . . . divested as it is, in too
many cases, of all that is comprehensive and great and good,
is to me more revolting than the most helpless imbecility,'[17]
he said.

What he considered to be the chief ends of education he put
clearly in a letter to J. C. Platt:

I hold . . . that there are but two things of vital importance, . . .
our duties and affections towards God, and our duties and feelings
towards men; science and literature are but a poor make-up for
the want of these,[18]

and in a letter to an old pupil he gives his idea of the true
meaning of wisdom:

I call by the name of wisdom – knowledge, rich and varied,
digested and combined, and pervaded through and through by the
light of the Spirit of God.

To the Praeposters on one occasion he said:

What we must look for here is 1stly, religious and moral principles; 2ndly, gentlemanly conduct; 3rdly, intellectual ability.[19]

One of his assistant masters at Rugby, writing of Arnold's
days at Laleham, said:

Every pupil was made to feel that there was a work for him to
do – that his happiness as well as his duty lay in doing that work
well. . . . Pupils of the most different natures were keenly stimulated;
none felt that he was left out, or that, because he was not endowed
with large powers of mind, there was no sphere open to him, in
the honourable pursuit of usefulness. This wonderful power of
making all his pupils respect themselves, and of awakening in them
a consciousness of the duties that God assigned to them personally
. . . was one of Arnold's most characteristic features as a trainer of
youth.[20]

15. ibid, pp. 104–6.   16. ibid, p. 107.   17. ibid, p. 116.
18. ibid, p. 395.   19. ibid, p. 107.   20. ibid, p. 37.

Arnold Whitridge compares him with Vittorino da Feltre:

What a curious similarity between Vittorino da Feltre and Dr
Arnold. Both men set out to develop character rather than to
fashion scholars, both men emphasized moral thoughtfulness, and
both were rewarded by the personal devotion of their pupils. Profoundly English as Dr Arnold was, he had more in common with
this Italian humanist of the Renaissance than with the average
headmaster of his own time and nationality. The blight that fell
upon humanism, transforming it from a discipline which aimed at
drawing out all the mental and moral faculties of man to a meaningless display of pedantry disguised under the name of 'pure
scholarship', explains the decay of English secondary education.[21]

It was Dr Arnold, continued Whitridge, who 'restored confidence in public schools by inoculating them with the old
conception of humanism'.

21. WHITRIDGE, *Arnold of Rugby*, p. 61.

30

ALL the great educators realized to some degree the necessity for understanding children; many suggested the need for observation and study in order to adapt teaching methods to the varying natures of children, but, with the exception of Madame Necker de Saussure and one or two others, little systematic study was attempted until the last two decades of the nineteenth century. Then, influenced by Darwin's theory of evolution and the growth of scientific method, an attempt was made to study children with an exactness somewhat comparable to that of the physical sciences.

In this study, originating in America, from where it spread rapidly over the world, the pioneer was G. Stanley Hall. Gesell describes him as 'the greatest modern student of the child, the Darwin of psychology'. Hall describes the revolution in teaching methods which must be the consequence of a study of children:

Teachers as a rule do not study the nature of the children they instruct.[1]

A number of investigations was carried out, some by direct observation, some by questionnaire method, applied both to children and to adults, who were asked to remember their childhood experiences and thoughts. Some of the subjects covered were:

the children's relation to Nature, including their experience with light and darkness and day and night, the sky, sun, moon, clouds, storms, rocks and earths, flowers and animals;

the development of the sense of self and of the concept of soul; shame and modesty; the psychology of dress, clothes and ornaments; illness; children's ambitions; jealousy; egoism and altruism;

1. PREYER, *Mind of the Child*, Part 1, Intro. to American Edition, p. xxii.

pleasure and pain; children's fears; anger, sympathy, pity; gangs; only children; reactions to solitude; leadership, teasing and cruelty; plays and games; effects of co-education;

fun, wit and humour in children; children's dreams; curiosity and interest; fetishes; collections and punishments.

The result of his research among school children in Boston, on 'The Content of Children's Minds on Entering School', led him to the conclusion:

That there is next to nothing of pedagogic value, the knowledge of which it is safe to assume at the outset of school life. Hence the need of objects and the danger of books and word cram.[2]

The misconceptions in children's minds which came to light through this investigation confirmed this conclusion, for they suggested

how a child may be led, in the absence of corrective experience, to the most fantastic and otherwise unaccountable distortions of facts by shadowy word specters or husks.

*

'Among all the nearly fourscore studies of young children printed by careful empirical and often thoroughly scientific observers,' wrote Hall in his Introduction to Preyer's *The Mind of the Child*, 'this work of Preyer is the fullest and on the whole the best.'[3]

The Mind of the Child, published in 1881, was based on Preyer's study of his own son, of whom he kept a complete diary from birth to the end of his third year.

The conclusions he reached are of considerable significance for education:

The mind of the new-born child ... does not resemble a *tabula rasa*, upon which the senses first write their impressions, ... but the tablet is already written upon before birth, with many illegible, nay, unrecognizable and invisible, marks, the traces of the imprint of countless sensuous impressions of long-gone generations.[4]

2. *Aspects of Child Life and Education*, p. 23.
3. *Mind of the Child*, Part 1, Intro. to American Edition, p. xxiii.
4. Ibid, p. xiv.

He saw that all learning must come through play and through the child's own experience.

'What a schooling the child goes through in his play . . . has not yet been by any means investigated psychologically,'[5] he suggests.

Children ought not to be disturbed when they are playing harmlessly, without imperative reasons. They should not be hindered . . . from teaching themselves through their own perceptions.[6]

For a long time and widely the error prevailed, that for the child's first learning there was absolute necessity of a teacher. . . . Herein lies a gross fallacy. . . . Because the highest culture can not be attained without thorough instruction in language, the inference was drawn that this culture is attained exclusively through instruction in language. Our schools are still suffering from this error. In the first period after birth, . . . instruction in language is of no account, because sense-perception is the means by which the child learns. His own seeing and feeling, his own experience . . . these are the natural teachers of the little child. Not even the best pictorial illustrations of the things surrounding the child have anything like the educational value of one single object seen or felt by himself.[7]

Thinking . . . can not be taught to any one by instruction through words. No child is instructed in it, but every one learns of himself to think, as well as to see and hear. . . . thinking is defective, judgment warped, and knowledge of one's relations to the world arrested, unless he is from childhood familiar with realities through his own experience. . . . The brain is developed only through activity.[8]

The great thing is . . . 'letting the child alone'. . . . We must therefore let the child alone while he is learning to see and hear, and for a considerable time after.[9] The beginning is made too soon with everything, . . . so that the word comes before the possibility of understanding at all the idea associated with it. . . .[10]

The process . . . of the formation of concepts may be brought a little nearer to our understanding from the physiological point of view by the consideration that all concepts . . . ultimately come to exist only after a great many sense impressions have been received.[11]

5. *Mental Development in the Child*, p. 44.
6. ibid, p. 47.   7. ibid, p. 66.
8. ibid, pp. 69–70, 72–3.   9. ibid, pp. 77–9.
10. ibid, p. 130.   11. ibid, p. 132.

It would .... be quite preposterous to suppose that the childish intellect may be screwed up beyond its ordinary tension by pressing words into it as early and as long as possible; ... for it is only when words designate things well understood that they can have the value they have been shown to have for the development of the intellect.[12]

He gives a definition of mental activity, in terms of balanced development of the emotions as well as the intellect:

By harmonious activity of mind I understand an activity in which the intellectual and the emotional are in equipoise.... Harmonious culture ... implies that the senses and therefore the observing powers, shall be exercised, and that the body, including the whole external personality, shall not be neglected as compared with the mind.

Preyer warns of the danger of an unbalanced education,

If we forget that neither one-sided concentration upon reading and writing ... nor occupation with anything and everything, continually changing ... is serviceable for the intellectual germs in the growing brain of the child, then we ought not to be surprised at the evil consequences which show themselves in the shape of arrested mental growth ... There are disturbances which do not appear on the surface and are not thought remarkable until great numbers of persons are seized at the same time as by an epidemic nervousness, and their intellectual activity is turned away from the natural, from the things that concern us in health ... So it is with children who are too early forced to become book-learned.[13]

*

In his work with idiots, which was to inspire and influence Mme Montessori, Edward Seguin put into practice many basic principles which are of significance in the education of normal children.

His aim was all-round development, with the object of producing goodness:

Education is the *ensemble* of the means of developing harmoniously and effectively the moral, intellectual, and physical capacities, as functions, in man and mankind.[14]

12. ibid, p. 161.   13. ibid, pp. 75–7.
14. SEGUIN, EDWARD, *Idiocy and Its Treatment*, p. 32.

Our system of education is the process of accumulating in children strength and knowledge; to create in men power and goodness.[15]

We confide mostly in the exercises borrowed from the daily labors and amusements common to all children. The spade, the wheelbarrow, the watering-pot, the bow, the wooden horse, the hammer, the ball, are greater favorites with us than the general gymnastics whose instruments are to be employed sparingly, and whose tendencies to exaggeration are to be avoided. The Grecians were using it to excess, for which Plato reprimands them, as well as for the other excesses in over-cultivating the intellectual faculties – the former making prize-fighters, the latter sophists. Nothing is so much to be discountenanced as this one-sided education.

In our case no excuse could be proffered to palliate a similar mistake, because we aim at a plain, comprehensive, harmonious training of the whole child.[16]

First

the individuality of the children is to be secured; for respect of individuality is the first test of the fitness of a teacher.[17]

From this it follows that

the beginning of the treatment of each child is where his natural progress stood still; so many children, so many beginnings.[18] We must teach every day the nearest thing to that which each child knows or can know.[19]

Contrary to the general belief, the best way to teach idiots is not by means of the memory:

Exclusive memory exercises do not actually improve idiots; rather the reverse; they impede their future progress. Better one thing thoroughly known than a hundred only remembered.[20]

The important thing is to teach not facts but the relations between them:

Teaching so many facts is not so fruitful as teaching how to find the relations between a single one and its natural properties and connexions.[21]

We must never confide to automatic memory what can be learned

15. ibid, pp. 97–8.   16. ibid, p. 99.   17. ibid, p. 33.
18. ibid, p. 97.   19. ibid, p. 95.   20. ibid, p. 91.
21. ibid, p. 91.

by comparison, nor teach a thing without its natural correlations
and generalizations; ... what enters the mind alone, dies in it
alone.[22]

Children must be allowed to learn in the way that is natural
to them, not by means of words, but by discovery and first-
hand observation.

Let our natural senses be developed as far as possible.... Then
the instruments of artificial senses are to be brought in requisition;
the handling of the compass, the prism,... the microscope and
others must be made familiar to all children, who shall learn how to
see nature through itself, instead of through twenty-six letters of the
alphabet; and shall cease to learn by rote, by trust, by faith, instead of by knowing.[23]

How often the teacher clumsily prevents the child from
learning:

We too often act or speak when the child might have acted or
spoken himself if we had more insisted upon his doing it; given
him a little time instead of hurrying; supported his hesitation
instead of prompting him; and given him no hint but a kind,
encouraging look.[24]

Children not only teach themselves but each other, and the
experience of teaching one another can be an excellent way of
learning:

The child who teaches another ... teaches himself more by the
reflex action of his will upon his own understanding.[25]

Seguin saw clearly the value of what is today called group
therapy. This principle, which he put into practice so successfully with idiots, has obvious implications for what are called
normal children, in particular as regards grading and streaming, and the organization of children considered backward:

What we cannot command, another child will incite; what we
cannot explain to a child, he will imitate from another; what a
group cannot do after our command, will be done after the example
of a small child. However incapable we consider idiots, they can
be made to act efficiently one upon another, if we know how to

22. ibid, p. 95.   23. ibid, p. 34.
24. ibid, p. 182.   25. ibid, p. 218.

oppose the vivacious to the immobile, the loquacious to the mute, the imitative to the careless, the affectionate to the indifferent.[26]

Seguin draws attention to the importance of rhythm, the balance of activity and rest, in living and learning:

Education must ... follow the great natural law of action and repose, which is life itself. To adapt the law to the whole training, each function in its turn is called to activity and to rest; the activity of one favoring the repose of the other; the improvement of one reacting upon the improvement of all others; contrast being not only an instrument of relaxation, but of comprehension also.[27]

Seguin's revolutionary ideas on the teaching of reading are now standard practice in the majority of modern infant schools, though there are still those, in other departments of our schools, who do not believe it is possible to teach children to read in this way:

Contrarily to school practice, and agreeably to nature, our letters are to be written before being read.... The instruments of the method are many. We have seen the best of all in operation; it is the hand, creating its own reading matter.[28]

Like all great educators he believed that the prime motive power in all teaching must be love:

To make the child feel that he is loved, and to make him eager to love in his turn, is the end of our teaching as it has been its beginning ... For our pupils science, literature, art, education, medicine, philosophy, each may do something; but love alone can truly socialize them; those alone who love them are their true rescuers.[29]

26. ibid, p. 218.   27. ibid, pp. 32–3.
28. ibid, p. 177.   29. ibid, pp. 244–5.

31

Thomas Huxley · Tolstoy

THOMAS HUXLEY, scientist and President of the Royal
Society, was one of the first members of the London School
Board of 1870. When, for the first time, the provision of elementary education for all was being widely discussed and
argued over, he had much to say, both on the need for such
provision and, more important, its quality. His influence upon
the scheme eventually put into practice by the Board was very
great. In his view

the whole object of education is, in the first place, to train the
faculties of the young in such a manner as to give to their profes-
sors the best chance of being happy and useful in their generation;
and, in the second place, to furnish them with the most important
portions of that immense capitalised experience of the human race
which we call knowledge of various kinds. I am using knowledge in
its widest possible sense.[1]

That man, I think, has had a liberal education who has been so
trained in youth that his body is the ready servant of his will; ...
whose intellect is a clear, cold, logic engine ... in smooth working
order ... ; whose mind is stored with a knowledge of the great
and fundamental truths of Nature; ... one who, no stunted ascetic,
is full of life and fire; ... who has learned to love all beauty ... to
hate all vileness, and to respect others as himself.[2]

Like many before him, Huxley rebelled against contemporary education.

The educational abomination of desolation of the present day is
the stimulation of young people to work at high pressure by in-
cessant competitive examinations.[3]

The present system of primary education

has the defect which is common to all the educational systems we
have inherited – it is too bookish, too little practical. The child

1. HUXLEY, THOMAS, *Science and Education*, p. 174.
2. ibid, p. 86.   3. ibid, p. 410.

is brought too little into contact with actual facts and things, and as the system stands at present it constitutes next to no education of those particular faculties which are of the utmost importance to industrial life – I mean the faculty of observation, the faculty of working accurately, of dealing with things instead of with words.[4]

Education at all levels suffers from this same defect. This, he says, is what the English tell their sons:

At the cost of from one to two thousand pounds of our hard-earned money, we devote twelve of the most precious years of your lives to school. There you shall toil, or be supposed to toil; but there you shall not learn one single thing of all those you will most want to know directly you leave school and enter upon the practical business of life. You will in all probability go into business, but you shall not know where, or how, any article of commerce is produced, or the difference between an export or an import, or the meaning of the word 'capital'. You will very likely settle in a colony, but you shall not know whether Tasmania is part of New South Wales, or *vice versa.*[5]

You will very likely get into the House of Commons. You will have to take your share in making laws which may prove a blessing or a curse to millions of men. But you shall not hear one word respecting the political organization of your country.... The mental power which will be of most importance in your daily life will be the power of seeing things as they are without regard to authority; and of drawing accurate general conclusions from particular facts. But at school and at college you shall know of no source of truth but authority; nor exercise your reasoning faculty upon anything but deduction from that which is laid down by authority.[6]

It is through this unsuitable kind of education that we, in fact, create backwardness and stupidity:

Stupidity, in nine cases out of ten,... is developed by a long process of parental and pedagogic repression of the natural intellectual appetites, accompanied by a persistent attempt to create artificial ones for food which is not only tasteless, but essentially indigestible.[7]

Those who today blame modern methods for what they consider the present low standards may be surprised to learn that

4. ibid, p. 431.   5. ibid, p. 95.
6. ibid, pp. 95–6.   7. ibid, p. 128.

Huxley had no great opinion of the results achieved by the traditional methods of his day. He wrote:

Every one knows that it is a rare thing to find a boy of the middle and upper classes who can read aloud decently, or who can put his thoughts on paper in clear and grammatical language.[8]

'What is education?' he asks. 'Above all things, what is our idea of a thoroughly liberal education?'[9]

If our lives and fortunes were to depend, one day, upon our winning or losing a game of chess, Huxley suggests

that we should all consider it to be a primary duty to learn at least the names and the moves of the pieces; to have a notion of a gambit, and a keen eye for all the means of giving and getting out of check. . . .

Yet it is a very plain and elementary truth that the life, the fortune, and the happiness of every one of us do depend upon our knowing something of the rules of a game infinitely more difficult and complicated than chess. . . . The chess-board is the world, the pieces are the phenomena of the universe, the rules of the game are what we call the laws of Nature.[10]

Education, then, must be something very different from what it has been in the past:

What I mean by Education is learning the rules of this mighty game. In other words, education is the instruction of the intellect in the laws of Nature, under which name I include not merely things and their forces, but men and their ways; and the fashioning of the affections and of the will into an earnest and loving desire to move in harmony with those laws.[11]

Education must not be from books but from first-hand discovery, in which the process of learning is of greater importance than the amount of information acquired. The boy

must handle the plants and dissect the flowers for himself; . . . you must be careful that what he learns he knows of his own knowledge. . . . Tell him that it is his duty to doubt until he is compelled, by the absolute authority of Nature, to believe that which is written in books. Pursue this discipline carefully and conscientiously, and you

8. ibid, p. 92.   9. ibid, p. 81.
10. ibid, pp. 81–2.   11. ibid, p. 83.

may make sure that, however scanty may be the measure of information which you have poured into the boy's mind, you have created an intellectual habit of priceless value in practical life.[12]

*

Tolstoy wrote: 'All agree that schools are imperfect; I, personally, am convinced that they are noxious.'[13]

Tolstoy's school, according to McCallister, was 'perhaps the first to be directly based upon a concept of freedom and is of considerable interest'.[14] He called it

a witness for all time to the success of a gifted artist who had faith in the child and in the simple values of humanity. ... He drew our attention to the fact that teaching, like all forms of art, is a mode of conveying our emotional selves and our deepest aspirations to the heart of the pupil.[15]

The school he founded at Yasnáya Polyána in 1859 held at first forty, later seventy, of the children of his serfs,

of innkeepers, clerks, soldiers, manorial servants, dramshop-keepers, sextons, and rich peasants.[16]

Aylmer Maude, his biographer, wrote in 1927:

His theories and practice were far more radical than any school system now existing, or likely to exist unless and until teachers are obtainable as able and as devoted ... as he was himself! [17]

[He] insisted that the success of the schools and the very rapid progress made by the pupils resulted not from any particular 'method' but from the free and natural relations that existed between teachers and pupils, and from the readiness of the teachers constantly to experiment and adapt their teaching to the changing requirements of the scholars.[18]

12. ibid, pp. 127–8.
13. TOLSTOY, Centenary Edition, Vol. 1, p. 244.
14. MCCALLISTER, The Growth of Freedom in Education, p. 391.
15. ibid, pp. 400–401.
16. TOLSTOY, Complete Works, Vol. 4, p. 256.
17. Centenary Edition, Vol. 1, p. 254.
18. ibid, pp. 258–9.

His principle was freedom:

The only criterion of pedagogy is freedom, the only method – experience.[19]

One need only glance at one and the same child at home or in the street, and at school. Here you see a vivacious inquisitive being, with a smile in his eye and on his mouth, seeking information everywhere as a pleasure, and clearly and often forcibly expressing his thoughts in his own way; while there you see a weary, shrinking, creature repeating merely with his lips some one else's thoughts in some one else's words with an air of fatigue, fear, and listlessness – a creature whose soul has retreated like a snail into its shell. One need but glance at these two conditions to see which of them is the more conducive to the child's development. That strange physiological condition which I call the 'School state of mind' and which unfortunately we all know so well, consists in the higher capacities: imagination, creative power, and reflection, yielding place to a semi-animal capacity to pronounce words without imagination or reflection.[20]

When I entered ... into the closest direct relations with those forty tiny peasants that formed my school, ... when I saw that susceptibility, that readiness to acquire the information which they needed, I felt at once that the antiquated church method of instruction had outlived its usefulness, and was not good for them. I began to experiment on other proposed methods of instruction; but, because compulsion in education ... [is] repulsive to me, I did not exercise any pressure, and, the moment I noticed that something was not readily received, I did not compel them, and looked for something else. From these experiments, it appeared to me ... that nearly everything which in the pedagogical world was written about schools was separated by an immeasurable abyss from reality.[21]

The less the children are compelled to learn, the better is the method; the more – the worse ... Everybody is agreed that just as in hygiene the use of any food, medicine, exercise, that provokes loathing or pain, cannot be useful, so also in instruction can there be no necessity of compelling children to learn anything that is tiresome and repulsive to them, and that, if necessity demands that children be compelled, it only proves the imperfection of the method.[22]

19. *Complete Works*, Vol. 12, p. 288.
20. *Centenary Edition*, Vol. 1, p. 242.
21. *Complete Works*, Vol. 12, pp. 286-7.
22. ibid, p. 293.

The school in which there is less compulsion is better than the one in which there is more. That method is good which ... does not necessitate any increase of discipline, while that which necessitates greater severity is certainly bad.[23]

Full liberty of study, that is, the permission given to the pupil to come to study when he wishes, is a *conditio sine qua non* of every fruitful instruction just as it is a *conditio sine qua non* of nutrition that he who feeds should feel like eating.[24]

In his school, therefore, there was no compulsion:

The pupil always had the right not to go to school, and even when in school not to listen to the teacher. The teacher had the right not to admit a pupil.[25]

No one brings anything with him, neither books nor copybooks. No homework is set them ... They are not obliged to remember any lesson, nor any of yesterday's work. They are not tormented by thought of the impending lesson.[26]

The results justified Tolstoy's belief in freedom. They

were always very good both for the teachers and the pupils; ... and this I assert boldly, for hundreds of visitors came to the Yasnáya Polyána school and know how it worked.[27]

For the pupils the results were that they learnt eagerly, always begged to have additional lessons on winter evenings, and were quite free in class ... we never had a single pupil who did not master the rudiments.[28]

In a letter to the Countess A. A. Tolstoy in July 1861, he wrote:

Just think, that during two years, and with a complete absence of discipline, not a single boy or girl has been punished, and there is never any idleness, rudeness, any silly tricks or improper words.[29]

He tells how the children once set themselves a target to learn to read in one week:

Suddenly mechanical reading became their favourite occupation. For an hour or an hour-and-a-half at a time they would sit without

23. *Centenary Edition*, Vol. 1, p. 247.
24. *Complete Works*, Vol. 23, p. 366.
25. *Centenary Edition*, Vol. 1, p. 253.
26. ibid, p. 251.   27. ibid, p. 274.
28. ibid, p. 274.   29. ibid, p. 276.

tearing themselves away from the books, which they did not understand; and they began taking books home with them, and really
within three weeks they made such progress as one could not have
expected.[30]

He gives a delightful description of how a heap of wrestling
boys transformed itself in the space of a few minutes, without
any outward compulsion, into a roomful of quiet children,
absorbed in reading:

To tear him [one of the boys] from his reading would now need
as much effort as formerly to tear him from his wrestling.[31]

This atmosphere of freedom entirely eliminated the furtive,
tale-telling behaviour often associated with the traditional
classroom:

During lessons I have never seen them whispering, pinching, gig-
gling, laughing behind their hands, or complaining of one another
to the teacher.[32]

Submitting naturally only to laws derived from their own
nature, children revolt and rebel when subjected to your premature
interference. ... The School should not ... reward or punish; ... the
best police and administration of a School consists in giving full
freedom to the pupils to learn and get on among themselves as
they like.[33]

This theory was based on, and confirmed by what he saw of
the behaviour of the children in his own school. With unusual
insight he describes the effect on two boys engaged in fighting
who are separated by the teacher. The boys, their anger still
smouldering, give each other a final, hate-filled whack. When
no one interferes they come to the end of their strife and are
soon laughing together. The interfering teacher says

'You are both to blame: kneel down!' ... and the teacher is
wrong, because one boy is to blame and that one triumphs while
on his knees and chews the cud of his unexpended anger, while the
innocent one is doubly punished.[34]

30. ibid, p. 260.   31. ibid, p. 252.   32. ibid, p. 252.
33. ibid, pp. 253, 254.   34. ibid, p. 254.

Tolstoy says: 'Leave them alone and see how simply and naturally the whole matter will settle itself.'[35]

The philosophy which underlay Tolstoy's belief in freedom was simple, but fundamental enough to strike at the roots of orthodox teaching methods:

A child, or a man, can learn when he has an appetite for what he studies. Without appetite, instruction is an evil – a terrible evil, causing people to become mentally crippled.[36]

That a man of any age should begin to learn, it is necessary that he should love learning.[37]

A child or man is receptive only when he is aroused, and therefore to regard a merry spirit in school as an enemy or a hindrance is the crudest of blunders.[38]

and the teacher's task consists 'in studying the free child', and adapting his methods to the child's needs.

To deal successfully with any object it is necessary to study it, and in education the object is a free child; yet the pedagogues wish to teach in their own way – the way that seems good in their own eyes, and when this does not act they want to alter not their way of teaching, but the nature of the child … Not till experiment becomes the basis of the School, and every school is, so to say, a pedagogic laboratory, will schools cease to lag behind the general level of the world's progress.[39]

Schools are not arranged to make it convenient for children to learn, but to make it convenient for teachers to teach. The voices, movements, and mirth of the children, which form a necessary condition of their studying successfully, incommode the teachers, and therefore in the prison-like schools of today, questions, conversation, and movement are forbidden.[40]

Such schools supply

not a shepherd for the flock, but a flock for the shepherd.[41] All instruction should be simply a reply to questions put by life. But School far from evoking questions, fails even to answer those which life suggests.[42]

35. *Complete Works*, Vol 4, p. 237.
36. *Essays and Letters*, AYLMER MAUDE, p. 38.
37. *Centenary Edition*, Vol. 1, p. 262.
38. ibid, p. 242.　　　　39. ibid, p. 243.
40. ibid, p. 243.　　　　41. ibid, p. 243.
42. ibid, p. 245.

Tolstoy gives two reasons why a freer method of education is not more generally practised:

First, this disorder, or free order, only frightens us because we were ourselves educated in and are accustomed to something quite different. Secondly, in this as in many similar cases, coercion is used only from hastiness or lack of respect for human nature. We think the disorder is growing greater and greater and has no limit. We think there is no way of stopping it except by force; but one need only wait a little and the disorder (or animation) calms down of itself and calms down into a far better and more durable order than we could devise.[43]

Tolstoy's faith in freedom was based on his belief in the age-old principle of the inner spring of growth in every man:

The need of education lies in every man; the people love and seek it as they love and seek the air for breathing.[44]
I believe that ... the desire to study is so strong in children that, in order to satisfy their desire, they will submit to many hard conditions and will forgive many defects.[45]

Education then becomes 'the exertion of influence upon the heart of those whom we educate'.[46]
The school must be

an all-sided and most varied conscious influence exercised by one man on another, for the purpose of transmitting knowledge without compelling the student by direct force or diplomatically to avail himself of that which we want him to avail himself of.[47]
But we can exert an influence upon the heart only by means of hypnotization ... – by the infectiousness of the example.[48]
Education presents itself as a complex and difficult matter, only so long as we wish, without educating ourselves, to educate our children ... But if we come to understand that we can educate others only through ourselves the question of education is made void, and only the question of life is left. How must I live myself?[49]

43. ibid, pp. 252–3.   44. *Complete Works*, Vol. 4, p. 5.
45. ibid, p. 246.
46. *Complete Works*, Vol. 23, p. 370.
47. *Complete Works*, Vol. 4, p. 150.
48. *Complete Works*, Vol. 23, p. 370.
49. ibid, p. 369.

Education to Tolstoy is a matter, not so much of the intellect and of the conscious mind, as of the feelings, the unconscious, a building up of attitudes, a growth of sensitivity:

Educators ... transfer what ought to take place unconsciously into the sphere of the conscious.[50]

'The first condition of a good education,' he wrote to a relative in 1903, 'is that the child should know that all he uses does not fall from heaven ready-made, but is produced by other people's labour.' [51]

As it was for Plato, so for Tolstoy, education is a natural miracle, a development of the light within, but the light cannot be developed except by those in whom it is growing:

I have just read N – s' letter, [he wrote] in which he says that medical help does not present itself to him as something good, that the continuation of many useless lives for many hundreds of years is much less important than the feeblest blowing upon the spark of divine love in the heart of another. In this blowing lies the whole art of education. But to fan it in others, we must first fan it in ourselves.[52]

I do not know a single act in the education of children which is not included in the education of oneself.[53]

50. ibid, p. 362.
51. *Essays and Letters*, Letter on Education, p. 339.
52. *Complete Works*, Vol. 23, p. 374.
53. ibid, p. 368.

32

John Dewey

IT is impossible to condense into a single chapter John Dewey's contribution to educational thought and practice. The reader must study his writings in order to make an adequate estimate. For the purpose of this survey a few outstanding points will be considered.

Dewey wrote:

'Our social life has undergone a thorough and radical change. . . .' [1] In the past

the household was practically the center in which were carried on, or about which were clustered, all the typical forms of industrial occupation.

The supply of all essential needs – clothing, lighting, food, furniture – was carried out by the family or by immediate neighbours.

The children . . . were gradually initiated into the mysteries of the several processes. It was a matter of immediate and personal concern, even to the point of actual participation.

We cannot overlook the factors of discipline and of character-building involved in this: training in habits of order and of industry, and in the idea of responsibility . . . Personalities which became effective in action were bred and tested in the medium of action.[2]

All this has passed away. 'If our education is to have any meaning for life, it must pass through an equally complete transformation,' [3] he said.

The introduction of active occupations, of nature study, of elementary science, of art, of history; the relegation of the merely symbolic and formal to a secondary position; the change in the

1. DEWEY, JOHN, *Dewey on Education, School and Society*, p. 49.
2. ibid, pp. 36 7.   3. ibid, p. 49.

moral school atmosphere, in the relation of pupils and teachers –
of discipline; the introduction of more active, expressive, and
self-directing factors – all these are . . . necessities of the larger
social evolution.[4]

The old education with 'its passivity of attitude, its mechanical massing of children, its uniformity of curriculum and
method' had its centre of gravity

outside the child . . . in the teacher, the text-book, anywhere and
everywhere you please except in the immediate instincts and activities of the child himself . . . Now the change which is coming
into our education is the shifting of the center of gravity. It is a
change, a revolution, not unlike that introduced by Copernicus,
when the astronomical center shifted from the earth to the sun. In
this case the child becomes the sun about which the appliances of
education revolve; he is the center about which they are organized.[5]

It is no longer a question of how the teacher is to instruct or
how the pupil is to study. The problem is to find what conditions
must be fulfilled in order that study and learning will naturally
and necessarily take place . . . The method of the teacher . . . becomes a matter of finding the conditions which call out self-educa-
tive activity, or learning, and of cooperating with the activities of
the pupils so that they have learning as their consequence.[6]

His educational philosophy, which was directly related to
his practical experience in the school attached to the University
of Chicago, is based on the belief that life is a self-renewing
process, in action and reaction upon its environment:

The most notable distinction between living and inanimate
beings is that the former maintain themselves by renewal. A stone
when struck resists. If its resistance is greater than the force of the
blow struck, it remains outwardly unchanged. Otherwise, it is
shattered into smaller bits. Never does the stone attempt to react
in such a way that it may maintain itself against the blow, much
less so as to render the blow a contributing factor to its own continued action. While the living thing may easily be crushed by
superior force, it none the less tries to turn the energies which
act upon it into means of its own further existence. . . . As long
as it endures, it struggles to use surrounding energies in its own

4. ibid, p. 49.   5. ibid, pp. 52–3.
6. *Dewey on Education, Progressive Education*, p. 125.

behalf. . . . Life is a self-renewing process through action upon the environment.[7]

Two opposing points of view are held by educators, states Dewey. One is the view that the child is

the immature being who is to be matured; . . . the superficial being who is to be deepened; his is narrow experience which is to be widened. It is his to receive, to accept.[8] The child's individual peculiarities, whims and experiences, . . . are what we need to get away from. . . . Our work is . . . to substitute for these superficial and casual affairs stable and well-ordered realities; and these are found in studies and lessons.[9]

The other point of view is that 'all studies are subservient' to the growth of the child. 'Personality, character, is more than subject matter.' The good is self-realization, not information. 'Learning is active.' The child, 'not the subject matter ... determines both quality and quantity of learning'.[10]

He contrasts these two ways of thinking as discipline versus interest, the logical versus the psychological, guidance and control versus freedom and initiative.

Both are extreme views of what, in fact, is the same thing:

The child and the curriculum are simply two limits which define a single process.[11] From the side of the child, it is a question of seeing how his experience already contains . . . elements . . . of just the same sort as those entering into the formulated study. . . . From the side of the studies, it is a question of interpreting them as outgrowths of forces operating in the child's life, and of discovering the steps that intervene between the child's present experience and their richer maturity.[12]

The new understanding of childhood makes imperative a new approach to education. In the past educators believed that:

the boy was a little man and his mind was a little mind – in everything but size the same as that of the adult. ... Now we believe in the mind as a growing affair, . . . presenting distinctive

7. *Democracy and Education*, pp. 1, 2.
8. *Dewey on Education, The Child and the Curriculum*, p. 95.
9. ibid, p. 94.   10. ibid, p. 95.
11. Ibid, p. 97.   12. ibid, pp. 96–7.

phases of capacity and interest at different periods.[13] The selection and grading of material in the course of study must be done with reference to proper nutrition of the dominant directions of activity in a given period.[14]

Education must meet the changing needs of children, but what is of greatest moment is that the right use be made of the needs and interests shown at any stage, to lead on to further development:

Since life means growth, a living creature lives as truly and positively at one stage as another, with the same intrinsic fullness and the same absolute claims. Hence education means the enterprise of supplying the conditions which insure growth, or adequacy of life, irrespective of age. . . .

Realization that life is growth protects us from that so-called idealizing of childhood which in effect is nothing but lazy indulgence. We must remember that manifestations are not to be accepted as ends in themselves. They are signs of possible growth. They are to be turned into means of development, of carrying power forward, not indulged or cultivated for their own sake. . . . What impulses are moving toward, not what they have been, is the important thing for parent and teacher. The true principle of respect for immaturity cannot be better put than in the words of Emerson:

'Respect the child. . . . Trespass not on his solitude. . . . Respect the child, respect him to the end, but also respect yourself. . . . The two points in a boy's training are, to keep his *naturel* and train off all but that; to keep his *naturel*, but stop off his uproar, fooling and horseplay; keep his nature *and arm it with knowledge in the very direction in which it points.*'[15]

Interest is indeed important – 'always the sign of some power below; the important thing is to discover this power'[16] – but it is not the end:

Interests . . . are but attitudes towards possible experiences; they are not achievements; their worth is in the leverage they afford.[17]

Any power . . . is indulged when it is taken on its . . . present

13. The School and the Child, p. 113.   14. ibid, p. 114.
15. *Democracy and Education*, p. 62.
16. *Dewey on Education, My Pedagogic Creed*, p. 29.
17. ibid, *The Child and the Curriculum*, pp. 99–100.

level in consciousness. Its genuine meaning is in the propulsion it affords toward a higher level.[18]

The problem which confronts educators is how, under the changed conditions of modern life, to 'introduce into the school occupations which exact personal responsibilities and which train the child in relation to the physical realities of life'.

As it is, the chief motive for learning in school is competition:

a comparison of results in the recitation or in the examination to see which child has succeeded in getting ahead of others in storing up . . . the maximum of information. So thoroughly is this the prevailent atmosphere that for one child to help another in his task has become a school crime.[19]

This must be replaced by cooperation and a 'genuine community standard of value'.

Life is the true educator:

The inclination to learn from life itself and to make the conditions of life such that all will learn in the process of living is the finest product of schooling.[20]

The only discipline that stands by us, the only training that becomes intuition, is that got through life itself . . . But the school has been so set apart, so isolated from the ordinary conditions and motives of life, that the place where children are sent for discipline is the one place in the world where it is most difficult to get experience – the mother of all discipline worth the name.[21]

But all this means a necessary change in the attitude of the school . . . Our school methods, and to a very considerable extent our curriculum, are inherited from the period when learning and command of certain symbols . . . were all-important . . . Our present education . . . is . . . dominated almost entirely by the mediaeval conception of learning. It is something which appeals for the most part simply to the intellectual aspects of our natures . . . not to our impulses and tendencies to make, to do, to create, to produce.[22]

18. ibid, p. 100.
19. ibid, *The School and Society*, p. 40.
20. *Democracy and Education*, p. 60.
21. *Dewey on Education, The School and Society*, p. 41.
22. ibid, p. 47.

Education must consider the child as a whole, not as a brain only:

> The older psychology was a psychology of knowledge, of intel-
> lect. Emotion and endeavour occupied but an incidental . . . place
> . . . Now we believe (to use the words of Mr James) that the in-
> tellect . . . can have but one essential function – the function of
> defining the direction which our activity . . . shall take.[23]

True education is an active process, based on the nature of the child:

> The primary root of all educative activity is in the instinctive,
> impulsive attitudes and activities of the child, and not in the pre-
> sentation and application of external material . . . and . . . accord-
> ingly, numberless spontaneous activities of children . . . are capable
> of educational use; nay, are the foundation-stones of educational
> method.[24]

Such education will call out the full co-operation of the principle of growth in the child:

> Immaturity designates a positive force or ability – the *power* to
> grow. We do not have to draw out or educe positive activities from
> a child, as some educational doctrines would have it. Where there
> is life, there are already eager and impassioned activities. Growth
> is not something done to them; it is something they do.[25]
>
> The child is already intensely active and the question of educa-
> tion is the question of taking hold of his activities, of giving them
> direction.[26]

The usual classroom provides little opportunity for the child to work.

> If we put before the mind's eye the ordinary schoolroom, with
> its rows of ugly desks . . . crowded together so that there shall be
> as little moving room as possible . . . we can reconstruct the only
> educational activity that can possibly go on in such a place. It is
> all made 'for listening' – for simply studying lessons out of a
> book is only another kind of listening. . . . The attitude of listen-
> ing means, comparatively speaking, passivity, absorption. . . .

23. *The School and the Child*, pp. 111–12.
24. ibid.
25. *Democracy and Education*, p. 50.
26. *Dewey on Education, The School and Society*, p. 54.

There is very little place in the traditional schoolroom for the child to work. The workshop, the laboratory, the materials, the tools with which the child may construct, create and actively inquire, and even the requisite space, have been for the most part lacking.[27]

The child must be aware of his own purpose – he must have 'a question of his own' – for through this he learns:

The problem of instruction is thus that of finding material which will engage a person in specific activities having an aim or purpose of moment or interest to him.[28]

The study of mathematics

is effectual in the degree in which the pupil realizes the place of the numerical truth he is dealing with in carrying to fruition activities in which he is concerned. This connection of an object and a topic with the promotion of an activity having a purpose is the first and the last word of a genuine theory of interest in education.[29]

In learning skills there must be a 'motive from within':

The *introduction* to technique must come in *connection with ends that arise within the child's own experience, that are present to them as desired ends, and hence as motives to effort . . .* The prime psychological necessity is that the child see and feel the end as *his own end*, the need as his own need, and thus have a motive from within . . . for . . . mastering the 'rules'.[30]

Teaching which isolates an act from its purpose is mechanical and must be avoided:

It is customary for teachers to urge children to read with expression, so as to bring out the meaning. But if they originally learned the sensory-motor technique of reading . . . by methods which did not call attention to meaning, a mechanical habit was established which makes it difficult to read subsequently with intelligence.[31]

Education must supply stimuli for response; the alternative is the unsatisfactory system of rewards and punishments:

27. ibid, pp. 50–51.
28. *Democracy and Education*, p. 155.
29. ibid, p. 158.
30. *The School and the Child*, p. 29.   31. ibid.

Healthy work, done for present reasons and as a factor in living, is largely unconscious. The stimulus resides in the situation with which one is actually confronted. But when this situation is ignored, pupils have to be told that if they do not follow the prescribed course, penalties will accrue; while if they do, they may expect, some time in the future, rewards for their present sacrifices. Everybody knows how largely systems of punishment have had to be resorted to by educational systems which neglect present possibilities in behalf of preparation for a future.[32]

Guidance and direction, however, are necessary, but

guidance is not external imposition. *It is freeing the life process for its own most adequate fulfilment.*[33] The problem of direction is . . . the problem of selecting appropriate stimuli for instincts and impulses.[34]

The teacher's problem is to discover the

ways in which [a] subject may become a part of experience; what there is in the child's present that is usable with reference to it; how such elements are to be used.[35]

The task of the educator is to plan the environment of the children he teaches, 'and thus by indirection to direct'. He must see that

the conditions are such that *their own activities* move inevitably in the direction of the capacities and the fulfilments that are open to the children.[36]

To some extent . . . all direction or control is a guiding of activity to its own end; it is an assistance in doing fully what some organ is already tending to do.[37]

There is to be nothing haphazard in this way of teaching:

It is the business of the school to set up an environment in which play and work shall be conducted with reference to facilitating desirable mental and moral growth. It is not enough just to introduce play and games, hand work and manual exercises. Everything depends upon the way in which they are employed. . .

32. *Democracy and Education*, pp. 64–5.
33. *Dewey on Education, The Child and the Curriculum*, p. 101.
34. ibid, p. 102.   35. ibid, p. 105.
36. ibid, p. 111 (amended).
37. *Democracy and Education*, p. 29.

The problem of the educator is to engage pupils in these activities in such ways that while manual skill and technical efficiency are gained and immediate satisfaction found in the work, together with preparation for later usefulness, these things shall be subordinated to *education* – that is, to intellectual results and the forming of a socialized disposition.[38]

Play should lead to educative growth, otherwise it is no more than amusement:

The peculiar problem of the early grades is ... to get hold of the child's natural impulses and instincts, and to utilize them so that the child is carried on to a higher plane of perception and judgment, and equipped with more efficient habits: so that he has an enlarged and deepened consciousness, and increased control of powers of action.[39]

Dewey stresses over and over again that education of this kind is not a matter of letting children do as they like, and of leaving them where they are:

It will do harm if child-study leave in the popular mind the impression that a child of a given age has a positive equipment of purposes and interests to be cultivated just as they stand ... Continuous initiation, continuous starting of activities that do not arrive, is ... as bad as the continual repression of initiative in conformity with supposed interests of some more perfect thought or will.[40]

Teaching of the most skilful kind is required. This is one of the points most frequently misunderstood in modern teaching methods. He gives an illustration in regard to children's painting:

All children like to express themselves through the medium of form and color. If you simply indulge this interest by letting the child go on indefinitely, there is no growth that is more than accidental. But let the child first express his impulse, and then through criticism, question and suggestion bring him to consciousness of what he has done, and what he needs to do, and the result is quite different.[41]

38. ibid, pp. 230–31.
39. *The School and the Child*, p. 58.
40. *Dewey on Education, The Child and the Curriculum*, pp. 99–100.
41. *Dewey on Education, The School and Society*, p. 56.

Dewey warns against another danger which has resulted from a fundamental misunderstanding of the aims of modern teaching:

The 'new education' is in danger of taking the idea of development in altogether too formal and empty a way. The child is expected to 'develop' this or that fact or truth out of his own mind. He is told to think things out, or work things out for himself, without being supplied any of the environing conditions which are requisite to start and guide thought. Nothing can be developed from nothing . . . Development does not mean just getting something out of the mind. It is a development of experience and into experience that is really wanted. And this is impossible save as just that educative medium is provided which will enable the powers and interests that have been selected as valuable to function.[42]

Purely external direction is impossible. The environment can at most only supply stimuli to call out responses. These responses proceed from tendencies already possessed by the individual. . . .

Speaking accurately, all direction is but re-direction; it shifts the activities already going on into another channel. Unless one is cognizant of the energies which are already in operation, one's attempts at direction will almost surely go amiss.[43] The child's own instincts and powers furnish the material and give the starting point for all education.[44]

The guidance of the group is one of the most effective forms of direction and education:

Knowledge that is worthy of being called knowledge, training of the intellect that is sure to amount to anything, is obtained only by participating intimately and actively in activities of social life.[45]

The school must provide

a genuine form of active community life, instead of a place set apart in which to learn lessons.[46] For when the schools depart from the educational conditions effective in the out-of-school environment, they necessarily substitute a bookish, a pseudo-intellectual spirit for a social spirit. Children doubtless go to school to learn,

42. *Dewey on Education, The Child and the Curriculum*, pp. 101–2.
43. *Democracy and Education*, pp. 30–31.
44. *Dewey on Education, My Pedagogic Creed*, p. 20.
45. *Schools of Tomorrow*, p. 63.
46. *Dewey on Education, The School and Society*, p. 39.

but it has yet to be proved that learning occurs most adequately when it is made a separate conscious business. When treating it as a business of this sort tends to preclude the social sense which comes from sharing in an activity of common concern and value, the effort at isolated intellectual learning contradicts its own aim. . . . Only by engaging in a joint activity, where one person's use of material and tools is consciously referred to the use other persons are making of their capacities and appliances, is a social direction of disposition attained.[47]

Discipline must be positive:

A person who is trained to consider his actions, to undertake them deliberately, is in so far forth disciplined. . . . To cow the spirit, to subdue inclination, to compel obedience, to mortify the flesh, . . . – these things are or are not disciplinary according as they do or do not tend to the development of power to recognize what one is about and to persistence in accomplishment.[48]

It is necessary to distinguish between physical results and moral results. Only educative influences which win the co-operation of the child can have any permanent and valuable effect:

A person may be in such a condition that forcible feeding or enforced confinement is necessary for his own good. A child may have to be snatched with roughness away from a fire so that he shall not be burnt. But no improvement of disposition, no educative effect, need follow. . . . When we confuse a physical with an educative result, we always lose the chance of enlisting the person's own participating disposition in getting the result desired, and thereby of developing within him an intrinsic and persisting direction in the right way.[49]

Dewey spotlights accurately the reason why so much educational practice lags far behind theory; few teachers have themselves experienced the kind of education in which they theoretically believe. It is therefore, for them, still in the realm of information and not of understanding; and the schools are not suitably equipped for active learning:

Why is it, in spite of the fact that teaching by pouring in, learning by a passive absorption, are universally condemned, that they

47. *Democracy and Education*, pp. 46–7.
48. ibid, pp. 151–2.   49. ibid, p. 32.

are still so intrenched in practice? That education is not an affair of 'telling' and being told, but an active and constructive process, is a principle almost as generally violated in practice as conceded in theory. Is not this deplorable situation due to the fact that the doctrine is itself merely told? It is preached; it is lectured; it is written about. But its enactment into practice requires that the school environment be equipped with agencies for doing, with tools and physical materials, to an extent rarely attained. It requires that methods of instruction and administration be modified to allow and to secure direct and continuous occupations with things.[50]

But what is this experience?

Experience is *trying*, ... *undergoing*. When we experience something we act upon it, we do something with it; then we suffer or undergo the consequences. We do something to the thing and then it does something to us in return. . . . Mere activity does not constitute experience. . . .

The very word pupil has almost come to mean one who is engaged not in having fruitful experiences but in absorbing knowledge directly. Something which is called mind or consciousness is severed from the physical organs of activity. The former is then thought to be purely intellectual and cognitive; the latter to be an irrelevant and intruding physical factor. . . .

It would be impossible to state adequately the evil results which have flowed from this dualism of mind and body. . . . In part bodily activity becomes an intruder . . . a distraction, an evil to be contended with. . . . A premium is put on physical quietude; on silence, on rigid uniformity of posture and movement; upon a machine-like simulation of the attitudes of intelligent interest. The teachers' business is to hold the pupils up to these requirements and to punish the inevitable deviations which occur. . . .

Physically active children become restless and unruly; the more quiescent, so-called conscientious ones spend what energy they have in the negative task of keeping their instincts and active tendencies suppressed, instead of in a positive one of constructive planning and execution; they are thus educated not into responsibility for the significant and graceful use of bodily powers, but into an enforced duty not to give them free play. It may be seriously asserted that a chief cause for the remarkable achievement of Greek education was that it was never misled by false notions into an attempted separation of mind and body.[51]

50. ibid, p. 46.   51. ibid, pp. 163–6.

Information, divorced from doing, is a dead thing:

Information severed from thoughtful action is dead, a mind-crushing load. Since it simulates knowledge and thereby develops the poison of conceit, it is a most powerful obstacle to further growth in the grace of intelligence.[52]

Wisdom has never lost its association with the proper direction of life. Only in education, never in the life of farmer, sailor, merchant, physician, or laboratory experimenter, does knowledge mean primarily a store of information aloof from doing.[53]

Words, the counters for ideas, are . . . easily taken for ideas. And in just the degree in which mental activity is separated from active concern with the world, from doing something and connecting the doing with what is undergone, words, symbols, come to take the place of ideas. . . . We get so thoroughly used to a kind of pseudo-idea, a half perception, that we are not aware how half-dead our mental action is, and how much keener and more extensive our observations and ideas would be if we formed them under conditions of a vital experience which required us to use judgment: to hunt for the connections of the thing dealt with.[54]

The fundamental fallacy in methods of instruction lies in supposing that experience on the part of pupils may be assumed. . . . The fallacy consists in supposing that we can begin with ready-made subject matter of arithmetic or geography, or whatever, irrespective of some direct personal experience of a situation. . . .

The first stage of contact with any new material, at whatever age of maturity, must inevitably be of the trial and error sort. . . .

To realize what an experience . . . means we have to call to mind the sort of situation that presents itself outside of school; the sort of occupations that interest and engage activity in ordinary life. And careful inspection of methods which are permanently successful in formal education . . . will reveal that they depend for their efficiency upon the fact that they go back to the type of situation which causes reflection out of school in ordinary life. They give the pupils something to do, not something to learn; and the doing is of such a nature as to demand thinking, or the intentional noting of connections; learning naturally results. . . .

No one has ever explained why children are so full of questions outside of the school . . . and the conspicuous absence of display of curiosity about the subject matter of school lessons. Reflection on this striking contrast will throw light upon the question of how far customary school conditions supply a context of experience

52. ibid, p. 179.   53. ibid, p. 218.   54. ibid, pp. 168, 169.

in which problems naturally suggest themselves ... where children are engaged in doing things and in discussing what arises in the course of their doing, it is found that children's inquiries are spontaneous and numerous, and the proposals of solution advanced, varied and ingenious. . . .[55]

The educational moral I am chiefly concerned to draw is not, however, that teachers would find their own work less of a grind and strain if school conditions favored learning in the sense of discovery and not in that of storing away what others pour into them; nor that it would be possible to give even children and youth the delights of personal intellectual productiveness – true and important as are these things. It is that no thought, no idea, can possibly be conveyed as an idea from one person to another. When it is told, it is, to the one to whom it is told, another given fact, not an idea. . . . Only by wrestling with the conditions of the problem at first hand, seeking and finding his own way out, does he think. When the parent or teacher has provided the conditions which stimulate thinking and has taken a sympathetic attitude towards the activities of the learner by entering into a common or conjoint experience, all has been done which a second party can do to instigate learning. The rest lies with the one directly concerned. If he cannot devise his own solution . . . and find his own way out, he will not learn, not even if he can recite some correct answer with one hundred per cent accuracy.[56]

Dewey gives an historical reason for the low regard in which practical activity and experience is generally held:

The notion that knowledge is derived from a higher source than is practical activity, and possesses a higher and more spiritual worth, has a long history. The history so far as conscious statement is concerned takes us back to the conceptions of experience and of reason formulated by Plato and Aristotle ... they agreed in identifying experience with purely practical concerns; and hence with material interests as to its purpose and with the body as to its organ. Knowledge, on the other hand, existed for its own sake free from practical reference, and found its source and organ in a purely immaterial mind; it had to do with spiritual or ideal interests. Again, experience always involved lack, need, desire; it was never self-sufficing. Rational knowing, on the other hand, was complete and comprehensive within itself. Hence the prac-

55. ibid, pp. 180–83.   56. ibid, pp. 187–8.

tical life was in a condition of perpetual flux, while intellectual knowledge concerned eternal truth. . . .

The philosophers soon reached certain generalizations from this state of affairs. The senses are connected with the appetites, with wants and desires. . . . They are important only for the life of the body. . . . Experience thus has a definitely material character. . . . In contrast, reason, or science, lays hold of the immaterial, the ideal, the spiritual. There is something morally dangerous about experience, as such words as sensual, carnal, material, worldly, interests suggest; while pure reason and spirit connote something morally praiseworthy.[57]

These ideas had a profound influence upon the course of education, giving rise to

the contempt for physical as compared with mathematical and logical science, for the senses and sense observation; the feeling that knowledge is high and worthy in the degree in which it deals with ideal symbols instead of with the concrete; . . . the disregard for the body; the depreciation of arts and crafts as intellectual instrumentalities. . . .

Medieval philosophy continued and reinforced the tradition. To know reality meant to be in relation to the supreme reality, or God. . . . Experience had to do with mundane, profane, and secular affairs. . . . When we add to this motive the force derived from the literary character of the Roman education and the Greek philosophical tradition, and conjoin to them the preference for studies which obviously demarcated the aristocratic class from the lower classes, we can readily understand the tremendous power exercised by the persistent preference of the 'intellectual' over the 'practical' not simply in educational philosophies but in the higher schools.[58]

A change began to appear in the seventeenth and eighteenth centuries:

The great need was to break away from captivity to conceptions which, as Bacon put it, 'anticipated nature' and imposed merely human opinions upon her, and to resort to experience to find out what nature was like. Appeal to experience marked the breach with authority. . . .

The change was twofold. Experience . . . became a name for something intellectual and cognitive. It meant the apprehension of

57. ibid, pp. 306–9.   58. ibid, pp. 310–11.

material which should ballast and check the exercise of reasoning.
. . . The result was an even greater 'intellectualism' than is found in
ancient philosophy, if that word be used to designate an emphatic
and almost exclusive interest in knowledge in its isolation. Practice was . . . treated as a kind of tag end or aftermath of knowledge. The educational result was only to confirm the exclusion of
active pursuits from the school, save as they might be brought in
for purely utilitarian ends — the acquisition by drill of certain
habits. In the second place, the interest in experience as a means
of basing truth upon objects, upon nature, led to looking at the
mind as purely receptive. The more passive the mind is, the more
truly objects will impress themselves upon it. . . .

Since the impressions made upon the mind by objects were
generally termed sensations, empiricism thus became a doctrine of
sensationalism — that is to say, a doctrine which identified knowledge with the reception and association of sensory impressions.
. . . John Locke, the most influential of empiricists . . . held that
the mind is a blank piece of paper, or a wax tablet with nothing
engraved on it at birth . . . so far as any contents of ideas were
concerned. . . . This notion was fostered by the new interest in
education as a method of social reform. . . . The emptier the mind
to begin with, the more it may be made anything we wish by bringing the right influences to bear upon it. . . .

A thoroughly false psychology of mental development underlay sensationalistic empiricism. Experience is in truth a matter of
activities . . . in their interactions with things. What even an infant 'experiences' is not a passively received quality impressed by
an object, but the effect which some activity of handling, throwing,
pounding, tearing, etc., has upon an object, and the consequent
effect of the object upon the direction of activities. . . .

It would seem as if five minutes unprejudiced observation of
the way an infant gains knowledge would have sufficed to overthrow the notion that he is passively engaged in receiving impressions of isolated ready-made qualities of sound, color, hardness,
etc. For it would be seen that the infant reacts to stimuli by activities of handling, reaching, etc., in order to see what results follow upon motor response to a sensory stimulation. . . . In other
words, what he learns are connections.[59]

Teaching is most effective when it follows the line of children's natural ways of learning, by engaging their activities:

Children do not set out, consciously, to learn walking or talking.

59. ibid, pp. 311–16.

One sets out to give his impulses for communication and for fuller intercourse with others a show. He learns in consequence of his direct activities. The better methods of teaching a child, say, to read, follow the same road. They do not fix his attention upon the fact that he has to learn something and so make his attitude self-conscious and constrained. They engage his activities, and in the process of engagement he learns.[60]

Children must be allowed to make mistakes:

Opportunity for making mistakes is an incidental requirement. . . . It is more important to keep alive a creative and constructive attitude than to secure an external perfection.[61]

Critics of modern methods, who regard freedom and activity as opportunities for licence and time-wasting, have failed to grasp the point which Dewey emphasizes again and again, that 'freedom is a *means*, not an end'.

overemphasis upon activity as an end, instead of upon *intelligent* activity, leads to identification of freedom with immediate execution of impulses and desires.[62]

Activities must be both orderly and progressive. It is fatal, he says,

to permit capricious or discontinuous action in the name of spontaneous self-expression. An aim implies an orderly and ordered activity, one in which the order consists in the progressive completing of a process ... it is nonsense to talk about the aim of education . . . where conditions do not permit of foresight of results, and do not stimulate a person to look ahead to see what the outcome of a given activity is to be.[63]

Contrary to the general belief held by those who only half understand the new approach to education, the teacher is not superfluous or passive:

There is no ground for holding that the teacher should not suggest anything to the child until he has *consciously* expressed a want in that direction. . . . But the suggestion must *fit in* with the dominant mode of growth in the child; it must serve simply as

60. ibid, pp. 198–9.   61. ibid, pp. 231–2.
62. *Experience and Education*, p. 81.
63. *Democracy and Education*, p. 119.

stimulus to bring forth more adequately what the child is already blindly striving to do.[64]

One thing that 'Nature' may be said to utter is that there are conditions of educational efficiency, and that till we have learned what these conditions are and have learned to make our practices accord with them, the noblest and most ideal of our aims are doomed to suffer.[65]

If we seek the kingdom of heaven, educationally, all other things shall be added unto us – which, being interpreted, is that if we identify ourselves with the real instincts and needs of childhood, and ask only after its fullest assertion and growth, the discipline and information and culture of adult life shall all come in their due season.[66]

64. *The School and the Child*, p. 60.
65. *Democracy and Education*, p. 135.
66. *The School and Society*, GARFORTH, p. 118.

33

Madame Montessori

'To stimulate life – leaving it free to develop, to unfold, – herein lies the first task of the educator.'[1]

Following in the great train of thinkers who, from the time of the Greeks, had demanded liberty in education, Madame Montessori made her outstanding contribution to the theory and practice of teaching by her successful work with little children in the slums of Rome, the results of which had a profound effect on the development of infant schools in the twentieth century.

In contrast to current methods where

the children, like butterflies mounted on pins, are fastened each to his place, the desk, spreading the useless wings of barren and meaningless knowledge which they have acquired,[2]

Madame Montessori believed that

the school must permit the *free natural manifestation of the child*.[3] . . . The fundamental principle of scientific pedagogy must be, indeed, the *liberty of the pupil*; – such liberty as shall permit a development of individual spontaneous manifestations of the child's nature.[4]

She is the first educator to give a clear and acceptable explanation of the value of freedom of movement. The old method, by which the child was 'disciplined' by immobility and silence,

hindered the child from learning to move with grace and with discernment, and left him so untrained, that, when he found himself in an environment where the benches and chairs were not nailed to the floor, he was not able to move about without overturning the lighter pieces of furniture.[5]

1. MONTESSORI, MME., *Montessori Method*, p. 115.
2. ibid, p. 14.   3. ibid, p. 15.
4. ibid, p. 28.   5. ibid, p. 84.

Liberty, however, was not to be unlimited, and was certainly not to be licence. It was Madame Montessori who, when she was shown part of the garden at Bedales set apart for the little ones, said that there must be a fence around it; there can be no freedom without limits:

Our idea of liberty for the child cannot be the simple concept of liberty we use in the observation of plants, etc. The child, because of the peculiar characteristics of helplessness with which he is born, and because of his qualities as a social individual, is circumscribed by *bonds* which *limit* his activity.

An educational method that shall have *liberty* as its basis must intervene to help the child to a conquest of these various obstacles.[6]

The first function of education is to lead the child to independence:

He who is served is limited in his independence. This concept will be the foundation of the dignity of the man of the future. 'I do not wish to be served, *because* I am not an impotent.' And this idea must be gained before men can feel themselves to be really free.

Any pedagogical action, if it is to be efficacious in the training of little children, must tend to *help* the children to advance upon this road of independence. We must help them to learn to walk without assistance, to run, to go up and down stairs, to lift up fallen objects, to dress and undress themselves, to bathe themselves, to speak distinctly, and to express their own needs clearly. We must give them such help as shall make it possible for children to achieve the satisfaction of their own individual aims and desires. All this is a part of education for independence.

We habitually *serve* children; and this is not only an act of servility toward them, but it is dangerous, since it tends to suffocate their useful, spontaneous activity. . . . We do not stop to think that the child *who does not do, does not know how to do.*[7]

In her description of the child in the park, filling his pail with stones, Madame Montessori shows remarkable insight into not only the difference between the child's purpose and that of the adult, but into the whole question of the distinction between spiritual and material values, which was so clearly understood by later educators such as Homer Lane. The child's

6. ibid, p. 95.   7. ibid, p. 97.

nursemaid, thinking to help him, filled it for him, and the child protested violently:

> The little boy did not wish to have the pail full of gravel; he wished to go through the motions necessary to fill it, thus satisfying a need of his vigorous organism. The child's unconscious aim was his own self-development; not the external fact of a pail full of little stones.[8]

The adult

> thinks that the child's wish is to obtain some tangible object, and lovingly helps him to do this: whereas the child as a rule has for his unconscious desire, his own self-development. Hence he despises everything already attained, and yearns for that which is still to be sought for. . . .
> A similar error is that which we repeat so frequently when we fancy that the desire of the student is to possess a piece of information. We aid him to grasp intellectually this detached piece of knowledge, and, preventing by this means his self-development, we make him wretched.
> To have learned something is for the child only a point of departure. When he has learned the meaning of an exercise, then he begins to enjoy repeating it, and he does repeat it an infinite number of times, with the most evident satisfaction.[9]

She draws attention to the important principle that each age, or stage, of childhood has its own particular needs, and that if these are not met at the time when they are most evident, some part of the child's development will forever remain arrested:

> The same exercises are not repeated by children of all ages. In fact, repetition corresponds to a *need*. . . . It is necessary to offer those exercises which correspond to the need of development felt by an organism, and if a child's age has carried him past a certain need, it is never possible to obtain, in its fulness, a development which missed its proper moment. Hence children grow up, often fatally and irrevocably, imperfectly developed.[10]

The child himself knows, even if only unconsciously, what these needs are, and behaviour which adults often regard as

8. ibid, p. 355.   9. ibid, pp. 356–7.   10. ibid, p. 358.

naughty and difficult, may in fact be his way of voicing his protest against treatment which fails to satisfy these needs:

> The child, like every other strong creature fighting for the right to live, rebels against whatever offends that occult impulse within him which is the voice of nature, and which he ought to obey; and he shows by violent actions, by screaming and weeping that he has been overborne and forced away from his mission in life. He shows himself to be a rebel ... against those who do not understand him and who, fancying that they are helping him, are really pushing him backward in the highway of life.[11]

The teacher, then, must be prepared to learn:

> From the child itself he will learn how to perfect himself as an educator.[12] The educator must be as one inspired by a deep *worship of life*, and must, through this reverence, *respect . . .* the *development* of the child life.[13]

Education is to guide activity; the work of the teacher is to provide an environment in which the children's own inner purposes may flourish in *self*-activity. It is the inner force which must be trusted and allowed to develop:

> All human victories, all human progress, stand upon the inner force.[14] We must know how to call to the *man* which lies dormant within the soul of the child.[15]
>
> *Environment* is undoubtedly a *secondary* factor in the phenomena of life; it can modify in that it can help or hinder, but it can never *create. . . .* The origins of the *development*, both in the species and in the individual, *lie within. . . .* Life makes itself manifest – life creates, life gives. . . . Life is a superb goddess, always advancing, overthrowing the obstacles which environment places in the way of her triumph.[16]

The child can only grow by means of his own activity. No teaching can do this for him, and the skill of the educator lies in being able to set this activity in motion, or rather in allowing it to take place. The emphasis must be on the child learning, not on the teacher teaching:

> We may liken the child to a clock, and may say that with the old-time way it is very much as if we were to hold the wheels of

11. ibid, p. 359.   12. ibid, p. 13.   13. ibid, p. 104.
14. ibid, p. 24.   15. ibid, p. 37.   16. ibid, pp. 105–6.

the clock quiet and move the hands about the clock face with our fingers. The hands will continue to circle the dial just so long as we apply, through our fingers, the necessary motor force. Even so it is with that sort of culture which is limited to the work which the teacher does with the child. The new method, instead, may be compared to the process of winding, which sets the entire mechanism in motion. . . .

Our educational aim with very young children must be to *aid the spontaneous development of the mental, spiritual, and physical personality.*[17]

In this process it will be found that children

soon *reveal profound individual differences* which call for very different kinds of help from the teacher. Some of them require almost no intervention on her part, while others demand actual *teaching,*

but, however great the difference, the principle remains

that the teaching shall be rigorously guided by the principle of limiting to the greatest possible point the active intervention of the educator.[18]

True discipline can only be achieved by this method, when children willingly take on a piece of work because of its appeal to their innate needs and interests:

The first dawning of real discipline comes through work. At a given moment it happens that a child becomes keenly interested in a piece of work, showing it by the expression of his face, by his intense attention, by his perseverance in the same exercise. That child has set foot upon the road leading to discipline.[19]

Madame Montessori illustrates this principle by telling of a boy of two and a half who kept up a game with letters for three quarters of an hour. The same principle is seen in operation in modern infant schools when a child becomes absorbed in some self-chosen task, sometimes termed play, through which he learns how to work. Then is the time for help from the teacher: 'Once the habit of work is formed, we must supervise it with scrupulous accuracy.'[20]

17. ibid, pp. 229–30.   18. ibid, p. 231.
19. ibid, p. 350.   20. Ibid, p. 330.

The best of our primary schools of today show the influence of this principle, by achieving discipline through 'developing activity in spontaneous work'.

Discipline

is not to be obtained by words; no man learns self-discipline 'through hearing another man speak'. . . . Discipline is reached always by indirect means. The end is obtained, not by attacking the mistake and fighting it, but by developing activity in spontaneous work. This work cannot be arbitrarily offered; . . . it must be work which the human being instinctively desires to do.[21]

The child . . . responds to nature because he is in action. . . . The child disciplined in this way is no longer the child he was at first, who knows how to *be* good passively; but he is an individual who has made himself better.[22]

Development comes through action, but this action must be orderly:

True rest for muscles, intended by nature for action, is in orderly action; just as true rest for the lungs is the normal rhythm of respiration taken in pure air. To take action away from the muscles is to force them away from their natural motor impulse, and hence, besides tiring them, means forcing them into a state of degeneration; just as the lungs, forced into immobility, would die instantly and the whole organism with them.

It is therefore necessary to keep clearly in mind the fact that rest for whatever naturally acts, lies in some specified form of action, corresponding to its nature.

To act in obedience to the hidden precepts of nature – that is rest.[23]

Rewards and punishments should not be used. Madame Montessori always treated a 'naughty' child as though he were ill, by isolating him from the other children and giving him special attention:

As for punishments, the soul of the normal man grows perfect through expanding, and punishment as commonly understood is always a form of *repression*. . . .[24]

The real punishment of normal man is the loss of the consciousness of that individual power and greatness which are the sources of his inner life.[25]

21. ibid, pp. 350–51.   22. ibid, p. 352.   23. ibid, p. 354.
24. ibid, p. 24.   25. ibid, p. 26.

True motivation must come from within, not from exterior compulsions:

He who accomplishes a truly human work, he who does something really great and victorious, is never spurred to his task by those trifling attractions called by the name of 'prizes', nor by the fear of those petty ills which we call 'punishments'.[26]

Man, disciplined through liberty, begins to desire the true and only prize which will never belittle or disappoint him, – the birth of human power and liberty within that inner life of his from which his activities must spring.[27]

It is perhaps unfortunate that to many people Madame Montessori is remembered chiefly as the inventor of a method of sense training, while many of these great principles, which have deeply influenced the education and treatment of young children, are forgotten. Nevertheless, the attention she drew to the importance of the senses and their training helped to enrich childhood, and to open the way to a practical and effective method of teaching children not only to read and write, but to develop judgement and sensitivity:

The education of the senses should be begun methodically in infancy, and should continue during the entire period of instruction which is to prepare the individual for life in society.[28]

Everyone knows in practical life the fundamental necessity of judging with exactness between various stimuli.[29] In many cases intelligence is rendered useless by lack of practice and this practice is almost always sense education. . . .

Aesthetic and moral education are closely related to this sensory education. Multiply the sensations, and develop the capacity of appreciating fine differences in stimuli, and we *refine* the sensibility and multiply man's pleasures.[30]

The senses of touch and hearing are of particular importance:

I have already learned, through my work with deficient children, that among the various forms of sense memory that of muscular sense is the most precocious. Indeed, many children who have not arrived at the point of recognising a figure by *looking at it*, could recognise it by *touching it*.[31]

26. ibid, p. 23.   27. ibid, p. 101.   28. ibid, p. 221.
29. ibid, p. 221.   30. ibid, p. 221.   31. ibid, p. 198.

I believe that after establishing silence it would be educational to ring well-toned bells, now calm and sweet, now clear and ringing, sending their vibrations through the child's whole body. And when, besides the education of the ear, we have produced a *vibratory* education of the whole body, through these wisely selected sounds of the bells, giving a peace that pervades the very fibres of his being, then I believe these young bodies would be sensitive to crude noises, and the children would come to dislike, and to cease from making, disordered and ugly noises.[32]

Madame Montessori was the first to point out what is now well understood by most teachers of young children, that 'Contrary to the usually accepted idea, writing *precedes reading*.' [33] She gives her reasons, and makes clear the difference between true reading and 'barking at print':

What I understand by reading is the *interpretation* of an idea from the written signs. . . . Until the child reads a transmission of ideas from the written words, *he does not read*. . . .[34]

In writing the child . . . *materially translates* sounds into signs, and *moves*, a thing which is always easy and pleasant for him. Writing develops in the little child with *facility* and *spontaneity*, analogous to the development of spoken language – which is a motor translation of audible sounds. Reading, on the contrary, makes part of an abstract intellectual culture, which is the interpretation of ideas from graphic symbols, and is only acquired later on.[35]

Nature study is of very real value:

Agriculture and animal culture contain in themselves precious means of education.

First. The child is initiated into observation of the phenomena of life. . . . Little by little, as interest and observation grow, his zealous care for the living creatures grows also, and in this way, the child can logically be brought to appreciate the care which the mother and teacher take of him.

Second. The child is initiated into *foresight* by way of *auto-education*; when he knows that the life of the plants that have been sown depends upon his care in watering them, and that of the animals, upon his diligence in feeding them; without which the

32. ibid, p. 206.   33. ibid, p. 296.
34. ibid, p. 296.   35. ibid, p. 267.

little plant dries up and the animals suffer hunger, the child becomes vigilant, as one who is beginning to feel a mission in life. Moreover, a voice quite different from that of his mother and his teacher calling him to his duties, is speaking here, exhorting him never to forget the task he has undertaken. It is the plaintive voice of the needy life which lives by his care. . . .

The rewards which the child reaps also remain between him and nature: one fine day after long patient care in carrying food and straw to the brooding pigeon, behold the little ones! behold a number of chickens peeping about the sitting hen, which yesterday sat motionless in her brooding place! behold one day the tender little rabbits in the hutch where formerly dwelt in solitude the pair of big rabbits to which he had not a few times lovingly carried the green vegetables left over in his mother's kitchen.[36]

The influence of Madame Montessori can be seen in the freedom of modern infant schools, where individual teaching has taken the place of class teaching, where children are allowed liberty to follow self-chosen occupations, and where the emphasis is on the children learning rather than the teacher teaching. Above all, it is evident wherever education is understood as the development of the whole personality, and where teaching follows the pattern of growth of the child:

By education must be understood the active *help* given to the normal expansion of life of the child. The child is a body which grows, and a soul which develops, – these two forms, physiological and psychic, have one eternal font, life itself. We must neither mar nor stifle the mysterious powers which lie within these two forms of growth, but we must *await from them* the manifestations which we know will succeed one another.[37]

36. ibid, pp. 156-7.   37. ibid, pp. 104-5.

34

The Twentieth Century · Arnold and Beatrice Gesell
Charlotte Bühler · Bertrand Russell · Susan Isaacs · Anna Freud
Piaget · Experimental Schools: The Little Commonwealth,
Summerhill, the Werkplaats, Bedales, Gordonstoun,
Leighton Park · William James · William McDougall
Sir John Adams · Sir Percy Nunn · Professor A. N. Whitehead
Gentile · Maritain · J. S. Brubacher · Sir Richard Livingstone
Professor M. V. C. Jeffreys · Dr Wall

WITH the coming of the twentieth century, the flame of education became a searchlight. The work of the psychoanalysts revealed the existence and importance of the unconscious. Freud, Jung and Adler emphasized the strength of the inner drives and the effect of inner conflict upon the personality.

This new understanding of the significance of unconscious influences had a profound effect on the growth of child psychology; and the study of childhood grew rapidly into a recognized science through the work of Arnold and Beatrice Gesell, Charlotte Bühler, Susan Isaacs, Anna Freud, Piaget and many others.

*

Arnold and Beatrice Gesell, writing in 1912, drew attention to the failure of the primary school to educate truly:

Although there is nothing finally established as to the ultimate healthy limits of achievement in the primary child, we do believe that he is at present far below his possibilities, and think it regrettable that the primary schools continue to turn out such hordes of pupils subnormal in personal power. The primary child has many untouched reservoirs of interest and capacity. He is ripe for unguessed avenues of activity and attainment.

The overzealous parent at the door and the relentless timepiece on the wall conspire to keep an artificially precocious atmosphere in the primary school. Order, system, detail, and prescription have replaced spontaneity, grace, initiative and investigation.[1]

The primary-school child comes to school with the belief that work is as lovely as play. See the zeal and pride with which he attacks his first intellectual problems, and the languour and discontent with which he often finishes them. Why is this? Why has the eager, buoyant, first-grade child often become the so-called lazy incorrigible of the grammar grades? What has become of the pride in work, the eagerness to help, the dominating curiosity, and the warm, unselfish affection for teacher and school? Why have these deep instincts been strangled in their very birth? Why have they not been preserved to brighten and inspire the effort of his later years? Chiefly because school work loses almost immediately its intimate, human touch. It is separated from all emotional incentive and becomes the dry tedium of accumulating facts.[2]

The feelings and emotions are an integral part of the personality and must have their full part in education:

The mind is a living unit, but a unit with three expressions; thinking, feeling and doing. . . . Hygiene recognizes the natural unity of the mind, and insists that mental health depends on a proper co-ordination of all three expressions. Pedagogy also must recognize this natural unity and beware of any practice which artificially dissociates thinking or doing from feeling. . . . Intellect, feeling, and will should function together, reinforcing one another.[3]

We are sometimes too much concerned with what is in the minds of little children, and too unconscious of what is in their hearts.[4]

The child's personality cannot emerge and develop unless his emotions are stirred in vital accompaniment to his intellectual work.[5]

Education must take into account the instincts as the driving force of all learning:

All development, both in the child, and in the race, is grounded in instinct. . . . It is time to have a reckoning, to realize before it is too late the futility of pushing nature. There are certain basic instincts implanted in childhood which wedge their way through

1. GESELL, BEATRICE and ARNOLD, The Normal Child and Primary Education, Preface and p. 305.
2. ibid, pp. 311–12.   3. ibid, pp. 291, 292.
4. ibid, p. 244.   5. ibid, p. 307.

obstacles to the accomplishment of their purpose. ... The part that mood and feeling and instinct play in school life and in mental hygiene is often utterly disregarded.[6]

What does the six-year-old care for print? his fingers are itching for contact with things, and his legs are set for chasing butterflies. Too much formalism in childhood kills spontaneity and interest. Education cannot, by formulating courses of study, force intellectual functions. The laws which govern the growth of mind are as immediate and irresistible in their operation as those which govern the growth of the body. If we force either the one or the other, personality is foiled.[7]

The source of energy lies in the instincts and in the right use of activity:

Energy wisely expended renews itself and accumulates power, which transfers itself into other lines of effort.[8]

The primary aim of education must be to lead children to think:

The business of the primary grades is not to give information, but to teach the children how to get it. To teach them how to work independently is of more importance than the technique of reading. The grammar grades and the high school need pupils who can think; they have plenty who can memorize words. But they will continue to be surfeited with lip workers until the primary school agrees to train the thought power of the child.[9]

The little child is so undeveloped intellectually that he needs material full of such suggestiveness that it is easily transformed and will invite expression and invention. See that his problem requires him to compare, judge, and formulate some conclusion. He must learn to think before he learns to study.[10]

The skilful teacher withdraws herself, and throws the burden of discovery and explanation upon the children. Give them a genuine problem, and then fairly turn them loose to solve and illustrate it in a variety of ways.[11]

The great and essential factor in the educative process is love. The child learns and develops because he feels loved and secure:

Little children must be led to the fulfilment of their possibilities

6. ibid, pp. 82, 308.   7. ibid, p. 309.   8. ibid, p. 231.
9. ibid, p. 236.   10. ibid, p. 232.   11. ibid, p. 308.

through a firm faith in the unselfish affection of those who care for them. The child is controlled by love. He understands love, for his heart is running over with it. It is incorporated into his being, for it was the force which first gave him life, and it is the energy which will continue to drive him on to excel himself.[12]

*

'The case for the greatest possible freedom in education is a very strong one,' wrote Bertrand Russell.

To begin with, absence of freedom involves conflicts with adults, which frequently have a much more profound psychological effect than was realized until very recently. The child who is in any way coerced tends to respond with hatred, and if, as is usual, he is not able to give free vent to his hatred, it festers inwardly, and may sink into the unconscious with all kinds of strange consequences throughout the rest of life. The father as the object of hatred may come to be replaced by the State, the Church, or a foreign nation, thus leading a man to become an anarchist, an atheist, or a militarist as the case may be. Or again, hatred of the authorities who oppress the child may become transferred into a desire to inflict equal oppression later on upon the next generation. . . .

Another effect of compulsion in education is that it destroys originality and intellectual interest. Desire for knowledge, at any rate for a good deal of knowledge, is natural to the young, but is generally destroyed by the fact that they are given more than they desire or can assimilate. Children who are forced to eat acquire a loathing for food, and children who are forced to learn acquire a loathing for knowledge. When they think, they do not think spontaneously in the way in which they run or jump or shout: they think with a view to pleasing some adult, and therefore with an attempt at correctness rather than from natural curiosity. The killing of spontaneity is especially disastrous in artistic directions. Children who are taught literature or painting or music to excess, or with a view to correctness rather than to self-expression, become progressively less interested in the aesthetic side of life.[13]

*

Charlotte Bühler and her colleagues in Vienna made detailed and continuous studies of children over many years, which

12. ibid, p. 247.
13. RUSSELL, BERTRAND, *Education and the Social Order*, pp. 32–3.

resulted in what she called 'a very complete scientific picture of mental development'.

Two principles grew directly from this work, both of which were to influence the practice of education in schools. The first was the importance of maturation, or the process of natural growth, and its effect on learning. She described the studies made on Albanian children in comparison with their own. These children, she wrote,

are so bandaged in their cradles during the first year that they can move neither hand nor foot. When at first unbound they are unable to hold anything and yet within a period of two hours they cover all those steps for which our children require many months and finally are able to perform the age characteristic test. The same holds good for the two- to five-year-olds. They of course are allowed to move about freely, but they have no playthings and are quite passive and lethargic. They are at first afraid of toys and are clumsy in handling them. And yet within a few hours they can almost achieve those performances that are normal for their age.[14]

Other studies which she describes underline the same point, that the acquisition of skills depends more on maturity than practice – an important principle for education, and one which has brought about such conceptions as 'reading-readiness' and 'number-readiness' in the teaching of young children. A group of two- and three-year-olds was trained, over a period of three months, to button, use scissors and to climb a ladder. At the end of this time a control group of children was trained in the same skills for a week. The control group achieved the same level of skill in the one week as the first group had achieved after three months. Charlotte Bühler wrote:

The dependency of sucessful learning on the level of maturation is even more pronounced in the case of intellectual activities than in the case of physical ones.[15]

Commenting on further experiments of this kind she said:

The degree of maturation and the innate capacities of the individual were much more decisive factors than the special training.[16]

14. BÜHLER, CHARLOTTE, *From Birth to Maturity*, p. 85.
15. ibid, p. 90.   16. ibid, p. 90.

The second principle is closely related. From her observations of children at play she discovered the importance of what she calls 'the work attitude'. Younger children, playing imaginatively, may start and finish their play whenever they like, but older children, in setting themselves a task, to construct something out of materials for instance, learn 'to accept and complete a task. The child understands this play activity as work.' When this stage has been reached the child is ready to work, for he is prepared to accept and complete a task given to him.

This is the foundation of the major prerequisite for successful school adaptation. An analysis of the work in the first grades of the Viennese elementary schools has demonstrated that eighty per cent of the first-grade children who fail, do so because they have not yet developed the work attitude in their games before entering school.[17]

*

Susan Isaacs, at the Malting House School at Cambridge, gathered data which threw much light upon the intellectual and social development of young children and confirmed her belief that children learn through their own activity and first-hand discovery.

In these years the child's intelligence is essentially practical. He thinks as much with his hands as with his tongue. . . . The whole of his education needs to be conceived in terms of his own activity. . . . The whole physical setting of the school and classroom should be based upon the creative value of the child's own movements. . . . When we ask children *not* to move, we should have excellent reasons for doing so. It is stillness we have to justify, not movement. . . . The end of education in these years is that the children should grow and develop, and to this, activity of one sort or another is the only key.[18] . . . We come back at every point to the view that it is the child's doing, the child's active social experience and his own thinking and talking that are the chief means of his education. Our part as teachers is to call out the children's activity, and to meet it when it arises spontaneously. We can give them the means

17. ibid, p. 119.
18. ISAACS, SUSAN, *The Children We Teach*, pp. 74, 76–7.

of solving problems in which they are actively concerned, but we cannot fruitfully foist problems upon them that do not arise from the development of their own interests. And their native interest in things and people around them – the street, the market, the garden, the railway, the world of plants and animals – do in fact offer us all the opportunities we need for their education. . . . Whatever activity brings light to the eye and eagerness to the voice and gestures can be taken as a clue to some inner need of growth.[19]

It is so . . . much easier . . . to keep the children relatively inactive and to 'teach' them, than it is to arrange for them to 'find out'. It is so much simpler to teach them reading and writing, . . . to tell them stories, or even to teach them rhythmic movement, than it is to go with them to see a bridge being built or a road being mended, to trace the course of the telephone wires or water-pipes, or to wait patiently while they experiment with water or gas or fire or cooking things. Reasons of this kind, of course, account for the general lag of our practice behind our theory in every direction. . . . We have long been familiar with the very young child's desire to touch and handle, to pull things to pieces, to 'look inside', to ask questions; but we have not taken much serious practical notice of all this, as regards the *direction* of our work, and our notion of what the school as a whole should be and do. We have been content to apply our new psychological knowledge of *how* the child learns, to the ways of getting him to learn the old things. We have not used it to enrich our understanding of *what* he needs to learn, nor of what experiences the school should bring to him. The school has on the whole remained a closed-in place, a screen between the child and his living interests.[20]

It is easy, in the schools, to forget or overlook the strength of the child's spontaneous impulses towards understanding. The weight of the traditional curriculum and traditional teaching lies so heavily upon us and upon the children that their spontaneous interests have little chance to show themselves, and we, little leisure to notice them. But look at the same children out of school. . . . Watch their interest then in motors and railways and the pneumatic road-drill, in the farm and animal life. Listen to their questions. And, especially, listen and watch in the Infants' School years, before the children have become quite sophisticated. Take them before they have been taught to separate learning from playing and knowledge from life. Then you will not be able to doubt the strength and

19. ibid, pp. 125, 170.
20. *Intellectual Growth in Young Children*, pp. 19–21.

spontaneity of the wish to know and understand, within the limits of the child's intelligence.[21]

One of the errors of the traditional curriculum and traditional teaching is the way in which knowledge is presented to children in separate 'subjects'. We need to appreciate the unity of the child's interests.

For him, especially in the early years of the Primary School, the field of knowledge does not divide itself spontaneously into separate departments – 'history', 'geography', 'nature study', 'arithmetic', 'English', and all the anatomy of the ordinary curriculum. ... He is concerned with *things* and with *activities* – things to understand and things to do – rather than with 'subjects'. . . .

When once this underlying unity of the child's interests is grasped, the time-table and the labelled curriculum both become good servants instead of the bad masters they have so often been.[22]

*

The observations made by Anna Freud and Dorothy Burlingham on children in Residential Wartime Nurseries stressed the importance of the early years of childhood and the relationships of children to their families, particularly to the parents. They concluded:

Early instinctive wishes have to be taken seriously, not because their fulfilment or refusal causes momentary happiness or unhappiness; but because they are the moving powers which urge the child's development from primitive self-interest and self-indulgence towards an attachment and consequently towards adaptation to the grown-up world. . . .

The normal and healthy growth of the human personality depends on the circumstances of the child's first attachments and on the fate of the instinctual forces (sex, aggression and their derivatives) which find expression in these early and all-important relationships.[23]

They suggested that if more use were made of the opportunities for observing children under conditions such as those of Residential Nurseries

21. *The Children We Teach*, pp. 112–13.

22. ibid, pp. 118, 123.

23. FREUD, A., and BURLINGHAM, D., *Infants without Families*, pp. 82, 83.

much valuable material about the emotional and educational response at these early ages might be collected and applied to the upbringing of other children who are lucky enough to live under more normal circumstances.[24]

*

The contribution of Professor Jean Piaget to education is only now being fully appreciated. For over thirty-five years he and his colleagues in Geneva have been carrying out detailed and systematic research into the development of reasoning and thought in young children. The results of this wealth of knowledge have shed new light on the question of the growth of understanding.

Nathan Isaacs sums up Piaget's thought:

The starting-point and crux of the child's intellectual growth is not – as it was long the fashion to assume – sensation or sensory perception or anything else passively impressed on him through his sense-organs from outside, but *his own action*. And action in the most literal, physical, observable sense of the term. From the beginning the infant sets out from patterns of active behaviour, and it is these that govern his life and shape his development. Through his own actions he takes in ever new experiences which become worked into his action-patterns and in turn continually help to expand their range and scope. It is through actively turning to look or listen, through following and repeating, through continually exploring by touch and grasping and handling and manipulating, through striving and learning to walk and talk, through dramatic play and the mastery of every sort of new activity and skill, that he goes on all the time both enlarging his world and organising it. His own physical activity thus enters profoundly right from the outset into his whole world-scheme and indeed fashions it, supports it and provides throughout the master-key to it.

In effect thought itself on this view is simply an internal version or development of outward action. It is action which becomes *progressively* internalized through the child's acquisition of language and his growing use of symbols, through imagination and representation; and which then goes on expanding under the guidance partly of social life, partly of the physical world, till it culminates in a great organized scheme of mental *operations*.[25]

24. ibid, p. 108.
25. ISAACS, NATHAN, *New Light on Children's Ideas of Number*, pp. 5–6.

It is impossible to give an adequate account of Piaget's work in the scope of this book, but his demonstration that 'the nature of children's thinking is basically different from that of adults', must have, in time, far-reaching effects on the education of young children.

*

Experimental schools, many of them connected with the Progressive Schools Movement, came into being in the present century and set a new pattern for education under the leadership of men and women such as Homer Lane in the Little Commonwealth, A. S. Neill at Summerhill, Kees and Betty Boeke at the Werkplaats in Holland, J. H. Badley at Bedales, Kurt Hahn at Gordonstoun, E. B. Castle at the Quaker School at Leighton Park, and others.

Homer Lane was described by his disciple, A. S. Neill, as 'the greatest child psychologist of our time', and by W. David Wills as 'half a century before his time'.[26] The community, known as 'The Little Commonwealth', consisted originally of young delinquents of fourteen years and over. The discipline and government were entirely in the hands of the children, and the community was run as a free democracy.

Lane shaped his highly successful practice on the belief in the basic goodness of the child. Delinquency and anti-social behaviour, in his view, were the result, not of an evil nature, but of a wrong direction of basic impulses. The way of salvation lies, not in punishment and treatment which would continue the process of warping, but in redirecting the energies, through freedom, love and the natural discipline of a community of one's peers:

'They must realize that I am on their side,' he said,

He followed [David Willis said] the path of freedom instead of imposed authority, of self-expression instead of a pouring-in of knowledge, of evoking and exploiting the child's natural sense of wonder and curiosity instead of a repetitious hammering home of dull facts. These ideas ... are all quite commonplace now, but we owe them as much to Lane as to anyone man.[27]

26. WILLS, W. DAVID, *Homer Lane, A Biography*, p. 19.
27. ibid, p. 20.

A. S. Neill

set out to make a school in which we should allow children freedom to be themselves. . . . We have been called brave, but it did not require courage: all it required was what we had – a complete belief in the child as a good, not an evil being.[28]

Possibly the greatest discovery we have made in Summerhill is that a child is born a sincere creature. We set out to leave children alone so that we might discover what they were. It is the only possible way of dealing with children, and the pioneer school of the future must pursue this way if it is to contribute to child knowledge and, more important, to child happiness.[29]

Summerhill began as an experimental school . . . it is now a demonstration school, for it demonstrates that freedom works and succeeds.

When my wife and I began it we had one main idea . . . to make the school fit the child instead of making the child fit the school.[30]

A school that makes active children sit at desks studying mostly useless subjects is a bad school.[31]

The function of the child is to live his own life – not the life that his anxious parents think he should live, nor a life according to the purpose of the educator who thinks he knows what is best. All this interference and guidance on the part of adults only produces a generation of robots.[32]

Parents are slow in realizing how unimportant the learning side of school is . . . All prize-giving and marks and exams sidetrack proper personality development. Only pedants claim that learning from books is education . . .

When I lecture to students . . . I am often shocked at the ungrownupness of these lads and lasses stuffed with useless knowledge . . . For they have been taught *to know*, but have not been allowed *to feel* . . . And so the system goes on, aiming only at standards of book learning – goes on separating the head from the heart.[33]

Children do not need teaching as much as they need love and understanding. They need approval and freedom to be naturally good.[34]

The classroom walls and the prisonlike buildings narrow the teacher's outlook and prevent him from seeing the true essentials of

28. NEILL, A. S., *That Dreadful School*, p. 10.
29. ibid, p. 17.   30. ibid, p. 8.
31. *Summerhill, A Radical Approach to Education*, p. 4.
32. ibid, p. 2.   33. ibid, pp. 25–6.   34. ibid, p. 118.

education. His work deals with the part of a child that is above the neck; and perforce, the emotional, vital part of a child is foreign territory to him.[35] There is never a problem child; there are only problem parents. Perhaps it would be better to say that *there is only a problem humanity*.[36] One day humanity may trace all its miseries, its hates, and its diseases to its particular form of civilization that is essentially anti-life ... my contention is that unfree education results in life that cannot be lived fully. Such an education almost entirely ignores the *emotions* of life ... Only the head is educated. If the emotions are permitted to be really free, the intellect will look after itself.[37]

The world *must* find a better way. For politics will not save humanity ... Most political newspapers are bristling with hate, hate all the time. Too many are socialistic because they hate the rich instead of loving the poor.

How can we have happy homes with love in them when the home is a tiny corner of a homeland that shows hate socially in a hundred ways?... All the Greek and math and history in the world will not help to make the home more loving, the child free from inhibitions, the parent free of neurosis ...

New generations must be given the chance to grow in freedom. The bestowal of freedom is the bestowal of love. And only love can save the world.[38]

Robin Pedley wrote:

Neill, more than anyone else, has swung teachers' opinion in this country from its old reliance on authority and the cane to hesitant recognition that a child's first need is love, and with love respect for the free growth of his personality: free, that is, from the arbitrary compulsion of elders, and disciplined instead by social experience ... Today's friendliness between pupil and teacher is probably the greatest difference between the classrooms of 1963 and those of 1923. The change owes much to Neill.[39]

The school founded by Kees and Betty Boeke in Holland was called a Workshop, for this should be the pattern for schools, where every child is a Worker and every grown up a Helper. Wyatt Rawson wrote:

35. ibid, p. 28.   36. ibid, p. 103.
37. ibid, p. 100.   38. ibid, p. 91.
39. PEDLEY, RODIN, *The Comprehensive School*, pp. 174–5.

The community will regulate its work by friendly discussion, but without compulsion, trying to give the utmost freedom to each individual to express himself in his own way, in so far this does not damage the whole. Spontaneous interest will be the underlying motive for all learning ... As for rewards and punishments, they will not be thought of, for threats and bribery will be considered unworthy. There will be no competition and no marks, since these make the quick conceited or reckless, while discouraging the slow. But everyone will get a chance to have his work recognized by the community.[40]

The school

encouraged spontaneity and freedom, secured order without appealing to force, and maintained a sense of equality and brotherhood among children varying widely in age, social background and intellectual capacity.[41]

It grew and flourished

until now (in 1956) it contains 850 boys and girls and is duly recognized and supported by the Dutch government ... Finally it became an outstanding success, securing a special position in Holland and arousing the interest of educators and psychologists in all the countries Kees Boeke has visited.[42]

*

'Scholarship, good-breeding and leadership no longer form the whole of our educational ideal,' wrote J. H. Badley, headmaster of Bedales.

We now recognize more clearly that education is concerned with the whole human-being, on every side of his nature, and cannot neglect any of his activities and needs. We recognize also that it is not merely a passive process of following tradition, absorbing the knowledge amassed by others, and doing as we are told by those older or more powerful than ourselves. Rather it is an active process on the part of the learner, who learns most not by what he is told but by what he finds out for himself and makes his own by practical use; and who learns not merely from books or from the formal lessons of the class-room but from the whole of his experience, both in the classroom and outside it. Thus the material

40. RAWSON, W. and others, *Kees Boeke*, p. 55.
41. RAWSON, W., *The Werkplaats Adventure*, Intro., p. 9.
42. ibid, pp. 9–10.

with which education has to deal is no less than his whole environment and way of life.[43]

The purpose of education is to give fulness of life ... Education
is concerned with every part of human nature, with feeling and
will no less than with thought. ... Wherever education is carried
on, it includes the whole of experience at the stage in question, and
must neglect nothing that contributes to the full growth and use
of the powers proper to that stage. Nor must it allow the needs
and interests of any stage of development to be lost sight of and
subordinated to the requirements of later stages, trying to make
young children into small editions of older, and these of adults.
The nature, order, and normal rate of mental development and
the inner life of the child are modern discoveries still in the
making. They have already transformed the conception and practice of education in its earlier stages; and continued psychological
investigation is bound to carry this transformation further into the
later stages also. In all that makes for health – health of mind as
well as of body – in the part played by freedom and happiness
in healthy development, in the need of satisfaction for the sense
of beauty and for the affections, in the far-reaching influence of
the emotions and the motives that are called into play – in all such
matters we have still much to learn of the full meaning of the
truism that life is only to be learnt by living.

Education, then ... is not only a matter of direct training of
body and mind and character; it depends much on the continual
influence of the environment ... By environment is to be understood not merely the actual surroundings of the school, or its
buildings and the rooms within which children have to spend so
much of their time, or the objects that meet their eyes, but also
the personal influences and human 'atmosphere' by which they
are surrounded ... And amongst the strongest influences of the
environment are the pressure-tendencies that are exerted by the
whole organization of the daily life, with the much or little variety
and freedom that it allows, and by the nature of the authority that
it is exercised, the compulsions and restraints that are felt, and
the presence or absence of a sense of strain. It is, in short, the whole
way of life, in school as elsewhere, that is the chief instrument of
education.[44]

*

E. B. Castle wrote of his work at Leighton Park: 'Unseemly

43. BADLEY, J. H., *A Schoolmaster's Testament*, p. 30.
44. ibid, pp. 36, 37-8.

conduct is less a matter of original sin than of unsatisfied appetite for appropriate occupation.'[45]

All our experience went to demonstrate that there can be no logical separation between moral, intellectual and aesthetic activity. Many instances come to mind of a boy gaining such confidence in non-academic work that its tonic effect spread into his studies, or transformed him from a fear-full little brat into a self-respecting boy . . .

This, of course, is a common experience in schools where such opportunities for individual release exist and where teachers know how to use them. What seems to be innate disability is frequently discovered to be emotional inhibition due to a variety of causes in the boy's home or school life. If diagnosis can be followed by special treatment of a purely educational kind, aiming at giving confidence in one area of achievement, the confidence gained will result in general achievement. . . .

We must surely agree that a major part of education consists in the enrichment of personality by tapping individual skills, and in relating knowledge, feeling, will, appreciation and skill into a total significant meaning. That is what we were trying to do, this is why we so often found that many of the non-academic occupations actually stimulated academic study rather than interfered with it.[46]

*

The practice of the ordinary schools was, in varying degrees, influenced by the results of these experiments. It was also influenced by the ever increasing flood of writings on education by philosophers, psychologists and practitioners, whose views helped to widen and broaden the concept of modern education.

William James and William McDougall both drew attention to the importance of the instinctive drives as the great springs of behaviour, and to the value of interest as a lever to learning. James wrote:

Without an equipment of native reactions on the child's part, the teacher would have no hold whatever upon the child's attention or conduct. . . . You may take a child to the schoolroom, but you cannot make him learn the new things you wish to impart, except

45. CASTLE, E. B., *People in School*, p. 30.
46. ibid, pp. 45–6.

by soliciting him in the first instance by something which makes him natively react.[47]

Since some objects are natively interesting and in others interest is artificially acquired, the teacher must know which the natively interesting ones are; for ... other objects can artificially acquire an interest only through first becoming associated with some of these natively interesting things.[48]

*

Sir John Adams was one of the early writers of the century who helped to shape educational thought. He emphasized the importance of putting the child in the centre. The teacher must know not only his subject, but the children he is teaching.

'Verbs of teaching govern two accusatives,' he wrote, 'one of the person, another of the thing; as, *Magister Johannem Latinam docuit* – the master taught John Latin.' [49]

Childhood is not merely a preparation for future life, but has its own importance, and children must live fully as children if they are to become fully developed adults:

Childhood has a meaning and a value in itself apart from its value as a stage on the way to maturity. The better the child is as a child, that is, the truer he is to his child nature as such, the better man will he make when the proper time comes.[50]

The purpose of education is not to supply information but so to act on the pupil that he becomes his own teacher:

Education has for its aim to modify the nature of the educand, and not merely to supply a certain amount of knowledge. ... The whole process of education may be said to be one in which the educand becomes gradually transformed into his own educator.[51]

This end can only be achieved

by obeying the laws of the educand's development. ... Our failures as men-makers result mainly from three causes: ignorance

47. JAMES, WILLIAM, *Talks to Teachers*, p. 39.
48. ibid, pp. 91–2.
49. ADAMS, SIR JOHN, *The Hebartian Psychology Applied to Educa-tion*, p. 16.
50. *The Evolution of Educational Theory*, p. 63.
51. ibid, pp. 16, 20.

of the laws of development, lack of power to modify the environment, and moral incapacity on the part of the educator.[52]

*

Sir Percy Nunn laid great emphasis on the importance of individuality and of creativity.

We must hold that a scheme of education is ultimately to be valued by its success in fostering the highest degrees of individual excellence of which those submitted to it are capable. . . .

Nothing good enters into the human world except in and through the free activities of individual men and women. . . .[53]

Education must be thought of as the means whereby the creative power of the individual is to be given the fullest opportunity for development and expression.

A school fails unless the spirit that pervades it gives its pupils a zest for at least some modest form of adventure in life and some confidence in their power to carry it through. Here the standing danger is that didactic and dogmatic methods of instruction should receive too large a place, too little room being left for freer methods of learning based upon a belief in the average pupil's gift of spontaneity and a due sense of the importance of developing it.[54]

The educator should take more note of the child's natural way of learning, through play:

It is hardly extravagant to say that in the understanding of play lies the key to most of the practical problems of education.[55]

No candid observer can doubt that school teaching would be immensely more efficient if teachers could learn to exploit the intellectual energy released so abundantly in play. . . . The child's impulses to experiment with life should be taken as our guide in teaching him.[56]

The highest types of work are those in which the worker chooses his own task and sets his own strict standards of achievement. . . . It can hardly be gainsaid that the highest type of school and the highest type of commonwealth would be a school, a commonwealth in which this kind of work, which is also play, prevailed.[57]

*

52. ibid, p. 307.
53. NUNN, SIR PERCY, *Education, Its Data and First Principles*, p. 12.
54. ibid, p. 36.   55. ibid, p. 99.   56. ibid, p. 96.   57. ibid, p. 100.

Professor A. N. Whitehead put again in a new form the principle that growth comes from within, and that the child is an active agent in his own education. He wrote:

The creative impulse towards growth comes from within.[58]

The mind is never passive; it is a perpetual activity, delicate, receptive, responsive to stimulus. You cannot postpone its life until you have sharpened it. Whatever interest attaches to your subject matter must be evoked here and now; whatever powers you are strengthening in the pupil, must be exercised here and now; whatever possibilities of mental life your teaching should impart, must be exhibited here and now.[59] The present ... is holy ground.[60]

In training a child to activity of thought, above all things we must beware of what I will call 'inert ideas' — that it to say, ideas that are merely received into the mind without being utilized, or tested, or thrown into fresh combinations. ... Education with inert ideas is not only useless; it is ... harmful.[61] The importance of knowledge lies in its use, in our active mastery of it — that is to say, it lies in wisdom. ... The habit of active thought ... can only be generated by adequate freedom.[62]

The pupil's mind is a growing organism. ... It must never be forgotten that education is not a process of packing articles in a trunk. ... Its nearest analogue is the assimilation of food by a living organism: and we all know how necessary to health is palatable food under suitable conditions. When you have put your boots in a trunk, they will stay there till you take them out again; but this is not at all the case if you feed a child with the wrong food.[63]

There can be no mental development without interest. Interest is the *sine qua non* for attention and apprehension. ... Now the natural mode by which living organisms are excited towards suitable self-development is enjoyment. ... We should seek to arrange the development of character along a path of natural activity, in itself pleasurable.[64]

Education must essentially be a setting in order of a ferment already stirring in the mind.[65] Education should begin in research and end in research ... An education which does not begin by

58. WHITEHEAD, A. N., *The Aims of Education*, p. 61.
59. ibid, p. 9.   60. ibid, p. 4.
61. ibid, pp. 1–2.   62. ibid, pp 49–50.
63. ibid, pp. 47, 51.   64. ibid, pp. 48–9.
65. ibid, p. 29.

evoking initiative and end by encouraging it must be wrong. For its whole aim is the production of active wisdom.[66]

The artificial divisions between subjects should be abolished.

The solution which I am urging, is to eradicate the fatal disconnection of subjects which kills the vitality of our modern curriculum. There is only one subject matter for education, and that is Life in all its manifestations.[67] You may not divide the seamless coat of learning.[68]

The kind of education offered to children at any time must conform to the stage of development they have reached.

Different studies and modes of study should be undertaken by pupils at fitting times when they have reached the proper stage of mental development.... Lack of attention to the rhythm and character of mental growth is a main source of wooden futility in education.[69]

Education, to Whitehead, is far more than the collecting of information.

Though knowledge is one chief aim of intellectual education, there is another ingredient ... more dominating in its importance. The ancients called it 'wisdom'. You cannot be wise without some basis of knowledge; but you may easily acquire knowledge and remain bare of wisdom.[70]

Culture is activity of thought, and receptiveness to beauty and humane feeling. Scraps of information have nothing to do with it. A merely well-informed man is the most useless bore on God's earth.[71]

We must rise about the exclusive association of learning with book-learning. First-hand knowledge is the ultimate basis of intellectual life. To a large extent book-learning conveys second-hand information ... The second-handedness of the learned world is the secret of its mediocrity.[72]

Much more than this is needed:

We can be content with no less than the old summary of educational ideal which has been current at any time from the dawn of our civilization. The essence of education is that it be religious.[73]

66. ibid, pp. 57–8.   67. ibid, p. 10.   68. ibid, p. 18.
69. ibid, pp. 24, 27.   70. ibid, p. 46.   71. ibid, p. 1.
72. ibid, p. 79.   73. ibid, p. 23.

Education is the guidance of the individual towards a comprehension of the art of life; and by the art of life I mean the most complete achievement of varied activity expressing the potentialities of that living creature in the face of its actual environment.[74]

*

'The school teaches, but often does not educate,' wrote Giovanni Gentile, Professor of Philosophy in the University of Rome, who became Italian Minister of Education and, in the course of two or three years, transformed education in his country.

The optimism of educators in the eighteenth century, their promise that marvels would come out of elementary instruction ... was constantly met in the course of the last century by an ever-growing mistrust of instruction generally restricted to the notion of mere instrumentality. For ... it was felt that this instrument might be put to a very bad use; that elementary learning might be a dangerous thing if it were not accompanied by something that instruction pure and simple cannot give, namely, soundness of heart, strength of mind, and conscience strong enough to uphold intelligence by the vigorous and uncompromising principles of moral rectitude. The hopefulness of that past optimism is fast yielding ground to the pessimistic denunciation of the insufficiency of mere instruction for the moral ends of life.[75]

True education must be essentially a spiritual matter.

Instruction ... which is not education is not even instruction. It is a denuded abstraction, violently thrust ... into the life of the spirit where it generates that monstrosity which we have described as material culture, mechanical and devoid of spiritual vitality.[76]

We must learn to loathe the scrappiness of education ... to react against a system of education which, conceiving its rôle to be merely intellectualistic ... proceeds to an infinite subdivision.[77]

Education must be concerned with the whole man, with the unity of life:

Unity ought to be our constant aim. We should never look away from the living, that is, the person, the pupil into whose soul

74. ibid, p. 61.
75. GENTILE, GIOVANNI, The Reform of Education, pp. 181–2.
76. ibid, p. 187.   77. ibid, pp. 190–91.

our loving solicitude should strive to gain access in order to help him create his own world.[78]

Education is union, communion; ... and unity is possible only because men spiritually convene. ... It is spirit that unites men. Education therefore cannot be a social relationship and a link between men except by being a spiritual tie among human minds. Therefore it is now, and has at all times been, what it naturally ought to be, education of the spirit.[79]

If education is to be truly spiritual, freedom is essential; children come before curricula.

Away with pre-established programmes ... of any description. Spiritual activity works only in the plenitude of freedom.[80]

A school without freedom is a lifeless institution.[81]

The pupil will absorb from his education 'only that much which is taken up by the autonomous growth of his personality', for he learns by means of the inner law of his own being.

The master, as St Augustine long ago warned us, is within us.[82] The real teacher is within the soul of the pupil.[83]

Gentile affirms that the Socratic ideal of the Truth within the soul, far from being outdated, is in our time confirmed by modern thought.

Modern philosophy and modern consciousness ... show to man that the lofty aim which is his law is within himself; that it is in his ever unsatisfied personality as it unceasingly strains upwards towards its own ideal.[84]

It is the ever unfinished task of education to provide the conditions in which each individual, through obedience to the inner law, may find his way towards completeness.

*

'The education of man is a human awakening,' [85] wrote Jacques Maritain. Its aim is

to guide man, in the evolving dynamism through which he shapes himself as a human person – armed with knowledge, strength of

78. ibid, p. 191.   79. ibid, p. 195.   80. ibid, p. 224.
81. ibid, p. 62.   82. ibid, p. 61.   83. ibid, p. 63.
84. ibid, p. 16.
85. MARITAIN, JACQUES, *Education at the Crossroads*, p. 9.

judgment, and moral virtues – while at the same time conveying to him the spiritual heritage of the nation and the civilization in which he is involved.[86]

Its goal is

the conquest of internal and spiritual freedom to be achieved by the individual person, or, in other words, his liberation through knowledge and wisdom, good will and love. . . .[87] The task of the teacher is above all one of liberation.[88]

The educational task is both greater and more mysterious and, in a sense, humbler than many imagine. If the aim of education is the helping and guiding of man towards his own human achievement, education cannot escape the problems and entanglements of philosophy, for it supposes by its very nature a philosophy of man, and from the outset it is obliged to answer the question: 'What is man?'[89]

What is of most importance in educators themselves is a respect for the soul as well as for the body of the child.[90]

The old education is to be reproached for its abstract and bookish individualism. To have made education more experiential, closer to concrete life and permeated with social concerns from the very start is an achievement of which modern education is justly proud. Yet in order to reach completion such a necessary reform must understand, too, that to be a good citizen and a man of civilization what matters above all is the inner center, the living source of personal conscience in which originate idealism and generosity, the sense of law and the sense of friendship, respect for others, but at the same time deep-rooted independence with regard to common opinion.[91]

Man's education must be concerned with the social group and prepare him to play his part in it. Shaping man to lead a normal, useful and co-operative life in the community, or guiding the development of the human person in the social sphere, awakening and strengthening both his sense of freedom and his sense of obligation and responsibility, is an essential aim. But it is not the primary, it is the secondary essential aim. The ultimate end of education concerns the human person in his personal life and spiritual progress, not in his relation to the social environment. . . .

The essence of education does not consist in adapting a potential citizen to the conditions and interactions of social life, but first

86. ibid, p. 10.   87. ibid, p. 11.   88. ibid, p. 39.
89. ibid, p. 4.   90. ibid, p. 9.   91. ibid, p. 16.

in *making a man*, and by this very fact in preparing a citizen.[92]

Maritain reiterates the age-old belief that growth is from within.

Ready-made knowledge does not, as Plato believed, exist in human souls. But the vital and active principle of knowledge does exist in each of us.... This inner vital principle the teacher must respect above all....

The mind's natural activity on the part of the learner and the intellectual guidance on the part of the teacher are both dynamic factors in education, but ... the principal agent in education, the primary dynamic factor or propelling force, is the internal vital principle in the one to be educated.[93]

Maritain distinguishes between two fields of the unconscious or subconscious: first, that explored by the Freudians, 'the unconscious or the irrational in man', and second, that which was missed by them,

the field of the root life of those spiritual powers, the intellect and the will, the fathomless abyss of personal freedom and of the personal thirst and striving for knowledge and seeing, grasping and expressing ... the preconscious of the spirit in man....

Reason does not consist only of its conscious logical tools and manifestations nor does the will consist only of its deliberate conscious determinations. For beneath the apparent surface of explicit concepts and judgments, of words and expressed resolutions or movements of the will, are the sources of knowledge and poetry, of love and truly human desires, hidden in the spiritual darkness of the intimate vitality of the soul....

Of course education has a great deal to do with the irrational subconscious dynamism of the child's psyche. But ... it is with the preconscious or the subconscious of the spirit that education is mainly concerned.[94]

Gerald Heard ... has expressed the opinion that after what he calls the 'eotechnic' stage of classical education and the present 'paleotechnic' stage of progressive education, a 'neotechnic' stage is now to come, which will be concerned with the subconscious powers and activity of the child.[95]

92. ibid, pp. 14, 15.   93. ibid, pp. 30, 31.
94. ibid, pp. 40–42.   95. ibid, p. 40.

We have good reason to believe that a particular weakness in our educational methods comes from the rationalistic approach which developed for two centuries, and from the Cartesian psychology of clear and distinct ideas which impaired traditional as well as progressive education. ... The pressure on the surface level of the mind of ready-made formulas of knowledge, as elaborated for the socialized intellectual life of adults, and only made cheaper and more rudimentary for the use of children, and the pressure on the surface level of the will, either of compulsory discipline or of extraneous incentives, motivated by self-interest and competition, have left the internal world of the child's soul either dormant or bewildered and rebellious.[96]

Education should be concerned with insights.

What matters most in the life of reason is intellectual insight or intuition. There is no training or learning for that. Yet if the teacher keeps in view above all the inner center of vitality at work in the preconscious depths of the life of the intelligence, he may center the acquisition of knowledge and solid formation of the mind on the freeing of the child's and the youth's intuitive power. By what means? By moving forward along the paths of spontaneous interest and natural curiosity, by grounding the exercise of memory in intelligence, and primarily by giving courage, by listening a great deal, and by causing the youth to trust and give expression to those spontaneous poetic or noetic impulses of his own which seem to him fragile and bizarre, because they are not assured by any social sanction.[97]

The whole work of education and teaching must tend to unify, not to spread out; it must strive to foster internal unity in man.

This means that from the very start, ... hands and mind should be at work together. ... There is no place closer to man than a workshop, and the intelligence of a man is not only in his head, but in his fingers too.

Not only does manual work further psychological equilibrium, but it also furthers ingenuity and accuracy of the mind, and is the prime basis of artistic activity.[98]

What is learned should never be passively or mechanically received, as dead information which weighs down and dulls the mind. It must rather be actively transformed by understanding into the very life of the mind, and thus strengthen the latter, as wood thrown into fire and transformed into flame makes the fire stronger.

96. ibid, pp. 39–40.   97. ibid, p. 43.   98. ibid, p. 45.

But a big mass of damp wood thrown into the fire only puts it out.[99]

The material of education must be adapted to children and their needs.

The child is not a dwarf man. . . . We try to cram young people with a chaos of summarized adult notions which have been either condensed, dogmatized, and textbookishly cut up or else made so easy that they are reduced to the vanishing point. As a result we run the risk of producing either an instructed, bewildered intellectual dwarf, or an ignorant intellectual dwarf playing at dolls with our science. . . .

The knowledge to be given to youth *is not* the same knowledge as that of adults, it is an intrinsically and basically different knowledge, . . . the specific knowledge fitted to quicken and perfect the original world of thought of the child. . . . Consequently I should like to emphasize that at each stage the knowledge must be of a sort fitted to the learners and conceived as reaching its perfection within their universe of thought during a distinct period of their development.[100]

*

J. S. Brubacher gave a warning of the danger resulting from the psychological and educational testing of children which has been a feature of research in this century and which has given rise to a science of educational statistics, from which it is tempting to draw all kinds of conclusions which may not necessarily follow, and to alter educational practice accordingly.

The danger of viewing human nature from a purely scientific angle is that the teacher may fail to take account of facts which do not lend themselves to isolation and objective statement. Educational psychology is all the more likely to be guilty of this shortcoming because it has tended to restrict itself to just those aspects of human nature which enable it to state its conclusions with an exactness aping the physical sciences.[101]

It may appear to be emphasizing the obvious to state . . . that human nature is, in the main, dynamic, active. . . . Yet in spite of this apparently obvious fact, there are some who think of youth as a rather passive recipient of the educative process.[102]

99. ibid, p. 50.   100. ibid, pp. 58–60.
101. BRUBACHER, J. S., *Modern Philosophies of Education*, p. 44.
102. ibid, p. 51.

He reminds us of the view of St Thomas Aquinas that

the principle of life which animates man is fundamentally active. Therefore when the psyche or soul, which embodies this principle of life, engages in learning, it must be an active process. ... He made this very clear in the analogy he drew between the offices of the doctor and the teacher. Getting well, he pointed out, is something which the patient has to do for himself. By prescribing a regimen of medicine or exercise the doctor can only aid the potentialities of the natural processes of the body to heal themselves. Similarly with education and getting to know. The student must do it himself; the teacher cannot do it for him. The teacher can teach him but, to put it ungrammatically, he cannot 'learn' him. Education, accordingly, is not so much an imparting of knowledge as it is a soliciting or prompting of the student to exert his native potentialities for knowing or learning.[103]

The whole art of education lies in knowing how to solicit the student to learn. This is the question of motivation. The modern biological approach to human nature

directs greater attention to the forces which motivate human conduct. With a knowledge of what motives have been operating from the beginning in child nature, the adroit teacher can better learn how to harness them to draw varying curriculum loads. Some think these drives so important that they should guide the formulation of educational aims. Schools, they think, should provide for the release of the energies which are pent up in these native drives.[104]

The efficiency of learning increases directly in proportion to the extent to which the learner is wholly bound up in his task. If he is united in a singleness of purpose, if he is absorbed and engrossed in his occupation, he begins to possess a mental integrity which is invaluable for learning.[105]

Instruction is usually dull and mechanical just in the proportion that the curriculum, as presented, lacks connection with present reservoirs of pupil energy. ... The loss in learning efficiency under such circumstances very much resembles the way in which a slipping clutch fails to deliver the full power of a motor to its load of work. And let no one think that he can teach without tapping and applying the pupil's powers. No activity, no learning. Somehow, sometime, motive must be enlisted.[106]

*

103. ibid, p. 90,   104. ibid, p. 55.
105. ibid, p. 247.   106. ibid, p. 248.

To Sir Richard Livingstone, education must provide a philosophy of life, a sense of values:

Education is atmosphere as well as instruction; it is not an assemblage of piecemeal acquisition and accomplishments, but the formation, largely unconscious, of an outlook and an attitude.[107]

The prior task of education is to inspire, and to give a sense of values and the power of distinguishing in life ... what is first-rate from what is not.[108]

As Plato says, the ignorance most fatal to states and individuals is not ignorance in the field of technology or of the professions, but spiritual ignorance.[109] The crown of Plato's education is the vision of the Idea of the Good.... The crown of our education is the vision of the Idea of Engineering, or the Idea of Physics, or the Idea of Economics, or the Idea of Exact Scholarship.[110]

The most important task of education is to bring home to the student the greatest of all problems – the problem of living – and to give him some guidance in it. Nations and individuals are ultimately judged by the values and standards by which they are ruled.[111] Can anyone deny the truth of Plato's words: 'The noblest of all studies is what man is and how he should live.' But how much time is devoted to that study by the ordinary undergraduate? [112]

At times, the right motto for our education seems to be ...: 'For the sake of livelihood to lose what makes life worth living.' The material in life tends to dominate it.... Spiritual and moral life is forgotten; wisdom and even judgment recede into the background. An age appears which can use hand and eye, follow its vocations with increased efficiency, masters nature and subdues her to its will, but, lacking ultimate convictions, misuses its illimitable opportunities.[113] States collapse, schemes fail for many reasons: but the commonest and most fatal cause is the weakness of human character. I should be ashamed to utter such a truism if modern political thought did not habitually build its imposing palaces without foundations and ignore the cause of their brief duration and calamitous fate. That error reflects the weakness of an education preoccupied with knowledge, with the intellectual aspect, to the exclusion of any other.[114]

107. LIVINGSTONE, SIR R., *The Future in Education*, p. 51.
108. ibid, p. 56.
109. *The Rainbow Bridge*, p. 118.
110. ibid, p. 127.
111. ibid, pp. 23, 24.   112. ibid, p. 128.
113. ibid, p. 125.   114. ibid, pp. 128–9.

Knowledge, information should never be the end of education. He writes of

the overcrowded curriculum which leads to intellectual dyspepsia, hopeless malnutrition, and often to a permanent distaste for knowledge and incapacity to digest it; to the plastering ideas and facts on the surface of the pupil's mind from which they rapidly peel off; to mistaking information, which never becomes an organic part of his experience, for education which is absorbed by his mind and transforms it. The test of a successful education is not the amount of knowledge a pupil takes away from school, but his appetite to know and his capacity to learn. If the school sends out children with a desire for knowledge and some idea of how to acquire and use it, it will have done its work. Too many leave school with the appetite killed and the mind loaded with undigested lumps of information.[115]

Education, that maid-of-all-work, has to set her hand to as many duties as a general servant. But two things she should give everybody before her work is complete – an intellectual attitude to life and a philosophy of life. I would define the right intellectual attitude as threefold: to find the world and life intensely interesting; to wish to see them as they are; to feel that truth, in Plato's words, is both permanent and beautiful. And a philosophy of life? The right intellectual attitude to life is already a partial philosophy of it. It is complete, if you extend it to cover Goodness, Truth and Beauty, and define Goodness to cover those words which have been trumpet-calls to many generations, and, once sounded by unknown men far back in history, have been borne round the world on the waves of the spiritual air, now loud, now low, but never wholly silent: love, justice, courage, self-mastery, mercy, liberty.[116]

What lines will education follow in the near future, what will be its general direction and aim? I have no doubt that it will concentrate far more than hitherto on the training of character.[117]

To see what Whitehead calls 'the vision of greatness', and to acquire the right habits – these are the foundations of the education of character. ... Education – of a sort – can exist without vision. It is possible to get full marks in examinations and first classes at the university and miss it. ... Hence the importance in

115. *The Future in Education*, p. 28.
116. *Education for a World Adrift*, p. 31.
117. *The Rainbow Bridge*, p. 148.

education of developing and feeding not only the intellect but the imagination by which the vision of greatness is seen.[118]

*

'Behind all modern experiments in the reform of the curriculum,' wrote M. V. C. Jeffreys,

> is the principle that education should be grounded in the general concerns of the pupil, and should help him, by means of material and activities appropriate to his present stage of development, to get his bearings in the world.[119]

The aim of education is the 'full and balanced development of persons' and its purpose is the

> *Nurture of Personal Growth.* . . . The law of growth demands the fulfilment of each stage of development for its own sake . . . and not only as a preparation for some hypothetical end-product. . . . The duty of the educator is to enable the growing person to make the best of himself at the stage he has reached. The best preparation for the future is to respond fully to the challenge of the present.[120]

> The educator's function, like the gardener's, is to provide the best possible conditions for right development – that is, to create opportunity. Growth is something that the organism itself does. No one can grow for another, nor learn for another.[121]

Education, generally, is unsure of its ultimate aims, and in this it reflects society:

> The most serious weakness of modern education is the uncertainty about its aims. . . . Education in the liberal democracies is distressingly nebulous in its aims.[122]

> Our age has been described as one in which mastery of techniques has been developed at the expense of conviction about ultimate meaning and purpose. If that is the character of our world, it is not remarkable if our education exhibits a preoccupation with means rather than with ends.[123]

Never was the redemption of personal values so desperately necessary in a world that denies them. Herein is the special educational urgency of the contemporary situation – the special aim of education for our time. . . .

118. ibid, p. 176.   119. JEFFREYS, M. V. C., *Glaucon*, p. 78.
120. ibid, p. 4.   121. ibid, p. 5.
122. ibid, p. 61.   123. ibid, p. 61.

The prevailing intellectual and moral relativism of our time is rotting the roots of deep conviction from which alone personal life can grow.[124]

If we are to educate people to be persons and not only technical and executive instruments, we must produce people not only who do their own thinking, but who do the kind of thinking that springs from deep convictions. . . .[125]

Education should seek to reveal what has been called the 'Vision of Greatness'. . . . It is probable that right thinking is connected with right feeling even more closely than we realize, and that the Vision of Greatness can release intellectual as well as emotional forces. That is to say, behaviour which is influenced by the right values will tend to be not only nobler but more intelligent. If that is so, the problem of how to educate a people to be capable of intelligent and responsible behaviour is not solely a question of Intelligence Quotients.[126]

*

Dr Wall's book, *Education and Mental Health*, puts the question of education into a setting of world affairs which must demand the attention of anyone whose thought stirs beyond his own immediate concerns.

The book grew from the work of the Regional Conference on Education and the Mental Health of Children in Europe, held by UNESCO in Paris in 1952.

The purpose of the Conference was to consider the effect on mental health and development of the changing values of society which resulted from two world wars, and to seek for means of solving the problems consequent upon this by a reconsideration of current methods of education.

Professor Piaget wrote, in his Preface:

Since they were ultimately concerned with social adaptation and international understanding, the author of this volume and the experts invited to the regional conference did not hesitate to turn their attention to early childhood. They were rightly convinced that the internal conflicts which may be caused in the kindergarten or in the home by mistaken methods or failure on the part of adults to understand the child, may have a greater effect than is generally imagined on his later development. For this reason

124. ibid, p. 56.   125. ibid, p. 63.   126. ibid, pp 71–3.

too, they made a detailed study of the basic problem of co-ordination between school and home, and devoted special attention to the general evil of overstrain at school, the serious nature of which is not fully realized by those responsible for public education.[127]

Dr Wall wrote:

International tensions, like tensions between individuals, do not arise solely from rational causes. They are coloured by, and indeed may sometimes spring from deep, unconscious feelings of insecurity, and from maladjustments and hostilities in the lives of the men and women who constitute nations and the leaders of nations.

The family, the school, the community, the nation, are aggregates of individuals, whose behaviour and attitudes are influenced by unconscious elements and by the interplay of personalities in ways as yet obscurely known. . . .

Anything therefore which contributes to the healthy emotional development of human personality, which frees men's minds from prejudice and from fear, is a direct contribution to the maintenance of peace. . . .

Conceived as the whole shaping process of development, education in the family, the school and the community has, therefore, a heavy responsibility. Satisfactory human development depends upon the success with which the fundamental emotional needs of each individual are met within the framework of the demands of the society in which he grows up. . . .

Underlying many post-war educational reforms lies recognition that the task of the school has considerably changed in the past fifty years, and that the old formulae and attitudes are insufficient for current needs . . . we can no longer equate school education with instruction . . . we cannot escape the fundamentally emotional aspect of all learning.[128]

In general, . . . healthy development will only be assured if acceptable outlets for (a young child's) basic drives are offered by his environment and if the affection of his mother and his family are there to sustain him.[129]

Activity and experience are . . . the very food of intellectual growth, and the task of the home and of the school is to provide both in variety.[130]

*

127. WALL, W. D., *Education and Mental Health*, Preface.
128. ibid, pp. 17–21.   129. ibid, p. 24.   130. ibid, p. 66.

These, then, are some of the voices speaking for education in the present century. The task is now to make the ideals of the past and present effective in the work of the schools. Both theory and practice have shown the way.

The work of education today makes greater demands than ever before on those who are responsible for it. No longer is it enough only to teach skills and to pass on information. The children of our time require more help than this to live in their world. They must be helped to find purpose and stability. This is particularly urgent for the so-called less academic children, whose experience has often included more than a little failure and frustration. In the Primary schools they learned to read last, and were either in lower streams or at the end of the class. Now in the Secondary schools their contemporaries have moved away from them into Grammar schools or academic streams. The sharing of a common building and school name does not remove the differences; it may be that children in these schools are more aware than ever of their educational position.

Some will find here a new belief in themselves, in their abilities and in their worth in the eyes of others, but for many the years between eleven and fifteen may be years of frustration, ill-adapted, in their eyes at least, to their needs and interests, as manhood and womanhood approach. To add to their troubles, too many carry a legacy, from early childhood, of rejection and frustration, from homes which, if not actually broken, had little to give them of stability or a sense of values.

These children, or rather young men and women, need the wisest possible direction and understanding, if the unhappy tale of futility and aimlessness, with its familiar behavioural consequences, is ever to be brought to an end. They need the finest teachers and the best provision. Their teachers have to be more skilled, more patient, more resilient, than those who teach the able, the stable and the successful. They must have a vision and a faith, beyond the ordinary, to carry them through what is the most difficult and demanding task in the schools.

But to make this provision at the secondary stage is something like shutting the door after the horse has gone. It is urgent that something should be done before the children pass out of any kind of organized control, but the opportunity was there fourteen or fifteen years ago. Lip service is paid to the idea, but too few fully appreciate the importance of the first years of life. Many, educators included, take serious notice of the influence of education only after the age of eleven. If half the attention and money were expended on provision for the early years that is spent at the secondary stage, many of the problems which now have to be dealt with would never appear.

If parents knew more about the development of their children and the effect of what they say and do upon mental and spiritual growth, the change would be noticeable in the children who come into our infant schools. It is not too early, in the Secondary school, to lead boys and girls to some understanding of themselves and of the right treatment of children. As it is, pupils leave school unprepared, apart from some knowledge of hygiene, for the experience of family life, on which many of them embark within a few years, or even months, of leaving school. Ignorant of themselves and the springs of their own behaviour, they repeat in their own children the mistakes of their parents, and the circle begins again.

What, then, may be the pattern of the future in education? The ideals of the great educators still await full implementation. Put into practice from the earliest stages, the results would be far reaching.

Provision of the right kind of pre-school experience, especially for children deprived of space to play and a stimulating home life, would be a priority. The practice of the best infant schools would be better understood and more appreciated, where it is realized that the task of these years is not just to teach children to read and write, important as these skills are, but to help them to feel accepted, loved and secure, confident to try new experiences, stable enough to face failure and frustration, able to talk and to think for themselves. These needs met, the learning of skills follows.

In the years between seven and eleven, when the urges of curiosity, construction, collecting and working together, and the strong force of imagination, are at their height, ways would be found of harnessing the energies associated with those drives in a programme of work based on first hand experience and discovery of the world around.

In the secondary school, new purposes would be developed, closely related to the needs and interests of children passing out of childhood and into manhood and womanhood, particularly in developing some understanding of themselves. Opportunities would be given for a more active share in the government of the school as a community. Ways would be found of developing and educating the feelings. The needs of the less mature for security, for success and for acceptance, would be considered of first importance. Those who fail to find satisfactory outlets in the usual school world of words and books would be helped, as many indeed are, to find themselves in new forms of expression through movement, drama, art and cooperative experiences, and, most of all, by the knowledge that each has his own unique contribution to make to the community, and that this contribution is needed and valued as much as that of the child who shines in academic work.

But it is not only the less academic whose education needs to be of the finest. The highly intelligent children are always at the mercy of a society which sets so high a value on intellect that it is prepared to sacrifice their stability, and even integrity, for the prize. There have been plenty of clever devils in the past, and the incidence of suicides at the universities, and the overcrowding of mental hospitals, are evidence that we are yet very far indeed from achieving the balanced development of the whole man that has been the goal of enlightened educators from the Greeks onwards. The history of the growth of this ideal in education, and especially the contribution of educators in this century, has made clear that development of the intellect cannot take place in isolation, and where the attempt is made, it is likely to be at the expense of other qualities. The growth of intellect comes about when all other aspects of man's educational needs have been met. The intelligence is then free to develop to its full extent. Those who work with young children confirm this. The child who is starved of creative and imaginative experiences, or who has not had his need for security and confidence fully met, who is under pressure, or who is deficient in language, is frequently stunted intellectually, unable to make use of the ability he has. Such a child rarely makes progress at all in the intellectual field until these needs have been met.

As a new understanding of the purposes of education comes about, it may be that our present ideas of levels of intelligence and ability will be radically changed as we come to have a different, and less materialist, view of man, but as long as examination successes and academic achievements are held to be the only, or even the chief, results of education, so long will there be the failures, amongst both the intelligent and the so-called non-intelligent, those for whom education is not only meaningless but harmful.

There is need for a change in the attitude of society towards personal worth. An honours degree is esteemed, so perhaps should be the ability to do an honest day's work. The willingness to cooperate unselfishly with others may be of more practical use than the possession of a certificate. To be able to think for oneself and take responsibility, are worthy ends in education, even though there is nothing that can be tabulated. The history of the growth of educational ideals brings to serious notice the value of qualifications of the spirit. These, though not measurable by any test, may one day rank with those that can be examined, and in that day education may begin to achieve its purpose of the making of men and the establishment of a stable and harmonious society.

BIBLIOGRAPHY

EDUCATION in all its aspects has been the subject of a very great number of books. For a general background history probably the mos, useful are WILLIAM BOYD, *A History of Western Education*, Blackt 1947; W. J. MCCALLISTER, *The Growth of Freedom in Education*, Constable, 1931; and P. MONROE, *Textbook in the History of Education*, New York, 1906. R. H. QUICK gives a readable account of the chief educationists as far as Herbert Spencer, with an assessment of their influence in *Educational Reformers*, Longmans Green, 1868. BARNARD, *English Pedagogy*, Hartford, 1876 is also worth reading, as is G. COMPAYRÉ, *The History of Pedagogy*, 1895, and F. V. N. PAINTER, *History of Education*, Appleton, New York, 1904.

More recent books on the general subject of education are: J. ADAMS, *The Evolution of Educational Theory*, Macmillan, 1912 and *Modern Developments in Educational Practice* by the same author, University of London Press, 1922, and nearer our own time, J. S. BRUBACHER, *Modern Philosophies of Education*, McGraw Hill, New York, 1939 (new edition 1962); S. J. CURTIS, *History of Education in Great Britain*; and S. J. CURTIS and M. E. A. BOULTWOOD, *A Short History of Educational Ideas*, both published by University Tutorial Press, the first in 1948 and the second in 1953.

GREEKS, ROMANS AND HEBREWS.

For the Greek period the best general work is W. W. JAEGER, *Paideia, the Ideals of Greek Culture*, Blackwell, 1939. Others which will be found of interest are: E. B. CASTLE, *Ancient Education and Today*, Penguin Books, 1961, and P. MONROE, *Source Book of the History of Education, Greek and Roman Period*, New York, 1906.

For Plato the reader should see J. ADAMSON, *The Theory of Education in Plato's Republic*, Swan and Sonnenschein, 1903; *Plato's Theory of Education* by R. C. LODGE, Kegan Paul, Trench, Trubner, 1947; B. BOSANQUET, *A Companion to Plato's Republic*, Revington, 1895; R. L. NETTLESHIP, *The Theory of Education in Plato's Republic*, Oxford, 1935; F. M. CORNFORD, *The Republic of Plato*, Oxford, 1941; and the *Meno* and *Protagoras* of Plato, both published by Penguin Books, 1956 and the *Iliad* trans. Lang, Leaf and Myers, Macmillan 1883.

Useful books giving general background are:
J. C. STOBART, *The Glory that was Greece*, Four Square Books, 1962;

H. D. F. KITTO, *The Greeks*, Penguin Books, 1951; G. LOWES DICKIN-SON, *The Greek View of Life*, Methuen, 1957, and C. M. BOWRA, *The Greek Experience*, Weidenfeld & Nicolson, 1957.

The reader should also see ARISTOTLE, *Ethics*, trans. F. H. PETERS or B. JOWETT; *Politics*, trans. by B. JOWETT; C. WINN, and M. JACKS, *Aristotle*, Methuen, 1967; XENOPHON, *Memorabilia*; and SENECA, in any of the following:

SENECA, *Epistulae Morales,* trans. by R. M. GUMMERE, Loeb Classical Library, Heinemann, first printed 1920; *Selections from Seneca*, arranged by R. DIMSDALE, Stocker, 1910; *The Epistles of Lucius Anneus Seneca*, trans. by T. MORELL, 1786, *Seneca, Select Letters*, ed. W. C. SUMMERS, Macmillan, 1910; and *A Frutefull worke of Lucius Anneus Senecae Called the Myrrour or Glasse of Maners and Wysdome,* 1547 (B.M.).

For the Roman Period, BONNER, *The Education of a Roman*, Liverpool University Press, 1950, will be found useful, and P. MONROE, *Source Book of the History of Education, Greek and Roman Period,* New York, 1906; *Roman Education,* by A. GWYNN, Oxford, 1926; *A History of Education in Antiquity*, H. I. MARROU, trans. G. LAMB, Sheed & Ward, 1956; also CICERO, *De Oratore*, A. S. Wilkins, Stuttaford & Sutton, 1879–92, and QUINTILIAN, *Institutes of Oratory*, trans. J. S. WATSON, London, 1882–5, or by H. E. BUTLER, London, 1921–2; *Quintilian on Education*, W. M. SMAIL, Oxford, 1938.

PLUTARCH, *The Education or bringinge up of children*, trans. SIR THOMAS ELIOT. KNYGHT C. 1535 (in B.M.), also printed in *Ethical Essays*, trans. A. R. SHILLETO BELL, 1898.

F. H. SWIFT writes of Hebrew education in *Education in Ancient Israel*, Chicago, 1919.

THE MIDDLE AGES

The following will all be found useful:

A. T. DRANE, *Christian Schools and Scholars*, Burns & Oates, first published 1867; AUGUSTINE, *Concerning the Teacher* in *Basic Writings of St Augustine,* Vol. 1, W. J. Oates, Random House Publishers, New York, 1948; AUGUSTINE *Confessions*, trans. R. S. PINE-COFFIN, Penguin Books, 1961; G. J. B. GASKOIN, *Alcuin: His Life and Work*, Clay & Sons, London, 1904.

16TH AND 17TH CENTURIES

General background is given in W. H. WOODWARD, *Contributions to the History of Education During the Age of the Renaissance*, and *Studies in Education During the Age of the Renaissance*, by the same author, Cambridge University Press, 1906; COMPAYRÉ, *History of Pedagogy*,

ed. PAYNE, G. H. TURNBULL; *Hartlib, Dury and Comenius*, edited by
KERMODE, University Press of Liverpool, 1947; and J. W. ADAMSON,
Pioneers of Modern Education, Cambridge, 1921.

Books on individual educators of this period are given in alphabetical
order according to the educator's name:

ASCHAM, R., *The Scholemaster*. E. B. Mayor, Bell & Daldy, 1863.

BACON, FRANCIS, *The Advancement of Learning*, ed. G. W. KITCHIN,
Everyman, 1915. *Novum Organum*, trans. ELLIS and SPEDDING,
Routledge, 1905.

BRINSLEY, JOHN, *Ludus Literarius or the Grammar Schools*, ed. E. T.
CAMPAGNAC, Liverpool University Press, Constable, 1917.

CASTIGLIONE, B., *The Courtier*, Tudor Library, London, 1900.

COMENIUS, J. A., *The School of Infancy*, trans. MONROE, Boston, 1906,
or a later edition, ed. E. M. ELLER, University of North Carolina
Press, 1956. JELINEK, V., *Analytical Didactic of Comenius*, Univ. of
Chicago, 1953; SADLER, J. E., *J. A. Comenius and the Concept of
Universal Education*, Allen & Unwin, 1966; COMENIUS, J. A., *Orbis
Sensualium Pictus,* intro. J. BOWEN, Sydney Univ. Press, 1967.

BUTLER, NICHOLAS MURRAY, *The Place of Comenius in the History of
Education*, Bardeen, 1892.

LAURIE, S. S., *John Amos Comenius*, Cambridge, 1904.

KEATINGE, M. W., *The Great Didactic of John Amos Comenius*, Black,
1910.

COWLEY, ABRAHAM, *A Proposition for the Advancement of Experimental Philosophy*, J. M. for Henry Herringman, London, 1661, reprinted in Abraham Cowley, *The Essays and other Prose Writings*,
Oxford, 1915.

DURY, J., *The Reformed School*, ed. H. M. KNOX, 1650, Liverpool
University Press, 1958.

ELYOT, SIR THOMAS, *Of the Knowledge which Maketh a Wise Man*, 1533,
trans. E. J. HOWARD, Oxford, Ohio, The Anchor Press, 1946. *The
Boke Named the Governour*, 1531, also available in Everyman, 1907

LEHMBERG, S. E., *Sir Thomas Elyot, Tudor Humanist*, University of
Texas Press, Austin, 1960.

ERASMUS, *That children oughte to be taughte and brought up gently in
vertue and learnynge*, 1550; also in SHERRY, R., *A Treatise of Schemes
and Tropes*, 1961.

WOODWARD, W. H., *Erasmus Concerning Education*, Cambridge, 1904.

WOODWARD, W. H., *Vittorino da Feltre*, Cambridge, 1905.

HARTLIB, S., *A Faithfull and Seasonable Advice*, London, 1643.

HOOLE, CHARLES, *A New Discovery of the old Art of Teaching Schoole*,
originally published 1660, ed. E. T. Campagnac, Liverpool University Press, Constable, 1913. *Children's Talk*, London, 1659.

374   BIBLIOGRAPHY

HUARTE, JUAN, *The Examination of Men's Wits*, 1698, with an intro-
    duction by C. ROGERS, Gainesville, Florida, Scholars' Facsimiles and
    Reprints, 1959.
HUGHES, T., *Loyola and the Educational System of the Jesuits*, London,
    1892.
KEMPE, W., *The Education of Children in Learning*, 1588.
LOCKE, J., *Conduct of the Understanding*, ed. T. FOWLER, Oxford, 1901.
    Some Thoughts Concerning Education, ed. E. DANIEL, London, 1880,
    or R. H. QUICK, Cambridge, 1934, or F. W. GARFORTH, Heinemann,
    1964.
JEFFREYS, M. V. C., *John Locke, Prophet of Common Sense*, Methuen,
    1967.
PAINTER, F. V. N., *Luther on Education*, Philadelphia Lutheran Pub-
    lishing Society, 1889.
EBY, F., *Early Protestant Educators*, McGraw Hill, New York, 1931.
MILTON, J., *Tractate on Education*, ed. O. BROWNING, Cambridge,
    1905.
Montaigne's Essays, trans. JOHN FLORIO, Everyman, 1965.
Complete Works, W. HAZLITT, Templeman, 1842.
Complete Works, D. FRAME, Stanford University Press, California,
    1948.
The Living Thoughts of Montaigne, presented by ANDRÉ GIDE, Long-
    mans, 1939.
MONTAIGNE, M. de, *The Education of Children*, ed. L. E. RECTOR,
    Appleton, New York, 1899.
HODGSON, G., *The Teacher's Montaigne*, Blackie, 1915.
MULCASTER, R., *Positions*, first pub. London 1581, ed. with an appen-
    dix by R. H. QUICK, Longmans, 1888.
Mulcaster's Elementarie, originally pub. London, 1582, ed. E. T.
    CAMPAGNAC, Oxford, 1925.
PETTY, W., *Advice of W. P. To Mr Samuel Hartlib*, 1647.
BARNARD, H. C., *The Port Royalists on Education*, Cambridge, 1918.
    The Little Schools of Port Royal, Cambridge, 1913.
BEARD, C., *Port Royal*, Longmans Green, 1861.
Logic or the Art of Thinking, being the Port Royal Logic, trans. BAYNES,
    T. S., 1662.
CADET, F., *Port Royal Education*, trans. A. D. JONES, Swan, Sonnen-
    schein & Co., 1898.
CLARK, W. R., *Pascal and the Port Royalists*, Clark, Edinburgh, 1902.
COUSTEL, *Rules for the Education of Children*, 1687.
NICOLE, P., *Moral Essays, Vol. 2, Of the Education of a Prince*, printed
    for Samuel Manship, 1696.
PASCAL, *Regimen for Children*, 1657.

RABELAIS, *Works*. The Navarre Society, 1931; another translation is published by Penguin Books.

Peter Ramus His Dialectica, trans. R. FAGE, 1632.

GRAVES, F. P., *Peter Ramus and the Educational Reformation of the Sixteenth Century*, Macmillan, New York, 1912.

ROLLIN, C., *The Method of Teaching and Studying the Belles Letters*, London, 1804.

SADOLETO, *On Education*, trans. E. T. CAMPAGNAC and K. FORBES, Oxford, 1916.

SALIGNAC, de la MOTHE FÉNELON. *On the Education of Daughters*, Darton, London, 1812.

BARNARD, H. C., *Fénelon on Education*, Cambridge University Press, 1966.

VERGERIO, P. P., *On the Manners of a Gentleman and On Liberal Studies*.

VIVES, J. L., *Tudor Schoolboy Life*, trans. FOSTER WATSON, Dent, 1908. *An Introduction to Wisedome*, trans. RICHARD MORSYNE, 1544. *De Anima et Vita*.

WATSON, F., *The Father of Modern Psychology*, reprinted from the *Psychological Review*, Vol. XXII, No. 5. *Vives on Education*, Cambridge, 1913.

WATSON, F., *J. L. Vives and the Renaissance Education of Women*, Arnold, 1912.

WATTS, ISAAC, *Improvement of the Mind*, London, 1782. Vol. 2.

WOODWARD, HEZEKIAH, *A Light to Grammar*, London, 1641. *Of the Child's Portion*, London, 1649.

WOTTON, SIR HENRY, *A Philosophical Survey of Education*, originally pub. 1672, Liverpool University Press, Hodder & Stoughton, 1938.

18TH AND 19TH CENTURIES

Books are listed alphabetically, according to the name of the educator:

FINDLAY, J. J., *Arnold of Rugby*, Cambridge, 1897.

STANLEY, A. P., *The Life and Correspondence of Thomas Arnold, D.D.*, John Murray, 1901.

STRACHEY, L., *Eminent Victorians*, Chatto, 1915.

WHITRIDGE, A., *Dr Arnold of Rugby*, Constable, 1928.

WORBOISE, E. J., *Life of Thomas Arnold*, D. D. Hamilton, 1859.

The Miscellaneous Works of Thomas Arnold, ed. A. P. STANLEY, Fellowes, London, 1845.

DE CROUSAZ, J. P., *New Maxims concerning the Education of Youth*, first pub. 1718, English trans. G. S. TACHERON, London, 1740.

EDGEWORTH, R. L., *Essays on Professional Education*, Johnson & Co., London, 1809. *Memoirs*, 1820.

EDGEWORTH, MARIA and R. L., *Essays on Practical Education*, Hunter, London, 1815.

The Establishments of M. E. de Fellenberg at Hofwyl by the COUNT LOUIS DE VILLEVIEILLE, Longman, Hurst, Orme & Brown, 1820.

Translation of the Reports of M. le Comte de Capo D'Istria and M. Rengger, Upon the Principles and Progress of the Establishment of M. de Fellenberg at Hofwyl, Switzerland, by J. ATTERSOLL, London, 1820.

RENGGER, A., *Report upon the Institutions for the Education of the Poor at Hofwyl*, 1815.

RENGGER, A., *Reports of the School of Industry at Hofwyl, in the Canton of Berne, Switzerland*, Dublin, 1817.

Second Numbers of Papers on the Rural Economy of Hofwyl, 1809.

FICHTE, J. G., *Addresses to the German Nation*, trans. R. F. JONES and G. H. TURNBULL, Chicago and London, The Open Court Publishing Co., 1922.

TURNBULL, G. H., *The Educational Theory of J. G. Fichte*, Liverpool University Press, 1926.

FORDYCE, DAVID, *Dialogues concerning Education*, London, 1745. *Elements of Moral Philosophy*, London, 1755.

FROEBEL, F., *The Education of Man*, trans. W. N. HAILMANN, Sidney Appleton, 1905.

Froebel's Chief Writings on Education, S. S. F. FLETCHER and J. WELTON, Educational Classics, 1912.

LAWRENCE, E. M., *Friedrich Froebel and English Education*, University of London Press, 1952.

JARVIS, *Froebel. The Education of Man*, Lovell, New York, 1885.

FROEBEL. *Education by Development*, Arnold, 1899.

MICHAELIS & MOORE. *Autobiography of Friedrich Froebel*, Swan, Sonnenschein, 1903.

FROEBEL, *Letters on the Kindergarten*, Swan, Sonnenschein, 1891.

GODWIN, WILLIAM, *An Enquiry Concerning Political Justice*, first pub. 1793, ed. H. S. SALT, Allen & Unwin, 1929. *The Enquirer*, London, 1797.

HAMILTON, E., *The Cottagers of Glenburnie*, Manners & Miller, Edinburgh, 1808.

HERBART, J. F., *The Science of Education*, trans. H. & E. FELKIN, Sonnenschein & Co., London, 1897. *The Application of Psychology to the Science of Education*, trans. B. C. MULLINER, Swan, Sonnenschein & Co., 1895, *Letters and Lectures on Education*, trans. Felkin, 1908.

HILL, ARTHUR, *Public Education. Plans for the Government and Liberal Instruction of Boys in large numbers*. 2nd ed, C. Knight, 1825. *Hints on the Discipline Appropriate to Schools*, Longmans, Brown, Green & Longmans, 1855.

HUXLEY, T. H., *Science and Education*, Macmillan, 1893.

Kant on Education, trans. A. CHURTON, Kegan Paul, Trench, Trubner, 1899.

The Educational Theory of Immanuel Kant, trans. and ed. E. F. BUCHNER, Lippincott & Co., London, 1904.

LA CHALOTAIS, *Essay on National Education*, trans. H. R. CLARK, Arnold, 1934.

OWEN, ROBERT, *A New View of Society*, London, 1813, also in Everyman, 1927.

anon. *Robert Owen at New Lanark*, 1839.

The Life of Robert Owen, By Himself. G. Bell & Sons, 1920.

OWEN, R. D., *An Outline of the System of Education at New Lanark*, Glasgow University Press, 1824.

COLE, G. D. H., *Life of Robert Owen*, London, 1925.

COLE, M., *Robert Owen of New Lanark*, Batchworth Press, 1953.

PODMORE, F., *Robert Owen*, Allen & Unwin, 1906.

MONROE, *Essential Thought of Pestalozzi*.

PESTALOZZI, *Leonard and Gertrude*, trans. E. CHANNING, Cambridge, Mass., 1885. *How Gertrude Teaches Her Children*, trans. L. E. HOLLAND and F. C. TURNER, Swan Sonnenschein & Co., 1900.

Pestalozzi's Educational Writings, trans. J. A. GREEN, London, 1912.

PESTALOZZI, J. H., *The Education of Man*, aphorisims, intro. W. H. KILPATRICK, New York Philosophical Library, 1951.

ROUSSEAU, J. J., *Émile*, trans. B. Foxley Dent, 1911.

Rousseau on Education, trans. R. L. ARCHER, Arnold, 1912.

MONROE, P., *Fundamental Teachings of Rousseau*.

RICHTER, J. P. F., *Levana or the Doctrine of Education*, George Bell & Sons, 1901.

ROLLIN, CHARLES, *Method of Teaching and Studying the Belles Lettres*, English trans., London, 1804. *New Thoughts Concerning Education*, Bettesworth & Hitch, London, 1735.

ROSENCRANZ, J. K. F., *The Philosophy of Education*, trans. A. C. BRACKETT, Appleton & Co., New York, 2nd ed. 1902.

ROSMINI, S., *Origin of Ideas*, Kegan Paul, 1883–4.

SPENCER, HERBERT, *Social Statics*, Williams & Norgate, 1902. *Education*, Watts & Co., 2nd imp., 1935.

SAUSSURE, MME. NECKER de, *Progressive Education*, Longmans, Orme, Brown, Green & Longmans, 1839.

SEGUIN, E., *Idiocy and its Treatment by the Physiological Method*, William Wood, New York, 1866. *Report on Education*, 1875.

STOW, DAVID, *The Training System*, Longmans, Brown, Green & Longmans, 1854.

TOLSTOY, LEO, *Essays and Letters*, trans. AYLMER MAUDE, Grant Richards, London, 1903. *Complete Works of Count Leo Tolstoy*, ed. L. WEINER, Dent, London, 1905.

TOLSTOY, L., *Tolstoy Centenary Edition*, Oxford, 1929.

WATTS, ISAAC, *A Discourse on the Way of Instruction by Catechism*, 3rd ed. London, 1736. *The Improvement of the Mind*, London, 1741. *Communication of Useful Knowledge. A Discourse on the Education of Children and Youth*, London, 1782.

WILLIAMS, DAVID, *A Treatise on Education*, London, 1774. *Lectures on Education*, John Bell, London, 1789.

WYSE, THOMAS, *Education Reform*, Longmans, Rees, Orme, Brown, Green & Longmans, 1836.

20TH CENTURY

General Books

JAMES, W., *Talks to Teachers on Psychology*, Longmans Green, 1899.

JEFFREYS, M. V. C., *Glaucon*, Pitman, 1950. *Beyond Neutrality*, Pitman, 1955.

LIVINGSTONE, R. W., *The Future in Education*, Cambridge, 1941. *Education for a World Adrift*, Cambridge, 1944. *The Rainbow Bridge*, Pall Mall Press, 1959.

MANNHEIM, K., *Diagnosis of Our Time*, Kegan Paul, 1943.

MANNHEIM, K., and STEWART, W. A. C., *An Introduction to the Sociology of Education*, Routledge & Kegan Paul, 1962.

MARITAIN, J., *Education at the Crossroads*, Oxford, 1943.

NUNN, SIR PERCY, *Education, Its Data and First Principles*, Arnold, 1945.

RANK, OTTO, *Beyond Psychology*, Dover Publications Inc., New York, 1958.

RAWSON, W., *The New Education*, Heinemann, 1965.

RUSSELL, B., *On Education*, Allen & Unwin, 1926. *Education and the Social Order*, Allen & Unwin, 1932.

VAIZEY, J., *Education for Tomorrow*, Penguin, 1966.

WALL, W. D., *Education and Mental Health*, UNESCO, Harrap, 1955.

WHITEHEAD, A. N., *The Aims of Education*, Benn, 1932.

Books on Child Development and Psychology

ADLER, A., *Education of Children*, Allen & Unwin, 1930.

BÜHLER, CHARLOTTE, *From Birth to Maturity*, Kegan Paul, 1935. *The Child and His Family*, Kegan Paul, Trench & Trubner, 1940.

BURLINGHAM, D., and FREUD, A., *Infants Without Families*, Allen & Unwin, 2nd ed. 1965.

COMPAYRÉ, G., *Intellectual and Moral Development of the Child*, trans. M. WILSON, D. Appleton & Co., New York, 1902.

GESELL, ARNOLD and BEATRICE, *The Normal Child and Primary Education*, Ginn, 1912.

HALL, G., *Aspects of Child Life and Education*, Longmans, 1899.

HEMMING and BALL, *The Child is Right*, Longmans, 1947.

ISAACS, N., *New Light on Children's Ideas of Number*, E.S.A., 1961.

ISAACS, S., *The Children We Teach*, U.L.P., 1932. *Intellectual Growth in Young Children*, Routledge & Kegan Paul, 1930. *Social Development in Young Children*, Routledge, 1933.

JUNG, C. G., *Psychology of the Unconscious*, 1st English ed. Routledge & Kegan Paul, 1921.

PREYER, *Mental Development in the Child*, trans. H. W. BROWN, Appleton & Co., New York, 1894. *The Mind of the Child*, trans. H. W. BROWN, Appleton & Co., New York, 1888.

Individual Educators

BADLEY, J. H., *A Schoolmaster's Testament*, Blackwell, 1937.

CASTLE, E. B., *People in School*, Heinemann, 1953.

DEWEY, J., *Democracy and Education*, Macmillan, New York, 1915. *Experience and Education*, Macmillan, New York, 1951. *The School and the Child*, ed. J. J. FINDLAY, Blackie, 1906.

Dewey on Education. Intro. and notes M. S. DWORKIN, Bureau of Publications, Teachers College, Columbia University, New York, 1959, includes *The School and Society* and *The Child and the Curriculum. Selected Educational Writings*, F. W. GARFORTH, Heinemann, 1966.

GENTILE, G., *The Reform of Education*, Benn, London, 1923.

LANE, HOMER, *Talks to Parents and Teachers*, Allen & Unwin, 1928.

WILLS, W. D., *Homer Lane: A Biography*, Allen & Unwin, 1964.

BAZELEY, E. T., *Homer Lane and the Little Commonwealth*, Allen & Unwin, Heinemann, 1948.

MONTESSORI, *The Montessori Method*, trans. A. E. George, Heinemann, 1912.

STANDING, E. M., *Maria Montessori*, Hollis & Carter, 1957.

MCLEAN, D., *Nature's Second Sun*, Heinemann, 1954.

NEILL, A. S., *Summerhill, a Radical Approach to Education*, Gollancz, 1962. *Problem Parents*, Jenkins, 1932. *That Dreadful School*, Jenkins, 1937. *Hearts Not Heads in the School*, Jenkins, 1944.

RAWSON, W., and others, *Kees Boeke*.

RAWSON, W., *The Werkplaats Adventure*, Stuart, 1956.

INDEX

MORE ABOUT PENGUINS
AND PELICANS

Penguinews, which appears every month, contains details of all the new books issued by Penguins as they are published. From time to time it is supplemented by *Penguins in Print*, which is a complete list of all books published by Penguins which are in print. (There are well over three thousand of these.)

A specimen copy of *Penguinews* will be sent to you free on request, and you can become a subscriber for the price of the postage – 4s. for a year's issues (including the complete lists). Just write to Dept EP, Penguin Books Ltd, Harmondsworth, Middlesex, enclosing a cheque or postal order, and your name will be added to the mailing list.

Some other books published by Penguins are described on the following pages.

Note: *Penguinews* and *Penguins in Print* are not available in the U.S.A. or Canada

THE ORIGINS AND GROWTH
OF PHYSICAL SCIENCE
(In Two Volumes)

Edited by D. L. Hurd and J. J. Kipling

The Origins and Growth of Physical Science (based on *Moments of Discovery*, by Schwartz and Bishop) records the stepping-stones along which, in the Western world, man has slowly advanced out of a morass of superstition. Today science orders a large area of human life. But it has required the brilliance and originality of many great men in many ages to discover the truth about the nature of things and to profit by it.

The beginnings of the scientific approach are described in Volume 1, from the ideas and discoveries of Aristotle, Archimedes, and the ancient Greeks down to the more specialized work which followed the Renaissance – the theories of Copernicus, Brahe, Kepler, Galileo, and Newton in astronomy, and of Pascal, Boyle, Priestley, Cavendish, and Lavoisier in chemistry. In Volume 2 the story is continued, by way of modern chemistry and electricity, to the atomic physics of today.

THE ORIGINS AND GROWTH
OF BIOLOGY

Edited by Arthur Rook

The Origins and Growth of Biology (based on *Moments of Discovery*, by Schwartz and Bishop) is a history of the science of life and the struggle against disease. It was Hippocrates, in the fifth century B.C., who first pronounced that disease, far from being an Act of God, had natural causes and could be treated scientifically. Later Aristotle made formidable additions to the knowledge and understanding of nature. Though the torch of science burned very low in the Dark Ages, it began to flare once again with the dissection work of Andreas Vesalius in the sixteenth century, and thereafter the study of the human body, of animals and plants proceeded at a mounting tempo, in the hands of such great men as Harvey, Linnaeus, Darwin, Mendel, Pasteur and Lister.

Included in this excellent outline are extracts from the most important writings of the great biologists, as well as brief biographies.

UNDERSTANDING SCHOOLS

David Ayerst

A revealing survey of the nature and scope of modern education, which should help parents to understand the reality of their children's school lives, and break down the barrier that often exists between the school and the home.

EDUCATING THE INTELLIGENT

Michael Hutchinson and
Christopher Young

Two experienced teachers outline an alternative curriculum for secondary schools which would meet the needs of the intelligent child. They go on to discuss fully the sixth-form syllabus, the examination system, university selection, and the choice, training and salaries of teachers.

UNIVERSITY CHOICE

Edited by Klaus Boehm

A guide for sixth-formers to the question 'what will you read at University?' Articles on thirty representative university subjects specially written by heads of faculties, lecturers and others, explaining in each case what studies consist of, how they are taught, and where they lead. 'This book will be bought by anxious parents; it should also be bought by every sixth form teacher, for it contains much good advice' – *Sunday Times*

THE GRAMMAR SCHOOL

Robin Davis

The grammar school problem lies at the heart of the future of secondary education, yet a defence of public and grammar schools based on real knowledge and rational argument continues to go by default. This important new book considers the role of policies in secondary education, analyses the conflicting claims of the comprehensive and selective principles, and discusses the semi-independent and public schools in the light of the question of 'integration'.

THE COMPREHENSIVE SCHOOL

Robin Pedley

Arguing that the best alternative to the 11-plus is a good comprehensive school, Dr Pedley gives a clear and critical picture of such schools as they exist in England and Wales today. 'Should certainly be read by all teachers' – *Teacher's World*

LIFE IN A SECONDARY MODERN SCHOOL

John Partridge

A disquieting survey of the type of education which is provided for two-thirds of British schoolchildren. The author, who taught at a Midlands secondary modern, gives a trenchant critique of streaming, corporal punishment, lack of vocational training, and general authoritarianism.